KU-158-745

# Global Business Strategy

# Global Business Strategy

Edited by Robin John

*Head, Division of Strategy and Marketing,*
*South Bank University*

**THOMSON**

Australia · Canada · Mexico · Singapore · Spain · United Kingdom · United States

**Global Business Strategy**

**Copyright © 1997 Robin John, Howard Cox, Grazia Ietto-Gillies, Nigel Grimwade, Michael Allen, Edward Finn**

The Thomson logo is a registered trademark used herein under licence.

For more information, contact Thomson, High Holborn House; 50-51 Bedford Row, London WC1R 4LR or visit us on the World Wide Web at: http://www.thomsonlearning.co.uk

All rights reserved by Thomson 2002. The text of this publication, or any part thereof, may not be reproduced or transmitted in any form or by any means, electronic or mechanical, including photocopying, recording, storage in an information retrieval system, or otherwise, without prior permission of the publisher.

While the publisher has taken all reasonable care in the preparation of this book the publisher makes no representation, express or implied, with regard to the accuracy of the information contained in this book and cannot accept any legal responsibility or liability for any errors or omissions from the book or the consequences thereof.

Products and services that are referred to in this book may be either trademarks and/or registered trademarks of their respective owners. The publisher and author/s make no claim to these trademarks.

*British Library Cataloguing-in-Publication Data*
A catalogue record for this book is available from the British Library

**ISBN 1-86152-352-1**

First published 1997, reprinted 1998 by International Thomson Business Press

Reprinted 2000 by Thomson Learning

**Reprinted 2002 by Thomson**

Printed in China by L-Rex

# *Contents*

# Notes on the contributors

**Michael Allen** is Teaching Fellow in the Centre for Strategic Trade Union Management at Cranfield School of Management. Previously Senior Lecturer in Employment Relations at South Bank University Business School, he has published widely on international labour and employment issues.

**Howard Cox** is Principal Lecturer in Economics at South Bank University and a visiting Fellow of the Economics Department at Reading University. He is the author of a number of papers in the fields of international business and business history, and joint editor of the *Growth of Global Business* which was published by Routledge in 1993.

**Edward Finn** is a management consultant who has extensive experience working with various business organizations throughout Europe. Since 1992 he has been a visiting Teaching Fellow at South Bank University Business School.

**Nigel Grimswade** is Principal Lecturer in Economics and Head of the Economics Division at South Bank University Business School. He is author of *International Trade* (1989) and *International Trade Policy: A Contemporary Analysis* (1996), both published by Routledge. He has written extensively on international trade and trade policy, and is an expert on the trade policy of the European Union.

**Grazia Ietto-Gillies** is Professor of Applied Economics and Director of the Centre for International Business Studies at South Bank University. She is author of *International Production: Trends, Theories, Effects* (Polity Press, 1992), joint editor of the *Growth of Global Business* (Routledge, 1993), and has published many articles on international business and applied economics.

**Robin John** is Principal Lecturer in Business Strategy and Head of the Strategy and Marketing Division at South Bank University Business School. He is the editor of *The Consumer Revolution: Redressing the Balance* published by Hodder Headline in 1994.

# Acknowledgments

The authors would like to thank the following publishers and publications:

Professor Stanley Chapman and Professor S. Pollard for Tables 1.1 and 1.2; William Heinemann Ltd for Table 1.3; *Business History* (Frank Cass & Co. Ltd) for Table 1.4 and 1.11; Harvard University Press for Table 1.6 and Figures 8.4 and 8.6; Professor Ansoff for Table 1.8 and Figure 7.7; Addison-Wesley Longman for Table 1.9; *Oxford Bulletin of Economics and Statistics* (Blackwell Publishers) for Table 2.3; the World Bank for Table 2.13; Cambridge University Press for Figure 3.3; *The Economist* for Boxes 5.8 and 11.1; Macmillan Press Ltd for Figure 6.1; Simon & Schuster for Figures 7.2, 7.4, 8.1 and 8.6; Paul Chapman Publishing Ltd for Box 8.1 and Figures 8.8 amd 8.9; The New Lexington Press for Figures 8.2 and 8.5 and Box 9.2; JAI Press for Figure 8.3; Box 9.1 and Table 10.2; *Strategic Management Journal* (John Wiley & Sons) for Figures 9.2 and 10.8; Basic Books, a division of HarperCollins for Figure 10.7; *Journal of International Business Studies* for Figure 11.1, University of Tokyo Press for Table 1.10, Allen & Unwin for Box 5.4; *The Financial Times* for Table 1.5 and Boxes 5.5, 5.6 and 8.3; Prentice Hall for Figures 7.5 and 10.1; Houghton Mifflin for Figures 7.6 and 8.11; Harvard Business School Press for Figure 8.10 and Box 8.2; *Sloan Management Review* for Figure 10.9; Institute of Personnel and Development for Figure 11.2; Centre des Études Industrielles for Table 1.7, and the National Institute for Economic and Social Research.

Every reasonable effort has been made to contact the copyright holders of all material reproduced in this book.

# Introduction

## Focus and approach

*Global Business Strategy* seeks to investigate and analyse the strategic decision-making processes of international firms. The book draws upon the authors' collective experience teaching programmes in international business at South Bank University, London.

The study of international business is essentially multidisciplinary in nature. This text was written with the intention of bringing together a range of viewpoints and analytical techniques including perspectives from applied economics, international economics, international business history, strategic management, organizational behaviour and human resource management. It aims to combine a discussion of relevant areas of theory with evidence and the evaluation of the contemporary international business literature. As a text written by several specialists and aimed at final year undergraduate and postgraduate students it deliberately avoids presenting a single, simplified overview of the international firm and international business strategy. It seeks instead to capture a diversity of theories, explanations and perspectives. There are some differences of viewpoint between the authors of particular chapters, but these are seen as a strength rather than a weakness. An important theme is the shifting dynamics and complexity of global business strategy and to that extent contradictions and diversity are to be expected. Part of the challenge of international business is to make sense of complex, changing and multifaceted phenomena.

The text focuses mainly on international strategic decision-making and the international business environment (including the institutional and policy environment) in which decisions are made by multinational firms. In such an important and expanding field there are inevitably significant limitations to the scope of the book. Functional-level strategies relating to decision-making in specific functional areas, such as international finance and marketing, are touched upon at various points but do not have full chapters in their own right. Interested readers are referred to specific texts in the fields of international marketing and finance.

## Terminology

Global business strategy is concerned with the important long-term policy decisions of international firms operating across frontiers in the world economy. The terms 'global' and 'globalization' have been used in many different ways in the international business literature. For some writers they are simply synonyms for 'international' and 'international-ization', referring to the tendency observed in the last 50 years for large firms to become much more international in outlook and in the geographical scope of their business activities. Other writers, however, have used the term 'global' in a special sense to identify a new stage of strategic orientation towards the end of the twentieth century, involving a paradigm shift in which global integration and co-ordination of activities become central to competitive strategy. Among the writers who have advanced this latter perspective is Peter Dicken:

> Globalization of economic activity is qualitatively different. It is a more advanced and complex form of internationalization which implies a degree of functional integration between internationally dispersed activities. (Dicken, 1992, p.1)

A central aim of this book is to explore and question the nature of global business strategy and the paradigm shift that may have taken place.

Both the terminology for, and definition of, the international firm are important issues. They have resulted in lengthy discussion in the literature, this being particularly concerned with distinguishing between 'multinationals', which engage in foreign direct investment, and 'firms', which simply serve foreign markets through exports. Both Hood and Young (1979, Chapter 1) and Ietto-Gillies (1992, Chapter 1) contain useful summaries of this debate. Some of the literature uses the terms 'multinational corporation' (MNC) and 'transnational corporation' (TNC) interchangeably. The term 'transnational corporation' is the one preferred by the United Nations and may be defined as '. . . a corporation that organises and controls production and/or related activities in more than one country' (Ietto-Gillies, 1992, p.8). Some writers, for example Martinez and Jarillo (1989) and Bartlett and Ghoshal (1989), use the term 'transnational' in a special sense, however, to describe an international firm that has reached a more advanced state where it is striving to be both globally integrated and responsive to local needs and conditions.

It is important that the student of international business should be sensitive to these nuances of meaning. No single term is used for the international firm throughout the text. Some chapters employ the term 'multinational corporation', others 'transnational corporation'. The context makes clear when either of these terms are being used in a particular sense.

## Organization and structure

The book is divided into two parts. Part One: The environment, growth and development of international firms, comprises six chapters. Chapter 1,

'The Evolution of the International Business Enterprise', plays a very important role in developing historical perspectives on the contemporary multinational corporation. It examines the causation and development of international business activity and foreign investment flows from the early nineteenth century until the late 1960s. Chapter 2, 'Internationalization Trends', analyses the qualitative and quantitative changes in various aspects of internationalization in the 50 years following the Second World War, including the structure and pattern of foreign direct investment (FDI).

Chapter 3, 'The Environment of International Business' and Chapter 4, 'The International Trading Environment', are concerned with analysing the environmental context of the multinational firm and its decision making. Chapter 3 is particularly concerned with identifying the variety of factors and conditions that have favoured the significant increase in internationalization during the last 50 years. Chapter 4 examines the pattern and structure of world trade and its institutional framework, including the General Agreement on Tariffs and Trade and the World Trade Organization. Chapter 5, 'Alternative Approaches to the Explanation of International Production', discusses and evaluates alternative theories of FDI and internationalization.

Part One concludes with Chapter 6, 'International Trade and Global Competition', which effectively acts as a bridge between the concerns of Parts One and Two.

Part Two, 'International Business Strategy and Management', comprises five chapters. Chapter 7, 'Strategic Planning and Management in International Firms', is an overview chapter setting out the international strategic management decision-making process as a whole, and analyses this in terms of three components: international strategic analysis, strategy formulation and strategy implementation, with its main emphasis on the first, strategic analysis, stage. Chapter 8, 'International Business Strategy', focuses on the strategy-formulation process, the range of international strategic choices, and the dual pressures of global integration and local responsiveness. Chapter 9, 'International Business Strategy Implementation', is concerned with strategy implementation, the third component of the international strategy process. Among a range of possible implementation concerns it focuses on three main issues: the importance of strategic alliances and joint ventures as methods of achieving strategic objectives, the significance of inter-national acquisitions and mergers and alternative methods of foreign market entry and development.

Designing an organizational structure that achieves the multiple strategic objectives of international business is one of the greatest challenges faced by multinational corporations in recent decades. The problem of international organizational structure is explored in Chapter 10. Chapter 11, 'Globalization and Human Resource Management', examines the functional areas that are least amenable to global integration and standardized policies.

## Suggestions for teaching and study

There are mini-case studies and examples throughout the book. Each chapter ends with suggestions for further reading as well as student discussion questions and activities designed to reinforce the student's understanding of the chapter. The type of exercise involved varies considerably, reflecting the range of, and the different disciplines underlying, various chapters. For example the questions and tasks in Chapter 5 are concerned with reinforcing and testing the student's knowledge of the alternative theories of internationalization whereas the main exercise for Chapter 7 involves the student in applying financial performance techniques to selected financial data from IBM's annual reports and accounts.

When the book is used in relation to a formal taught course in international business we suggest that the lectures be followed by informal group work. This allows students to revise the topics raised in the lectures, assisting them to absorb what is, in places, quite demanding material. At least one hour per week should be devoted to these follow-up sessions, in which students could be asked to work in groups of four or five.

Over several weeks these groups should be asked to work through the discussion questions of different chapters and to answer similar questions devised by the tutor. They should be encouraged to co-operate and discuss these questions among themselves, consulting their lecture notes as well as this book.

The group should have a convener or chairperson, in charge of time management, keeping discussion to the point and reporting back. This is a role that should rotate among the group members.

One possibility might be to divide the student body into several such groups, each chairperson reporting back to a plenary session. During this session the tutor could take the opportunity to give feedback, clarification and assistance. We recommend that, to encourage student co-operation and a relaxed study environment, these group activities should not be formally assessed.

One assessed group exercise that the authors use in teaching international business is an 'international corporate project'. The students work in project teams consisting of four or five members, but they study one specific multinational corporation of their choice for the duration of the course. The group's early meetings are concerned with agreeing the choice of company and allocating tasks among the group members. Students should gather information from a range of sources including company annual reports, databases including CD Roms and the Internet, journal articles and press reports.

As far as possible the MNC's activities should be examined in the light of theory and using analytical concepts from the course. As well as an initial SWOT analysis of the company's strategic position (see Chapter 7), topics which might be examined include: industry structure and competitors; resource and financial performance analysis; strategic capability and competitive advantage; international strategies including the use of alliances, joint ventures and acquisitions; the corporation's effects on home and host countries in which it operates; organizational structure and human resource management. A number of the book's chapter-end discussion topics have prompts for the international group project. In terms of assessed output, each group is expected to produce a 7000 word written report on its multinational company and make an oral assessed presentation of its main findings to a plenary session of all the students. Important learning outcomes include the ability to apply theory to corporate practice and to engage in company analysis. By the end of the course students should have become familiar with the operations and activities of several important international firms.

The international corporate project is best facilitated by the tutor. A degree of tutor intervention may be necessary to guide the initial choice of multinational companies to ensure wide sectoral and geographic coverage. Examples of United States', European and Asian MNCs should be included among the projects as far as possible. The tutor may need to assist in directing the students to information sources, ensuring that the project is sufficiently analytical and helping students to organize their presentations.

# Part One

## The environment, growth and development of international firms

# The evolution of international business enterprise

*1*

## 1.1 Introduction

During the latter half of the 1960s economic analysts became increasingly aware that multinational companies had become the primary engines of growth in many modern industries. The identification of this phenomenon, which is now regarded as commonplace, had been hindered by the prevailing Keynesian economic methodology. This placed the focus of analysis upon national economies, as the economic model of international trade formulated by Ricardo had done over a hundred years earlier, and thus tended to obscure the growth in importance of extra-national entities such as multinational companies. Even the models of monopoly and oligopoly, which had been developed in the area of microeconomic analysis to account for the observed increase in the size of firms, represented a response to rising industrial concentration in product markets that were measured in relation to *national* output and consumption patterns. By the end of the 1960s, however, many of these markets were served, and in some cases dominated, by the local manufacturing subsidiaries of firms whose headquarters lay abroad.

Given this prevailing tendency towards nationally based forms of analysis in economics it is perhaps not surprising to discover that much of the early work relating to the operation of multinational corporations characterized them as a quintessentially American form of foreign investment. The studies of Dunning (1958) and Servan-Schreiber (1968) and more theoretical work by Hymer (1960) and Kindleberger (1969) all concentrated on the activities of American companies operating abroad. The work of Hymer, which is discussed in greater detail in Chapter 5, was especially influential in promoting a new approach towards the analysis of multinationals. He achieved this reorientation by linking together what he saw as the two essential features of multinationals: they were large-scale oligopolistic producers and they managed international flows of investment as part of their global competitive strategy. Hymer's crucial insight was to demonstrate that multinationals, by linking together their production know-how with overseas-based investment, had created a seemingly new type of foreign investment.

Up to this point international transfers of capital were viewed as financial transactions in which investors sought the best return available for a given level of risk. Such international capital flows were called *portfolio investments,* a term that indicated that the investors discharged control for the use of their capital to a third party, as for example when they purchased securities issued by a foreign government. According to Hymer, multinationals generated a different form of foreign investment: foreign direct investment (FDI). The firms that engaged in FDI retained direct responsibility for managing their foreign investments, frequently through the creation of subsidiary companies registered abroad and hence, unlike portfolio investors, they did not surrender control of their capital. Foreign investment by these companies did not simply consist of financial transfers but rather involved transfers of a package of production techniques under the firm's operational control. Thus the modern definition of multinationals as companies that own, manage and control productive assets in countries other than the one that constitutes their home base, began to permeate the literature of economics. Moreover, the terms 'multinational corporation' and 'foreign direct investment' began to be treated synonymously, as two labels for the same phenomenon.

By the 1970s, as confidence in Keynesian policies of national demand management began to wane, multinationals came to be viewed as one of the main forces preventing national governments from successfully managing their economies. Books such as *Global Reach: the Power of the Multinational Corporations* by Barnet and Müller (1974) began to popularize the view that multinationals represented a pernicious element in the world economic system, developing as alternative centres of power to democratically elected governments and acting to reinforce the unequal distribution of wealth between the industrialized and less-developed countries. It also began to be recognized that multinationals had a history that predated the Second World War and that Europe, as well as America, had spawned companies that were engaged in FDI.

No data had ever been systematically collected on the growth of multinationals over time because they transcended national boundaries. To help rectify this omission a vast research project was initiated at the

Harvard Business School during the 1960s under the direction of Raymond Vernon. This traced the development of 187 United States-based firms (from the Fortune 500 of 1963–4) that controlled six or more foreign manufacturing subsidiaries. Data on 209 of the most important non-United States industrial corporations which, at one time or another, had controlled at least one foreign subsidiary, were added to this.

Altogether, the study collected information on a total of 28 318 foreign subsidiaries and it remains the single most comprehensive statistical account of the growth of multinationals. The main statistical results from the Harvard study were published by Vaupel and Curhan (1974).

## 1.2 Early forms of FDI

The findings of the Harvard study provided a useful guide to the origins of many of the world's most important multinational companies. However, by adopting the methodology of projecting backwards from the present, the study obscured the fact that other less enduring forms of FDI had developed during the nineteenth century. More recent research has clearly illustrated that FDI predated multinational corporations. Moreover, the database in the Harvard study was limited to *manufacturing* subsidiaries and did not include companies whose activities involved, for example, the provision of services. Thus the study captured the development of manufacturing multinationals but excluded many other forms of FDI.

Until quite recently it was assumed that foreign investments that preceded the rise of multinational companies invariably took the form of portfolio investments. It is certainly the case that, prior to the First World War, many foreign governments took advantage of the London capital market to raise the funds they needed for social overhead capital, and that the foreign investors who subscribed to these issues did so without in any way assuming responsibility for their management.

A great many companies were created in the United Kingdom before 1914, however, which operated abroad but which were in practice ultimately controlled by directors based in Britain. For example, a study by Houston and Dunning (1976) showed that of the 13 500 enterprises quoted on the London Stock Exchange in 1914, 3373 operated exclusively or mainly abroad, and 78 per cent of these were registered in the United Kingdom. Wilkins (1988) has termed these enterprises 'free-standing' companies. Unlike conventional multinationals they were set up as operations with no parallel organization in Britain itself. Although most of the shareholders who subscribed to these joint stock companies did not exert control over the companys' activities (for which reason they have in the past been incorrectly categorized as portfolio investments) their affairs were nevertheless frequently managed by a board of directors based in Britain. Hence they did constitute a genuine form of foreign *direct* investment. Box 1.1 gives some examples of typical free-standing companies.

---

**Box 1.1**   Free-standing companies

The term 'free-standing company' was introduced by the American business historian Mira Wilkins (1988) in order to provide a means of classifying forms of FDI that were different from those emanating from the standard American-style multinational corporation. The main point of distinction, and the reason why the term 'free-standing' was utilized, lay in the fact that these foreign investments were not a development of a domestic company's existing operations. Rather, they represented a situation in which a joint stock company was floated as a means of allowing capital holders in one country to take advantage of an investment opportunity abroad. These were not, therefore, subsidiary companies of an existing domestic enterprise but were independent (free-standing) entities. They were, however, forms of direct (rather than portfolio) investment as long as managerial control of the operation ultimately resided in the country which had provided the investment funds. This appears to have frequently been the case amongst the many companies floated on the London stock exchange before the First World War whose operations took place largely or exclusively abroad.

Between the passing of the Limited Liability Act and the First World War (1856–1914), a total of 154 817 joint stock companies were floated in the United Kingdom. A detailed study by Payne (1980) showed that of the 2936 companies formed in Scotland between 1865 and 1895, a little over 10 per cent (318) were concerned with operations overseas. Breaking down this sample of companies by industrial classification shows that the most important activities engaged in were mining and quarrying (37 per cent), finance, insurance and real estate (25 per cent) and agriculture (20 per cent). Manufacturing, on the other hand, was relatively limited (7 per cent), being confined mainly to food and textile products and oil refining.

Particularly prominent among the overseas companies formed at this time were metal mining concerns. Financial institutions, both in Scotland and in London, had gained experience in raising capital for domestic mining concerns and were able to respond with alacrity in the face of potential opportunities abroad. Encouraging reports of potential gold deposits in Madras, India, at the beginning of the 1880s, for example, led within the space of 19 months to the flotation in Britain of 41 companies, 33 of which were successfully launched with an aggregate nominal capital value of over £4.0 million. Before any crushing had actually taken place, a speculative bubble developed which swiftly inflated the share prices of these concerns based upon overoptimistic predictions of the gold yield. As soon as the true yields became apparent share prices collapsed and, within a year, 15 of the 33 companies had been wound up.

The example of the Indian gold rush speculation illustrates a weakness of this form of overseas investment, namely that the capital holders have inadequate access to accurate information and rely upon the trustworthiness of those promoting and managing the enterprises. It would be mistaken, however, to assume that such problems could not be overcome and by no means all of the gold mining companies formed in India at this time were financial failures. Free-standing companies such as the Mysore Gold Mining Company Ltd and the Nundydroog Gold Mining Company Ltd, both formed in 1880, drew on the experience of John Taylor & Sons, a London-based mining engineering company, to oversee the management of their organizations and, with the introduction of improved techniques for deep mining, the operations were eventually highly remunerative. Even with good management, however, gold mining remained something of a lottery.

In general, the key to the success of free-standing companies was their ability to draw together the sources of capital, the knowledge of investment opportunities and the required expertise. As Harvey and Press (1990, pp.109–10) explain: 'The situation in mining was little different to that in shipping, railways, tramways, water, manufacturing and financial services. A merchant house with British connections would become aware of a potentially lucrative investment, often through influential local contacts; details would be sent back to London and a syndicate formed; a concession would be floated [usually] in London to exploit the syndicate. The main promotional gains accrued at the point of transfer of a concession from a syndicate to a newly-formed operating company. Usually a substantial price was paid for the concession in cash, debentures or shares, and besides this contracts for construction, management services and supplies might well be granted to syndicate members.' According to a contemporary report, the typical profile of the directors of an Indian gold-mining company formed around 1880 would comprise:

- solicitor to the company

- financial agent (promoter)

- consulting engineer

- engineering agent in London

- syndicate members

- broker

- partner in firm to provide machinery

- contractor to supply tools and stores

- company secretary

- vendor of property in India.

Mining companies of world renown, such as De Beers and Rio Tinto Zinc, as well as Burmah Oil and Shell, were formed in just this way as free-standing companies. Over time, the role of company promoter seems to have become more and more concentrated into the hands of specialized investment houses and the 1890s saw the formation of a number of joint-stock mining finance companies (Turrell and Van Helten, 1986). These financiers included engineering firms like John Taylor & Sons, and Bewick, Moreing & Co.; merchants such as Julius Wernher, Alfred Beit and Barney Barnato in South Africa; as well as merchant bankers such N.M. Rothschild & Sons.

*Sources: Harvey and Press (1990, pp.98–119); Payne (1980); Turrell and Van Helten (1986, pp.181–205); Wilkins (1988, pp.259–82).*

Although each of the individual free-standing companies was nominally an independent concern, a number of informal links existed between groups of them, drawing them into clusters. Particularly important in this respect were financial institutions in the City of London that developed from commission agencies (supervising the trade of other firms for payment of a commission) into investment houses and which promoted a series of free-standing companies during the nineteenth century. These investment houses, as Chapman (1985, 1992) has explained, provided international networks that linked sources of capital, from London and elsewhere, with investment opportunities abroad. This ability to connect domestic sources of capital and expertise (comprising both technical expertise and financial management skills) with influential contacts abroad enabled investment groups like Finlay & Co., Butterfield & Swire, Antony Gibbs & Co. and De Beers to emerge as strategic actors in the growth of FDI during the nineteenth century.

Although these institutions were international in scope, the organizational structures that they used to manage their overseas assets were clearly different from the conventional form of multinational corporation that developed in the United States. Table 1.1 lists some of the major British-based investment groups that were operating around the turn of the nineteenth century.

**Table 1.1**  Activities of selected British-based investment groups c.1900–14

| Group | Overseas base | Activities |
|---|---|---|
| **Far East** | | |
| Finlay & Co. | Bombay 1862 | Banking, cotton mills, coal mines, shipping, silk mills, tea estates |
| Jardine, Skinner | Calcutta 1840 | Indigo mills, jute mills, paper mills, coal mines, sugar mills, tea estates |
| Butterfield & Swire | Shanghai 1867 | Harbour and docks, shipping, silk mills |
| M. Samuel & Co, | Yokohama 1878 | Banking, petroleum, shipping |
| **Latin America** | | |
| Antony Gibbs | Lima 1822 | Banking, railways, shipping, soda factories, nitrates |
| Dreyfus & Co. | Buenos Aires 1880 | Banking, shipping, warehousing |
| Knowles & Foster | Rio de Janiero 1886 | Banking, coal mines, flour mills |
| **Russia** | | |
| Knoop | Moscow 1840 | Banking, cotton mills |
| Rodocanachi | St Petersburg 1851 | Banking, breweries, cotton mills, iron works, flour mills, shipping |
| **South Africa** | | |
| Wernher Beit | Kimberley 1873 | Banking, diamond mines, gold mines |
| Barnato Bros | Kimberley 1873 | Banking, diamond mines, gold mines |
| De Beers | Kimberley 1874 | Diamond mines, gold mines, railways |

Note: overseas base refers only to the earliest or principal overseas location; in fact almost all investment groups operated simultaneously from several overseas centres of trade.

*Source: Chapman (1985).*

## 1.3 FDI and managerial capitalism

Portfolio investment and free-standing firms were both forms of foreign investment in which capital was raised in a piecemeal, rather than a strategic, fashion. Firms receiving this investment remained relatively small-scale businesses and did not develop particularly sophisticated forms of management or extensive internal organizations; family and other personal connections persisted and mutual trust in partners and colleagues remained important as an organizational mechanism.

In America, however, the process of rapid industrialization after 1870 brought forth organizational methods and structures that were quite novel. Beginning with the organization of the railways which, often being single track, required precise administrative co-ordination, American firms emerged as pioneers in the creation of large-scale corporations utilizing modern management hierarchies (Chandler, 1977, 1990). This structure delegated responsibility for the functional, day-to-day management of production, sales, purchasing, transport and finance to a newly created group of non-shareholding middle managers, separating control from ownership and creating a new social group of professional businessmen. Above these middle managers stood the company's top management for whom longer-term corporate strategy and growth became the principal concerns.

These new corporate structures were particularly suited to the needs of the high-volume production industries generated by the cluster of technical innovations that constituted the second industrial revolution of the late nineteenth century. The new technologies that engendered this revolution led to rapid changes in many fields of production. They transformed the processing of tobacco, grains, whisky, sugar, vegetable oil and other foods. They revolutionized the refining of oil and the making of metals and materials: steel, non-ferrous metals (particularly copper and aluminium), glass, abrasives and other materials. They created entirely new chemical industries that produced man-made dyes, fibres, and fertilizers. They brought a wide range of machinery into being: light machines for sewing, agricultural and office uses and heavier, standardized machinery, such as elevators, refrigerating units, and greatly improved printing presses, pumps and boilers (Chandler, 1990, p.62). To be successful, these innovations in technology required massive investments in plant and machinery. Moreover, the potential benefits of high-volume production also required complementary investments in management and marketing expertise. It was by bringing together all three of these crucial forms of investment (production, management and marketing) within the context of the organizational structure of the corporation that American firms gained the market positions that enabled many of them to expand from national to multinational concerns from 1870 onwards.

The corporate structures of American business adapted readily to multinational operations. They had already developed expertise in distribution and marketing across the rapidly expanding market of the United States and these skills could be adapted to other markets. Moreover, their organizational capacity could be replicated in their foreign subsidiaries, giving them the necessary structure to effectively manage the process of vertical integration in those industries where this was an important source of competitive advantage. By the time of the outbreak of the First World War, many more American than European firms had developed their own production and marketing organizations abroad, an observation which remained valid until at least the 1960s.

## 1.4 Britain's foreign investments, 1865–1914

The period 1815–1914, stretching from the end of the Napoleonic Wars to the outbreak of the First World War, is sometimes referred to as *pax Britannica* to signify the overwhelming supremacy British naval power held throughout the nineteenth century. This military advantage enabled Britain to administer and enforce the safe maritime passage of goods globally and, where necessary, to force reluctant trading partners such as the Chinese to allow access to foreign vessels for the purposes of trade.

The Napoleonic Wars also saw the City of London emerge as the unrivalled financial centre of world trade. Indeed, economic historians such as Rubenstein (1993) and Cain and Hopkins (1993a, 1993b) now argue that it was the financial and allied service industries that developed in the south-east of England, more than the manufacturing industries of the north of England, which served to shape Britain's economic destiny, especially from 1850 onwards. British banks were amongst the country's earliest multinational enterprises, as Jones (1993) has demonstrated.

The institutions of the City were of vital importance in promoting sterling as the linchpin of the free trading system. London's financial institutions provided the sources of funding and the services of accepting and discounting bills of exchange which combined to enable the smooth functioning of the international trading system, while the ability of the Bank of England to convert sterling to gold at a fixed rate meant that holding assets in sterling accounts in London offered investors both security and a rate of interest. As a result, sterling increasingly became adopted as the currency of international trade. The gold standard régime that supported the growth of trade during the second half of the nineteenth century was thus essentially a sterling standard, centred on London and underwritten by Britain's mercantile and military preeminence.

Underpinning its position of hegemony in international trade was the fact that Britain had entered the nineteenth century as the world's first industrial economy. This industrial breakthrough could not have been achieved without the resources and markets provided by the international trading system; the raw cotton required by Britain's expanding textile firms, for example, simply could not be grown in the British climate. As the century progressed, therefore, the majority of economic interests in Britain outside the agricultural sector became ever more closely identified with the policy of free trade. Trading patterns developed that were increasingly based on international specialization of production, as conjectured by Ricardo's model of comparative advantage, which saw Britain develop as an exporter of manufactures and an importer of primary commodities.

Britain's position in the world economy meant that much of its early, portfolio-type investment abroad was directed towards the infrastructure required to support primary production activities. Figures cited by Pollard (1985), reproduced in Table 1.2, show that, around 1870, Britain's capital investments abroad, which are estimated at about £1000 million, focused on transportation, utilities and public works. Many foreign government authorities, both national and provincial, used London to raise finance during the nineteenth century.

**Table 1.2** Percentage distribution of British portfolio investment abroad, 1865–73 and 1909–13

|  | 1865/73 | 1909/13 |
| --- | --- | --- |
| Agriculture | 1.7 | 5.6 |
| Mining | 5.2 | 9.3 |
| Manufacturing | 0.7 | 4.8 |
| Transportation | 47.6 | 46.6 |
| Utilities | 5.5 | 6.4 |
| Public works | 17.8 | 17.3 |
| Other, incl. defence | 21.5 | 10.0 |

*Source: Pollard (1985), Table 1.*

By the outbreak of the First World War, these foreign investments had roughly quadrupled in value compared with 1870 but the composition had changed somewhat. Infrastructural services remained of primary importance but lending to foreign governments had become relatively less common while direct investments in production (agriculture, mining and manufacturing) accounted for an increased share.

Table 1.3 looks at the changing geographical dispersion of Britain's foreign investments and shows that, between 1860 and 1913, the relative share of capital exports going to Britain's emerging industrial rivals in Europe and America fell (from 52 per cent to 25 per cent) while investments in the largely primary producing regions of the British Empire and Latin America grew in significance.

---

**Table 1.3** British investment abroad by region: percentage 1860–1913

|  | **1860–70** | **1911–13** |
|---|---|---|
| British Empire | 36.0% | 46.0% |
| Latin America | 10.5% | 22.0% |
| United States | 27.0% | 19.0% |
| Europe | 25.0% | 6.0% |
| Other | 3.5% | 7.0% |

*Source: Hobsbawm (1987), Table 8.*

---

A considerable portion of the investment flowing out from Britain at this time was clearly 'portfolio' in nature. However, the recognition of the role of free-standing companies (see section 1.2 above) has led analysts to reconsider the extent to which Britain's foreign investments were actually of a direct nature. Recent work by Corley (1994) has suggested that, in the period immediately before the outbreak of the First World War, as much as 45 per cent of Britain's foreign capital holdings may have been direct investments. Of this 45 per cent, Corley suggests that about 35 per cent probably took the form of free-standing quoted companies and the remaining 10 per cent were the overseas investments of those domestic manufacturers who constituted Britain's first group of multinational companies.

A breakdown of the capital invested abroad by quoted (free-standing) companies in terms of industry sector is provided in Table 1.4 for 1907, 1910 and 1913. Compared with the portfolio investments given in Table 1.2 it suggests that these direct investments showed a greater disposition towards extractive industries (mining and oil) and market-based manufacturing activities (food processing, metal manufacturing and other market-based activities), which together account for somewhere in advance of 30 per cent of the total. The geographical breakdown of this free-standing foreign direct investment given by Corley, excluding railway investments, suggests that for the year 1910 the bulk of this capital (56 per cent) was invested in the countries of the British Empire. Latin America received 16 per cent, China, Japan and Thailand 7 per cent, while the industrialized United States and Europe received only around 10 per cent each. Most of the free-standing investment in railways, excluded from this breakdown, was directed towards Latin America.

Although the details are even less precise in the case of Britain's early multinational manufacturing companies, evidence from the Harvard

**Table 1.4** Quoted British overseas companies by industry groups (percentages)

|  | 1907 | 1910 | 1913 |
|---|---|---|---|
| **Resource-based** | 29.1 | 27.2 | 25.2 |
| Of which: Mining | (25.1) | (21.0) | (18.5) |
| Oil | (1.4) | (1.9) | (2.6) |
| Plantations | (2.6) | (4.3) | (4.1) |
| **Market-based** | 9.3 | 11.2 | 12.6 |
| Of which: Food (a) | (1.7) | (1.4) | (1.2) |
| Metals (b) |  | (1.7) | (2.0) |
| Other | (7.6) | (8.1) | (9.4) |
| **Railways** | 27.4 | 28.9 | 29.5 |
| **Banking/Insurance** | 5.3 | 4.8 | 4.8 |
| **Utilities and services** | 28.9 | 27.9 | 27.9 |
| Of which: Tramways | (3.5) | (4.4) | (5.0) |
| Electric power | (0.8) | (1.1) | (1.8) |
| Gas and water | (2.2) | (1.9) | (1.9) |
| Telegraphs | (3.4) | (3.1) | (2.9) |
| Shipping, docks etc. | (0.6) | (0.3) | (0.5) |
| Land and other | (18.4) | (17.1) | (15.8) |
| **TOTAL** | 100.0 | 100.0 | 100.0 |

*Source: Corley (1994), Table 2.*

Notes: (a) especially brewing
      (b) including motor traction and manufacturing

Figures in brackets are breakdowns of the sector subtotals.

study (Stopford, 1974) and from studies by Nicholas (1982) and Jones (1986) all indicate a greater tendency for these firms to invest in the developed markets of Europe and the United States compared with their free-standing counterparts.

Another point of contrast between these two forms of FDI lies in the fact that the investments of Britain's early multinational firms tended to be trade-replacing rather than trade-enhancing. Jones (1986, pp.8–10) found that the most important factors encouraging foreign investment among the group of firms covered by his study were the attractions of the foreign market, the need to avoid tariffs or other forms of host government pressure and the desire to maintain patent protection. In contrast, the study finds little evidence that the companies were locating abroad in search of lower labour costs. For British manufacturing firms investing abroad before 1914, access to markets rather than factors of production seem to have been the primary consideration.

Interestingly, although three-quarters of the foreign investments by domestic manufacturers studied by Jones involved the creation, rather than the acquisition, of a foreign subsidiary, most foreign investments by these pioneering multinational companies (71 per cent) took the form of joint ventures either with local producers, other British firms or third-country partners. Weaknesses in management, the spreading of risks, and the perceived need to deflect nationalistic criticism all seem to have contributed to this tendency of British firms to favour joint ventures, along with the fact that many of the companies engaged in foreign expansion were relatively small-scale concerns. The relative smallness of British companies also seems to have encouraged a greater tendency towards the use of international product licensing during the years before the First World War when compared with American firms. Table 1.5 lists some of Britain's leading manufacturing multinationals which had overseas production in operation before the First World War.

To sum up, therefore, Britain's foreign investments on the eve of the First World War embraced three distinct categories. First, portfolio investments, accounting for at least one half of the total, were directed mainly towards trade-related activities in the pre-industrialized world. Second, free-standing companies, accounting for perhaps one-third of the total of Britain's foreign investments, were oriented more towards mining and utilities and, like the portfolio investments, were based mainly in the British Empire and Latin America. Since these investments were generally managed from Britain they represented the bulk (around three quarters) of Britain's foreign *direct* investment at this time. The third category of foreign investment, the overseas subsidiaries of domestic firms, remained relatively small before the First World War, accounting for perhaps as little as 10 per cent of Britain's total stock of foreign investment. These predominantly manufacturing investments showed a much greater tendency to seek market opportunities in the industrialized regions of Europe and the United States compared with the two other categories of Britain's foreign investments.

**Table 1.5** United Kingdom enterprises with production facilities in at least four countries in 1914

| Industry/firm | Later identity/owners |
|---|---|
| **Oil** | |
| Royal Dutch Shell | |
| | |
| **Mining and metal manufacture** | |
| Consolidated Gold Field | Hanson Trust |
| British South Africa Co. | Chartered Consolidated |
| Borax | RTZ |
| | |
| **Household goods, food, tobacco** | |
| Lever Bros | Unilever |
| British American Tobacco | BAT Industries |
| Bryant and May | Wilkinson Match |
| Liebig Extract of Meat | Brook Bond/Unilever |
| Reckitts | Reckitt & Colman |
| Union Cold Storage | Western United Investments |
| | |
| **Textiles** | |
| J. & P. Coats | Coats Viyella |
| Bradford Dyers Assoc. | Coats Viyella |
| Calico Printers | Tootal |
| Courtaulds | |
| English Sewing Cotton | Tootal |
| Fine Spinners and Doublers | Courtaulds |
| Linen Thread | L Industries/Hanson Trust |
| | |
| **Other materials** | |
| Assoc. Portland Cement | Blue Circle Industries |
| Dunlop | BTR |
| Pilkington Bros | Pilkington |
| Vanesta (tea chests) | Carnaud Metalbox S.A. France |
| | |
| **Engineering, etc** | |
| Vickers | |
| G. & J. Weir | |
| Claudius Ash | Amalgamated Dental Ind. |
| Gramophone Co. | Thorn EMI |
| Minerals Separation | Burmah Castrol |
| S. Pearson & Son | Pearson |

*Source: Houston & Dunning (1976).*

## 1.5 FDI from the United States and continental Europe before 1914

In Britain, therefore, genuine multinational corporations accounted for a small fraction of the stock of foreign investment that the country had built up by 1914. The pattern of foreign investment that had evolved in Britain reflected the importance of trade and finance to its economic performance. In contrast to this, economic development in the United States and Germany during the late nineteenth century had been founded on the rapid growth of domestic firms in the industries transformed by the innovations of the second industrial revolution. These circumstances materially affected the shape of foreign involvement that emerged in these two economies prior to the First World War.

Figures from Wilkins (1974) estimate that, of a total stock of long-term United States outward investment of around $3.5 billion in 1914, $2.65 billion (roughly three-quarters) of this took the form of FDI. This figure is in stark contrast to the $6.7 billion stock of inward long-term foreign investment that had accumulated within the United States at this time, of which only $1.3 billion is estimated to be FDI. Although the United States economy was still a net importer of investment capital by 1914, therefore, its corporate sector had helped to make America a substantial net exporter of FDI.

Table 1.6 provides a breakdown of American FDI on the eve of the First World War by both sector and region. One striking feature of this pattern of investment is the importance of geographical proximity exhibited by the more traditional forms of foreign investment. The proportion of United States FDI accounted for by Canada, Mexico, Central America and the Caribbean as a group is 68 per cent in mining, 90 per cent in agriculture, 77 per cent in utilities and 95 per cent in railroads. A great deal of American FDI in these activities therefore involved domestic producers 'spilling over' the (still relatively arbitrary) national borders into neighbouring regions. Moreover, these more traditional activities were undertaken principally by domestic firms extending their operations abroad, rather than through the medium of the free-standing firm. The success of the mining enterprises under the direct control of the Guggenheims in Chile contrasts with the problems encountered in the free-standing operations managed by the British-based investment house of Antony Gibbs (O'Brien, 1989).

In contrast to the geographical dispersion of FDI in the more traditional activities, American overseas investment in manufacturing, sales and petroleum-related activities focused much more sharply on the markets of Europe. One half of the investment in sales-based activities, and over 40 per cent of manufacturing investments, were located in Europe in 1914. American pre-eminence in manufacturing investment at this time is illustrated by the fact that roughly half of the foreign manufacturing subsidiaries established in Britain before 1920 were of American origin (Bostock and Jones, 1994). These included Singer Sewing Machines, which set up an assembly plant in Glasgow in 1867,

**Table 1.6** Estimates of United States direct foreign investments, 1914 (book value in US $ million)

| Country/region | Total[1] | Manufacturing | Sales[2] | Petroleum[3] | Mining[4] | Agriculture | Utilities | Railways |
|---|---|---|---|---|---|---|---|---|
| Europe | 573 | 200 | 85 | 138 | 5 | – | 11 | – |
| Canada | 618 | 221[5] | 27 | 25 | 159 | 101[6] | 8 | 69 |
| Mexico | 587 | 10 | 4 | 85 | 302 | 37 | 33 | 110 |
| Cuba/W.Indies | 281 | 20 | 9 | 6 | 15 | 144 | 58 | 24 |
| C. America | 90 | – | 1 | – | 11 | 37 | 3 | 38 |
| S. America | 323 | 7 | 20 | 42 | 221 | 25 | 4 | 4 |
| Asia | 120 | 10 | 15 | 40 | 3 | 12 | 16 | 10 |
| Africa | 13 | – | 4 | 5 | 4 | – | – | – |
| Oceania | 17 | 10 | 5 | 2 | – | – | – | – |
| **TOTAL[7]** | **2652** | **478** | **170** | **343** | **720** | **356** | **133** | **255** |

*Source: Wilkins (1974), Table I.3.*

[1] Total includes banking investments of $30 million.
[2] Excludes petroleum distribution.
[3] Includes exploration, production, refining and distribution.
[4] Mining and smelting.
[5] Includes investments in paper and pulp ($74 million in 1914).
[6] Includes speculative investments.
[7] Total includes banking investments of $30 million.

Kodak (cameras), United Shoe Machinery (boot and shoe machinery) and Ford, which opened a car assembly plant in Manchester in 1911.

American industrial success before the First World War had been particularly marked in food processing, tobacco, drugs and other branded goods, light machinery (especially electrical and electronic equipment), transportation equipment, industrial chemicals, and vertically integrated industries of various kinds such as primary metals, rubber goods and, particularly, oil. Each of these industries had spawned corporations which, by 1914, had made major investments in plants abroad. Examples identified by Wilkins (1970) include American Tobacco, Coca Cola, H.J. Heinz, Quaker Oats and the meat packing enterprises of Armour and Swift in the food and tobacco goods sector, Du Pont and United Drug (later Rexall Drug) in chemicals and pharmaceuticals; General Electric, National Cash Register and International Harvester in machinery; Ford Motor and Westinghouse Air Brake in transportation equipment (motor cars and railway equipment respectively); Alcoa and Gillette (metal goods); US Rubber and Standard Oil of New Jersey (later the Exxon Corporation). Box 1.2 explores the contrasting forms of international growth that American and British tobacco companies adopted following the commercial success of the machine-made cigarette.

**Box 1.2** International growth in the cigarette industry

The formation of the British–American Tobacco Company provides an excellent example of the different ways in which firms in Britain and America responded to the potential benefits of mechanized production in the late nineteenth century. During the 1880s, a number of mechanical devices were developed in an effort to reduce the high costs of semi-skilled labour required to manufacture cigarettes. The most successful of these machines, named after its American inventor James A. Bonsack, was able to turn out 125 000 cigarettes per day compared with the 3000 that the fastest hand-roller could produce (Chandler, 1990, p.49).

Up until this time, cigarettes had represented only a tiny segment of the manufactured tobacco industries of Britain and America. However, the cost savings that were made possible by the Bonsack machine enabled cigarettes to be produced and sold at prices that placed them on a competitive footing with other forms of manufactured tobacco. In Britain, for example, the Bristol firm of W.D. & H.O. Wills which first gained exclusive control of the Bonsack patent for the British market, was able to market brands of cigarettes (notably Woodbine) at a price of 5 for 1 old penny. The Wills' cigarette sales were dramatic: in 1880 the company held 4.5 per cent of the United Kingdom market for tobacco products, none of which was accounted for by cigarettes; by 1900 Wills' share of the UK tobacco market had risen to 11 per cent and no less than 57 per cent of the company's sales (by weight) were now accounted for by cigarettes. (Alford, 1973, Tables I and II).

Wills' position as market leader in the British cigarette market was mirrored in the United States by the American Tobacco Corporation (ATC). ATC was the creation of James B. Duke, an entrepreneur who had turned his father's tobacco company, W. Duke & Sons, into the main American cigarette manufacturer by virtue of his acquisition of the Bonsack machine on favourable terms. Duke appreciated the benefits of economies of scale that could be gained by manufacturers of cigarettes. He also recognized, however, that under competitive conditions these benefits would not result in profits to the manufacturers unless they were able to control the market. Duke's strategy, therefore, was to embark upon cut-throat competition with rival firms until they agreed to a merger. In 1890, he succeeded in bringing together the four largest cigarette manufacturers in the United States with his own firm under the auspices of the ATC (Porter, 1969). Having thus succeeded in monopolizing the American cigarette market, Duke began to look for new cigarette markets abroad.

During the 1890s the exploitation of foreign markets had also become increasingly important to Wills. Using import/export agencies based in various countries, both Wills and ATC began to compete for market share in places such as Australia, Canada, Japan, India and China. It soon became apparent, however, that the different strategies that the companies had adopted in their home markets would colour their approach to exploiting foreign markets. Whereas Wills were prepared to deal with their rivals on the basis of market competition, Duke's ATC was perfectly prepared to advance its cause through the acquisition of rivals. Thus the decision of the Japanese government to place a tariff on imported cigarettes in 1898 was greeted by Wills with a scheme that was designed to reduce the invoice price of exported cigarettes to their agent, while ATC responded by simply buying the controlling share in Japan's largest cigarette manufacturer (Cochran, 1980, pp.40–1).

Hence ATC was already an established multinational corporation when, in 1901, Duke made the decision to invade the British market by purchasing control of the Liverpool-based cigarette manufacturer Ogdens. The ploy was countered by Wills, who adopted Duke's own strategy of amalgamation. The Imperial Tobacco Company was formed as an alliance of 13 British tobacco companies under the leadership of Wills in order to fight off the American threat. A year of commercial conflict, which affected the tobacco markets of all the countries in which the two giant firms competed, was brought to an end in September 1902 by the formation of the British–American Tobacco Company (BAT). This new organization became the focus for the overseas operations of both ATC and Imperial, although it was Duke's company that held the controlling interest.

During the first four decades of the twentieth century, BAT grew to become the leading manufacturer of cigarettes in over 40 countries. The story of BAT has a twist in the tail, however, since in 1911 the American Supreme Court dissolved Duke's ATC trust, forcing the company to sell off its interest in BAT. Over the course of the next few years the company's shares passed largely into British hands, and hence the company which provided Britain with its most geographically extensive multinational corporation between the wars actually had its origins in the USA.

*Sources: Alford (1973); Chandler (1990); Cochran (1980); Porter (1969), pp.59–76.*

In continental Europe, the most important source of corporate FDI prior to 1914 was Germany. Estimates of the stock of German foreign investment (both portfolio and FDI) on the eve of the First World War have recently been revised upwards as new evidence has become available and is currently placed at around $7.3 billion, of which some $2.6 billion is calculated to have been in the form of FDI (Schröter, 1993a). The success of German companies in the rapidly developing chemical and electrical industries is reflected in the extensive network of foreign manufacturing subsidiaries operated by firms such as Siemens, AEG and Bosch (electrical) and BASF, Hoechst, Bayer, Agfa and Degussa (chemicals) before 1914 (Franko, 1974). In addition to these large-scale investments by the firms in Germany's heavy industry, a variety of smaller manufacturers, such as the pharmaceutical firm of E. Merck, also made foreign investments at the beginning of the century (Hertner, 1986). Wilkins (1989) has recently uncovered a great deal of new evidence regarding the investments of German companies in America before 1914 and Schröter (1993a) cites a study claiming to have traced 336 German enterprises that were operating in the United States before 1914, including those involved in activities such as banking and insurance; indeed a number of Germany's early foreign direct investments were undertaken by financial institutions such as Deutsche Bank and insurance companies such as Allianz and Victoria. German enterprises were also the second largest source of FDI in Britain after American firms between 1890 and 1914 (Bostock and Jones, 1994).

Outside Germany and Britain, the development of European companies engaging in FDI was more limited. French firms, in particular, showed great preference for exports over foreign investment. Even in industries where French firms were strong, such as the motor industry, it was left to German companies (Daimler) and Italian companies (Fiat) to play the role of international pathbreakers. Much of the foreign investment of the leading French motor car producers

(Renault, Panhard, Darracq) before the First World War was limited to a network of sales agents (Fridenson, 1986). In many cases France developed more as a market in which foreign firms, particularly American companies, set up their own subsidiaries (Kindleberger, 1974). By 1914, France had emerged as the most popular location for Belgian multinationals (Devos, 1993) and the second, behind Germany, for Swiss FDI (Schröter, 1993b). Both the electrical industry and the chemical industry in France fell under the domination of American and German multinational firms before 1914 (Broder, 1986).

Among the smaller European nations, both Swiss and Swedish companies had developed impressive international profiles by the time of the First World War. Schröter (1993b) calculates that, by 1914, 160 Swiss multinational companies had established 265 foreign subsidiaries. Particularly important among these were the chemical firms of Ciba and Geigy, the electrical products manufacturer Brown-Boveri, and the food processing company Nestlé. Between them, these four firms could boast of foreign manufacturing operations in Russia, France, Germany, the United States, the United Kingdom, Spain, Austria, Italy, Holland, Norway and Australia by 1914 (Franko, 1974).

As with the Swiss, limitations in the size of the domestic market encouraged a number of Swedish manufacturers to move abroad in search of customers for their products. When SKF, manufacturers of ball and roller bearings, began production in 1907 it was purely to serve foreign clients; domestic firms preferred the traditional type of bearing produced in Germany. The importance of being physically close to the end users of its products soon led SKF to set up plants abroad. In 1910 the company began production in Britain and during the First World War it extended operations still further to the United States in 1915 and France in 1917. Most of the Swedish firms that invested abroad during the early part of the twentieth century were involved in the rapidly growing engineering industries. The limited size of the domestic market for such goods, coupled with the advantages that close proximity to their customers and direct control of the production process gave them, meant that many of Sweden's successful manufacturers around the turn of the century evolved into multinationals. Locating production abroad also made it much easier for these firms to win government contracts, a factor that greatly helped L.M. Ericsson to expand its sales of telephone equipment (Lundström, 1986).

## 1.6 FDI before 1914

It is hazardous to generalize about the patterns of FDI that developed prior to the First World War but, at the risk of oversimplification, some general points can be made. The late nineteenth century was a period of international economic and political stability in which both capital and labour were relatively mobile. The free flow of people and resources helped to encourage firms to expand their production activities beyond the confines of their domestic markets. Increasingly well-developed capital markets allowed investors in the capital-rich economies of West Europe to access investment opportunities abroad through the medium of free-standing companies formed specifically for the purpose. This form of FDI, neglected until recently, helps to explain why Britain was the world's largest source of FDI in 1914 while, at the same time, America played home to most of the world's emerging multinational corporations. Since free-standing companies seem mainly to have linked capital from the industrialized countries with investment opportunities in the peripheral regions, it may also be an explanation for the relatively high level of French FDI in 1914, which seems to have been directed largely towards the underdeveloped regions of South-East Europe and North and West Africa, and for the fact that around one-third of Dutch FDI was tied up in the Dutch East Indies (Gales and Sluyterman, 1993) where Royal Dutch pursued its oil production as a free-standing company that had first been floated on the Amsterdam capital market in 1890 (Sluyterman and Winkelman, 1993).

Another feature of international investment before 1914 was the variability in the forms and activities that the fledgling multinationals took. In Europe as a whole, most of the foreign investment that was generated by domestic firms seems to have been directed towards expanding sales through local production instead of exports. This investment therefore seems to have been predominantly directed towards relatively high-income markets. Obviously there were exceptions to this: a number of British companies made supply-related investments in developing countries before 1914: Lever Brothers in the Solomon Islands and the Belgian Congo, Dunlop in the Malay Peninsular and Ceylon (Sri Lanka), and Cadbury in Trinidad, for example. For the most part, however, Europe's demand for raw materials could be met through international commodity markets, often serviced by free-standing firms, without the need for long-term supply-related investments on behalf of the end users. Backward vertical integration was not a major objective for most of the European firms' early foreign investment policies.

The distinction between free-standing FDI and the activities of multinational corporations was much less important in the United States, where the latter form tended to dominate foreign investment. In America, most of the industries that were transformed by the second industrial revolution underwent a process of horizontal integration through mergers and takeovers which led to the creation of large-scale firms, or trusts, in a range of industries. To effectively manage such large organizations, the trusts developed a hierarchical managerial structure which Chandler (1977, 1990) has termed the multiunit, multifunctional enterprise. The principal benefit of such a structure lay in the fact that an administrative hierarchy could perform the co-ordinating role between different functions that, up until this point, had either been performed by the market mechanism or had simply not been required given the relatively simple methods of production. The advent of such a hierarchical managerial structure enabled large firms in America to control much more extensive production processes. Both horizontal and vertical integration could be taken much further than had previously been the case. Before the First World War, American firms in the oil industry (Standard Oil), industrial chemicals (Du Pont), the rubber industry (US Rubber, Firestone, Goodyear), primary metal production (Alcoa, Anaconda, Kennecott, American Smelting and Refining – the Guggenheim's concern), and in industrial materials (Pittsburgh Plate Glass) had utilized managerial hierarchies to achieve vertical integration of the production process.

Vertical integration by firms in many of these industries, and others such as United Fruit in fruit processing, meant that the co-ordination of production extended over national boundaries. Rather than simply using a foreign subsidiary to substitute foreign production for exports, these firms began to internalize the production process itself. Few European firms had developed the same kind of organizational structure as American corporations. The operations of their foreign subsidiaries were held on a much looser rein and relatively little international vertical integration was successfully undertaken.

## 1.7 Foreign investment from the First World War to the Great Crash

In 1914, the era of international economic stability that had ushered in the rapid expansion of FDI came to an abrupt and violent end. The immediate consequences of the war in Europe for many of the multinational corporations from the belligerent countries was that some of their foreign assets now lay in enemy territory. In most instances, the ultimate result of this situation was a process of repatriation. The Anglo-American cigarette manufacturer BAT, for example, had built up substantial manufacturing capacity in Germany shortly before the war broke out. During the conflict the company was able to negotiate the sale of its German assets to the Deutsche Bank, one of the group of large-scale German banks that held interests in a range of industries. After the end of the war, BAT received compensation totalling just over £1 million but did not reinvest in the German economy until 1926. Hence, one direct effect of the war was the nationalization of many foreign subsidiaries.

Whilst this seems mainly to have involved compensation, investors with assets in Russia after the Bolshevik revolution of 1917 were less fortunate. Indeed, the loss of the Russian market was a severe blow for many European firms, notably those from Sweden, which had sought the potential market there as a major location for their foreign activities.

The First World War proved to be a major setback for the international ambitions of firms in Europe. Germany, in particular, was hard hit. During the course of the war, German business interests were seized by the Allied nations and the assets were sold off as part of the reparation payments. Subsidiaries of German multinationals were sold off to domestic interests, forming the basis for companies such as the English Electric Company of Great Britain (formerly Siemens Brothers Dynamo Works) (Panayi, 1990) and Sterling Drug of the United States (formerly the American subsidiary of Bayer) (Chandler, 1990). Threatened to the east by the rise of Bolshevism, stripped of its foreign colonies, and forced to pay reparations by the Allies through the Treaty of Versailles, Germany's foreign investments between the wars fell to negligible levels when compared with its rapid growth before 1914.

Elsewhere in Europe, the period between the wars did witness the international development of some major firms. The Nestlé and Anglo-Swiss Condensed Milk Company grew rapidly and by 1936 had acquired interests in more than 20 other companies in Europe, North and South America, Australia and Asia (Humes, 1993). The international expansion of the Dutch electrical giant Philips gathered pace after the First World War when the need to secure inputs and the opportunities presented by the loss of markets by German competitors led it to adopt a policy of vertical and horizontal integration that saw it organize affiliates across Europe and in the US (Sluyterman and Winkelman, 1993).

Table 1.7 illustrates the number of new foreign subsidiaries formed between 1920 and 1939 by the 87 continental European manufacturing firms included in the Harvard study. These 87 firms were drawn from Germany (32), France (21), Belgium and Luxembourg (6), Holland (5), Switzerland (7), Italy (7) and Sweden (9). Table 1.7 shows that this relatively small group of companies created a total of 249 traceable subsidiaries between 1920 and 1929 and concentrated largely on inter-European growth. Continental European investors in Britain during this period included Philips from Holland, and the car assembly and manufacturing plants of the French firms Citroën (1926), Renault (1927) and Michelin, which established a tyre factory at Stoke-on-Trent in 1927. Investments were also made in Britain by firms that were not included in the Harvard study, such as the Swedish firm Electrolux and a small Dutch manufacturer of raincoats, N.V. Hollandia Fabrieken Kattenburg. Altogether, Bostock and Jones (1994) have been able to trace 34 new subsidiaries set up in Britain during the 1920s by firms from Switzerland (2), Sweden (5), Germany (6), France (7) and the Netherlands (14). The minor renaissance of German manufacturing FDI that began in the late 1920s was based partly on the re-acquisition of former subsidiaries.

British firms were more inclined to resume international growth after the war than their continental counterparts. The 47 British companies included in the Harvard study were found to have made a total of 118 foreign subsidiary investments during the 1920s and the majority of these were spread equally between Europe (42, excluding Ireland) and

**Table 1.7** Establishment or acquisition of foreign subsidiaries by US, UK and contintental European firms included in the Harvard study (by number of subsidiaries), 1920–29 and 1930–39

| | 1920–1929 | | | 1930–1939 | | |
|---|---|---|---|---|---|---|
| | USA | UK | Europe | USA | UK | Europe |
| USA | – | 8 | 27 | – | 3 | 7 |
| Canada | 84 | 10 | 0 | 69 | 6 | 1 |
| Mexico | 7 | 1 | 1 | 19 | 0 | 1 |
| C. America/Carib. | 3 | 5 | 3 | 15 | 0 | 2 |
| South America | 29 | 8 | 11 | 33 | 6 | 13 |
| **America subtotal** | **123** | **32** | **42** | **136** | **15** | **24** |
| | | | | | | |
| United Kingdom | 48 | – | 18 | 53 | – | 14 |
| Germany | 24 | 14 | 30 | 18 | 8 | 7 |
| France | 25 | 4 | 11 | 20 | 3 | 7 |
| Italy | 6 | 2 | 28 | 5 | 1 | 2 |
| Belgium/Lux. | 5 | 2 | 13 | 7 | 2 | 3 |
| Netherlands | 5 | 2 | 5 | 6 | 5 | 8 |
| Scandinavia | 8 | 6 | 14 | 6 | 9 | 10 |
| Austria | 4 | 2 | 9 | 4 | 3 | 6 |
| Spain | 9 | 1 | 12 | 4 | 0 | 8 |
| Switzerland | 1 | 2 | 8 | 3 | 2 | 3 |
| **Europe subtotal[*]** | **141** | **46** | **186** | **131** | **42** | **78** |
| | | | | | | |
| South Africa | 5 | 6 | 0 | 13 | 4 | 0 |
| British Africa[1] | 0 | 7 | 0 | 0 | 5 | 0 |
| French Africa[2] | 0 | 3 | 1 | 0 | 0 | 0 |
| Egypt/Middle East[3] | 2 | 1 | 0 | 1 | 1 | 2 |
| **Africa subtotal[*]** | **7** | **17** | **4** | **14** | **10** | **5** |
| | | | | | | |
| Japan | 3 | 0 | 3 | 2 | 0 | 1 |
| China | 2 | 0 | 2 | 0 | 0 | 2 |
| India | 3 | 5 | 3 | 2 | 8 | 1 |
| Philippines | 5 | 1 | 0 | 2 | 0 | 1 |
| **Asia subtotal[*]** | **15** | **10** | **10** | **9** | **14** | **5** |
| | | | | | | |
| **Australia and N.Z.** | **13** | **13** | **7** | **25** | **18** | **0** |
| | | | | | | |
| **Total** | **299** | **118** | **249** | **315** | **99** | **112** |

Notes:
[*] Includes investments in countries not listed separately.
[1] Includes Rhodesia, Zambia, Tanzania, Kenya, Nigeria.
[2] Includes Morocco, Algeria, Tunisia.
[3] Includes Libya

*Source: Vaupel and Curhan (1974), Tables 1.17.2, 1.17.3, 1.17.4.*

the Empire (41). Particularly striking in Table 1.7, however, is the small number of subsidiaries set up by British manufacturers in the booming 1920s American market, lending credence to the argument that British firms in the leading industries lacked a competitive edge. Firms that bucked this trend and invested in America between the wars included the now British-controlled British–American Tobacco (cigarettes), Dunlop (rubber), EMI (records), Baker Perkins (machinery), Distillers (alcoholic drinks), and Turner & Newell (asbestos) (Stopford, 1974).

The main beneficiary of the war was undoubtedly the United States. Between the outbreak of the war and 1919, America's foreign investment position was transformed as the figures from Wilkins (1974) demonstrate. During this brief period the United States' $4.6 billion deficit in portfolio foreign investment was turned into a surplus of $1.0 billion whilst its net surplus in foreign direct investment rose from $1.4 billion in 1914 to $3.0 billion in 1919. Not surprisingly, the share of this FDI that was invested in Europe fell as American firms moved particularly into South America but this was purely a relative decline and American firms continued to invest in Europe even during the years of the conflict.

Over the course of the 1920s the book value of United States' foreign direct investment doubled and the amount of this FDI devoted to manufacturing grew by a still larger proportion. It has been argued that by the end of the 1920s the size of United States' investments in both Canada and Latin America exceeded those of British investors for the first time and that more than 1300 companies or organizations in Europe were either owned or controlled by United States' capital (Wilkins, 1974, p.155). It was during this era that the American multinational truly first came of age. American companies did not simply set up parallel operations in foreign markets but many actually created international holding companies that co-ordinated production across national boundaries. Among these new 'international companies' of the 1920s were American & Foreign Power (1923), ARMCO International (1924), International B.F. Goodrich (1924), Crown Cork International (1928), and Aluminium Limited (1928) (Wilkins, 1974, p.148).

Vertically integrated American multinationals were established across a wide range of industries between the wars. Perhaps the most extreme example of these, and one of the few cases in which European firms had developed along similar lines, was the oil business in which seven multinationals dominated world output between the wars (Sampson, 1993). This rapid expansion of vertical integration meant that by 1929 numerous examples existed of American firms that had developed both supply-oriented and market-oriented investments (although these latter operations often constituted only sales-based investments).

America was not the only beneficiary of the diversion created in Europe by the First World War. Table 1.8 illustrates that Europe's share of world production and trade between 1913 and 1923/4 each fell by 9 per cent. One of the main consequences of the war was thus the decentralization of the international economy. North America in

**Table 1.8** Production and world trade, 1913–24 (regional distribution in percentages)

|  | Share of world production | | Share of world trade | |
| --- | --- | --- | --- | --- |
|  | 1913 | 1923 | 1913 | 1924 |
| Europe | 43 | 34 | 59 | 50 |
| North America | 26 | 32 | 14 | 18 |
| Asia | 20 | 21 | 12 | 16 |
| Latin America | 7 | 8 | 8 | 9 |
| Africa | 2 | 3 | 4 | 4 |
| Australia | 2 | 2 | 3 | 3 |

*Source: Hardach (1977), Table 36.*

particular raised its share of world output, but both North America and Asia increased their share of international trade at Europe's expense. In the case of Asia it was Japan's export industries that took advantage of the withdrawal of European goods from these markets (Hardach, 1977). The large scale industrial conglomerates, the *zaibatsu*, and their trading houses the *sōgō shōsha*, made particular progress in the Chinese market by rapidly expanding Japan's share of textiles there. By the end of the 1920s, Japanese producers had made substantial investments in China, most especially in Manchuria, and had forged complete control over China's coal and iron ore industries and pig iron production. Box 1.3 looks at the organization and growth of Japan's pre-war *zaibatsu* and their trading operations, the *sōgō shōsha*.

**Box 1.3** The Japanese *zaibatsu* and *sōgō shōsha*

The origins of Japanese industrial modernization can be dated from the political upheavals of 1868 during which the rule of the Tokugawa family was brought to an end and the authority of the Meiji Emperor was restored. This event, commonly known as the Meiji Restoration, represented an acknowledgment amongst many of the ruling classes in Japan that the country was faced with a choice of industrial modernization or colonial domination by the Western powers.

An immediate concern of the new government was to place the economy on a stable financial basis. To this end it instituted a policy of land reform designed to provide revenues derived from the collection of a land tax. These moves toward macroeconomic stability were coupled with an industrial policy in which state investment in infrastructure and modern factories played a central role during the 1870s. The authorities were also quick to introduce and disseminate the institutional form of the joint stock company and the growth of by far the most important of Japan's industrial sectors during the nineteenth century, silk and cotton textiles, was based upon a large amount of small-scale investment centred on the joint stock structure (Francks, 1992, p.37).

During the 1880s, as the burden of large-scale industrial investment began to weigh over-heavily on the Japanese state's revenue base, the government began to seek to engage the capital resources of the wealthy merchant groups who had been a major source of economic power during the preceding Tokugawa period. Thus the Japanese government began a series of privatization programmes which began to transfer the responsibility for developing the country's heavy industries to the private sector. This policy thus set in motion a train of events which saw the modern sector of the Japanese economy – mining, shipping and shipbuilding, and the manufacture of machinery, metals and chemicals – dominated between the late nineteenth century and the Second World War by the so-called *zaibatsu*.

The *zaibatsu* have been defined as a group of diversified businesses owned exclusively by a single family or extended family (Morikawa, 1992, p.xvii). The founders of the *zaibatsu* used their influence and personal connections with members of the Meiji government to gain the patronage necessary to establish new industrial enterprises. From this basis the largest of the groups developed into huge pyramid organizations with their own banking and trading arms, extending their activities through the formation of diversified subsidiaries which were linked to the main holding company through interlocking shareholdings and directorships, or through the personal ties of family relations and marriage. Following the end of the First World War, the Japanese economy suffered from a period of prolonged depression as a result of which many smaller firms were forced into bankruptcy. These conditions allowed the largest of the *zaibatsu*, in particular the enormous Mitsui and Mitsubishi groups, to gain substantial influence over the Japanese economy.

Nowhere was the influence of Mitsui and Mitsubishi greater than in the area of Japan's international economic growth. Early in their development, the two had both been heavily involved in the effort to wrest control of Japan's coastal shipping away from foreign interests. In 1885 the two companies merged their shipping interests to form the Nippon Yusen Kaisha (NYK), providing Japan with a shipping company which was sufficiently strong to challenge the cartel arrangements for transoceanic shipping organized by the European shipping companies. NYK's first success beyond Japan was to establish its own line between Bombay and Kobe following a commercial battle with Britain's P&O company which dominated lines to India (Wray, 1984).

The opening up of shipping lines run by the leading *zaibatsu* allowed Japan the opportunity to extend its activities in international trade. NYK's access to Bombay was used by Mitsui to develop an import trade under the control of its own trading arm, Mitsui Bussan, to supply Japanese textile manufacturers with raw cotton. Military successes over China (1894/5) and Russia (1905) further strengthened Japan's trading position, allowing it much greater leverage to dictate terms of trade and to gain increasing influence in the economic affairs of China. During the dislocations to international trade created by the First World War, Mitsui Bussan provided the mechanism through which Japan gained a large share of the Chinese market for cotton piece goods.

The Mitsui Bussan represented the first example of a *zaibatsu* developing a general trading company (*sōgō shōsha*) as part of its organizational structure. The *sōgō shōsha* represent trading companies, rather like the old-style chartered trading companies of Europe such as the British East India Company, which set up branches abroad to deal with Japan's import and export trade (Mirza, 1993). Although Japanese firms engaged in very little foreign direct investment before the Second World War, these general trading companies were of great importance in allowing Japan's manufacturing industries to develop a substantial export trade. The Mitsui Bussan retained central importance in Japan's trading performance between the wars, accounting for 15.2 per cent of the country's total exports and 14.4 per cent of total imports around 1930 (Morikawa, 1992, p. xix).

When the *zaibatsu* were dismembered by the Allied Occupying Force at the end of World War Two, the *sōgō shōsha* were spun off to become independent trading organizations. Although they subsequently re-established links with the reformed postwar industrial groups, the *kieretsu*, the traditional *sōgō shōsha* retained an important function in the postwar trade success of the Japanese economy, nowadays handling worldwide sales in excess of even the largest Western multinational corporations.

*Sources: Francks (1992); Mirza (1993); Morikawa (1992); Wray (1984).*

## 1.8 International firms in depression and war

The growth of Japanese influence in Asia and United States' influence in Latin America which occurred during the 1920s represented the beginning of a process of economic regionalism that came increasingly to the fore after the Great Crash of 1929. The 1920s had seen the gradual reconstruction of the prewar gold standard (Britain restored sterling to gold in 1925) and this had been an important factor in stabilizing the world economy, encouraging firms to engage once again in international trade and investment. The structure was never as secure after the war as it had been before 1914, however (Aldcroft, 1977), and when, in 1929, the Wall Street Crash provoked a financial crisis in the United States, the fragile nature of the reconstructed order quickly became apparent. By 1931, the system lay in tatters.

The reconstructed gold standard suffered from a number of structural weaknesses (Drummond, 1987). As noted earlier, one of the consequences of the First World War had been the emergence of the United States as net exporter of capital. During the 1920s the United States ran an almost permanent surplus on its current account and, as a result, built up large stocks of gold. In order for the fixed exchange rates of the gold standard to remain in parity, indeed for the continued stability of the international economy as a whole, it was necessary for America to continuously engage in foreign lending. One result of this was that, during the 1920s, New York began to eclipse London as the principal source of international investment funds. However, much of this lending, upon which a number of European governments relied for their financial stability, was short-term and unreliable. The emergence of New York as the *de facto* international financial centre in the 1920s, therefore, tended to increase the degree of international financial instability. This became particularly clear when in 1928/9 the market for United States domestic stocks boomed, squeezing out the funds required to support foreign issues and threatening the stability of the international monetary system. A great deal of short-term American foreign assets were repatriated with the crash in October 1929. An international effort was made to revive foreign lending from America in the wake of the crash, partly to counter the deflationary pressures caused by the domestic liquidity crisis. A recovery in portfolio lending was engineered during 1930, partly through the United States-sponsored Young Plan but a crisis of confidence amongst private business had now been provoked by the collapse in United States stock prices and the lending effort could not be sustained. The contrast between portfolio and FDI lending to the countries of Latin America and Asia, Africa and Oceania during 1930 is indicative of this loss of commercial confidence. While United States portfolio lending to the 'periphery' rose between 1929 and 1930 (from $71 million to $225 million for Latin America, and from $17 million to $77 million for Asia, Africa and Oceania), direct investment declined. In 1929, United States' firms had invested $205 million in businesses in Latin America; in 1930 this fell to only $41 million. The comparable figures for Asia, Africa and Oceania were $65 million and $14 million, respectively (Kindleberger, 1986, p.122).

Figures from Wilkins (1974) suggest that a decline, or at least a levelling off, in FDI on behalf of American firms remained a feature of the 1930s as a whole. By 1940, the book value of foreign direct investments by United States' firms had fallen slightly from its 1929 level of $7.5 billion to $7.0 billion. In fact manufacturing- and sales-based investments held up quite well during the 1930s. Table 1.7 indicates that the group of American firms included in the Harvard study slightly increased the number of new subsidiaries compared with the previous decade. This conclusion is corroborated by the findings of the Bostock and Jones (1994) study of manufacturing FDI into Britain which shows 118 acts of FDI by American firms between 1920 and 1929 (from a total of 158) being followed by 110 acts during the 1930s (from a total of 157). Indeed, the activities of American manufacturing and sales subsidiaries, including the Ford Motor Company's massive investment in its Dagenham plant, operational from 1931, represented some of the most dynamic aspects of Britain's economy between the wars.

The sectors that witnessed the main retreat in FDI by American firms during the world depression were mining and agriculture and in each case Latin America was the region affected most. This fall in investment was undoubtedly linked to the collapse in the value of primary commodities as a consequence of the sharp decline in world demand between 1930 and 1932. Nevertheless, as the 1930s progressed, United States' firms continued to make investments in Latin American industry, switching progressively from export processing to domestic manufacturing (Abel and Lewis, 1985, p.285). The extent of this redirection of United States' FDI in South America can be gauged from the fact that in 1914 United States' manufacturing-based FDI in South America accounted for barely 2 per cent of the non-oil total invested in that subcontinent; by 1940 this ratio had risen to 25 per cent (Wilkins, 1974, pp.31, 182–3).

The tightening conditions for international investment flows and the tendency for these flows to become increasingly regionalized after the collapse in the volume of world trade after 1929 was particularly marked in the case of Great Britain. The policy of according Imperial Preference in trading relations towards the nations of the British Empire hardened after the decision had been taken to withdraw sterling from the gold standard in 1931. Britain's foreign trade consequently became much more focused on these Empire economies, together with the handful of foreign countries whose currency remained linked in value to sterling and which together with the Empire countries formed the so-called Sterling Area.

The same regionalization was also true of Britain's foreign investments between the wars. Table 1.9 shows that the level of new overseas capital issues both declined in value and became increasingly focused on the Empire. By the mid-1930s, the small trickle of money going to foreigners went largely to those within the Sterling Area (Cain and Hopkins, 1993b, p.47). A similar bias can be seen in Britain's foreign direct investment flows. The tightening of the capital market, and a greater tendency towards investment in domestic firms, appears to have considerably slowed down the growth of the free-standing type of FDI, whilst

**Table 1.9** New capital issues in Britain: Empire and foreign 1900–38 (average per year)

| | Empire | | Foreign | | Total | |
|---|---|---|---|---|---|---|
| | £m. | % | £m. | % | £m. | % |
| 1900–14 | 53.5 | 39.1 | 83.9 | 60.9 | 137.4 | 100 |
| 1919–23 | 65.4 | 66.4 | 27.9 | 33.6 | 93.3 | 100 |
| 1924–28 | 72.5 | 58.8 | 50.8 | 41.2 | 123.3 | 100 |
| 1929–33 | 44.0 | 69.6 | 19.2 | 30.4 | 63.2 | 100 |
| 1934–38 | 25.6 | 86.2 | 4.1 | 13.8 | 29.7 | 100 |

*Source: Cain and Hopkins (1993b), Table 3.7.*

Britain's pioneering multinationals displayed an increasing disposition towards directing their investments at Empire markets between the wars (Nicholas, 1989). In India, for example, the managing agencies that had provided the institutional framework for managing Britain's free-standing foreign investments were largely bypassed in the wave of investments by British-based multinationals which Tomlinson (1986) identifies as having effectively begun in the 1920s.

The impact of the depression was most severe on the international development of firms in continental Europe. Table 1.7 indicates that the number of foreign subsidiaries created by the sample of manufacturing firms in the Harvard study fell by over one half after 1929. In place of competition, international cartels were instituted between the national firms in many industries, most notably in chemicals, plate glass, iron and steel and electrical goods. Table 1.10 illustrates the extent to which corporations from continental Europe had subscribed to such international agreements by the late 1930s. According to Casson (1985, p.64):

> During the 1930s in Europe, *laissez faire* capitalism was written off in political terms: centralised control was widely believed to hold the key to the restoration of economic stability, and the only questions were how tight the control should be, and whether it should remain in private hands or be vested in the state.

This kind of arrangement served to consolidate in economic terms the growing sentiment towards nationalism that became increasingly evident politically during the 1930s. It is hardly surprising that, by the time these political forces culminated in the Second World War, the notion of 'global corporations' had receded to the faintest echo of a seemingly bygone age.

Table 1.10    Number of international cartel member corporations by country, 1937

| Country | Number of participants | | |
|---|---|---|---|
| | Direct | Indirect/partial | Total |
| France (and colonies) | 67 | 2 | 69 |
| Germany | 57 | | 57 |
| Great Britain | 31 | 9 | 40 |
| Switzerland | 25 | | 25 |
| Holland | 20 | | 20 |
| Belgium | 20 | | 20 |
| Czechoslovakia | 17 | 3 | 20 |
| Norway | 16 | 1 | 17 |
| Sweden | 16 | | 16 |
| Austria | 15 | 3 | 18 |
| Italy | 15 | 1 | 16 |
| Poland | 13 | 2 | 15 |
| Finland | 10 | 1 | 11 |
| Yugoslavia | 9 | 1 | 10 |
| Hungary | 8 | 3 | 11 |
| United States | 8 | 3 | 11 |
| Japan | 2 | 2 | 4 |

*Source: Kudō and Hara (1992), p.3.*

## 1.9 American multinationals and the postwar recovery

Six years of global warfare, involving the occupation and seizure of assets together with economic dislocation on an unprecedented scale, left even the most robust of international corporations in a precarious state by the end of 1945. By and large, however, the Western hemisphere managed to escape from the destruction inflicted elsewhere, and American firms with investments in Latin America were, relative to European multinationals, enormously strengthened as a result of the war. Moreover, the main bridgehead that these firms had established in Europe, Great Britain, had remained allied and unoccupied throughout the course of the conflict. On these foundations, American corporations consolidated into the position of world leaders across almost the entire range of the advanced industries during the 1950s.

The key to the success of American firms during this period lay in the decisive lead that they had gained in technology. The Second World War spurred technical progress across a wide range of industries. Particularly important were advances in transport (notably the jet engine) and communications, both of which served to make the operation of international business far easier to manage in the postwar period. A great deal of progress in electronics was also achieved by American firms after the war, based upon the development of semi-conductors (and later integrated circuits) which greatly stimulated the rate of product innovation and heralded the start of the computer age (Auerbach, 1988, pp.298–310).

The postwar recovery also benefited from the absence of the international cartel agreements that had served to restrict competition and innovation during the 1930s. Coupled with the liberal reforms in world trade ushered in through the Bretton Woods agreements (Chapter 2), the 1950s saw a restoration of competition for market share between both domestic producers and foreign firms in many product markets. American producers, technically advanced and competitively more adept than most of their European rivals, quickly increased their market presence in the expanding markets of Western Europe. Beginning with exports but finding constraints on growth due to the shortage of dollars in Europe, many United States firms were encouraged to replace this trade-led competition with overseas branch plants, allowing them both to service foreign markets and to promote their goods more effectively. Reflecting on his survey of American foreign direct investment in Europe in the 1950s, Dunning (1983) has argued that, in the main, United States manufacturing subsidiaries at this time were truncated replicas of their parent organizations which, after a brief learning period, tended to operate with the minimum of parental interference. Whilst this may still have been the case for its European subsidiaries, it is important to note, as Chandler (1990) has pointed out, that American corporations were also developing the more flexible multidivisional structure which would enable them to effectively harness the advantages of product diversification that their substantial commitment to research and development had began to generate.

As we will see later (Chapter 5), this role of technological leadership, promoting foreign investment by American firms, was used by Vernon (1966) to develop one of the earliest theories of international production based on the model of the product life cycle. The growth of oligopolistic rivalry amongst United States' firms was also taken to be a cause of FDI. Knickerbocker (1973) noted a tendency for FDI to be used as part of the competitive strategy of American firms against their domestic rivals. This oligopolistic reaction model of FDI argued that foreign investment by firms within an industrial sector would tend to cluster at a narrow point in time as rival firms in an oligopoly found themselves obliged to follow the lead of the first-mover. Vernon and Knickerbocker's work provide examples of how the American experience heavily influenced the development of theories of international production in the 1960s.

The dominance of American firms in the early postwar growth of FDI and international production in manufacturing is clearly indicated by the Bostock and Jones (1994) study of inward FDI in Britain. Of the 376 new subsidiaries identified in Britain between 1950 and 1962, 303 (81 per cent) represented investments by United States-based firms. Given that United States' firms had exerted almost the same degree of foreign penetration in Britain between the wars, it is hardly surprising to find commentators identifying multinational corporations as an effectively American phenomenon during the 1960s.

Table 1.11 provides a sectoral breakdown of these predominantly American investments in Britain between 1950 and 1962, and compares them with the pattern of those made between the wars. The most striking feature of this table is the fact that practically half of all the subsidiaries created between 1950 and 1962 were based in two sectors: the chemical industry and mechanical engineering. In fact these investments were yet more concentrated within the sectors themselves. Foreign chemical companies were heavily clustered in basic industrial chemicals and pharmaceuticals; those in mechanical engineering were concentrated on machine tools and mechanical equipment. The apparent decline in electrical engineering after the war is a little misleading because the main boom for FDI in this sector was in the 1960s; indeed, of the 38 subsidiaries noted in Table 1.11, 18 had been created between 1960 and 1962. Here also, investments were clustered in telecommunications equipment, electronic capital goods and passive electronic components. It should also be noted that, although numerically small, foreign investments in the motor vehicle industry were of great significance in terms of output and employment: in 1963, 31.1 per cent of sales and 25.6 per cent of employment in the British motor industry were accounted for by these foreign subsidiaries (Bostock and Jones, 1994, pp.95–9).

The geographical distribution of United States' manufacturing firms' foreign investments in the early postwar period was highly skewed. The Latin American markets that had increased in importance between the wars accounted for around 30 per cent, whilst the growing industrial and consumer markets of Canada and Europe accounted for another 50 per cent of the foreign investments for those United States' firms included in the Harvard study. The investments of British manufacturing firms in the study were equally geographically concentrated. Based on the Harvard figures from Vaupel and Cuhran (1974), Dunning (1983) estimates that, in 1960, 70 per cent of United Kingdom multinationals' capital was invested in Commonwealth countries. Compared with British firms, manufacturing companies from continental Europe displayed a much greater tendency during the 1950s to direct their investments towards other parts of the Continent and the United States.

The threat of domination of European markets by American firms, which emerged as a focus of attention during the 1960s, soon subsided as European firms began to adopt an increasingly multinational form themselves. However, in the less developed regions of the world the (sometimes justified) hostility towards multinationals grew exponentially during the 1960s (cf. Turner, 1973). Frequently identified as a legacy of colonialism, or agents of neocolonialism, multinationals found their investments in the developing world subject to increasing political

**Table 1.11** New manufacturing subsidiaries in the United Kingdom by sector, 1920–39 and 1950–62

| | New subsidiaries created | |
| --- | --- | --- |
| Activity | 1920–39 | 1950–62 |
| Mineral oil processing | 3 | 0 |
| Production and distribution of oil and gas | 3 | 0 |
| Metal manufacturing | 13 | 15 |
| Manufacturing of non-metallic mineral products | 7 | 8 |
| Chemical industry | 66 | 93 |
| Production of man-made fibres | 3 | 8 |
| Manufacturing of other metal goods | 27 | 17 |
| Mechanical engineering | 41 | 91 |
| Manufacture of office machinery | 5 | 7 |
| Electrical and electronic engineering | 40 | 38 |
| Motor vehicles and parts | 12 | 4 |
| Other transport equipment | 3 | 2 |
| Instrument engineering | 16 | 21 |
| Food, drink and tobacco | 38 | 32 |
| Textiles | 5 | 1 |
| Leather and leather goods | 9 | 5 |
| Timber and wooden furniture | 3 | 0 |

| Activity | 1920–39 | 1950–62 |
|----------|---------|---------|
| Paper and paper products | 7 | 10 |
| Rubber and plastics | 10 | 10 |
| Other manufacturing | 4 | 7 |
| **TOTAL** | **315** | **376** |
| Number from US | 228 | 303 |

*Source: Bostock and Jones (1994), Table I.*

pressure as Third World governments attempted to institute economic planning as the route to development. Supply-based investments came under particular scrutiny as host governments attempted to wrest a share of the monopoly rents and became aware of practices such as transfer pricing being used to reduce the profitability of foreign subsidiaries of vertically integrated firms (Jenkins, 1987). Expropriations of foreign subsidiaries rose steadily through the 1960s, peaking in the wake of the OPEC crisis of the mid 1970s (UNCTC, 1988).

In the early postwar period, therefore, American firms took the leading role in helping to internationalize competition in many industries once again. As European firms, and later Japanese firms, took up the challenge, so the pace of internationalization accelerated. The extent to which economic recovery benefited from liberalization is indicated by the fact that trade consistently grew more rapidly than the value of world output before the energy crisis of the early 1970s, and that FDI grew more rapidly than both of these. However, difficulties in many developing countries, coupled with a tendency for much international investment to seek out lucrative markets, meant that the activities of multinational corporations in the postwar years tended to increase the polarization between industrialized and less-developed countries. Not until the 1960s was it possible to point to clear examples in which FDI by multinational corporations contained benefits as well as drawbacks and the concept of a newly industrialized country (NIC) began to emerge.

## 1.10 Further reading

Chapman, S.D. (1992) *Merchant Enterprise in Britain: From the Industrial Revolution to World War One*, Cambridge University Press, Cambridge.

(Describes the predecessors of the multinationals in Britain.)

Hertner, P. and Jones, G. (eds) (1986) *Multinationals: Theory and History*, Gower, Aldershot.

(Contains a useful combination of theory and case studies of multinationals.)

Jones, G. (ed.) (1986) *British Multinationals: Origins, Management and Performance*, Gower, Aldershot.

(Deals with British multinationals.)

Jones, G. (1996) *The Evolution of International Business: an Introduction*, Routledge, London.

(Provides an extremely good, detailed and up-to-date introduction to this subject.)

Jones, G. and Schröter, H. (eds) (1993) *The Rise of Multinationals in Continental Europe*, Aldershot: Edward Elgar.

(Discusses multinationals in continental Europe.)

Schmitz, C.J. (1993) *The Growth of Big Business in the United States and Western Europe, 1850–1939*, Macmillan, London.

(Contains a concise introduction to the subject of the growth of large, although not necessarily multinational, firms, together with a very helpful guide to sources.)

Wilkins, M. (ed.) (1991) *The Growth of Multinationals*, Edward Elgar, Aldershot.

(Provides a collection of key articles on the history of multinationals.)

Wilkins, M. (1970) *The Emergence of Multinational Enterprise*, Harvard University Press, Cambridge MA and Wilkins, M. (1974) *The Maturing of Multinational Enterprise*, Harvard University Press, Cambridge MA.

(These are classic studies of the American multinational.)

## 1.11 Questions for further discussion

1.    How did Britain's position as a leading trading nation influence the growth of foreign investment in that country?

2.    Give examples of the industries that were transformed by the Second Industrial Revolution. What factors stimulated the growth of these industries in Germany and America?

3.    Distinguish between cartels and trusts. Why do you think that the interwar period witnessed industrial stagnation in many industries?

4.    What kind of organizational innovations helped American firms to become multinational? Contrast the developments which took place before the First World War with those that occurred mainly after the Second World War.

# 2

# *Internationalization trends*

## *2.1 Introduction*

This century has seen considerable qualitative and quantitative changes in the process of internationalization, most of which have been concentrated in the 50 years following the Second World War. The changes relate to trade and all aspects of activities by the transnational companies (TNCs). This chapter concentrates on the activities of TNCs rather than on trade, which will be examined in Chapter 4. It will only touch on some of the most important trends. The reader who would like more details should consult the various publications listed in section 2.7, especially those by the United Nations.

In order to assist the reader, the complex web of data will be grouped into various categories and, in particular, into evidence and trends related to the TNCs themselves (micro level) and those related to the macro level of countries and regions.

## *2.2 Transnational companies and the network of their operations*

In the early 1990s the number of TNCs in the world totalled more than 38 500, of which 89 per cent were based in developed countries (Table 2.1 and Figure 2.1a). Within the developed countries themselves, the largest percentage were in Germany followed by Japan, Sweden and Switzerland. Within the developing ones, the Republic of Korea is home to the largest number. Comparisons between countries must be made with some caution, however, as the quality of the data is very uneven across countries (cf. Notes to UNCTAD-DTCI, 1995: Table I.2, pp. 8–9).

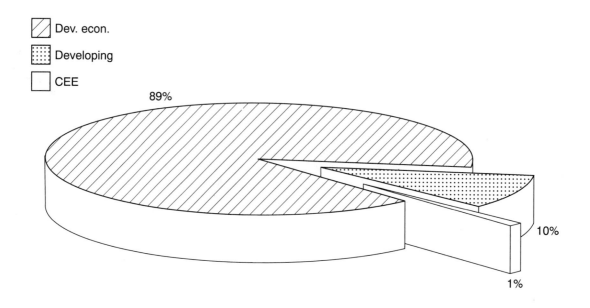

**Figure 2.1a**  Percentage of parent TNCs by area – early 1990s.

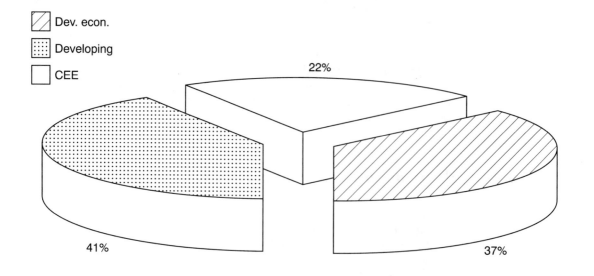

**Figure 2.1b**  Percentage of foreign affiliates by area – early 1990s.

The information in Table 2.1 relates to all TNCs, large and small. The overall picture looks rather different when only the largest companies are considered as in Table 2.2 and Figure 2.2. The United States, Japan and the United Kingdom are home to the highest percentage of the world's largest TNCs in both manufacturing and service industries. Germany falls into fourth position. This is an indication that many German TNCs are not very big companies. It is interesting to note that the concentration of the largest TNCs by country of origin is very similar for both manufacturing and services. The TNCs have collectively set up a network of almost 251 500 affiliates worldwide (Table 2.1 and Figure 2.1b). These affiliates are distributed more evenly than the headquarters of the TNCs themselves. Over 37 per cent are located in developed countries and the rest (approximately 40 per cent) in developing countries and in Central and Eastern Europe (almost 22 per cent). The Republic of China hosts almost 18 per cent of the world's affiliates. Recent years have seen a considerable increase in the proportion of affiliates located in Central and Eastern Europe (CEE). For example the proportion of affiliates there in 1992 – reported in UNCTAD-DTCI (1994) Table I.1, p. 4 – is 10.5 per cent, while the corresponding figure for 1995 was almost 22 per cent (as in our Table 2.1). These percentages refer to total number of affiliates and are therefore no guide to the value of the investment behind them (this is discussed further in sections 2.2 and 2.3).

There is evidence of an increasing trend in the number of small- and medium-size companies that become transnationals (cf. UNCTNC, 1988, Chapter 2 and UNCTAD-DTCI, 1995, Chapter I). This is both a sign of and an outcome of greater internationalization. The increasingly favourable conditions (see Chapter 3) that lead to the spreading of activities of large TNCs are also likely to enhance the opportunities for smaller companies. Moreover, the international activities of large TNCs may themselves help to improve the opportunities for similar activities by smaller companies. A tradition of internationalization in a particular country may generate an environment of social, political, legal and cultural advantages that further enhances the opportunities for international activities by both large and smaller companies (Ietto-Gillies, 1996).

There is evidence that companies, particularly the largest ones, are spreading their activities wider and wider. Vernon (1979) provided evidence of the trend towards an increased network of operations by the largest American and European TNCs between 1950 and the 1970s (Table 2.3). Research into similar trends for Britain (Ietto-Gillies, 1996) demonstrates even more dramatic changes between 1963 and 1990. Table 2.4 shows that, between 1963 and 1990, the percentage of United Kingdom companies with a network in less than 6 countries declined from 23 per cent to 3 per cent while the percentage of companies with a network in more than 21 countries increased from 20 per cent to 72 per cent. The network refers to affiliates and therefore gives no indication of the spread in terms of the value of investment. Evidence of the increase

**Table 2.1** Number and percentage of parent TNCs and foreign affiliates by area and country, early 1990s

| Area/country | Parent corporations based in country | | Foreign affiliates located in country | |
|---|---|---|---|---|
| | No. | % | No. | % |
| **Developed economies** | **34 353** | **89.1** | **93 311** | **37.1** |
| Of which: | | | | |
| Australia | 732 | 1.9 | 2 450 | 1.0 |
| Canada | 1 447 | 3.8 | 4 475 | 1.8 |
| Finland | 1 200 | 3.1 | 1 050 | 0.4 |
| France | 2 216 | 5.7 | 7 097 | 2.8 |
| Germany | 7 003 | 18.2 | 11 396 | 4.5 |
| Japan | 3 650 | 9.5 | 3 433 | 1.4 |
| Netherlands | 1 608 | 4.2 | 2 259 | 1.0 |
| Norway | 1 000 | 2.6 | 3 000 | 1.2 |
| Sweden | 3 700 | 9.6 | 6 150 | 2.4 |
| Switzerland | 3 000 | 7.8 | 4 000 | 1.6 |
| United Kingdom | 1 443 | 3.7 | 3 376 | 1.3 |
| United States | 2 966 | 7.7 | 16 491 | 6.6 |
| **Developing economies** | **3 788** | **9.8** | **101 139** | **40.2** |
| Of which: | | | | |
| Brazil | 797 | 2.1 | 9 698 | 3.9 |
| China | 379 | 1.0 | 45 000 | 17.9 |
| Hong Kong | 500 | 1.3 | 2 828 | 1.1 |
| Republic of Korea | 1 049 | 2.7 | 3 671 | 1.5 |
| **Central and Eastern Europe** | **400** | **1.0** | **55 000** | **21.9** |
| **WORLD (total)** | **38 541** | **100.0** | **251 450** | **100.0** |

*Source: Adapted from UNCTAD-DTCI (1995), Table I.2, pp.8–9.*

(See notes to original table for comparisons and discrepancies.)

**Table 2.2**  World's largest transnational companies by country of origin and sector (percentage)

| Country | Percentage of total companies in | |
|---|---|---|
| | Mining and manufacturing | Services |
| United States | 46 | 46 |
| Japan | 16 | 20 |
| United Kingdom | 10 | 10 |
| Federal Republic of Germany | 6 | 5 |
| France | 4 | 6 |
| Netherlands | 1 | 3 |
| Switzerland | 2 | 2 |
| Italy | 1 | 1 |
| Others | 14 | 7 |
| Total | 100 | 100 |
| **No. of companies in sample** | **600** | **365** |

*Source: Ietto-Gillies (1993). Original data from UNCTNC.*

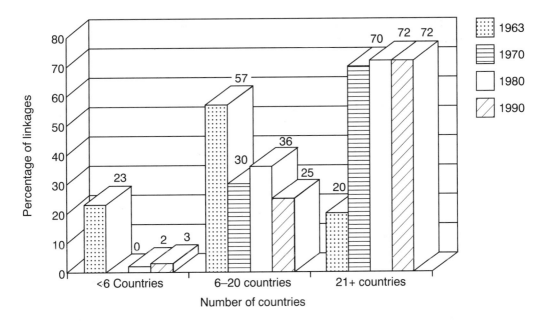

**Figure 2.2**  United Kingdom's largest TNCs in manufacturing and mining: percentage of network affiliates abroad by number of countries. Source: Ietto-Gillies (1996), Table 1, p.200.

**Table 2.3** Network of foreign manufacturing subsidiaries of MNCs. Total and percentages, 1950 and 1970

| Area of origin | Year | Companies with a network in | | | | | |
| | | < 6 countries | | 6–20 countries | | 21+ countries | |
| | | Total | % | Total | % | Total | % |
|---|---|---|---|---|---|---|---|
| United States | 1950 | 138 | 76 | 43 | 24 | 0 | 0 |
| | 1975 | 9 | 5 | 128 | 71 | 44 | 24 |
| Europe | 1950 | 116 | 86 | 16 | 12 | 3 | 2 |
| | 1975 | 31 | 23 | 75 | 56 | 29 | 21 |

*Source: adapted from Vernon (1979), Table I, p.258.*

**Table 2.4** UK largest TNCs in manufacturing and mining. Network of affiliates abroad by number of countries (totals and percentages)

| Year | Companies with a network in | | | | | |
| | < 6 Countries | | 6–20 countries | | 21 + countries | |
| | Total | % | Total | % | Total | % |
|---|---|---|---|---|---|---|
| 1963 | 10 | 23 | 25 | 57 | 9 | 20 |
| 1970 | 0 | 0 | 14 | 30 | 32 | 70 |
| 1980 | 1 | 2 | 20 | 36 | 35 | 72 |
| 1990 | 2 | 3 | 16 | 25 | 45 | 72 |

*Source: Ietto-Gillies (1996), Table 1, p.200.*

**Table 2.5** Growth in strategic alliance formation, 1980–89 (number and percentage)

|  | 1980–84 | | 1985–89 | | 1980–84 to 1985–89 |
| --- | --- | --- | --- | --- | --- |
|  | Number | % | Number | % | % change |
| **Automobiles** | 26 | 100 | 79 | 100 | 203 |
| US – Europe | 10 | 39 | 24 | 30 | 140 |
| US – Japan | 10 | 39 | 39 | 49 | 290 |
| Europe – Japan | 6 | 23 | 16 | 20 | 167 |
| **Biotechnology** | 108 | 100 | 198 | 100 | 83 |
| US – Europe | 58 | 54 | 124 | 63 | 114 |
| US – Japan | 45 | 42 | 54 | 27 | 20 |
| Europe – Japan | 5 | 4 | 20 | 10 | 300 |
| **Information technology** | 348 | 100 | 445 | 100 | 28 |
| US – Europe | 158 | 45 | 256 | 58 | 62 |
| US – Japan | 133 | 38 | 132 | 30 | −1 |
| Europe – Japan | 57 | 16 | 57 | 13 | – |
| **New materials** | 63 | 100 | 115 | 100 | 83 |
| US – Europe | 32 | 51 | 52 | 45 | 63 |
| US – Japan | 16 | 25 | 40 | 35 | 150 |
| Europe – Japan | 15 | 24 | 23 | 20 | 53 |
| **Chemicals** | 103 | 100 | 80 | 100 | −22 |
| US – Europe | 54 | 52 | 31 | 39 | −43 |
| US – Japan | 28 | 27 | 35 | 44 | 25 |
| Europe – Japan | 21 | 20 | 14 | 17 | −33 |

*Source: UNCTAD–DTCI (1994), Table III.12, p.139.*

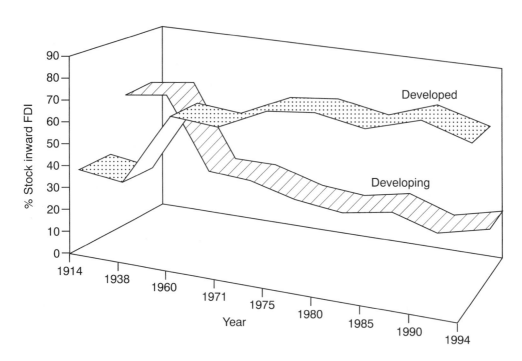

**Figure 2.3** Percentage stock of inward FDI by selected years 1914–94 for developed market economies and developing countries (sources: for 1914, 1938, 1960 and 1971 – Dunning (1983), Table 5.2; for 1975 – UNCTC (1988), Table I.3; for 1980, 1985, 1990, 1994 – UNCTAD-DCTI (1995), Annex, Table 3, pp.401–6).

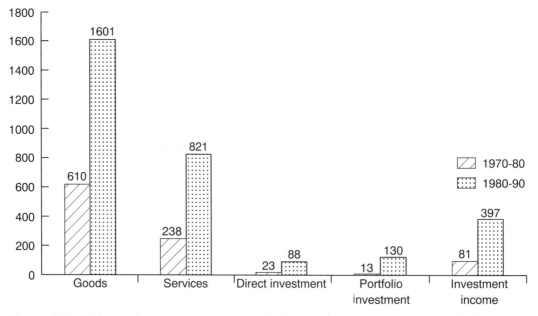

**Figure 2.4** Values of main components of flows in international transactions. Adapted from OECD (1994), p.19.

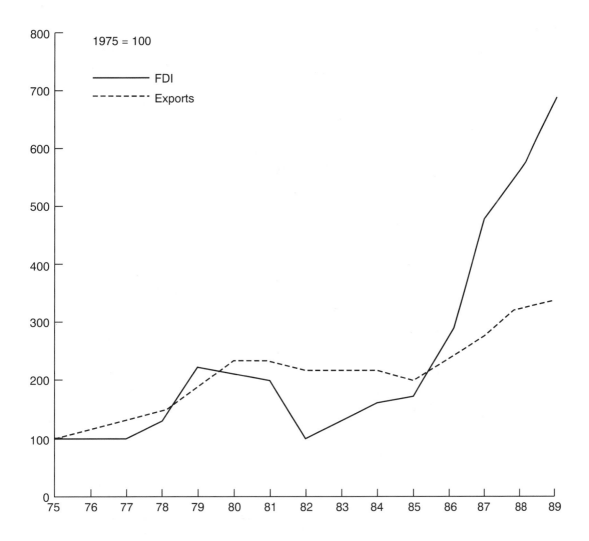

**Figure 2.5** Index of current value of exports and foreign direct investment outflows, 1975–1989. Source: UNCTC (1991), Figure I, 9.5.

in the spread of outward activities of United Kingdom transnational companies both in terms of value of the investment and in terms of the number of affiliates is in Ietto-Gillies (1996).

The last 20 years have also seen a growing tendency towards collaboration between companies. This takes various forms, ranging from strategic alliances to joint ventures and subcontracting. The reasons for these global networks vary and tend to be linked both to technological elements and to the oligopolistic structure of the industries in which most large TNCs operate. Reich (1991b, Chapters 8, 9, 10) analyses this tendency towards what he calls 'global webs'.

Table 2.5 shows evidence of considerable growth in strategic alliances between the first and second half of the 1980s (UNCTAD-DCTI, 1995, Table III.4 and III.5, p.156). The industries most involved seem to be the ones at the forefront of technological applications (information technology and biotechnology) and the automobile industry, where the problems of overcapacity may have encouraged companies to co-operate rather than compete in many cases.

Joint ventures have become prominent in the relationships between TNCs and local companies from host countries in developing countries and Central and Eastern European regions. There are numerous reasons for these ventures. They include the ease of penetration into a country in terms of many elements that range from understanding the host country's business culture and its regulatory framework, to compliance with the host governments constraints and regulations. Joint ventures can, therefore, be seen as a necessary means to penetrate some new countries as well as a learning process for such penetration. Joint ventures and strategic alliances will be discussed at greater length in Chapter 9. See also Ietto-Gillies (1992, Chapter 2) and Contractor and Lorange (1988). Details of evidence and motivations for joint ventures in Central and Eastern Europe are in (UNTC, 1988, Chapter XVIII).

Subcontracting and licensing agreements usually involve a large company as the principal/licensor and smaller ones as sub-contractors/licensees. The reason why companies are increasingly involved in these contractual arrangements are many and span from a desire to minimize risks of fluctuation of demand to the externalization of labour involved in production. (On subcontracting, reasons and trends, see also Ietto-Gillies, 1992, Chapters 12 and 14; Germidis, 1980.)

Table 2.6   Average annual growth rates of outward foreign FDI and exports, 1981–93 (percentages)

| Period | Outward FDI flows | Outward FDI stocks | Export of goods and non-factor services |
|--------|------------------:|-------------------:|----------------------------------------:|
| 1981–85 | 0.8 | 5.4 | −0.1 |
| 1986–90 | 28.3 | 19.8 | 14.3 |
| 1991–93 | 5.6 | 7.2 | 3.5 |

Source: UNCTAD–DTCI (1995), Table I.1, p.4.

Table 2.7   Exports and imports by employee of foreign affiliates and in the total economy, 1989 (US$ thousands)

|  | Exports by employee | | Imports by employee | |
|---|---|---|---|---|
|  | Foreign affiliates | Total economy | Foreign affiliates | Total economy |
| United States (1990) | 14.8 | 11.7 | 20.5 | 16.9 |
| Japan | 32.7 | 21.7 | 12.8 | 11.1 |
| France | 49.9 | 38.1 | – | 52.2 |
| Sweden | 66.1 | 50.4 | – | 50.8 |
| Finland | 47.0 | 56.1 | – | 53.3 |
| Portugal | 11.0 | 7.7 | 10.3 | 7.2 |

*Source: OECD (1994), Table 19, p. 78.*

## 2.3 Macro trends

Transactions across frontiers take many forms. There are flows of human resources but these will not be dealt with here. There are movements of products and financial assets across frontiers. In particular, there are trade flows (both goods and services), portfolio investments, foreign direct investments and incomes from investments (both portfolio and direct). Figure 2.1 gives the averages over two decades of these components for OECD countries. It should be noted that 'cross-countries transactions for goods and services' are still the most relevant component, although the growth rate of world exports has been considerable lower than the growth rate of FDI in the 1980s and 1990s (Figure 2.2 and Table 2.6). All the components of transactions show higher average values in the 1980s compared to the 1970s (Figure 2.4). Interestingly enough the flows of investment income are considerably larger than the flows for investment. This is due to the fact that the incomes relate to cumulative investment over long periods. For countries with a long tradition of foreign investment (and this includes many countries within the OECD group) the profits and dividends on cumulative overseas assets can be very substantial.

The large increase in FDI in the 1980s is mainly due to mergers and acquisitions. UNCTAD (1994, p.23) reports that:

Worldwide cross-border acquisitions accounted for approximately 70 per cent of the FDI inflows to the developed countries during the period 1986-1990; that share was significantly higher in the peak years 1988 and 1989, amounting to 86 and 73 per cent, respectively. In 1990, cross-border acquisitions declined by 7 per cent and, in 1991, by 56 per cent, leading to a comparable behaviour in worldwide investment flows. Indeed, growth and decline in worldwide investment flows have seemed to coincide broadly with the boom and decline of cross-border acquisitions.

On the trade side, according to UNCTNC (1988, Chapter VI), the TNCs are responsible for over 75 and 80 per cent of the total exports of the United States and Britain respectively. The figures on the imports side are lower. The TNCs tend to generate trade to a larger extent than companies operating in one country. This is highlighted by Table 2.7 which shows that the trade intensity of foreign affiliates of TNCs in OECD countries is higher than for the economy as a whole on both the export and import sides. The table only refers to foreign affiliates so, in theory, the difference could be ascribed to the trade activities of both the uninational companies and the home based TNCs. In reality, less trade-intensive companies are likely to be uninational. None the less the relative weight of exports in the sourcing of foreign markets is declining in favour of direct sales by foreign affiliates, as shown by the trend in the last row in Table 2.8. In the late 1980s, direct sales by foreign affiliates overtook sales through exports.

**Table 2.8** International production and world economic activity: selected indicators, 1960–93 (percentages)

| Item | 1960 | 1975 | 1980 | 1985 | 1991 | 1993 |
|---|---|---|---|---|---|---|
| World FDI stock as share of world output | 4.4 | 4.5 | 4.8 | 6.4 | 8.5 | 9.2 |
| World FDI inflows as share of world output | 0.3 | 0.3 | 0.5 | 0.5 | 0.7 | 0.9 |
| World FDI inflows as share of gross fixed capital formation | 1.1 | 1.4 | 2.0 | 1.8 | 3.5 | 4.0 |
| World sales of foreign affiliates as a share of world exports | 84 | 97 | 99 | 99 | 122 | 113[1] |

[1] 1992 data.

*Source: UNCTAD (1994), Table III.6, p.130 and UNCTAD (1995), Table I.1, p.4, GATT (1994).*

The TNCs generate substantial intra-firm trade. This consists of movements of goods and services across frontiers, but within the company. It is the result of all the goods and services transferred from affiliate to affiliate or between affiliate and parent company. It is both an indication and a result of the integration of production activities within a company with an international network of affiliates. Data on intra-firm trade are not widely available as most countries do not collect the relevant statistics. The United States, and Japan have data on both the imports and exports side. For the United States the share of intra-firm exports and imports in total exports and imports in the 1980s were of the order of 30 and 40 per cent respectively. For Japan, the corresponding figures are around 32 and 30 per cent. For the UK, data are available only on the export side and show a figure of around 30 per cent (UNCTC 1988: Table VI.1, p.92). UNCTAD-DTCI (1995, Table I.13, p.37) estimates worldwide intra-firm exports to be about a third of total world exports.

The prices at which the internal transfer of goods and services takes place within the company are *transfer prices*. There are situations when it is in the economic interest of the company as a whole to invoice these internal transfers at a price that is different from the price that might prevail in the market for the same good or service ('arm's length price'). The manipulation of transfer prices of components and services may be carried out by the company in order to increase its overall level of profits or for strategic reasons. It should be noted that the manipulation of transfer prices is not considered a fair or legal practice. Companies do not admit to such practices, which are difficult to detect. In fact, many components or services transferred internally are not sold on the open market and, therefore, do not have corresponding arm's-length prices for comparison. Motives that are particularly likely to lead to the overpricing or underpricing of internal transfers include:

- The minimization of tax liabilities. By reducing recorded profits in countries with high tax rates and increasing recorded profits in countries with low tax rates the company can minimize its overall tax liability worldwide.

- Over- or under-invoicing in order to take advantage of expected movements in exchange rates and/or in order to facilitate the repatriation of profits over and above the levels allowed by the host country.

- A strategy of reducing recorded profits in countries with high levels of industrial conflict may help the company in arguing for a lower wage settlement.

- A strategy leading to low prices of final products through low pricing of internal imported components may help the company to penetrate a new market.

**Table 2.9** Foreign direct investment inflows and outflows as percentage of gross fixed capital formation, 1981–93, by area and selected countries (averages)

| Region | Inward | | | Outward | | |
|---|---|---|---|---|---|---|
| | 1981–85 | 1986–90 | 1991–93 | 1981–85 | 1986–90 | 1991–93 |
| **Developed economies** | **2.2** | **4.6** | **3.3** | **2.7** | **5.6** | **5.1** |
| Western Europe | 2.6 | 5.8 | 5.5 | 4.3 | 8.8 | 7.5 |
| European Union of which: | 2.6 | 5.8 | 5.6 | 4.3 | 8.8 | 7.4 |
| Belgium/Luxembourg | 7.6 | 16.1 | 24.9 | 1.3 | 14.7 | 16.8 |
| Denmark | 0.4 | 2.5 | 6.9 | 0.9 | 4.7 | 8.7 |
| France | 2.0 | 4.1 | 7.7 | 2.5 | 8.5 | 10 |
| Germany | 1.2 | 2.0 | 1.4 | 3.4 | 6.8 | 5.3 |
| Ireland | 4.0 | 1.1 | 1.3 | 2.2 | 7.1 | 7.6 |
| Italy | 1.1 | 2.2 | 1.3 | 1.8 | 2.3 | 2.9 |
| Netherlands | 6.1 | 13.3 | 10.6 | 15.5 | 21.1 | 20.6 |
| Portugal | 3.0 | 10.0 | 10 | 0.2 | 0.5 | 2.1 |
| Spain | 5.3 | 9.4 | 7.3 | 0.9 | 1.7 | 2.2 |
| Sweden | 1.6 | 4.0 | 9.5 | 7.7 | 23.0 | 7.4 |
| UK | 5.7 | 14.6 | 9.6 | 12.0 | 18.7 | 13.2 |
| North America of which: | 2.9 | 6.9 | 3.4 | 2.0 | 3.0 | 5.7 |
| USA | 2.9 | 0.9 | 3.3 | 1.7 | 2.8 | 5.7 |
| Other developed economies of which: | 0.7 | 0.9 | 0.6 | 1.5 | 4.2 | 1.9 |
| Australia | 4.6 | 10.3 | 7.2 | 2.4 | 7.0 | 2.2 |
| New Zealand | 4.8 | 9.5 | 23.9 | 1.7 | 9.4 | 3.6 |
| Japan | 0.1 | 0.1 | 0.1 | 1.5 | 4.1 | 1.8 |
| **Developing economies** | **3.3** | **3.2** | **5.8** | **0.4** | **1.2** | **1.2** |
| Africa | 2.3 | 3.5 | 4.6 | 1.8 | 1.5 | 1.1 |
| Latin America/Caribbean | 4.1 | 4.2 | 6.5 | 0.2 | 0.9 | 0.7 |
| Asia | 3.1 | 2.8 | 5.6 | 0.3 | 1.3 | 1.4 |
| **Central/Eastern Europe** | – | **0.1** | **12.2** | – | – | **0.05** |
| **World total** | **2.3** | **4.1** | **3.8** | **2.1** | **4.7** | **4.3** |

*Source: adapted from UNCTAD-DTCI (1995), Annex Tables 5 and 6, p.411–26.*

**Table 2.10** Estimated employment in world transnational corporations, 1975, 1985, 1990 and 1992 (millions of employees)

|  | 1975 | 1985 | 1990 | 1992 |
|---|---|---|---|---|
| **Estimated employment in TNCs** | 40 | 65 | 70 | 73 |
| Employment in parent companies at home | – | 43 | 44 | 44 |
| Employment in foreign affiliates | – | 22 | 26 | 29 |
| Developed countries | – | 15 | 17 | 17 |
| Developing countries | – | 7 | 9 | 12 |
| China | – | – | 3 | 6 |

*Source: adapted from UNCTAD-DTCI (1994), Table IV.3, p.175.*

The increasing relevance of FDI in the domestic economies is highlighted by Tables 2.8 and 2.9. Table 2.8 shows increasing percentages over time for all the components. Table 2.9 shows the increasing weight of FDI in relation to the capital formation for the world as a whole and for major areas and countries. The data show a considerable increase between the early and late 1980s with stability or some decline in the early 1990s.

Some countries have high percentages on both inward and outward FDI: these are Belgium and Luxembourg, Netherlands, the United Kingdom and New Zealand. The inward percentage for the developing countries shows a considerable increase in the early 1990s; this is due partly to the effects of privatization programmes and partly to the large influx of FDI into China. The European Union as a whole has a higher outward than inward percentage, a pattern that is similar to that of the developed countries overall. It must be remembered that the FDI data include investment due to both 'greenfield' investment (new factories, equipment, machinery) and mergers/acquisitions. This means that the increased FDI does not necessarily correspond to increased productive capacity in the host country. In fact the figures for the 1990s in developing countries can be partially explained by the increase in FDI due to privatization in those regions. This issues will be reconsidered in Chapter 3.

The impact of TNCs' activities on employment is considerable as can be inferred from Table 2.10. It shows increased employment levels in TNCs worldwide from 40 million in 1975 to 73 million in 1992.

**Table 2.11** Inflows and outflows of foreign direct investment (percentage shares 1981–94)

| Inflows and outflows by area | Percentage share in total | | | | | |
|---|---|---|---|---|---|---|
| | 1981–85[*] | 1986–90[*] | 1991 | 1992 | 1993 | 1994[**] |
| **Inflows** | | | | | | |
| Developed countries | 74 | 84 | 72.6 | 65.2 | 61.9 | 59.8 |
| Developing countries | 26 | 16 | 25.8 | 32.1 | 35.1 | 37.4 |
| (of which China) | | | (2.8) | (6.5) | (13.2) | (15.0) |
| Central and Eastern Europe | 0.04 | 0.1 | 1.5 | 2.5 | 2.8 | 2.7 |
| **Total** | **100** | **100** | **100** | **100** | **100** | **100** |
| **Outflows** | | | | | | |
| Developed countries | 98 | 96 | 94.4 | 89.9 | 86.8 | 85.1 |
| Developing countries | 2 | 4 | 5.5 | 10.1 | 13.1 | 14.8 |
| (of which China) | | | (0.5) | (2.1) | (1.8) | (0.9) |
| Central and Eastern Europe | 0.01 | 0.01 | 0.01 | n | 0.03 | 0.03 |
| **Total** | **100** | **100** | **100** | **100** | **100** | **100** |

[*] Annual averages.    [**] Based on preliminary estimates.    n = negligible

*Sources: adapted from UNCTAD–DTCI (1994), Table I.4, p.12; UNCTAD–DTCI (1995), Annex Tables 1 and 2.*

**Table 2.12** Percentage stock of inward foreign direct investment, developed market economies and developing countries, selected years

| Host region | 1914 | 1938 | 1960 | 1971 | 1975 | 1980 | 1985 | 1990 | 1994[*] |
|---|---|---|---|---|---|---|---|---|---|
| Developed market economies | 37.2 | 34.3 | 67.3 | 65.2 | 75.1 | 77.5 | 73.5 | 80.3 | 74.0 |
| Developing countries | 62.8 | 65.7 | 32.3 | 30.9 | 24.9 | 22.5 | 26.4 | 19.6 | 25.2 |
| Unallocated | n.a. | n.a. | 0.4 | 3.9 | n.a | 2.3 | n.a. | n.a. | 0.8 |

[*] estimates    n.a. = not available    Unallocated amounts include FDI into Central/Eastern Europe.

*Sources: for 1914, 1938, 1960, 1971 – Dunning (1983), Table 5.2; for 1975 – UNCTNC (1988), Table I.3; for 1980, 1985, 1990, 1994 – UNCTAD-DTCI (1995), Annex Table 3, pp.401–6.*

**Table 2.13** FDI from privatization programmes as share of total FDI: developing regions and Central and Eastern Europe (percentages)

| Area | 1988 | 1989 | 1990 | 1991 | 1992 | 1993 |
|------|------|------|------|------|------|------|
| Developing region | 2.7 | 1.8 | 27.9 | 11.9 | 7.9 | 5.4 |
| Central and Eastern Europe | 1.4 | 31.2 | 33.5 | 49.8 | 46.4 | 49.0 |

*Source: developed from Sader (1995).*

## 2.4 Geographical patterns

The developed countries are responsible for most of the outward FDI. Table 2.11 shows outflows of FDI from developed countries of well over 85 per cent although there is a declining trend. On the inward side, one of the most remarkable changes that took place during the course of this century is the shift in the shares of foreign direct investment that went to developed and developing countries. Table 2.12 shows how the share in the stock of inward foreign direct investment into developing countries has moved from almost 63 per cent at the beginning of this century to 25.2 per cent in 1994.

This means that the developed countries are not only responsible for the largest share of outward foreign direct investment but are also the main receivers of foreign direct investment. Many developed countries thus experience a crossflow of investment. Notable among these countries are the United Kingdom, the United States and the Netherlands. A considerable amount of this investment also occurs on an intra-industry basis which means that often both inward and outward investment take place in products belonging to the same industrial categories. Estimates of intra-industry foreign direct investment are in Dunning (1982). A comprehensive review of evidence and motivations in intra-industry foreign direct investment is in Erdilek (1985).

The developing countries as a whole have none the less experienced considerable increases in the flow of foreign direct investment in the 1990s as is clear from Table 2.11. This is mainly due to two factors. The first of these is the effect of privatization programmes in developing countries. Table 2.13 gives evidence of the relevance of privatization in the inflow of foreign direct investment into developing regions and specially into Central and Eastern Europe where it constitutes more than half of the total foreign direct investment into the region. Secondly, there

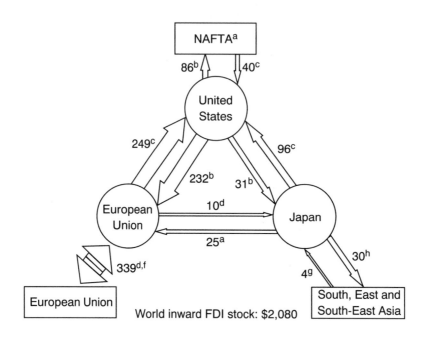

**Figure 2.6** FDI stock among Triad members and their clusters, 1993 (billions of dollars).

*Source: UNCTAD–DTCI, 1995.*

[a] Canada and Mexico.

[b] United States outward FDI stock.

[c] United States inward FDI stock.

[d] Outward FDI stock of Austria, Finland, France, Germany, Italy, Netherlands, Sweden and the United Kingdom. Data for Austria are for 1991 and data for France and the Netherlands are for 1992.

[e] Data from inward FDI stock of Austria, France, Germany, Italy, Netherlands and United Kingdom. Data for Austria and France are 1991 and data for Italy and the Netherlands are for 1992.

[f] For Sweden, the data reflect FDI to and from all European countries. Intra-European Union FDI, based on inward stocks, is $225 billion.

[g] Data are based on approval/notifications and represent those from countries other than those in north America and Europe.

[h] Estimated by multiplying the values of the cumulative flows to the region according to FDI approvals by the ratio of disbursed to approved/notified FDI in developing countries.

**Table 2.14** Foreign direct investment stock to/from the European Community, the United States and Japan, 1980, 1988, 1993 (percentages and world total values)

| | FDI stock | | | | | |
|---|---|---|---|---|---|---|
| | – Outward – | | | – Inward – | | |
| | 1980 | 1988 | 1993 | 1980 | 1988 | 1993 |
| **Country/region** | | | | | | |
| EC (including intra-EC/ EU FDI) | 38.7 | 43.4 | 45.1 | 36.9 | 32.7 | 40.0 |
| United States | 42.0 | 30.4 | 26.2 | 16.3 | 27.0 | 21.4 |
| Japan | 3.8 | 9.8 | 12.2 | 0.6 | 0.8 | 0.8 |
| Triad (including intra-EC/ EU FDI) | 85.5 | 83.6 | 83.5 | 54.0 | 60.6 | 62.2 |
| Intra-EC/EU FDI | 9.5 | 14.1 | 15.9 | 8.8 | 13.1 | 16.3 |
| **World total (including intra-EC/EU FDI)** | **524.0** | **1134.0** | **2135.0** | **509.0** | **1219.0** | **2080.0** |

Source: adapted from UNCTC (1991), Table 10, p.32 and UNCTAD-DTCI (1995), p.11.

is what we may call the 'China' effect. The Republic of China has experienced enormous growth in inward flows and in the 1990s it became the second largest recipient of FDI worldwide. Moreover, FDI has also had considerable effects on China's trade and exports in particular. The UN Report (UNCTAD-DTCI 1994, p.68) states:

> The export share of foreign affiliates in total national exports increased from 13 per cent in 1990 to 28 per cent in 1993, amounting to $25.2 billion. China now ranks as the eleventh exporter in the world and second largest exporter among the developing countries; its exports accounted for 17 per cent of its GNP in 1992. There is no doubt that FDI has fuelled China's export boom and contributed to sharpening its international competitiveness.

The 1980s have brought considerable changes to the structure of the United States' foreign direct investment. The United States has moved from its traditional position as an outward investor to the position of a large recipient of foreign direct investment.

**Table 2.15** Sectoral distribution of outward and inward foreign direct capital stock for largest developed and developing countries (percentage shares 1970–90)

| Group of countries and sectors | 1970 | 1975 | 1980 | 1985 | 1990 |
|---|---|---|---|---|---|
| **A. Outward stock** | | | | | |
| Developed countries | | | | | |
| Primary | 22.7 | 25.3 | 18.5 | 18.5 | 11.2 |
| Secondary | 45.2 | 45.0 | 43.8 | 38.7 | 38.7 |
| Tertiary | 31.4 | 27.7 | 37.7 | 42.8 | 50.1 |
| **Total outward** | **100.0** | **100.0** | **100.0** | **100.0** | **100.0** |
| **B. Inward stock** | | | | | |
| Developed countries | | | | | |
| Primary | 16.2 | 12.1 | 6.7 | 9.2 | 9.1 |
| Secondary | 60.2 | 56.5 | 55.2 | 46.2 | 42.5 |
| Tertiary | 23.7 | 31.4 | 38.1 | 44.5 | 48.4 |
| **Total inward (developed countries)** | **100.0** | **100.0** | **100.0** | **100.0** | **100.0** |
| Developing countries | | | | | |
| Primary | | 20.6 | 22.7 | 24.0 | 21.9 |
| Secondary | | 55.9 | 54.6 | 49.6 | 48.6 |
| Tertiary | | 23.5 | 22.7 | 26.4 | 29.5 |
| **Total inward (developing countries)** | | **100.0** | **100.0** | **100.0** | **100.0** |

*Source: adapted from UNCTAD – Programme on Transnational Corporations (1993), Table III.1, p.62 (a).*

See original source for specification of countries included. These countries account for approximately 90 per cent of outward stock in 1990, 72 per cent and 68 per cent of inward stock for developed and developing countries respectively.

**Table 2.16** Area distribution of inward stock of foreign direct investment by sector: largest developed and developing countries, 1970–90 (percentages)

| | Sectors and areas | | | | | |
|---|---|---|---|---|---|---|
| | Primary | | Secondary | | Tertiary | |
| Year | Developed | Developing | Developed | Developing | Developed | Developing |
| 1975 | 70.8 | 29.2 | 80.6 | 19.4 | 84.6 | 15.4 |
| 1980 | 51.4 | 48.6 | 78.3 | 21.7 | 85.7 | 14.3 |
| 1985 | 55.7 | 44.3 | 75.3 | 24.7 | 84.7 | 15.3 |
| 1990 | 67.1 | 32.9 | 81.1 | 18.9 | 88.9 | 11.1 |

*Source: c.f. Table 2.14.*

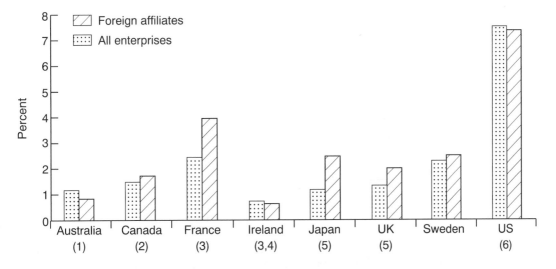

**Figure 2.7** Research and development intensities[7] of foreign affiliates and of all firms in manufacturing, 1989. Source: OECD (1994). Diagram 18, p.65.

[1] 1986/87 including minority foreign-owned affiliates.
[2] 1990.   [3] Based on total national enterprises.
[4] R&D expenditure on 1991 turnover invluding minority foreign-owned affiliates
[5] R&D expenditure on production.   [6] R&D intensity is based on value added in 1987.
[7] R&D expenditure on production or turnover.

**Table 2.17** Research and development expenditure of selected countries and top companies (percentage shares)

| Country | Percentage share of country's R and D expenditure in GDP | R and D expenditure by company as percentage of sales | Number of companies in sample |
|---|---|---|---|
| Canada | 1.3 | 4.6 | 6 |
| France | 2.3 | 4.2 | 17 |
| Germany (Federal Republic) | 2.6 | 6.1 | 19 |
| Italy | 1.3 | 4.2 | 8 |
| Japan | 2.7 | 4.9 | 74 |
| Netherlands | 2.1 | 3.0 | 7 |
| Sweden | 2.9 | 6.5 | 10 |
| Switzerland | 2.9 | 5.9 | 10 |
| United Kingdom | 2.4 | 2.1 | 33 |
| United States | 2.7 | 4.7 | 28 |

*Source: adapted from UN Transnational Corporations and Management Division, Development (1992), Table VI.2, p.136.*

The data refer to various years during the 1980s.

The main investors into the United States have been Japan, the United Kingdom and the Netherlands. There has been what some economists call a 'transatlantic reversal' with the United States moving from a position of a major outward investor into the United Kingdom to becoming a major recipient of British investment. The foreign direct investment into the USA has mainly occurred through mergers and acquisitions of existing American companies by Japanese and European TNCs (OECD, 1994, Annex 2.I; UN, 1994, Chapter I).

Another major geographical development is the tendency for the formation of regional clusters of integration in terms of both foreign direct investment and trade as highlighted in Chapter 4. There are three major regions within which international flows tend to conglomerate.

The regions are the United States, Japan and the European Union. Figure 2.6 gives the cluster of countries pertaining to each region while Table 2.14 gives the values and percentages of FDI stock within each cluster. The triad as a whole is responsible for over 80 per cent of the outward stock of FDI and around 60 per cent of the inward stock.

## 2.5 Sectoral changes

This century has seen major sectoral changes in FDI flows. Before the Second World War the bulk of FDI was resource-based as companies moved abroad with a view to securing their supplies of raw materials through internalization in a process of backward vertical integration. This meant that FDI tended to be directed towards developing countries (often colonies or former colonies of the developed investing country). This phenomenon explains the geographical pattern of FDI and its distribution between developed and developing countries before the Second World War as highlighted in section 2.4 and Tables 2.11 and 2.12. After the Second World War FDI moved from resources to manufacturing. Since the mid-to-late 1970s, however, the major increases have been in FDI in the services sector. The breakdown between the three sectors (primary, secondary and tertiary) is shown in Tables 2.15 and 2.16.

Table 2.15 shows that, while the relevance of the primary sector has declined considerably for the developed countries, its share in the developing countries has remained fairly steady at just over 20 per cent. The relative importance of primary inward FDI for the developing countries is also confirmed by the data in Table 2.16. It shows that these regions have their highest share of inward FDI in the primary sector.

The move towards manufacturing and services is accompanied by increased research intensity. Table 2.17 shows that the top TNCs have high research intensity in relation to the research and development expenditure of their home countries. Figure 2.7 shows similar results for selected developed countries.

We are witnessing what some experts call 'technoglobalism' (OECD, 1994, Chapter IV). This term denotes the fact that technology itself is becoming more global in two aspects. First, research and development laboratories are being spread in more off-shore facilities. Second, there has been a tendency to spread the network of research and development worldwide via collaborative agreements between large TNCs or large companies and smaller ones or between companies and universities. However, the OECD report (1994, Chapter IV) shows that, on the whole, the involvement in research by foreign affiliates tends to be proportionally lower than their involvement in production. Moreover, it is applied research that tends to be located in foreign affiliates rather than basic research, which has remained fairly centralized.

## 2.6 Conclusions

This chapter considered the main trends in the components of internationalization and particularly in foreign direct investment.

It first dealt with the major developments at the micro level and therefore with the changes in the universe of transnational companies, their network of affiliates and with their overall geographical spread of activities. It then considered the major macro trends in terms of both the geographical and sectoral patterns of FDI.

The big surge of investments in the 1980s and 1990s mainly had a basis in the acquisition strategies that companies used. In many cases activities may have reduced productive capacity in the rationalization process following the acquisition. The privatization programmes of many developed and developing countries have also encouraged considerable cross-border flows.

It is very difficult to make any predictions. However, as the privatization momentum slows down this may have effects on the amounts and patterns of FDI worldwide.

China is responsible for a very large influx of FDI and has become the second largest host country. Whether this trend will continue or not will depend on economic and political factors. Either way, China is going to be a major determining factor in the level and pattern of future FDI.

## 2.7 Further reading

Dicken, P. (1992) *Global Shift. The Internationalization of Economic Activity,* Paul Chapman Publishing Ltd, London (second edition, Chapter 2).

Ietto-Gillies, G. (1992) *International Production. Trends, Theories, Effects,* Polity Press, Cambridge (Chapter 2).

Organization for Economic Co-operation and Development (OECD) (1994) *The performance of Foreign Affiliates in OECD Countries,* OECD, Paris.

United Nations Centre on Transnational Companies (1988) *Transnational Corporations in World Development. Trends and Prospects,* United Nations, New York.

United Nations Conference on Trade and Development, Division on Transnational Corporations and Investment (DTCI), Programme on Transnational Corporations, Department of Economic and Social Development, *World Investment Reports,* United Nations. Various issues.

## 2.8 Questions for further discussion

1. List the three most important changes in the universe of TNCs. How do you see the trends moving in the next decade?

2. Highlight the main trends in FDI in developing countries and their characteristics.

3. How does technology affect the main trends in FDI?

4. What is intra-firm trade? Why do companies manipulate transfer prices?

# 3

# *The environment of international business*

## *3.1. Introduction*

Chapter 2 presented evidence of the growth in MNC activities. The underlying conditions that have led to such growth are considered in the current chapter.

Until the Second World War, the international economy and the study of international economics were traditionally seen as being related to trade. Economic activities between nations mainly took the form of the movement of goods across frontiers. The theory of international trade was therefore developed with the basic assumption that products were internationally mobile while factors of production were not. In practice some mobility of factors always existed, in particular the considerable amount of labour mobility in the form of large waves of migration from Europe into the American continent and Australia. Considerable cross-border capital flows also existed.

After the Second World War internationalization increasingly took the form of production activities and trade activities. International production has not been a substitute for international trade and both have increased at a remarkable pace as highlighted in Chapter 2. International trade trends are discussed further in Chapter 4.

What has happened, and is still happening, is a growing internationalization of economic life. The following points give a schematic and concise summary of the main patterns and forms of internationalization:

- Movement of capital across frontiers.

- Increase in the movement of goods across frontiers.

- Increasing movements of people across frontiers for leisure and productive activities. Labour mobility across frontiers has differed increasingly from the migration waves of a century ago. Where unskilled labour is concerned, in many cases it has resulted in some less permanent forms of migration. There have also been some considerable temporary relocations (that is short- to medium-term movements) of skilled labour and of high-level technical and managerial labour across frontiers.

- Some international convergence of demand as consumers across borders become aware of products available worldwide through the mass communication media.

- Internationalization of supply, with markets being sourced from production centres across the world.

- Organization of production on an international and global scale with internal cross-border flows of goods, services and factors.

Many conditions have been favourable to these developments and they will be considered in the following sections. Most of these conditions have interacted with the activities of TNCs as both cause and effect: the existence of these conditions has led to the growth of TNCs and their activities and the existence and growth of TNCs have contributed to create further favourable conditions in the technological, political and organizational spheres. This interaction of cause and effect has been cumulative in nature and thus has led to an upward spiral of international activities.

We can identify three main areas of development favourable to internationalization: the political environment, the technological environment and organizational developments. These three areas are all connected and they are all linked to the TNCs and their activities.

## 3.2 The political environment

The decades immediately following the Second World War saw an unprecedented period of co-operation, at least among 'First World' countries, the industrialized Western nations. Trade barriers came down as economies grew under the stimulus of reconstruction. The establishment and enhancement of international institutions such as the General Agreement on Tariffs and Trade (GATT) and International Monetary Fund (IMF), designed to smooth the path to economic co-operation, were both a product and a further cause of this international co-operative stance. The Cold War gave the Western powers further scope for co-operation.

Free trade came to be seen as an essential tool in securing growth in this political environment. Direct investment and production by TNCs from a foreign country was seen as a demonstration of that country's positive attitude towards other Western nations and their products.

A few countries had a tradition of foreign investment reaching back for many decades, particularly Britain, the Netherlands and the United States. As highlighted in Chapter 2, however, the post-Second World War period saw considerable changes in the following:

- The scale of operations increased to unprecedented levels.

- The geographical pattern changed. There was a movement away from the use of developing countries as hosts and towards the developed countries.

- The industry structure moved away from resource-based to manufacturing FDI.

- These changes were all interconnected to some degree.

The first big wave of FDI after the Second World War saw investment by the United States in the European manufacturing sector. This was something unprecedented in Europe. From the point of view of the United States, this new trend represented a considerable change from the geographical pattern of FDI that existed between the two World Wars. In that period, a large share of United States' FDI was directed towards Canada. Companies from other countries soon started catching up in foreign investment, particularly into other developed countries. Foreign investment was received with mixed feelings in host countries. While accepting some of the beneficial effects, some commentators expressed worries about the dominance of foreign capital in the domestic economy. The 1960s saw a considerable body of writing on the possible economic conflicts created by FDI in developed and developing countries. Concerns about American dominance over Europe were poignantly expressed in Servan-Schreiber (1968). Concerns over the effects on the developing countries (the so-called Third World) became even stronger and gave rise to a large amount of literature on economic imperialism, that is on the dominance of the developing countries by the developed ones through investment and trade rather than through political subjugation. One such example is the book by the American political economist Harry Magdoff (1966). None the less, the reality was one of co-operation and free movement of goods and capital. This was reflected in what was actually happening in terms of business activities as well as at the national and international political level.

The 1970s saw a less co-operative mood at the political level. The decade started with the United States unilaterally withdrawing the convertibility of the dollar which ended the era of fixed exchange rates and of stable relations among the Western industrialized countries. The oil crisis moved both developed and developing countries further away from their previous co-operative stance. This led, in many cases, to a more entrenched position in terms of trade: both transparent and non-transparent barriers re-emerged after a long period of co-operation.

Despite some problems at the political level between governments in various countries, the momentum for the growth of international production created in the 1950s and 1960s was not, on the whole, lost. Indeed it increased and, ironically, one of the factors that may have helped to enhance it was the lifting of trade barriers by national governments. The transparent or non-transparent trade barriers that governments were raising led companies to seek alternatives to exports for the sourcing of foreign markets. The obvious alternative was direct production. Companies that had already gained considerable expertise in direct production found it easier to follow this route and source their markets by producing directly in foreign countries rather than by home production and exports. At the same time, host governments became more welcoming to inward direct investment as they saw the employment and output benefits deriving from it. This was very relevant in a world in which unemployment grew monthly and words like 'recession' and 'stagflation' increasingly became part of everyday vocabulary.

The integration movements among nations linked by economic, historical and geographic ties led to regionalization which further helped the internationalization process in several ways (see Chapter 2, section 2.4). First, it created huge integrated markets. Second, it increased the harmonization in the standard of products and components at the level of production. Third, it encouraged inward investment from MNCs based in countries outside each region. These MNCs invested in other regions in order to prevent the exclusion of their products from large, profitable markets through trade barriers. On this point see UNCTC (1990) and Oman (1994) as well as Thomsen and Woolcock (1993).

The attitude of suspicion between governments in developing countries and MNCs (almost entirely drawn from the rich industrialized countries) remained until the late 1970s and early 1980s. The concerns that they expressed were many and included the following:

- whether the products and productive processes were appropriate to local culture and conditions, particularly in terms of the local supply of factors of production;

- doubts about the positive impact of FDI in terms of cumulative effects on investment and development;

- excessive profits and their repatriation;

- the effects of production methods that were seen as detrimental to the environment. It was often felt that production methods that would not be tolerated by governments and public opinion in the industrialized countries were being introduced in the poor ones without regard for the high social costs imposed on these countries in terms of health effects, safety standards and pollution.

The last 15 years have seen a more welcoming stance to inward investment from both developing and developed countries. Indeed, governments are increasingly competing for FDI and are boasting about their ability to attract it. The issue of confrontation versus co-operation between MNCs and governments is considered in Dunning (1993, Chapter 13, pp. 330–53). Many elements have contributed to this change:

- the high levels of unemployment worldwide have made any investment more attractive than none;

- the gradual shift in the share of FDI towards developed countries (see Chapter 2, section 2.4) has made governments in developing countries more aware of the dangers of missing opportunities. Most developing countries are now competing for inward investment not only with developed countries but also with the 'new industrializing countries' (NICs) and with the countries of Central and Eastern Europe (CEE). Competition for investment has recently become very fierce with developed, developing, socialist and former socialist countries all seeking their share;

- TNCs themselves have become more aware of the need to pay attention to local cultures and to work co-operatively with local businesses and governments in order to win them over. One effect of this new stance has been the increase in joint ventures mentioned in Chapter 2. These collaborative agreements are required by some national governments as a condition for allowing foreign investors into their countries. They are often welcomed by foreign TNCs as a passport and as a means of learning about local procedures, customs, bureaucracies;

- as information spreads rapidly and widely there is an awareness that environmental issues are no longer local issues: they are world issues. Global environmental issues have strengthened the perception of interdependence between nations. Outcries over environmental degradation can cause worldwide damage to the reputation of companies wherever they operate and so TNCs are becoming a little more environmentally aware whether their production is located in developed or developing countries;

- the deregulation of financial markets and the privatization programmes of most countries have created a further opportunity and stimulus to activities across countries.

The change from confrontation to co-operation that has characterized the political relationship between governments and TNCs is strongly highlighted by trends in nationalization and privatization programmes shown in Figure 3.1.

The growing nationalization programmes of the 1960s were reversed in the 1970s. The 1980s saw great leaps in privatization. This generated opportunities for FDI through the direct acquisition of privatized assets; it also signalled a changed political environment that favoured private enterprises including foreign multinational corporations and their FDI.

The late 1980s and the 1990s have seen a 'confrontation reversal'. It is now governments, researchers and commentators in developed countries who express concern over competition for jobs by the developing countries (in this connection see the impressive theoretical and empirical work by Wood (1994) and the survey by Woodall (1994)). This is undoubtedly the effect of the protracted high levels of unemployment in industrialized countries.

Concern has also been expressed about the changes in the competitive environment worldwide. It should be noted that since the early 1980s most foreign direct investment has taken place through mergers and acquisitions across borders. This has implications for the degree of monopoly that can be observed in many industries, both worldwide and regionally, and it has prompted calls for tighter competition policy across borders.

The political climate after the Second World War has, on the whole, been very favourable to the internationalization of economic activities in all their forms and particularly to foreign direct investment by multinational corporations.

## 3.3 *The technological environment*

The decades after the Second World War saw considerable technological improvements in many areas. The changes that most affected internationalization and which created the necessary conditions for internationalization on a large scale were those related to the space-shrinking technologies of transportation and communication. Those two areas provided what Dicken (1992, p.103) calls the 'enabling technologies'. Dicken writes:

> Transport and communication technologies perform two distinct, though closely related and complementary roles. Transport systems are the means by which materials, products and other tangible entities (including people) are transferred from place to place. Communication systems are the means by which information is transmitted from place to place in the form of ideas, instructions, images, and so on. For most of human history

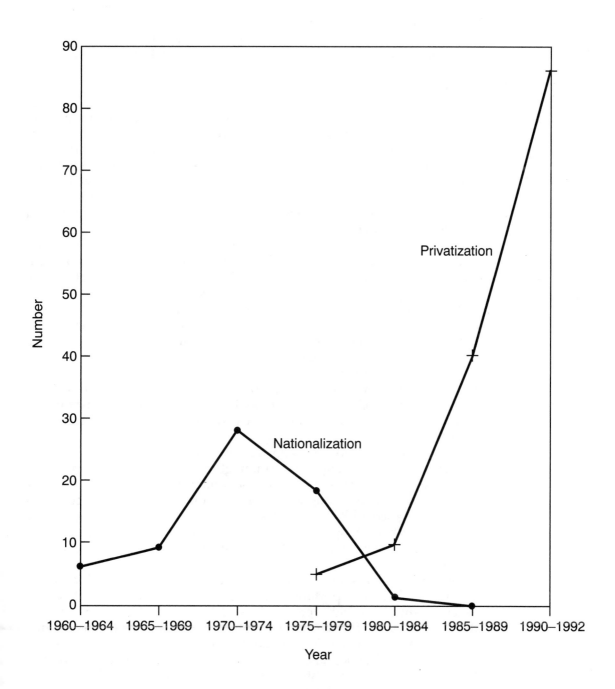

**Figure 3.1** The number of nationalization acts and privatization activities, 1990–92.

transport and communication were effectively one and the same. Prior to the invention of electric technology in the nineteenth century, information could move only at the same speed, and over the same distance, as the prevailing transport system would allow. Electric technology broke that link, making it increasingly necessary to treat transport and communication as separate.

Improvements in the technology of transportation and communication and the related reduction in the relative costs of such services, were necessary conditions for full-scale internationalization to take off.

Transportation refers to the whole system of moving people and goods. In the post-Second World War period, improvements were made in sea transport with the development of larger vessels and much of the containerization systems which allow speedier and cheaper loading and unloading. The major developments, of course, have been in air travel with larger and quicker systems being introduced. We should not underplay the role that faster trains have for continental transport, however. Indeed their role may increase unless the problems of speedy access to airports and noise pollution can be solved.

These two problems may be interconnected as the need for quick access to airports could discourage planners from locating airports at a reasonable distance from urban centres. Currently, this seems to be one of the major bottlenecks in the air transport system. An old and inefficient transport medium, the motor car, could thus be seen to be responsible both for large social costs in terms of health hazards and environmental pollution and for holding back the full utilization and further development of more advanced and efficient transport systems.

The communication system relates to the ability to transmit information across distances. As highlighted by Dicken (1992, p.103) in the passage cited above, the speed of communications and transportation was the same throughout most of human history. For centuries people struggled to be able to transmit information at a higher speed than the transport system would allow. Examples of this are the attempts to convey messages through flags, smoke signals and carrier pigeons.

However, it was only with the discovery and wide adoption of electricity that transportation and communications could take on independent and fairly separate lives of their own. Electricity allowed the development of much faster communication systems (such as radio, telegraph and telephone) and made them independent from the systems that transported goods and people. Moreover, the wide application of faster and more efficient communication systems facilitated, and continues to facilitate, the adoption of better transportation systems (cf. Dicken, 1992, p.105).

More recently the 'electricity era' has developed into the 'information technology era':

> Information technology is the outcome of the convergence between two
> initially distinct technologies: communication technology, which is
> concerned with the transmission of information, and the computer
> technology, which is concerned with the processing of information.
> (UNCTAD 1994, p.125.)

There are two aspects to information technology of interest here. First,
there is the impact it has on the speed of communication and
transmission of information and the scope it gives to transmit large
amounts of information at high speed. There is a massive quantitative
change both in the speed of transmission and in the type and the amount
of information that can be conveyed. The relationship between
communication and transportation technology and their convergence
or divergence through time is illustrated in Figure 3.2. Secondly, there is
a qualitative change that is the result of the interaction between
communication technology and computer technology. This combination
has greatly raised the scope for the elaboration of information (written
work, images, data processing) and its transmission.

Figure 3.2 highlights the changes in the speed of the transportation
and communication systems and their interrelationships through
different technological eras. Prior to the development of electricity there
was no distinction in terms of the speed of movement between
transportation and communication. The two system were fully
convergent; indeed they were one and the same (boxes a and b belong
to the same transmission system and have the same speed). Messages
could only travel at the speed allowed by the transportation system.
With the introduction of electricity, communication took on a life of its
own and messages could be transmitted independently of the
transportation system for humans and goods. This allowed communication (box d) to be transmitted much faster than would have been allowed
by the prevailing transportation system (box c).

The information and communication technology (ICT) era gave rise to
three different and interconnected trends.

First of all the speed of transmission on the communication side (box f)
has been raised beyond anything experienced previously: paper, sound
and images can be transmitted more-or-less in real time, simultaneously.
The much longer arrow next to box f indicates this great leap in the speed
of transmission.

Secondly, the range of what can be transmitted is much wider: images,
large documents as well as voice, letters, messages; thus many elements
previously listed under the transportation system (box c) can now be
transmitted at the very high speed of the communication system (box f).
The broken line from box c to box f indicates this shift of some elements
from the transportation to the communication systems. Space-time
compression has been pushed to unprecedented levels in terms of speed
and scope. Images of persons as well as places and objects (including
paper work) can now travel as fast as any other piece of information.

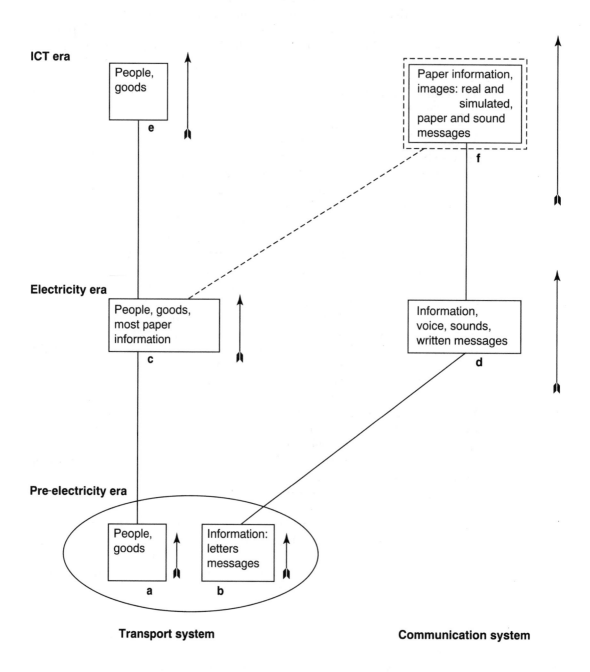

**Figure 3.2** Transport and communication systems: convergence and divergence through time (arrows denote different speed).

Before the introduction of electricity, communications could only travel as fast as transportation would allow humans to travel. With electricity, the communications system became separated from transportation and took on a momentum and a faster speed of its own. Now documents and all types of paper information, which were previously sent by transportation systems, are conveyed almost instantly via fax machines and electronic mail. Moreover, images can be transmitted simultaneously and in an interactive way; in many activities such images become a kind of substitute for the transport of people/objects.

Thirdly, the combination of communication and computer technology is giving scope for completely new developments such as simulation and networking. The use of computers to process information (data, written work, images) allows the simulation of real and planned situations, objects and people. The combination of high speed transmission and processing of information allows simultaneous networking across the world between people and their work. This new situation is highlighted in Figure 3.2 by the dashes around box f.

The scope for new developments arising from this is very considerable. We are, in a sense, at the beginning of a revolution in terms of the development of productive forces and lifestyles. Freeman (1993, p.2) states that:

> ICT affects every function within the firm as well as affecting every industry. Since it facilitates much greater integration of research, design, development, production and marketing it leads to a new style of management and a new pattern of organization within and between firms. This change is so fundamental that it amounts to a change of techno-economic paradigm.

There are also profound effects on the process of internationalization. These will be discussed in section 3.5.

## 3.4 Organizational developments

The new macroenvironment created the favourable conditions necessary for internationalization to take off on a big scale. Moreover, some microeconomic changes also helped this process. Companies needed to adjust their internal organization to the new wider geographical network of their operations. The post-Second World War period saw the gradual spread of the multidivisional form of organization to the international arena, with divisions based on countries' operations rather than on product lines. This argument is developed further in Chapter 10.

From the 1970s onwards we have seen the establishment of the so-called flexible production system (cf. Oman, 1994). This new concept in production is closely tied to advances in information technology and would not have been possible without them. Among its basic tenets are the following:

- The organization of production on a wide geographical scale is combined with a move away from mass production in favour of shorter production runs. These shorter runs allow the customerization of production and adaptation to cultural conditions and demand, while organization within a single structure allows economies of scope to be made.

- Design and manufacturing are linked by simultaneous engineering carried out through computer technology.

- 'Just-in-time' production replaces the system of buffer stock (the 'just-in-case they are needed' approach) that required large expensive stocks.

- Implementation of quality controls at the point of production rather than sale; high reliance on continuous incremental improvements rather than large-scale changes.

- Supply chains become more integrated into the design and manufacturing of the whole product.

In order to be effective the new production system needs strong support from computer technology and infrastructure at the points of design, production, distribution and sale. It also needs adequate backup from the human and physical infrastructure. The physical infrastructure consists of IT and adequate transportation and communication networks. The human infrastructure required is a skilled and well-trained labour force. These conditions make it less efficient for modern production systems to be located in many developing countries given their low levels of education and training. This contrasts with the large-scale production runs of the 1950s and 1960s when standardized products required large capital investment and unskilled labour. The link between the standardization of production, the demand for unskilled labour, and FDI in developing countries is analysed in the product cycle theory of international production, which is discussed in Chapter 5.

One essential feature of flexible production systems is that they require production to be organized in different ways in various respects because they rely more on (a) team work and on communication between various experts; (b) a closer liaison between suppliers along the production chain; (c) closer involvement between management and technical experts. Attention to the human resources aspects of production is essential for its success. Oman (1994, p.64) expresses the essence of flexible production:

In sum, the 'secret' of flexible organizations is their emphasis on the elimination of waste through better management and organization of work, and overcoming the under-utilization of knowledge, creativity and human capabilities that tends to characterise taylorist forms of organization.

## 3.5 Implications of various favourable conditions

(a) In the last three sections we have highlighted the major developments at the macro and micro levels that have made the international activities of companies possible and, indeed, have enhanced those activities. We have stressed the line of effects going from these changes in the economic, political and technological environment to the MNCs and their activities. However, we would like to re-emphasize something that has already been mentioned. The effects also flow in the opposite direction, from the MNCs and their activities to the macro and micro environment with a web of interaction that has helped internationalization to move almost in an upward spiral. Political, technological and organizational developments should not be considered as exogenous developments that happened to move in the direction of internationalization; it is probable that they are all to a greater or lesser extent developments that have been pushed by the combined interests, activities and actions of the MNCs.

(b) One of the byproducts of the growth in internationalization is that economists are increasingly discovering the relevance of economic geography. Particularly important here is the work of Paul Krugman (see, for example, Krugman 1991). Internationalization has not just emphasized the role of geography in trade and in the location of production highlighted by Krugman; it has also raised the issue of the role of 'ownership' and geography. The issue of where production is to be located is of the utmost relevance for countries as it is central to their growth and development. Is ownership relevant? Does it matter whether the investment is made by a national company or foreign company? Answers cannot be given without asking 'For whom does it matter?' and 'What effects are we considering?' For example, the ability of foreign companies to produce directly in the host country may pose a bigger threat than the threat of sourcing the market through exports for local companies that see the competition becoming stronger. In terms of labour, however, employment created by foreign companies may be as good as employment generated by investment from domestic companies. Moreover, TNCs may bring further advantages to the host country's workforce by upgrading skills. This issue has been brought to some prominence through the writings of Robert Reich (particularly Reich, 1991). Reich points out that the dilemma of foreign versus American capital should be addressed by considering which companies contribute to the employment and growth of the country. These issues are considered in Ietto-Gillies (1993).

(c) The two issues considered so far in this section highlight the relevance of TNCs in any discourse on economic policy, general politics and international politics. This point is clearly brought out in Stopford and Strange (1991) where the relevance of TNCs in international politics is emphasized as the advent of new 'triangular diplomacy' (p.2). They express the 'new diplomacy' with a simple revealing graph given here as Figure 3.3. They write (p.22):

> Changes in the international political economy create new sources of asymmetry in the relative importance of the three sides of the triangle. The growth of global competition can be seen as moving the world towards a position where events are conditioned more by an emerging managerial technocracy than by traditional notions of state power. In this new technocracy, firms feature prominently but are only one component of a wider network that links them to the educational and skills infrastructure and the financial system.

These problems are of the utmost relevance for developing countries. We have seen changes in attitude towards the effects of the activities of TNCs in developing countries. None the less, there is new concern about the terms of competition for FDI as both developed and developing countries fight for a share of this investment.

Concern is being expressed at the weak position of most developing countries in view of the following: (a) the high levels of human and physical infrastructure required by the new flexible production systems (Oman 1994, Stopford, Strange and Henley, 1991); (b) the availability of production sites in former socialist countries; (c) the increasing attractiveness of China as a location for production and as a market.

One of the questions that arise concerns the extent to which FDI and international production in general are 'games' with zero, positive or negative outcomes. This issue involves analysing the extent to which foreign investment merely replaces domestic investment or unleashes forces that have positive or negative effects on further investment and thus on growth and productivity. The methodological issues involved in assessing some of these effects are considered in Ietto-Gillies (1992, Chapter 14).

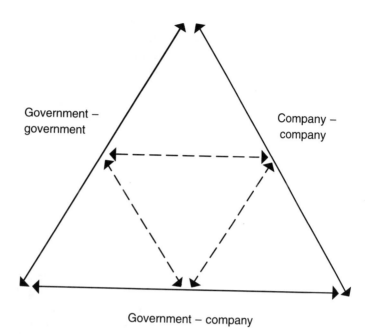

Government –
government

Company –
company

Source: Stopford and
Strange (1991), p.22.

Government – company

**Figure 3.3** Triads of relationships.

(d)  Information technology has already transformed parts of the production process and its control and management. All the signs are that the transformation is in its infancy. Whole countries, continents, and sectors of production are, as yet, very little affected by information technology so the scope for the spread of new methods and related organizations are considerable. Besides this spreading effect, there are still considerable deepening effects in the sense that technology can allow further improvements in fields of production where the full potential in terms of applications has yet to be developed.

One of the effects of information technology is that it allows, to a very large extent, the analysis of problems and their solutions 'at a distance'. Experts can work in a different location from the problem that they are working on. Through computing networks and simulation they can analyse, give advice, and intervene at a distance and without loss of time. This is already happening to some extent. Engineering at a distance and medical assistance (including surgery) at a distance are already with us. The application of 'virtual reality' systems will enhance these possibilities further by giving the expert a stronger feel for the place, person, and object of his or her analysis and intervention. Will this further transform the organization of production by increasing the opportunities for management at a distance? The answer appears to be affirmative.

One of the constraints to further internationalization seems to be the willingness of managers to become expatriates or to become so for a substantial period of time. Scullion (1994), following a survey of British TNCs, finds various barriers to international mobility; they are clustered among two main areas: (a) effects on the family, and (b) concern about work and career structure after repatriation. These concerns generate problems both for the expatriates themselves and for the companies. Difficulties in recruiting expatriates may, in fact, go hand-in-hand with low performance from disgruntled and unhappy expatriates and repatriates. The solution may be to look at radical alternatives and to start querying whether the current levels of substantial expatriate work (both in terms of number of people involved and length of the assignments) are really necessary. More extensive and better use of local managers not only avoids the problems concerned with the use of expatriates, but generates better feelings towards the foreign company at the local level. New technology that simultaneously brings images together from a long distance (the conferencing system) can be a reasonable substitute for some, if not all, the personal communication needed in management. This does not, of course, deny the need for personal contact; it just means reassessing the overall need for the current levels of expatriate work in the light of the new information systems.

Advances in transportation and communications have made growth in international activities possible on the scale highlighted in Chapter 2. We are now expecting further substantial changes from the introduction of new technologies. These further changes will not only facilitate further internationalization; they will increasingly introduce new systems for the planning, organization and management of production on a global scale. Thus the new technologies will have a 'quantity' impact on internationalization and will also transform the 'quantity' elements into 'quality' ones.

In conclusion, technology is moving economic systems in the direction of internationalization by removing constraints. This is happening through the changes in the relations between space and time and their effects on the work of experts, including managers.

## 3.6 Conclusions

This chapter dealt with the conditions that facilitated internationalization on the scale we have witnessed in the last 50 years. Three main elements have been identified: changes in the political environment, technological changes and organizational developments. They have all contributed to the growth in internationalization. These elements are all interconnected and are linked, in a cause/effect interrelationship, to the activities of

TNCs themselves. The three elements identified are all complex and involve various issues. They have each progressed historically and we have tried to highlight some of these changes. The scope for further changes in the years to come is very considerable and some potential future changes have been highlighted.

## 3.7 Further reading

Dicken, P. (1992) *Global Shift. The Internationalization of Economic Activity*, Paul Chapman Publishing Ltd, London (second edition, particularly Chapter 4).

Dunning, J.H. (1993) *The Globalization of Business*, Routledge, London (particularly Chapter 13).

Stopford, J., Strange, S. and Henley, J.S. (1991) *Rival States, Rival Firms. Competition for World Market Shares*, Cambridge University Press, Cambridge (particularly Chapter 1).

## 3.8 Questions for further discussion

1.  Highlight the changing attitudes towards TNCs in developing countries since the 1960s. Give the main reasons for the changes in attitudes.

2.  List the various phases of development of the communication technologies and their impact on internationalization.

3.  Give the major internal organizational changes in the last 30 years and how they may have affected a company of your choice and its activities.

# 4

# *The international trading environment*

## *4.1 Introduction*

Various aspects of the international environment affecting international firms were discussed in the previous chapter. This chapter will focus on the trading environment.

The structure of world trade constitutes a major factor external to the international firm and governs the firm's decisions about what to produce, where to produce and where to sell. The international firm is also a key player in the world trading system, however. As such, it determines the pattern and direction of world trade. This latter aspect is explored more fully in later chapters of this book. In this chapter, trade is viewed more as an environmental factor: it is treated as an exogenous variable to which firms must react. Informed and therefore effective decision-making requires a knowledge and understanding of the main trends occurring in world trade.

First, we discuss the growth in world trade. It is necessary to know how quickly total trade and the different components of trade have increased in recent decades. Over the past 50 years trade has played a leading role in world economic growth. This, in turn, reflects an increase in the degree of international specialization. Second, we discuss the regional or geographical structure of world trade. A distinction will be drawn between trade *between* regions (inter-regional trade) and trade *within* regions (intra-regional trade). One issue that will be addressed concerns the tendency for world trade to become more regionalized; that is, for intra-regional trade to increase relative to inter-regional trade. Third, the network of world trade will be examined. This is important in showing which countries or regions trade most with each other. Fourth, we shall discuss the changing commodity structure of world trade and will identify the main factors that have caused changes in the proportion of world trade accounted for by different product groups.

Fifth, the chapter discusses the related issue of the industries or product groups in which different countries specialize. It will be necessary to explain the methods most commonly used for measuring the degree of a country's specialization in a particular industry or product group. Much international specialization in recent decades has tended to take the form of product (intra-industry) specialization rather than industry (inter-industry) specialization. The chapter will discuss some of the main reasons for intra-industry specialization and will comment on the possible future direction of international specialization. Finally, the chapter will discuss the institutional framework that governs world trade. Institutions play a crucial role at both the multilateral or global level and at the regional level in shaping patterns of world trade. An interesting question concerns the relative strengths of institutions at these two levels in shaping the future pattern of world trade.

## 4.2 The growth in world trade

World trade is made up of trade in both goods (merchandise) and services. In 1992, world merchandise exports amounted to $3640 billion or roughly 79 per cent of total world exports. Exports of commercial services amounted to $1000 billion or 21 per cent of world trade. Significantly, the share of commercial services in total world exports rose from 19 to 21 per cent between 1970 and 1991 (GATT, 1994). We begin with merchandise trade.

### 4.2.1 Merchandise trade

The growth in world trade may be measured by the rate of increase in either the value of world exports (or imports) or the volume of world exports (or imports). The rate of increase in the volume of exports takes into account any change in the average price or unit value of exports over the period in question. It therefore provides a better picture of the *real* increase in trade. Table 4.1 sets out the annual average rate of growth in the *volume* of world merchandise exports. These may be compared with the equivalent series for world *production*. The third section of the table shows the ratio of world export growth to world production growth for each category.

In the decade 1960–9 world trade grew by 8.5 per cent per year in terms of volume. In the following decade (1970–9), however, it fell to 5.5 per cent and then to 3.9 per cent for the period 1980–92. This rate of growth has nevertheless been consistently faster than the growth in world production which has averaged 6 per cent, 4 per cent and 2.1 per

Table 4.1 Growth of world merchandise trade and production, 1960–62 (average annual percentage change in volume)

| | 1960–69 | 1970–79 | 1980–92 |
|---|---|---|---|
| **Production** | | | |
| Total | 6.0 | 4.0 | 2.1 |
| Agriculture | 2.5 | 2.5 | 2.1 |
| Mining | 5.0 | 3.5 | 0.1 |
| Manufacturing | 7.5 | 4.5 | 2.5 |
| **Exports** | | | |
| Total | 8.5 | 5.5 | 3.9 |
| Agriculture | 4.0 | 3.0 | 1.9 |
| Mining | 6.5 | 2.5 | 1.0 |
| Manufacturing | 10.5 | 7.5 | 5.2 |
| **Ratio of export growth to production growth** | | | |
| Total | 1.4 | 1.4 | 1.9 |
| Agriculture | 1.6 | 1.2 | 0.9 |
| Mining | 1.3 | 0.7 | 10.0 |
| Manufacturing | 1.4 | 1.7 | 2.1 |

*Source: GATT (various issues).*

cent for the three periods in question. Trade has thus grown faster than output throughout the past three decades. Trade can only grow faster than output if countries are undertaking more specialization. It follows that international specialization has been increasing. The lower part of the table shows that the ratio of world export growth to world output growth in fact grew over the period from 1.4 in the 1960s and 1970s to 1.9 in the 1980s and in the early 1990s. Despite a decline in the rate of growth of world trade, therefore, the evidence suggests that an increasing degree of international specialization has been taking place.

The most dynamic element in world trade has clearly been trade in manufactures. Exports of manufactures have consistently grown faster than trade in non-manufactures (primary commodities). Moreover, these exports have grown considerably faster than world manufacturing output. The ratio of trade growth to output growth has risen from 1.4 in 1960-9 to 1.7 in 1970-9 and 2.1 in 1980–92. Since 1970, this ratio has exceeded that for merchandise as a whole. This suggests a deeper level of specialization has been taking place in manufacturing and this has increased in recent decades despite slower trade growth. Throughout the period, exports of primary commodities have grown at a much slower rate than trade as whole and mostly at a rate slower than the growth in world output. It follows that, whereas exports of manufactures have *led* the growth of world output, exports of primary commodities have tended to *follow* the growth of world output. Exports of agricultural products grew more slowly than world output for the entire period, while exports of mining products grew at a slightly faster rate than world output between 1960–9 but thereafter these exports grew at a consistently slower rate.

The reasons for this are not surprising. The demand for food in the advanced industrialized countries is income-inelastic. It follows that agricultural output in these countries is unlikely to rise as fast as real incomes. Moreover, the markets of the advanced industrialized countries have all been highly protected by heavy subsidization of farming and high import barriers. These have all served to reduce trade in farming products. On the other hand, overproduction of food in the advanced industrialized countries, encouraged by excessive subsidies, combined with inadequate production in other parts of the world including the poorest, less-developed countries, have acted as offsetting factors. The demand for raw materials is necessarily limited by the growth of production in the advanced industrialized countries so imports of raw materials can never exceed the growth in output. Moreover, reductions in the amount of raw materials used to produce a given level of output due to technological change may result in the demand for raw materials lagging behind output. Nevertheless, on some occasions, exports of primary commodities have grown faster than the output of these sectors, which indicates that some increased specialization has been taking place.

### 4.2.2 Services

Services are difficult to distinguish from goods. Most economists refer to characteristics such as intangibility, invisibility, non-storability or transience as being unique to services. One feature of many services is that, because they cannot be stored, they must be produced and consumed at the same time. This feature means that many services are not capable of being traded across borders. Increasingly, however, as a result of technological progress, it is possible to export services produced in one country to a buyer in another country. For example, the modern fax machine has made it possible to transfer information across borders at relatively low cost. Services that can be traded across borders in this way are sometimes known as 'splintered' or 'separated' services. Where services cannot be sold in this way, however, either the buyer must move to where the service supplier is situated (tourism for example) or the service supplier must move to where the buyer is located (as is the case in banking, advertising and distribution). These have been referred to, respectively, as 'provider-located' and 'demander-located' services (Stern and Hoekman, 1987).

GATT now provides regular information covering trade in commercial services as well as goods. The data are obtained from the balance of payments statistics that countries submit each year to the International Monetary Fund on a reporting basis. It comprises transportation, travel, other private services and income (including temporary workers, income from royalties and other intellectual property and residual services). For a variety of reasons, these statistics significantly underestimate the true extent of trade in services. GATT (1994) gives five reasons for this. First, a number of important countries are not IMF members and therefore do not supply comparable data. Second, some countries do not provide information on certain specific services items. Third, a large number of service transactions go unrecorded. This is particularly true of services that are electronically transmitted and of services that are traded between a parent company and an overseas affiliate. Fourth, statistics are sometimes reported on a net (export minus import) rather than gross basis. Fifth, some trade in services is misclassified. Some trade in services is recorded as trade in goods, as factor incomes or as transfers.

A particular aspect of the problem concerns 'demander-located services'. As we have seen, these require a movement of capital and labour on a temporary or permanent basis from the exporting country to the foreign market. This shows up as foreign direct investment (FDI) where capital is exported. Strictly speaking, it is the receipt of income by the services supplier and not the export of capital that constitutes trade. This would be measured by the foreign investment income of the service-supplier or the wages of migrant workers. This kind of trade in services is missed in any measurement of commercial services. Moreover, although most countries record the 'interest, profits and dividends' from foreign investment in the invisible part of the current account of the balance of payments, no distinction is made between investment income derived from the sale of services and that derived from the sale of goods. Investment income from abroad also fails to capture the true extent of overseas earnings as some profits may be reinvested in the overseas subsidiary.

Despite these problems, it is possible, using the figures for officially recorded trade in commercial services, to conclude that trade in services is rising significantly faster than trade in manufactures. The share of services in world trade has consequently been growing. However, because of changes in data coverage during the 1980s, there was a slight upward bias imparted to the share of commercial services in total trade. Within the total, the biggest and fastest growing category of services has been 'other private services'. This accounts for roughly two-fifths of world trade in services and includes rapidly growing service industries such as insurance and banking, telecommunications, construction services and software and data processing. There is every reason to believe that these trends will continue and they may well accelerate in future decades.

## 4.3 The geographical composition of world trade

Table 4.2 sets out the regional structure of world merchandise exports. The regions defined are those used by the GATT in its annual trade statistics. The first section of the table shows the value of merchandise exports from the major regions of the world to other regions. Out of total exports of $3642 billion, West Europe accounted for $1711 billion or 47 per cent. The Asian region (which includes Pacific rim countries such as Australia and New Zealand) accounted for a further $885 billion or 24.3 per cent and North America for $583 billion or 16 per cent of the total. A comparison of these percentages with those from 30 years earlier shows that the Asian region's share has increased significantly from roughly 15.1 per cent in 1963 to 24.3 per cent today. The West European region's share has also increased less dramatically from 42.8 per cent in 1963 to 47 per cent today. The share of all other regions has declined.

The second section of Table 4.2 gives the share of each region's exports that passes to other countries in the region (intra-regional trade) and the share going to countries outside the region (inter-regional trade). It is noticeable that a high proportion (71.9 per cent) of West European exports are intra-regional when compared with other regions; 44.5 per cent of the exports of the Asian region but only 33.4 per cent of the North American region are intra-regional. The shares are even lower for the Latin American, Central/Eastern Europe, African and Middle Eastern regions. The final section shows the share of a region's total exports (intra- and inter-regional) in world exports. This tells us that trade between the countries of West Europe accounts for 33.8 per cent of total world trade.

Two tendencies have been particularly noticeable in the geographical structure of world trade in past decades. At first sight these may seem contradictory. First, there has been a tendency for trade to become more geographically dispersed. Second, trade has become more geographically biased or regionalized.

Let us take geographical dispersion first. This measures the proportion of world trade accounted for by the largest trading nations. In 1973, the top 20 exporters of manufactures accounted for 87.8 per cent of world

**Table 4.2** Regional structure of world merchandise exports, 1992 ($ billion and per cent)

| Origin | Destination | | | | | | | |
|---|---|---|---|---|---|---|---|---|
| **A. Values** | North America | Latin America | West Europe | C./E. Europe and USSR | Africa | Middle East | Asia | World[1] |
| North America | 195 | 78 | 129 | 7 | 11 | 18 | 146 | 583 |
| Latin America | 71 | 26 | 31 | 2 | 2 | 2 | 14 | 151 |
| West Europe | 126 | 36 | 1230 | 57 | 53 | 57 | 128 | 1711 |
| C. and E. Europe | 2 | 2 | 57 | 17 | 2 | 2 | 10 | 92 |
| Africa | 14 | 2 | 53 | 2 | 6 | 2 | 10 | 95 |
| Middle East | 16 | 4 | 33 | 3 | 6 | 10 | 52 | 125 |
| Asia | 232 | 21 | 170 | 10 | 14 | 31 | 394 | 885 |
| World | **655** | **169** | **1702** | **97** | **94** | **122** | **753** | **3642** |
| **B. Shares of intra- and inter-regional flows in each region's total exports** | | | | | | | | |
| North America | 33.4 | 13.4 | 22.1 | 1.2 | 1.8 | 3.1 | 25.0 | 100.0 |
| Latin America | 46.8 | 17.2 | 20.3 | 1.5 | 1.4 | 1.6 | 9.1 | 100.0 |
| West Europe | 7.3 | 2.1 | 71.9 | 3.3 | 3.1 | 3.3 | 7.5 | 100.0 |
| C. and E. Europe | 2.3 | 1.9 | 61.9 | 18.5 | 1.8 | 1.9 | 11.1 | 100.0 |
| Africa[1] | 14.4 | 1.9 | 56.3 | 2.0 | 6.7 | 1.7 | 10.1 | 100.0 |
| Middle East | 12.9 | 2.9 | 26.5 | 2.1 | 4.8 | 7.7 | 41.6 | 100.0 |
| Asia | 26.2 | 2.4 | 19.2 | 1.1 | 1.5 | 3.6 | 44.5 | 100.0 |
| World | **18.0** | **4.6** | **46.8** | **2.7** | **2.6** | **3.3** | **20.7** | **100.0** |
| **C. Shares of intra- and inter-regional trade flows in world exports** | | | | | | | | |
| North America | 5.3 | 2.1 | 3.5 | 0.2 | 0.3 | 0.5 | 4.0 | 16.0 |
| Latin America | 1.9 | 0.7 | 0.8 | 0.1 | 0.1 | 0.1 | 0.4 | 4.1 |
| West Europe | 3.4 | 1.0 | 33.8 | 1.6 | 1.5 | 1.6 | 3.5 | 47.0 |
| C. and E. Europe | 0.1 | 0.0 | 1.6 | 0.5 | 0.0 | 0.0 | 0.3 | 2.5 |
| Africa[1] | 0.4 | 0.0 | 1.5 | 0.1 | 0.2 | 0.0 | 0.3 | 2.6 |
| Middle East | 0.4 | 0.1 | 0.9 | 0.1 | 0.2 | 0.3 | 1.4 | 3.4 |
| Asia | 6.4 | 0.6 | 4.7 | 0.3 | 0.4 | 0.9 | 10.8 | 24.3 |
| World | **18.0** | **4.6** | **46.7** | **2.7** | **2.6** | **3.3** | **20.7** | **100.0** |

[1] Includes unspecified destination.

*Source: GATT (1994).*

manufacturing exports and the top 10 for 72.6 per cent. By 1983, these proportions had fallen to 85.5 per cent and 68.1 per cent. Since that time there has been a slight increase in the share accounted for by the top 20 exporters to 87.8 per cent in 1991 and of the top 10 to 69.4 per cent.

Let us next consider the tendency towards greater regionalization of world trade. One approach to measuring geographical bias in world trade is to observe the trend in the share of intra-regional trade (trade within the region) to a region's total trade. This is shown for various regions of the world in the first section of Table 4.3.

Taking all regions of the world, it is clear that intra-regional trade has been increasing since 1948 after falling in the inter-war period. Intra-regional trade was highest in West Europe and has risen faster than in any of the other regions. In East Europe the intra-regional share rose sharply after 1948 but has fallen back to its former level since 1968. In North America the intra-regional share also rose significantly after 1948 but fell back between 1968 and 1978. In Asia, there has been a similar increase in the share since 1968 but over the period as a whole it has been less stable than in other regions. In Latin America, Africa and the Middle East, the intra-regional share is much lower and no sustained upward trend is discernible.

One problem with using the intra-regional trade share as the measure of geographical bias is that it is affected by the region's share in total trade. If the latter is increasing over time, the intra-regional share will also increase. For example, suppose there are two regions each made up of two countries, A and B in Region 1 and C and D in Region 2. A, B and C each account for 20 per cent of world trade and D for 40 per cent. Each country exports an amount to each other country in proportion to the importer's share of world trade. Because Region 2's share of world trade is greater, its intra-regional trade share is higher (40 per cent) than that of Region 1 (25 per cent). To correct for this distortion, Andersen and Norheim (1993) proposed the use of an intensity of intra-regional trade index. This is obtained using the following formula:

$$Iij = Xij/Mj$$

where $I$ and $j$ are two countries making up a region. $Xij$ is the share of country $I$'s exports going to country $j$ (intra-regional trade) and $Mj$ is the share of country $j$ in world imports. If the index gives a value greater than one, this would indicate a geographical trade bias.

Section 2 of Table 4.3 gives Anderson and Norheim's results. Taking the world as a whole, the index has increased since 1928, although it has fallen somewhat since 1968. This would suggest that world trade has become more geographically biased. In Western Europe the index rose steadily throughout the period. In North America, the index rose after 1948 before falling slightly after 1978. The index for the Asian region has fluctuated a great deal but has been on a declining trend since 1958.

**Table 4.3** Measures of the regionalization of world trade, 1928–90

|  | 1928 | 1938 | 1948 | 1958 | 1968 | 1978 | 1990 |
|---|---|---|---|---|---|---|---|
| **1. Intra-regional trade share (%)** | | | | | | | |
| West Europe | 51 | 49 | 43 | 53 | 63 | 66 | 72 |
| East Europe | 19 | 14 | 47 | 61 | 64 | 54 | 46 |
| North America | 25 | 23 | 29 | 32 | 37 | 30 | 31 |
| Latin America | 11 | 18 | 20 | 17 | 19 | 20 | 14 |
| Asia | 46 | 52 | 39 | 41 | 37 | 41 | 48 |
| Africa | 10 | 9 | 8 | 8 | 9 | 6 | 6 |
| Middle East | 5 | 4 | 21 | 12 | 8 | 7 | 6 |
| **Total, world** | **39** | **37** | **33** | **40** | **47** | **46** | **52** |
| **2. The index of intra-regional trade** | | | | | | | |
| West Europe | 1.13 | 1.14 | 1.21 | 1.38 | 1.51 | 1.57 | 1.60 |
| East Europe | 4.36 | 2.61 | 10.22 | 7.62 | 7.30 | 7.88 | 10.88 |
| North America | 2.59 | 2.91 | 2.39 | 3.07 | 3.57 | 3.63 | 3.50 |
| Latin America | 1.37 | 2.30 | 1.71 | 1.95 | 3.55 | 3.80 | 3.53 |
| Asia | 2.61 | 2.83 | 2.74 | 3.15 | 2.84 | 2.77 | 2.31 |
| Africa | 2.37 | 1.73 | 1.27 | 1.38 | 1.91 | 1.24 | 2.48 |
| Middle East | 7.56 | 3.47 | 9.55 | 4.25 | 3.00 | 1.17 | 2.23 |
| **Total, world** | **1.85** | **1.92** | **2.43** | **2.65** | **2.81** | **2.64** | **2.62** |
| **3. The share (%) of GDP traded** | | | | | | | |
| West Europe | 33 | 24 | 35 | 33 | 34 | 48 | 46 |
| East Europe | 30 | 25 | 25 | 25 | 40 | 40 | 41 |
| North America | 10 | 8 | 11 | 9 | 10 | 19 | 19 |
| Latin America | 45 | 30 | 30 | 30 | 21 | 27 | 28 |
| Asia | 32 | 27 | 25 | 26 | 21 | 27 | 29 |
| Africa | 60 | 50 | 50 | 58 | 37 | 56 | 53 |
| Middle East | 60 | 50 | 50 | 46 | 38 | 48 | 49 |
| Total, world | **24** | **19** | **19** | **22** | **22** | **35** | **34** |

*Source: adapted from Anderson and Norheim (1993).*

Although trade does appear to have become more regionalized, this has in part been offset by a tendency for countries and regions to become more 'open'. Openness may be measured by the proportion of gross domestic product (GDP) which a country trades. The last section of Table 4.3 shows that, whereas regions became less open in the inter-war period, this trend has been reversed since 1948. This was true for all the developed regions and for all other regions since 1968. Western Europe, which had the highest intra-regional share, was also the most open region measured in this way except for Africa and the Middle East. It follows that, whereas trade does appear to have become more regionalized, this has not yet been achieved by regions doing less trade with the rest of the world. Global trade has expanded as regions have become more open but this has gone hand-in-hand with an increased geographical bias in world trade. There is no certainty that this will continue to be the case in the future.

## 4.4 The regional network of world trade

Table 4.2 also shows the value and share of trade that each region conducts with other regions or what is usually referred to as the network or directional flow of world trade.

This is useful for identifying the most important bilateral flows of trade occurring in the world and for an understanding of the balance of trade between different regions. The figures show that the greater part of world merchandise trade occurs between three regions: North America, West Europe and Asia. Bilateral trade flows between these three regions account for 75 per cent of world trade. Trade between North America and West Europe is almost balanced. However, Asia enjoys a large surplus on its merchandise trade with both North America ($86.64 billion in 1992) and West Europe ($42.19 billion in 1992). This is because 59 per cent of Asia's imports are from regions other than North America or West Europe. Of these, roughly three-quarters are from the Middle East. The surplus in Asia's trade with North America and Europe is thus offset by the region's deficit in its trade with the Middle East. This largely reflects the dependence of Asia (Japan in particular) on the Middle East for energy. The point is often not understood in either Europe or North America where debate tends to focus only on the bilateral balance.

Other regions of the world are of necessity heavily dependent on one or more of the three dominant regions for trade. Thus, 56.5 per cent of Latin American exports go to North America, with North America enjoying a small surplus in 1992; 76 per cent of the exports of Central/East Europe and the former USSR go to West Europe, with West Europe enjoying a small surplus. It is interesting to observe that this region is much less important as a market for West Europe (only 3.3 per cent of its exports) than vice-versa. It can be seen that 60.3 per cent of Africa's exports go to West Europe and 45 per cent of Middle Eastern exports go to Asia (with the Middle East enjoying a sizeable surplus). Whereas the bulk of Middle Eastern exports to Asia and most African exports to West Europe are non-manufactures (mainly mining products), a sizeable proportion of Latin America's exports to North America and the Central and East European countries' exports to West Europe are manufactures.

## 4.5 The commodity composition of world trade

Table 4.4 shows the product or commodity composition of world trade. It gives the share of different product groups in world trade for the period 1980 to 1992 and the annual average change in the value of exports. In 1992, manufactures accounted for $2653 billion or 72.8 per cent of world trade. This compares with 61.2 per cent in 1985 and 54 per cent in 1980. By way of contrast, the share of primary products (agricultural and mining products) has been falling steadily. In 1992, agricultural products accounted for $444 billion of world trade or 12.2 per cent compared with 13.7 per cent in 1985 and 14.7 per cent in 1980. In 1992, mining products accounted for $446 billion or 12.2 per cent of world trade, compared with 21.9 per cent in 1985 and 27.6 per cent in 1980. Agricultural products comprise food and agricultural raw materials (such as natural rubber, textile fibres, hides and skins). Mining products are ores and other minerals, fuels and non-ferrous metals. Of these, the share taken by fuels has in the past been highly volatile being affected by fluctuations in world oil prices. After rising sharply in the mid-1970s and early 1980s, oil prices have fallen steadily (rising slightly in 1988 and 1989) contributing to the decline in the share of fuels in the world total.

In general, changes in the share of a particular product group in world trade may be due to either a faster or slower growth in the *volume* of exports or a relative rise or decline in the *unit value* or price of the product. As noted above, exports of manufactures have grown much faster than those of primary commodities in volume as well as value terms, hence the increase in the share of manufactures in the world total. As noted above, the demand for food is income-inelastic so that the growth in output of food products can never exceed the growth of real incomes. The volume of trade in food products may grow faster than output if countries are prepared to allow greater specialization. In practice, few countries are prepared to allow free trade in food products and so specialization is impeded. An offsetting factor might be a sudden sharp rise in food prices. In fact, over the period, 1980 to 1992, the export prices of food products have been falling (rising until 1984, then falling steadily despite a small reversal in 1985).

The volume of trade in raw materials (agricultural, minerals and metals) is heavily dependent on output in the advanced industrialized

**Table 4.4** World merchandise exports by product, 1980–92

| | Value | Shares — | | | Annual average change | | |
|---|---|---|---|---|---|---|---|
| | 1992 | 1980 | 1985 | 1992 | 1980–92 | 1991 | 1992 |
| All products* | 3642 | 100.0 | 100.0 | 100.0 | 5.0 | 1.6 | 5.9 |
| **Agricultural products** | 444 | 14.7 | 13.7 | 12.2 | 3.3 | 0.8 | 6.1 |
| Food | 349 | 11.0 | 10.4 | 9.6 | 3.8 | 3.3 | 7.3 |
| Raw materials | 95 | 3.7 | 3.3 | 2.6 | 1.9 | −7.2 | 2.1 |
| **Mining products** | 446 | 27.6 | 21.9 | 12.2 | −1.9 | −5.1 | −2.0 |
| Ores/other minerals | 47 | 2.1 | 1.8 | 1.3 | 0.9 | −6.7 | −3.2 |
| Fuels | 331 | 23.0 | 18.2 | 9.1 | −2.8 | −4.8 | −1.8 |
| Non-ferrous metals | 67 | 2.5 | 1.8 | 1.8 | 2.4 | −5.6 | −1.7 |
| **Manufacturers** | 2653 | 54.0 | 61.2 | 72.8 | 7.6 | 3.3 | 7.6 |
| Iron and steel | 103 | 3.8 | 3.6 | 2.8 | 2.5 | −1.1 | −1.2 |
| Chemicals | 327 | 7.0 | 7.8 | 9.0 | 7.2 | 3.1 | 7.4 |
| Other semi-manufactures | 280 | 6.8 | 6.4 | 7.7 | 6.1 | 0.8 | 5.9 |
| Machinery/transport equipment | 1359 | 25.8 | 31.0 | 37.3 | 8.3 | 3.8 | 8.0 |
| Office and telecom equipment | 349 | 4.2 | 6.8 | 9.6 | 12.5 | 7.6 | 8.8 |
| Automotive products | 361 | 6.5 | 8.6 | 9.9 | 8.8 | 1.5 | 10.7 |
| Other machinery | 649 | 15.2 | 15.5 | 17.8 | 6.4 | 3.1 | 6.2 |
| **Textiles** | 117 | 2.7 | 2.8 | 3.2 | 6.3 | 4.2 | 6.9 |
| **Clothing** | 131 | 2.0 | 2.5 | 3.6 | 10.2 | 9.7 | 12.0 |
| **Other consumer goods** | 337 | 5.9 | 7.1 | 9.3 | 9.0 | 2.9 | 8.8 |

* Including unspecified products.

*Source: GATT (1994).*

countries. In fact, due to a tendency towards reduced consumption of certain kinds of natural materials per unit of manufacturing output as technology has made the substitution of synthetic for natural materials possible, trade in raw materials has lagged the growth in world manufacturing output. As with food, a rise in raw material prices could offset this tendency. This was the case for the period after 1985 when both agricultural raw material prices and the prices of minerals and non-ferrous metals rose significantly. This was sufficient to stabilize the share of these products in world trade. Trade in fuels fell in value terms between 1980–92 due largely to falling world oil prices.

The largest component of world manufacturing trade is machinery and transport equipment. In 1992, this accounted for $2653 billion or 37.3 per cent of world trade. It has also been the second fastest growing product group within manufacturing trade. In particular, trade in office and telecommunications equipment has been rising rapidly in recent years. Trade in clothing products and other consumer goods have also increased quite fast. By way of contrast, the share of iron and steel products has been falling in value terms. Exports of iron and steel products grew at a noticeably slower rate than other manufactures over the period as a whole. Textiles and other semi-manufactures were also growing more slowly.

## 4.6 Patterns of international specialization

One interesting aspect of world trade concerns the nature of international specialization. To what extent do countries specialize in particular industries? To the extent that they do, can any pattern of specialization be detected? It is not the purpose of this chapter to examine the different theoretical explanations for why countries specialize in particular industries. Instead, we are concerned with how this can be measured and what the results of measurement reveal.

The concept most widely used by economists for measuring a country's specialization in a particular product group is that of 'revealed comparative advantage' (RCA). This can be measured in one of two ways. Firstly, the share of the country in total world exports of a particular product group may be compared with its share of world exports of all commodities. Alternatively, it is possible to estimate a country's export-import ratio for a particular product group relative to its export-import ratio for all products. In both cases, a number greater than one would indicate a degree of specialization. If the number is increasing over time as trade barriers are lowered, this would indicate increasing specialization in that product group.

Table 4.5 contains some estimates for a select group of countries. Products in which countries appeared to have a clearly discernible RCA are listed along with the value of the specialization index and the export-import ratio. The United States has a strong specialization in agricultural products (both food and raw materials) and in certain branches of manufacturing, most notably 'other transport equipment', chemicals, power-generating machinery and 'other non-electrical machinery'. Canada's strength is found in agricultural products (particularly raw materials), mining products (especially non-ferrous metals) and a few branches of manufacturing. France also has a strong revealed comparative advantage in food products as well as in 'other transport

**Table 4.5** Patterns of international specialization for selected countries

| Country | Specialization index | Export/import ratio |
| --- | --- | --- |
| United States | Food 1.125 | Food 1.8443 |
| | | Agric. raw materials 1.8996 |
| | Chemicals 1.417 | Chemicals 1.9153 |
| | | Power generating machinery 1.6368 |
| | | Other non-electrical machinery 1.5445 |
| | | Other transport equipment 3.9697 |
| Canada | Food 1.0 | Food 1.4750 |
| | | Agric. raw materials 5.5985 |
| | | Mining products 2.4272 |
| | | Other semi-manufactures 1.2584 |
| | Automative products 2.3611 | Automative products 1.0802 |
| France | Food 1.6349 | Food 1.4758 |
| | Chemicals 1.5238 | Chemicals 1.2287 |
| | | Automative products 1.2984 |
| | | Other transport equipment 1.9085 |
| Germany | Chemicals 1.4435 | Chemicals 1.4739 |
| | | Power generating machinery 1.5767 |
| | | Other non-electrical machinery 2.1930 |
| | | Electrical machinery and apparatus 1.4668 |
| | Automative products 1.7826 | Automotive products 1.6808 |
| Italy | | Other semi-manufactures 1.8570 |
| | | Other non-electrical machinery 2.6389 |
| | | Electrical machinery and apparatus 1.5089 |
| | Textiles 2.2895 | Textiles 1.9070 |

| Country | Specialization index | Export/import ratio |
|---------|---------------------|---------------------|
|  | Clothing 1.9583 | Clothing 3.0204<br>Other consumer products 2.2600 |
| United Kingdom | Chemicals 1.5686 | Fuels1.516<br>Chemicals 1.4980<br>Power-generating machinery 1.8463<br>Other non-electrical machinery 1.2691<br>Other transport equipment 1.4922 |
| Japan |  | Iron and steel 2.4424<br>Other non-electrical machinery 4.0398 |
|  | Office and telecom equipment 2.4835 | Office and telecom equipment 4.0160<br>Electrical machinery and apparatus 3.1534 |
|  | Automative products 2.3846 | Automative products 8.4002<br>Other transport equipment 2.8984 |

equipment', chemicals and automotive products. Germany's strength is entirely in manufacturing, in particular power-generating machinery, 'other non-electrical machinery', electrical machinery and apparatus and automotive products. Italy specializes in clothing, textiles, other consumer goods, other semi-manufactures and electrical machinery and apparatus. The United Kingdom specializes mainly in manufacturing (power-generating machinery, chemicals and other transport equipment) and it has a modest (but declining) strength in fuels. Finally, Japan's strength is concentrated in manufactures with generally much higher degrees of specialization in selected industries. These are automotive products, office and telecommunications equipment, 'other non-electrical machinery' and electrical machinery and apparatus.

One feature of the estimates shown in Table 4.5 is that, with a few exceptions, they are quite low. This would suggest that countries specialize to quite a low degree. Although there are some industries in which one or more countries have a strong specialization (Japan in automotive products for instance), for many of the countries shown in the table there were few if any industries in which this was the case. The growth of world trade, especially in manufactures, would suggest an increase in the degree of specialization, however. The solution is to be found in the *type* of specialization that has been taking place as world trade has expanded. Rather than countries specializing in whole *industries* (so-called inter-industry specialization), specialization has taken place at the *product level* (intra-industry specialization). In other words, specialization has taken a narrower form than in the past.

There now exists a wide literature on the subject of intra-industry trade. One of the first contributions towards an understanding of the subject was by Grubel and Lloyd (1975). They proposed the following formula:

$$Bij = \frac{(Xij + Mij) - |Xij - Mij|}{(Xij + Mij)}$$

where *Xij* and *Mij* stand for the export and import of product *i* by country *j* (see Grimwade, 1989, for a discussion of this formula and other approaches to the measurement of intra-industry trade). *Bij* will vary between 0 and 100. The higher the value of *Bij*, the greater the importance of intra-industry trade. Essentially, *Bij* measures the proportion of country *j*'s trade which is 'matched' or balanced. At one extreme, if country *j* merely exported product *i* but imported nothing at all, *Bij* would equal zero. At the other extreme, if exports equal imports, *Bij* would have a value of 100. Grubel and Lloyd (1975) found that the average level of intra-industry trade for the ten most advanced industrialized countries had risen from 36 per cent to 48 per cent between 1959 and 1967. Using a formula which was more fully adjusted for an imbalance in a country's overall trade, Aquino (1978) found a generally higher level of intra-industry trade for manufactured goods than that obtained by Grubel and Lloyd. Later empirical work shows that intra-industry trade continued to increase during the 1970s, but tapered off and in some countries was even partially reversed (see Globerman and Dean (1990) for example).

Intra-industry specialization can take one of two forms: horizontal and vertical. Horizontal intra-industry specialization occurs when each country specializes in a particular group or range of products belonging to the same industry. For example, in the pharmaceuticals industry it is not uncommon to find one country specializing in one type of drugs (antibiotics for example) and another country in an entirely different sort (such as vitamins). This is essentially the result of product differentiation. Products are not homogeneous but differ in appearance, style, performance and technology. In such industries, unit costs tend to fall with output over a significant range so it is not profitable for manufacturers to produce all products demanded by consumers. Specialization enables each producer to produce a larger quantity of each type. In this way, consumers are able to choose between a greater variety of the same product. Prices may also be lower because of lower unit costs.

Vertical intra-industry specialization involves countries specializing in particular processes or stages in the manufacture of a group of products. This is already much in evidence in the automobile industry. It reveals itself essentially in high levels of intra-industry trade in intermediate goods. While technological change in product design and methods of transport and communication facilitated the growth of this type of specialization, its basis often resides in differences in factor intensities. Since the different stages or processes require different factor proportions and because factor costs differ between countries it is profitable to situate the separate processes or stages of manufacture at different geographical locations. In some cases, the presence of decreasing unit costs may also favour concentrated production of particular components and parts at highly specialized, large-scale establishments located in a particular country.

It remains to be seen whether there will be further increases in the extent of intra-industry specialization in future decades. Given the high levels of intra-industry specialization already in evidence it would not be surprising if there were no further expansion. The returns from further specialization may have reached their maxima so that any further expansion might yield negative returns. Another relevant consideration is the possible effects of the growth of new methods of manufacturing such as computer-aided production, 'just-in-time' methods of stock control and flexible manufacturing. These reduce the importance of economies of scale, permit more rapid switching from one process or product to another within the same establishment and make more customized production possible. They might therefore reduce the necessity for intra-industry specialization, at least of the horizontal type. They might also favour less offshore assembly and more concentration of production in highly automated plants closer to the biggest markets. In this case, vertical intra-industry specialization could also decline. (See Dicken (1992) for an interesting discussion of the possible effects of the application of new technologies to manufacturing industry.) Another factor that might lead to less intra-industry specialization in the future is the tendency for world trade to become more geographically dispersed. One result of this is a greater heterogeneity of consumer tastes and preferences favouring more inter-industry trade. (This point is discussed by Globerman and Dean (1990) as a possible factor contributing to the tapering off of intra-industry specialization in recent decades although, in empirical testing, it was not found to have had a statistically significant effect on the level of intra-industry trade.)

## 4.7 *The institutional framework*

The institutions that determine the arrangements for trade between different countries and regions of the world are a key factor shaping the volume and pattern of world trade. At the *global* level the most important of these institutions is the GATT (General Agreement on Tariffs and Trade) which on 1 January 1995 was replaced by the newly-created World Trade Organization (WTO). (Technically, the WTO brings together three separate agreements: the GATT itself which largely covers trade in goods, a new General Agreement on Trade in Services (GATS) and the new agreement covering Intellectual Property Rights.) The WTO has two broad functions (as did GATT). The first is to establish precise rules or disciplines to govern world trade. These proscribe certain kinds of practices and set limits on or regulate the use of others. These are intended to ensure that trade is conducted in an environment of certainty in which exporters and importers know that some actions by governments are not acceptable under international law. They include mechanisms for dealing with cases where disputes arise because of a particular practice adopted by another country. Under the rules of the newly established WTO, where an independent panel is convened that upholds the complaint of one party against another, the offending party must remedy the situation or face possible sanctions.

The second role of the WTO is concerned with the liberalization of world trade through multilateral negotiation. By 1996 there were eight so-called 'rounds' of the GATT, the last of which (the Uruguay Round) was successfully concluded in December 1993. Although the range of issues covered by the more recent rounds has broadened considerably, the primary objective of these rounds is to increase the volume of world trade through a reciprocal lowering of trade barriers. Countries negotiate with each other offering 'concessions' in the form of lower tariffs or non-tariff barriers and in return expect to receive equivalent concessions from partner countries in the form of improved access for their exports in foreign markets.

A key principle on which the GATT/WTO is based is that of non-discrimination, the so-called 'most favoured nation' principle. Countries agree to apply equal treatment to each other in areas such as tariffs and non-tariff barriers. It follows that where countries *bilaterally* negotiate a lowering of import barriers, these concessions must automatically be extended to all other member states. Although this principle has not always been applied and in some cases has created problems, it has permitted a more rapid rate of trade liberalization than might otherwise have been possible. In particular it has resulted in a lowering of tariffs on industrial products from an average of around 40 per cent in 1947 to roughly 3 per cent when the cuts made in the Uruguay Round are included. This has contributed to the rapid growth in the volume of world trade over the past 40 years. On the other hand, since the early 1970s these gains have been increasingly threatened by the growth of non-tariff protectionism, particularly on the part of the Western industrialized economies. Much of it has been targeted at the emerging developing economies in the Asian region.

At the *regional* level, a similar process of geographically defined liberalization has been taking place through the establishment of regional trading blocs. GATT/WTO rules permit the formation of free trade areas (FTAs) and customs unions (CUs) on the grounds that these constitute stepping stones in the direction of free trade. Both involve the elimination of tariffs on internal, intra-regional trade, but a CU goes further in establishing a common or harmonized external tariff. GATT/WTO rules require that the average level of external tariffs should not exceed that which existed before the FTA/CU was formed. It is also a requirement that internal tariffs should be wholly eliminated on 'substantially all trade' although a transitional period during which tariffs are gradually lowered is permitted. Although these requirements help to ensure that the trade-diverting effects of regional trading blocs are minimal, they are not completely satisfactory in this respect (see Bhagwatti (1992) for a good discussion of the arguments involved). Since FTAs/CUs are necessarily discriminatory they will cause some diversion of trade away from low-cost suppliers outside the area to higher-cost suppliers inside the area. As Viner (1950) first explained, such trade diversion is harmful and could under certain circumstances exceed the beneficial trade-creating effects resulting from the elimination of internal barriers.

Regional trading blocs were popular in the late 1950s and early 1960s. Few of these schemes lasted apart from regional integration in West Europe through the European Community (EC) established in 1958 and the European Free Trade Area (EFTA) set up in 1960. Many totally failed to achieve their original objectives. More recently, there has been a renewed interest in the creation of regional trading blocs. In West Europe, there was the creation of the Single Market in 1993 and, simultaneously, the European Economic Area (EEA). Following the passage of the Maastricht Treaty in December 1991, the EC has begun the process of transforming itself into an Economic Union. In North America, the United States, previously the primary custodian of multilateralism, has been converted to regionalism, signing free trade agreements with Israel (1985) and Canada (1987) and then setting up the North American Free Trade Area (NAFTA) with Canada and Mexico (1993). More recently, the USA has declared its desire to bring about an all-Americas free-trade zone including both North and South America by the year 2006. The South American countries have also been actively seeking to deepen their regional trading arrangements. In January 1995, Brazil, Argentina, Paraguay and Uruguay set up a customs union known as Mercosur. The Andean Pact countries of South America are similarly seeking to create a common market with a common external tariff. Finally, the Asian region has also taken some steps towards closer regional trading arrangements. Australia and New Zealand are already members of ANZCERTA (the Australian and New Zealand Closer Economic Relations Trade Agreement) established in 1983. Along with the ASEAN countries, Japan and the United States they are also members of the Asia-Pacific Cooperation (APEC) organization. In November 1994, APEC committed itself to creating a free trade area of 17 nations by no later than 2020. In January 1993 the ASEAN countries themselves launched an Asian Free Trade Area (AFTA) designed to eliminate tariffs on industrial goods within 15 years.

Regionalism has thus become a powerful institutional factor influencing the volume and direction of world trade. It remains to be seen whether the pull towards regional trading promoted by the proliferation of regional trading blocs will prove stronger than the tendency towards globalism that multilateral trade liberalization fosters. Much will depend on the arrangements created for the formation of the new regional blocs. It will also depend on the extent to which the new blocs create higher external barriers through devices other than tariffs. If this were to happen, the result would be that world trade would become more geographically biased. If countries then become preoccupied with regional negotiations the momentum towards multilateral trade liberalization might be lost.

## 4.8. Conclusion

This chapter provided a survey of the international trading system in which international firms must operate. It sought to show how this system has grown, viewing the growth of world trade in recent decades as the result of increased specialization, mainly in manufacturing industry. The regional and commodity structure of world trade has also been examined. This was seen to be a constantly shifting structure in which clear trends are discernible. The chapter also discussed the pattern of specialization in which countries have clear revealed advantages in certain particular sectors. These advantages are not always very pronounced, however, reflecting the fact that much of the specialization of recent decades has been of a narrower type. It remains uncertain whether increased intra-industry specialization will take place in the future. Finally, the chapter discussed the changing institutional background to trade. Particular attention was drawn to the growing importance of regional trading arrangements and the possibility that these could become sufficiently powerful to counteract multilateral liberalization measures.

## 4.9 Suggestions for further reading

Anderson K and Blackhurst R (eds) (1993) *Regional Integration and the Global Trading System,* Harvester Wheatsheaff, Hemel Hempstead, is one of the best texts on regional integration.

Grimwade, N. (1989, new edition 1997) *International Trade,* Routledge, London, deals with trends in world trade and intra-industry trade.

Grimwade, N. (1996) *International Trade Policy: a Contemporary Analysis,* Routledge, London, should be consulted by the reader interested in contemporary developments in international trade policy.

Nielsen J., Madsen E. and Pedersen K. (1995) *International Economics, the Wealth of Open Nations,* McGraw-Hill, London, is a useful text on trade theory.

Schott J. (1994) *The Uruguay Round: an Assessment*, Institute for International Economics, Washington DC, gives a recent assessment of the Uruguay Round.

World Trade Organization (bimonthly) *Focus,* World Trade Organization, Geneva, students should consult this for information on current developments in trade policy.

World Trade Organization (1995) *1995 International Trade – Trends and Statistics,* World Trade Organization, Geneva, is the most important source on trends in world trade.

## 4.10 Questions for further discussion

1. Can we expect world trade to grow faster than world output in the next decade or more?

2. What major changes do you envisage in patterns of international specialization in the next century?

3. What major changes do you envisage will take place in the regional structure of world trade?

4. Do you expect the trend towards increased intra-industry specialization to continue in the next century?

5. What might be the consequences for the world trading system of a further proliferation and strengthening of regional trading blocs?

# 5

# *Alternative approaches to the explanation of international production*

## *5.1 Introduction*

This chapter considers various approaches that have been developed to explain foreign direct investment and international production. The decades after the Second World War have seen considerable developments in direct investment in terms of its growth, its geographical and industry patterns and also in its different forms as highlighted in Chapter 2. It is therefore not surprising that there has been a simultaneous growth in the theories put forward to explain these changes. The main theories have been developed since the mid-1960s. Some theories only relate to FDI; others relate to wider forms of international involvement such as franchising and licensing. In some the focus is on FDI as such; in others the focus is the MNC its organization, development and activities.

In order to do some justice to the wealth of theories put forward and in order to help the reader see the connections between theories, we shall group the various theories within overall general approaches. (Cf. also Cantwell, 1991.)

This is necessarily a broad and rough method of classification. The number and type of approaches could have been chosen differently and not every author embarking on such a task would necessarily have grouped the theories in the same way. The task is made more fluid and difficult by the fact that some theories, by their very nature and/or because of the richness of their content, lend themselves to inclusion in more than one approach.

Four major approaches are considered here: the *neoclassical approach;* the *macroeconomic approach;* the *market structure and market power approach* and the *eclectic* approach. This last approach is a composite one that draws on a variety of theories to develop a framework of analysis.

The rest of this chapter is structured in the following way. Section 5.2 deals with the reasons why theories and explanations are relevant. Sections 5.3, 5.4, 5.5 and 5.6 deal with the neoclassical, macroeconomic, market structure and power and the eclectic approaches respectively. Section 5.7 draws conclusions. Section 5.8 gives advice on further reading. Section 5.9 gives suggestions for issues and questions to be discussed in small group work.

## 5.2 Why do we need theories?

In business and economics the world is characterized, *inter alia,* by the fact that people operate in situations in which current decisions have effects and repercussions in the future. Sometimes such repercussions are deliberate and planned; sometimes they are not. In either case, business people and economic actors in general need to form opinions as to what is likely to happen in the future in order to be able to plan and take appropriate decisions and actions. The future, however, is characterized by uncertainty. In order to counteract this uncertainty, decision-makers need to make predictions. They can then take action on the basis of such predictions.

All this is particularly important in the realm of investment which, by its very nature, has considerable impact on the future in two different ways. First, because the implementation of investment activities usually extend into the medium- to long-term: for example a factory has a long gestation period and may require months or years to be built. Second, because the effects of investment on production extend well into the future: the new factory will be used for production for many years. The uncertainties related to investment range from the costs of building the factory to the demand conditions for the product that is going to be produced, to the reactions by competitors to the prices of inputs whether raw materials or labour and to current and future developments in technology.

Predictions are thus essential for business people, firms, labour organizations, governments and their policy makers. Predictions are not always consciously made and expressed; they are nevertheless always present as an essential ingredient of business and economic life.

In order to make meaningful predictions business people and

economists need to begin by explaining why certain phenomena occur. By explaining what has happened in the past or present they will then be able to make predictions for the future within the constraints of suitable assumptions and conditions.

Does this mean that the task of explaining business and economic phenomena is an impossible one and that all we have are alternative positions – indeed, positions that may be heavily influenced by ideological issues? I believe that this is not the case. Theories can be assessed for their applicability to certain situations in terms of their ability to describe and explain real phenomena and to make predictions. Some theories may be more applicable than others to specific historical situations, countries, industries and firms. It is the role of the expert to assess the situation using appropriate tests and to decide which theory he or she considers most applicable and why. The assessment of the situations must relate to both the explanatory and predictive power of the theory against observed facts.

This raises a more general question in the philosophy of science. Are theories mere instruments for calculations and predictions or are they (and should they be) descriptions and explanations of the real world? In other words, should they attempt to express 'truths' about the world? This question has been the subject of considerable debate in the literature on the methodology of science. The 'instrumentalists', in contrast to the 'realists', maintain that predictions are possible despite unrealistic theories and assumptions. This 'instrumentalist' position is not very widely accepted by philosophers of science. However, it has some powerful supporters among economists, with Friedman (1953, Part I, pp.3–43) as the main advocate. A very good critique of Friedman's position may be found in Musgrave (1981). The realist versus instrumentalist debate is lucidly explained in Popper (1963, pp.97–119).

When it comes to explanations, however, neither natural scientists nor social scientist have ready-made answers that can be applied with certainty to all times and situations. What they do have are theories: conjectures about how the world operates. Conjectures must be tested against observable facts for confirmation before they are accepted; they may be refuted by the weight of counter-evidence at any time and may eventually be replaced by competing theories.

Very often, when attempting to answer the question 'why invest abroad?' business people, the financial press and many textbooks offer simple, snappy explanations that appear to make a lot of sense. On both the demand and the supply side there are many simple explanations that appear, at times, to be very plausible including: the search for new markets, the search for locations with lower input costs (in particular labour and raw materials) or suitable infrastructure, jumping trade barriers (that is the use of international production to source a market when exports are excluded or difficult because of trade barriers), and government incentives in the host country.

These explanations seem to make much sense in many cases so why bother to resort to more complex theories? There are various reasons for this. For a start, what is to be explained is very complex. It is necessary to try to explain (a) the choice between international production, exports and franchising or licensing in terms of sourcing of markets; (b) why, in some cases, the penetration of a market may require a strategy of joint ventures; (c) the choice between green field investment and mergers and acquisitions in terms of growth strategy; (d) in terms of the organization of production, the strategy of internal expansion versus a strategy that favours outsourcing of components including the use of subcontractors; (d) the different patterns between industries and between companies in the same industries.

At the macro level we need to explain the industrial and geographical pattern of FDI shares through time. There are also differences between the behaviour of a company/industry in the short and long term: a market may be sourced by exports in the short run and by FDI and/or franchising later.

A simple explanation (such as tariff jumping) may thus apply to a specific industry/company at a specific period of time but may not – or not by itself – give enough insight into the wider patterns and trends and their interrelationships. This is the task of more complex theories.

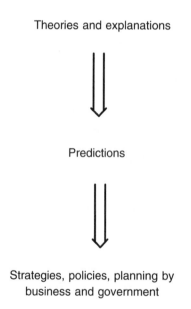

Theories and explanations

Predictions

Strategies, policies, planning by
business and government

**Figure 5.1** Theories as facilitators of strategies, policies and planning.

## 5.3 The neoclassical approach

### 5.3.1 The pre-Second World War neoclassical approach

The neoclassical economic paradigm is the most widely used in teaching and research. Its origin goes back to the 1870s and its early developments are particularly due to economists in Britain, France, Austria, Switzerland. The general principles on which it is based are:

- People act rationally and have full knowledge of markets and economic conditions; there is no uncertainty in the system.

- Consumers want to maximize the utility derived from consumption given their budgetary constraints.

- Firms are profit maximizers.

- Markets are perfectly competitive

- Resources are scarce and their allocation to various uses is done through the price mechanism.

- Given the initial distribution of wealth, the distribution of income between the various factors of production occurs via the price mechanism and it is based on the principle of the contribution to production of each factor of production (particularly labour and capital), via its productivity level and growth. The system as a whole will be in equilibrium, or move towards it, at both the micro and macro levels. These general principles and conclusions are applied in all aspects of economic life from goods to factors (including labour) markets, to the behaviour of investors, consumers and households.

The application of the neoclassical theory to foreign investment developed along the following lines. Prior to the Second World War there was no theory of foreign direct investment as such. There was a general theory of foreign investment that made no distinction between portfolio investment and direct investment. Foreign investment was considered to involve a transfer of funds and was explained under the general theory of capital movements. This theory followed the same general principles and assumptions as the theory of movements of goods and services across frontiers through international trade, of which it became an extension. For example Ohlin (1933) deals with capital movements in the context of his more well-known theory of international trade.

The general thrust of this neoclassical theory of foreign investment was that movements of funds between countries would take place in response to differentials in interest rates and rates of return on investment. The rate of return was related to the relative endowment of capital by each country in relation to its demand at home. Capital-abundant countries would have lower rates of return and interest than capital-scarce countries. Funds would thus move from capital-abundant to capital-scarce countries. These movements would gradually change the relative endowment of capital in the two countries. The new situation as regards the scarcity or abundance of capital in the two countries would lead to a decline in the rate of return and interest rates in the outward investor's country and an increase in the rates in the country receiving funds, with eventual equalization of interest rates and rates of return on investment across the two countries. Ohlin (1933), Nurkse (1933), and Iversen (1935) were the main proponents of this theory before the Second World War.

This theory stresses the relative endowment of capital in the countries as the main stimulus for the movement of capital across frontiers and thus for foreign investment. There is a parallel in the theory of international trade. This explains movements of products across frontiers in terms of the relative endowment of factors of production in the two countries (Grimwade, 1989, Chapter 1). It is therefore basically a macroeconomic theory within the overall neoclassical approach. The approach is neoclassical in various respects:

- It emphasizes scarcity and the relative factor endowment of countries.

- It emphasizes profit maximization as the objective and the price mechanism (interest rates) as the main vehicle in encouraging activity.

- It assumes certainty and perfect knowledge of the markets on the part of the operators.

- It leads to final equilibrium and price equalization through capital movements.

- The approach is essentially static and involves comparative static analysis (that is comparisons between two static equilibrium positions) in relation to the situation before and after the movements of capital.

### 5.3.2 Hymer's critique

Steven Hymer was a Canadian economist who, in the late 1950s and in 1960, was working at the Massachusetts Institute of Technology (MIT) as a research student. This was the period when a big wave of American investment into Europe and Canada was well under way. Hymer (1960) researched the international operations of national firms for his dissertation. His work, published in 1976 after his death, begins with a powerful critique of the then-prevalent neoclassical theory.

He distinguishes between portfolio and direct investment according to whether the investor wants to (and does) acquire control over the acquired firm and the activities in which it invests. This distinction proved to be of great relevance and has been used ever since. He noted that direct investment shows peculiarities that do not correspond with the assumptions of the neoclassical theory nor corroborate its conclusions. In particular he notes the following:

- Direct investment does not necessarily involve movement of funds from country to country as the investor company can borrow money elsewhere and often uses funds in the host country for new investment. These funds can be raised on the host country's capital markets or they may originate from profits in existing affiliates of foreign companies.

- Direct investment often shows a cross-countries pattern with both countries involved being simultaneously home and host country to the other's investment.

- Direct investment tends to be industry specific rather than country specific. This means that the flow of investment tends to concentrate in specific industries across countries rather than specific countries across many industries.

His first point invalidates the whole basis of the neoclassical theory of foreign investment which assumes that funds move from the investor to the inward country. Moreover, if the investment is in response to differentials in capital endowment and interest rates it is not clear how both countries could invest into each other. The relative scarcity of capital in a country should also show a country-specific pattern, not a pattern linked to industries.

Hymer's critique applies mainly to the ability of the theory to deal with direct investment, not so much with portfolio investment. This was a distinction that was absent in the original neoclassical analysis.

### 5.3.3 Transaction costs, internalization and the MNE

In the 1970s a new strand of neoclassical theory was developed by researchers working on both sides of the Atlantic. The new development has come to be known as the 'internalization' theory of international production and FDI. Unlike the pre-Second World War approach, this new strand is closely based on the firm, its activities and objectives and its organization rather than on the macro economy.

The theory builds on Coase's criticism of conventional neoclassical theory in relation to the firm and the market. Coase (1937) noted the inconsistency between the assumption that the market and its price mechanism is the best allocator of resources and the fact that in real life a large and increasing amount of resources is allocated internally to firms via internal planning and directives within the organization. The riddle was solved by introducing the concept of 'transaction cost'. Market transactions are costly because the parties need to search for the best opportunities in terms of quality, reliability, prices and so forth. Thus firms will prefer to internalize their activities whenever the cost of carrying the transaction in the market exceeds the possible internal diseconomies of scale and organization that may be involved in the larger firm. Any development (technological and/or organizational) that reduces the cost of internal and/or spatial organization will favour internalization, so the organization of production and transactions will be undertaken within the firm, as discussed in Chapter 3.

On the other hand, excessive internalization has its own costs and disadvantages. These can be assessed in terms of managerial and organizational constraints and diseconomies, including possible diseconomies of operating on an excessively large scale. There may also be a cost attached to the control of a large workforce and its increasing power due to the concentration of labour employed in the same company and country (cf. Ietto-Gillies, 1992, Chapter 14 as well as the brief comments at the end of 5.5.3). Coase's analysis opened the way for a whole new approach to the working of markets, firms and institutions in both the private and public sectors. Developments by Williamson (1975 and 1981) further extended his work. The focus of research began to shift from the theory of the firm towards the development of an overall theory of the organization of production and business. Indeed Williamson attempted to interpret the whole history of the firm and its changing organization in terms of economies in transaction costs. This new twist in the theory of the firm opened the way for a new, less critical, view of large organizations and monopoly power, and a more critical view of anti-trust legislation (cf. Pitelis, 1993). Coase himself (1991) clarified the origin of the debate as well as some analytical issues within it.

Coase (1960) takes the debate into the links between economics and law. On the assumption that the costs of transactions are the problem, it is important to have a legal framework that allows clear contracts to be drawn that minimize uncertainties about quality and prices of supplies. The economic relevance of the legal framework and related contracts takes on a double meaning: the contract may be a guarantee that encourages more market transactions and less internalization but the contract involves legal and other expenses that become part of the transaction costs of dealing in the market. Coase (1991, p.62) summarizes his views as follows:

> Transaction costs were used in the one case to show that if they are not included in the analysis, the firm has no purpose, while in the other I

showed, as I thought, that if transaction costs were not introduced into the analysis, for the range of problems considered, the law had no purpose.

---

**Box 5.1** Examples of transaction costs

**1. Consumer**

Acquiring a new car involves you in:

- Research to find which products respond to your needs and specifications and which are the most reliable manufacturers.

- Finding the best dealers.

- Finding who offers the best after-sales service and who offers the best prices and credit conditions.

- Expenses involved in the purchase, including the legal expenses concerning contracts.

**2. Producer: vertical chain**

You are the chief executive of a major French company that produces furniture and you want to buy wood. You want to review your strategy for obtaining a supply of wood from South America. Possible transaction costs include:

- Time and expenses in finding out about the best suppliers in terms of quantity, prices and delivery time.

- Expenses associated with contracts.

- Costs of acquiring knowledge of, and adaptation to, different business cultures.

---

The 'transaction costs' approach to the relationship between markets and firms has had considerable influence on both economic theory and policy. On the theory side, the period since the mid-1960s has seen a move towards the reinterpretations of many economic concepts, theories and facts in terms of economies of transaction costs. As regards policies, the approach had considerable effects on issues of competition policy. A possible conclusion seems to be that if the growth of the firm occurs as a result of the wish to economize on transaction costs it follows that the concentration of production in large units can be efficient and we need not worry too much about excessive market power of large firms.

The applications of this new approach to the MNE and international production came through the works of McManus (1972), Buckley and Casson (1976), Teece (1977), Rugman (1981) and Caves (1982). The general assumption behind the application of the approach is that markets are imperfect mechanisms in terms of the information they convey. In particular, buyers and sellers have asymmetrical positions as regards access to information. Buyers do not have full information about the product they wish to buy. There are uncertainties in relation to the quality, reliability and relative prices of the products offered by various producers. Costs are incurred in searching for information about products. In order to cut the uncertainties and reduce the transactions costs, firms will prefer to internalize the transaction, carrying out production themselves.

Two situations can arise: vertical and horizontal integration. The firm will prefer to internalize the various vertical stages of the production process whenever it wants to cut the uncertainty over supplies of raw materials or components. This explains vertical internalization both at the national and international levels. International horizontal integration (direct production in different countries of the same or similar products) is explained in terms of the need to protect the firm's knowledge from competitors. The firm's knowledge may be in terms of research and development and/or in terms of superior managerial, organizational or marketing skills. This type of knowledge is characterized by the following:

(a) its acquisition is likely to require large initial costs in research and development;

(b) it is embodied in intangible assets that are difficult to value and exchange at arm's length on the market; within the firm, these assets become a 'public good'. A public good has low or zero marginal cost although its fixed costs may be high. This means that once the knowledge is acquired it may be in the interest of the firm to utilize it as widely as possible within its own ownership borders. However, if knowledge goes outside the firm, the firm itself will lose its monopoly over it and its advantage over rivals, and thus eventually the profit which derive from it. In the circumstances, franchising or selling the patent may become risky. The firm may therefore prefer to expand into new markets by producing directly rather than by selling on the market for fear of losing its superior knowledge to its competitors.

Any institutional arrangement that does not threaten the loss of the monopoly over knowledge and its related profits for the firm will favour the externalization of production, however. Thus a patents system that offers strong protection against imitators will favour licensing rather than internal production as a means of expansion and market sourcing (cf. Hennart, 1991, p.87). The externalization of production through various inter-firm contractual arrangements, such as licensing or sub-contracting, may be encouraged for other reasons such as the following:

- The large-scale expansion of the firm through internalization may create organizational and managerial problems that result in diseconomies.

- A large firm means often employing a large labour force which may then become too powerful and costly (cf. Ietto-Gillies, 1992, Chapter 14).

It should be noted that the choice between internalization/externaliza-tion is not necessarily an 'either/or' situation. Companies have developed a whole array of inter-firm relationships with various degrees of externalization (cf. Chapter 2 in this book as well as OECD, 1994, pp.12–13).

The theory presents some difficulties, however. For example it cannot fully explain internationalization because, after all, the firm could internalize by producing at home and exporting in order to source foreign markets. The theory may thus explain the choice between FDI and licensing but not the choice between exports and FDI. If foreign production is more profitable or efficient due, for example, to transportation costs or to trade barriers, then the choice between different sourcing strategies becomes a choice between internalization and externalization. There are, however, different degrees of internal or external co-ordination from full ownership of all the co-ordinated units to inter-firm co-ordination. On the whole, vertical integration is easier to explain with the internalization theory than horizontal integration. Caves (1971 and 1982) explains vertical integration through internaliza-tion, and horizontal integration in terms of the desire or need for product differentiation in oligopolistic markets.

The internalization/externalization debate has come into sharp focus since the early 1980s with the debate about the desirability of achieving more streamlined organizations that concentrate on core activities while externalizing the more peripheral activities (often by subcontracting). This has had a big impact and has affected public organizations to an even larger extent than private ones.

It may be interesting to note the relationship between the development of the Coasian analysis and the changes in the political and economic macro environment. Coase put forward his theory about the determi-nants of the limits between the expansion of the firm (internalization) versus market transactions. The limits are set by the relative costs of operating within the two structures. In 1937 and in the following decades firms were growing; the advantages of economies of scale were taken for granted. There was not much debate about the efficiency of large-scale organizations. In the 1970s, when the Coasian analysis was resurrected by economists, there was concern about the issue of excessive monopoly power brought about by the growth of firms in the previous decades. Transaction costs analysis was partly used to show how internalization led to lower transaction costs and therefore had private and social benefits that should be balanced against the social costs of excessive market power.

The big success of Coase's theory came in the 1980s. This is the period when the wisdom of having larger and larger organizations in both private and public sectors was hotly debated. The benefits of externalization and market transactions became more and more fashionable and expressions like 'downsizing' of firms and 'outsourcing' of production became everyday business vocabulary. The search for a more flexible organization of production went hand-in-hand with the search for the flexibility of employment of labour by firms.

The internalization theory would, *prima facie*, appear to be quite different from the traditional neoclassical theory. In what sense can they be grouped together? What are their common characteristics? They certainly differ in the following elements:

(a)   the traditional neoclassical theory of foreign investment is centred on the macro economy while the internalization theory is based on the firm and on the organization of production;

(b)   the neoclassical approach assumes perfect markets and certainty while the internalization theory considers imperfect markets and uncertainty. The imperfections in the markets exist mainly in terms of asymmetry between buyer and seller and market transaction versus internal transaction within the firm.

(c)   The traditional neoclassical theory deals with typical economic concepts; the internalization theory enters new territory with its attempt to developing a theory of the organization of production.

Their common ground is the following.

(a)   Both theories deal with exchange more than with production (cf. Cantwell, 1991).

(b)   Both theories are concerned with profit maximization and efficiency. In one case these objectives are achieved through the reallocation of capital across nations; in the other they are achieved through the balance between internal allocation and allocation through the market. In the internal allocation theory, profit maximization is achieved through economies in transaction costs.

The drive for efficiency is neatly explained in the following passage from McManus (1972, p.84):

> In summary, we have argued that the international firm is one of the methods by which interdependent activities in different countries can be co-ordinated. There are two equivalent statements of the conditions under which the international firm will be chosen by interdependent producers in different countries: the producers will choose to centralize control if the international firm is the least expensive way in which to obtain a given level of efficiency within the joint activity; the producers will choose to centralize control if the international firm yields the highest level of efficiency for a given cost of co-ordinating their joint activity.

---

**Box 5.2** Internalization and integration

The internalization theory of the multinational company uses economies in transaction costs to explain

- vertical integration across frontiers within the same firm;

- horizontal integration across frontiers within the same firm.

---

## 5.4 Macroeconomic approaches

This section addressed some theories that have been developed, to a considerable extent, around macroeconomic features of the system in terms of the way they deal with causes and/or effects of foreign direct investment. The traditional neoclassical approach was macroeconomic in nature but it will not be included in this section because its prevalent feature is considered to be its strictly neoclassical assumptions and conclusions.

### 5.4.1 The product life-cycle theory

In the 1960s Raymond Vernon was working at the Harvard Business School, Cambridge MA, not far from the MIT where Steven Hymer had been working. Vernon (1966) had outlined the 'product life cycle' (PLC) theory of international production, investment and trade. The theory goes back to existing approaches to the life of the product (at the micro level) and to the technological gap theories of trade at the macro level. In particular Posner (1961) considers the technological gap between

---

**Table 5.1** Characteristics of the product cycle

| Characteristics | Cycle phase – | | |
| --- | --- | --- | --- |
| | Early | Growth | Mature |
| Technology | Short runs. Rapidly changing techniques. Dependence on external economies. | Mass production methods gradually introduced. Variations in techniques frequent. | Long runs and stable technology. Few innovations of importance. |
| Capital intensity | Low. | High, due to high obsolescence rate. | High, due to large quantity of specialised equipment. |
| Industry structure | Entry is know-how determined. Numerous firms providing specialised services. | Growing number of firms. Many casualties and mergers. Growing vertical integration. | Financial resources critical for entry. Number of firms declining. |
| Critical human inputs | Scientific and engineering. | Management. | Unskilled and semi-skilled labour. |
| Demand structure | Sellers' market. Performance and price of substitutes determine buyers' expectations. | Individual producers face growing price elasticity. Intra-industry competition reduces prices. Product information spreading. | Buyers' market. Information easily available. |

*Source: Hirsch (1965), p.92.*

countries and its effect on trade. At the micro level the various phases of the product's life are analysed by Kuznetz (1953) and later by Hirsch (1965). The characteristics of the product life cycle as set up by Hirsch (1965, p.1) are reproduced in Table 5.1.

Vernon noticed that new products are likely to be developed in a country with high per capita income, relatively scarce labour and relative abundant capital. The United States was such a country at the time when Vernon was writing. The new product at first requires high-skill labour; it is produced in a relatively monopolistic position and this helps to make it a product which has, at first, a high income elasticity of demand and a low price elasticity of demand. The product is soon exported, by the originating company, to other developed countries and is later produced there directly in order to thwart competitors who might try to imitate it. This is the mature phase of the product, when all the required technological adaptations have been made and when mass production will gradually begin. The product eventually becomes easy to imitate; at this point its demand becomes more price elastic and the firm that initiated production has to find ways to meet competition through prices; it therefore looks for reductions in costs. This makes location in developing countries attractive, particularly since the product is now standardized, mass produced and therefore requires mainly unskilled labour. The shift of production to developing countries is likely to be accompanied by a pattern of trade in which the developing countries export the product to developed countries including the original one (the United States).

One of the interesting conclusions of the theory concerns the transfer of technology between developed and developing countries. Outdated technology is transferred to the developing countries and this lengthens the life of some plants which might otherwise have to be abandoned.

Many writers further developed and refined the theory and many criticized it. Vernon (1979) himself wrote a critique that set limits to the validity of his (1966) theory. He explained that his theory was no longer as valid in the late 1970s as it had been in the 1960s due to macroeconomic developments. The gap between the United States and other developed countries, particularly Europe, had declined; this meant a decline in the technological gap and in per capita income between the United States and European countries. At the same time companies had acquired the ability to locate worldwide almost from the birth of the new product. Corroboration on this point was to be found in two relevant trends: the widening network of worldwide linkages by the largest American and European companies and the tendency towards the shortening of the lag between the beginning of production of a new product at home and the location of its production abroad. Thus the product life cycle theory, as a theory of international production, was no longer valid or not as widely applicable as in the 1960s.

What seem to have changed, however, are mainly the relationships within developed countries and between the technological advanced country (the United States) and other developed countries. We could maintain that the theory is still applicable in many cases including the following ones:

(a)    the development of relatively low-demand, luxury, niche markets;

(b)    the cycle between developed and developing countries in general;

(c)    the relationship between developed countries and countries from the former socialist bloc.

It is generally true that it is easier to detect a life cycle sequence in some products than others. For example the motor car industry seemed to fit the model better than consumer audio equipment. In the first industry, the production of some automobile models has been discontinued in developed countries and relocated to developing countries (the Volkswagen Beetle and the Fiat 600). With regard to audio equipment, however, it is noticeable that items such as the Walkman have appeared throughout the world in terms of both consumption and production almost simultaneously.

The more recent move towards flexible production systems may have dealt a further blow to the validity of Vernon's original approach. Flexible systems rely on economies of scope to be achieved through smaller production runs rather than through large scale standardized production. This means that the last phase of Vernon's cycle may no longer be fully applicable to a large number of products. It also means that the advantages of developing nations for this phase of the product cycle may be lost since flexible production requires more skilled labour and higher level infrastructure as highlighted in Chapter 3. Further criticisms of product life-cycle theory are also emerging in terms of the technological gap element. There is some evidence that technological developments tend to cluster in specific countries and industries (Cantwell, 1989 and 1993). Moreover, companies are increasingly involved in some decentralization of research and development activities (OECD, 1994). All this seems inconsistent with the PLC theory of technological superiority by one country, as pointed out in Cantwell (1994).

The theory has a strong macroeconomic emphasis in that it is linked to the gap in technology and per capita income between countries as well as to the relative scarcity of factors of production and labour skills. The theory also manages to deal with both FDI and trade flows within developed countries as well as between developed and developing ones. The theory also assumes an imperfect market structure and this will be discussed later in section 5.5.

### 5.4.2 Aliber's theories

Two different and strictly macroeconomic approaches were developed by Robert Aliber. The first one was developed in Aliber (1970). It is strongly based on financial flows between countries and on the division of the world into customs areas and currency areas. Countries with high trade barriers will attract FDI because firms will try to bypass the barriers and enter the barred markets by producing directly in the countries concerned. Countries with strong currencies will invest in weak-currency countries in order to maximize the profit from the invested capital. The value of the acquired assets in weak-currency countries is higher for the investor operating from a strong-currency country.

There are various problems with this approach. For example Dunning (1991) notes that overvaluing a currency is likely to explain the timing of outward direct investment but not necessarily its long-term trend and industry structure. We could add that Aliber's theory, if valid at all, is more likely to apply to the acquisition of existing capacity abroad than to the creation of new capacity through 'greenfield' plants. Greenfield capacity requires a medium- to long-term gestation period which is unlikely to be influenced by short-term issues linked to currency valuation. It is also worth noting that, in some respects, Aliber seems to go back to the financial flows aspects of foreign investment stressed by the traditional neoclassical theory; in fact they both deal with movements of funds rather than with international production.

A more recent work by Aliber (1993) puts stronger emphasis on the real economy and less on its financial side. Here Aliber explains patterns of FDI worldwide by looking at differentials in growth rates of national production.

He notices that countries experience periods of rapid growth at different times as their industrialization phase occurs at different times. Rapid growth is characterized by an increase in the share of manufacturing output and in high productivity growth as well as a high rate of technological innovation. High growth rates are also associated with high profit rates and high interest rates. As a result, countries with high growth rates attract foreign investment as this seeks growth in the demand for products and high profit/interest rates.

A very detailed analysis of the relationship between different phases of development and international trade has been developed by Rowthorn and Wells (1987). Interestingly enough Rowthorn and Wells link development and growth to trade although not to foreign investment. Aliber links it to foreign investment although not to trade to any great extent.

### 5.4.3 Stagnationist views

Some authors link problems on the demand side of the macroeconomy to foreign investment. Pitelis (1991) traces the lack of effective demand and stagnation to the monopolistic structure of the economy. The lack of effective demand coupled with the connected increase in the liquidity of companies is likely to lead to foreign investment, particularly through mergers and acquisitions often across borders. Investment through mergers and acquisitions increases capacity for the acquiring firm though not for the world economy as a whole. It also leads to the concentration of market shares in fewer companies worldwide. The consequence of this strategy at the companies' level is an increase in the degree of monopoly in the economy with consequent longer-term stagnation problems.

Cowling and Sugden (1987) link their theory of international monopoly capitalism to firms' strategic behaviour in an oligopolistic structure. We shall deal more extensively with the micro and industry side of their theory in section 5.5.2. On the macro side, they conclude that the behaviour of companies leads to an increase in the degree of monopoly and to a consequent lack of effective demand. Cowling and Sugden (1987) follows on from Cowling (1982) and it links the strategic behaviour of companies in 'monopoly capitalism' to some macroeconomic features. In particular, the high and increasing degree of monopoly in the economic system leads to overcapacity and stagnation and therefore leads to unemployment. This is a theme that has long and strong antecedents in the economics literature. It goes back to Hobson (1902), Luxemburg (1913) Kalecki (1939) Baran and Sweezy (1966) and others.

The stagnationist view differs from Aliber's (1993) view in many respects. Both of these approaches consider growth rates and related levels of demand to be relevant. In the case of Aliber, however, the growth rates differ across countries and they are linked to different phases of development and industrialization. In the case of the more recent stagnationist writers (Kalecki, Baran and Sweezy and Cowling and Sugden) growth is linked to the monopolistic structure of the economy.

## 5.5 Market structure, power and conflicts

### 5.5.1 Introduction

Many theories have been developed by looking at what happens within the individual firm – by examining its internal organization and the organization of production in general. The internalization theory could be included in this microeconomic group. It has been included in the first group of theories – those constituting the neoclassical approach – to highlight the efficiency side of its conclusions and of its assumptions in relation to the firm's objectives.

Other authors have placed the working of the firm within the industry in which it operates and developed theories that see FDI as the outcome of interplay between the firm, its objectives and organization, and its rivals within the industry. This approach, which concentrates on the industry rather than the micro or macro economy, has been very fruitful. The authors working within this broadly 'mesoeconomic' (intermediate between macro and micro) background differ in many respects, in particular in relation to whether they stress market power on the part of the company and whether they consider the structure of the market to be an exogenous variable or to be endogenous and thus affected by the behaviour of the companies. The extent to which the macro environment is a given, fixed variable or can be affected by the action of companies is also an important issue; it can be relevant to both the macro approaches and the 'mesoeconomic' ones (that is those based on the working of the industry).

### 5.5.2 Hymer's contribution

One of Hymer's most fruitful insights was to shift the focus of analysis from the macro economy, on which the conventional neoclassical theory was based, to the industry, its market structure and the behaviour of firms. He noticed that FDI had a tendency to be industry specific and that the industries concerned were characterized by imperfect markets. In particular they had an oligopolistic structure. In such a structure the behaviour of firms is affected by the power that they have and by the strategies they want to follow *vis-à-vis* their rivals.

Foreign production involves specific additional costs and disadvantages. If companies engage in it they must derive counterbalancing advantages. These are to be sought in terms of the advantages over rivals that their presence in a foreign country can give. These advantages can be fully exploited through the direct control of production abroad; this is why they engage in FDI. Hymer's theories are considered in Yamin (1991).

### 5.5.3 American perspectives on oligopolistic structures

Vernon's (1966, 1974 and 1979) contributions, while set in a broadly macroeconomic framework, also have strong industry and market structure elements. The innovative firm in Vernon (1966) operates in an imperfect market and has a monopolistic advantage deriving from its new product that is reflected in a low price elasticity of demand. The moves towards FDI in European countries and later in developing countries, are largely motivated by strategic behaviour toward rivals, whether these are actual or potential. The first move towards FDI, directed at Europe, aims to stop potential rivals from operating in the large European markets. The second move, at the stage when the product is standardized, is designed to reduce costs and thus avert price competition in a product that is no longer new and which can, at this stage, be imitated widely.

Vernon's (1974) contribution links his general theory on the MNE's decisions and behaviour to oligopolistic structures even more strongly and explicitly than in Vernon (1966). In an *innovation-based oligopoly* firms compete through innovation; their demand tends to be price inelastic and they tend to locate production in their home base. In a *mature oligopoly* the advantages derive not from innovation but from the scale of operations. Companies tend to fear each other and open war is avoided by tacit or explicit collusion on prices and location of production. In situations where economies of scale are not, or are no longer, strong enough to act as barriers for actual or potential rivals, competition will take the form of cost cutting and this affects the location of production. Developing countries are now likely to be favoured as sites for investment. Vernon calls this a *senescent oligopoly*. The three types of oligopoly clearly match the three phases in the life of the product.

There may be an interesting link between the phases of oligopoly highlighted by Vernon and the trends towards strategic alliances. Alliances and joint ventures may affect the competitive structure of the industry. However, it could be that, like the structure of oligopoly, some alliances are innovation-based, some may be more typical of mature industries looking to share costs and risks, while others may be collusive in nature and thus more akin to Vernon's senescent oligopolies.

The strength of Vernon's approach is largely due to its richness. It contains macro as well as industry elements; it deals with technology and production as well as marketing aspects; it deals with foreign production as well as trade.

Frederick Knickerbocker worked as research student with Vernon at the Harvard Business School. Knickerbocker (1973) developed Vernon's model further in looking for explanations of the geographical pattern of FDI. Companies become skilled at pioneering new products and this leads them to invest in other developed countries along the lines suggested by the product life cycle model. Knickerbocker noted that FDI tends to 'bunch up' in particular countries and industries and thus the location of investment tends to have a bandwagon pattern. His approach, strongly rooted in the assumption of an oligopolistic market structure, led him to conclude that 'bunching up' is the result of defensive and aggressive behaviour of oligopolists towards each other. Oligopolists operate in uncertain conditions; following the leader in terms of location of investment gives them a sort of assurance of being able to maintain their overall world position. Knickerbocker stresses the risk and uncertainty faced by firms operating in an oligopolistic environment. Foreign direct investment is a risky strategy but doing nothing to counteract a rivals' move may be even riskier.

Graham (1978 and 1985), also working at Cambridge Massachusetts, uses similar assumptions in respect of the oligopolistic structure of industries and the aggressive or defensive behaviour of firms. His aim is to explain the so-called 'transatlantic reversal', that is the shift in the position of the United States from a net outward investor to a net inward investor (cf. Chapter 2). Graham concludes that it is the defensive behaviour of European companies that leads to investment in the USA within the same industry. Thus intraindustry FDI is seen as the result of an 'exchange of threats' between rival oligopolists. This behaviour avoids a price war which means that competition for locations takes the place of price competition; thus the more aggressive (mutually destructive) pricing strategies are avoided. Interpenetration of markets reduces the likelihood of price wars but also avoids full collusion.

**Box 5.3** Oligopolistic structure and FDI: American perspectives

| | | |
|---|---|---|
| Vernon | explains | • FDI |
| | | • international trade. |
| | | • relations between USA Europe and developing countries at different stages. |
| Knickerbocker | explains | • bandwagon effect and clustering of FDI in the same industries and locations. |
| Graham | explains | • cross-country FDI explained as an exchange of threats between rivals |

The oligopolistic structure also plays a very relevant role in the work of Caves (1971 and 1982). Product differentiation is the outcome of competitive behaviour among rivals in an oligopolistic structure. A general strategy of product differentiation is also likely to lead to horizontal integration across countries and therefore to FDI in the same products.

A variation on the earlier work emanating from Harvard University was provided in the 1980s by Michael Porter (1980, 1985, 1986, 1990). Porter's work placed the emphasis for the unit of analysis on the industry. In order to understand the nature of competitive threats and opportunities and hence derive an appropriate competitive strategy, firms need to appreciate the competitive forces that impinge on their performance. According to Porter, these competitive forces are industry specific in that they vary in strength and significance from one industry to another.

Porter's approach to understanding the nature of global competition, therefore, is based on a structural analysis of the competitive forces that operate across the industry in question. Globalization will be of significance in an industry whenever competitive conditions dictate that there is an advantage to be gained by the firm from engaging in either global configuration, global co-ordination, or both. Global configuration involves adopting a policy of optimizing the location of a given activity from a worldwide perspective (for example locating labour-intensive assembly operations in cost-efficient regions such as export processing zones). Global co-ordination, by contrast, refers to the benefits to be gained from linking operationally-distinct parts of the firm's value-adding activities (referred to by Porter as the firm's 'value chain'). These dimensions of global performance, configuration and co-ordination, allow Porter to distinguish between a range of global competitive strategies. Industries in which neither dimension is of great significance for providing a firm with competitive advantage are termed 'multidomestic' industries by Porter. Global co-ordination, on the other hand, is an essential feature of industries that have come to be dominated by multinational corporations. In contrast, industries where global configuration is of major significance for providing economies of scale, such as in the case of shipbuilding, represent arenas of global competition (the firms compete with one another for the same group of international customers) in which multinational firms may not be of great importance.

This last observation represents an important distinction between Porter's work and that of economists whose traditional focus for an analysis of internationalization has been the firm. For Porter, global competition, and hence a global industry, is not necessarily concomitant with the emergence of multinational corporations. It is the nature of the industry, rather than the shape of the firms within it, which is the crucial determinant of internationalization in his model. The advantage of such an approach is that it allows for international trade and foreign direct investment to be treated as aspects of competition in global industries rather than as mutually exclusive alternatives available to the firm.

A similar line of approach has recently been followed by a British economist working at the University of Reading. John Cantwell has developed a theory of FDI based on 'technological competence'. For Cantwell (1989 and 1993) technology is the key to internalization within firms, to the location of FDI and to the behaviour of companies towards rivals, and to the development and growth of countries. Companies internalize in order to retain their proprietary knowledge but technology and technological competence have considerable spill-over effects. This means that companies can benefit from each other's technological advances and from a macro environment that is favourable to specific technologies. This leads companies to locate production where the macro environment gives them advantages of the spill-over effects. They thus tend to locate where companies in the same technological league have located. In the long run this creates technological poles and clusters of FDI location. This approach leads to some decentralization of technological applications within the company as well as to clusters of technology-based FDI in some countries. The tendency towards agglomeration in some countries/locations generates a vicious circle of growth.

Cantwell's approach has elements of internalization theory linked to some macro elements and to elements of behaviour and performance typical of an oligopolistic market structure. It has similarities with Knickerbocker in terms of its use of the concept of clustering. However, while in Knickerbocker the clustering of FDI is due to the rivalistic behaviour of oligopolists who adopt a follow-my-leader approach, in Cantwell it is due to the wish to locate in technological poles and benefit from the spill-over effects of technology. There are also analogies with Vernon's theory in that both stress the role of technology in FDI. However, in Vernon we have a theory based on the technological superiority of one country over others while in Cantwell we have poles of technological development that attract production from companies based in many countries and in the same technological league.

### 5.5.4 Power and conflict: European perspectives.

Two British economists, Keith Cowling and Roger Sugden from the University of Warwick, have also been working within an oligopolistic framework. Section 5.4.3 highlighted the macroeconomic consequences of the workings of modern capitalism within this framework and, in particular, the stagnationist tendency in modern economic capitalist systems. According to Cowling and Sugden, transnationalism makes the situation worse because TNCs have what they call 'special detection powers' – the ability to find the best locations for production – and take advantage of competing bids for inward investment on the part of governments. This is a concept not dissimilar from Vernon's notion of 'global scanners'. They note, moreover, that transnationalism is spreading throughout the world. Small and medium-sized companies work as subcontractors for large TNCs. Since the large TNCs are the ultimate controllers of production, however, this new development, far from leading to a more competitive macro and industry environment, tends to increase the overall degree of monopoly in the system. Location in developing countries and the actual or potential threat of withdrawal of investment from developed countries leads to a divided and more compliant workforce. The advantages of a 'divide and rule' strategy can be used as defensive or aggressive weapons in competition with rivals.

Cowling and Sugden see companies engaged in strategic games of defence and attack, sometimes colluding to avoid open destructive wars, sometimes attacking if they feel strong enough to gain. They all have some retaliatory power. The fear that this might be used by their rivals may lead to collusive behaviour regarding prices or location of production.

It is interesting to note how different theories within the market structure approach may lead to different conclusions. Cowling and Sugden (1987) as well as Hymer, particularly in his later work such as Hymer (1971), and Jenkins (1987) follow a more Marxist tradition. They conclude that transnational strategies increase the monopolistic tendency in the economy. For them market imperfections are endogenous and therefore the conduct and strategies of companies lead to imperfections.

On the other hand, other authors, who also emphasize the oligopolistic structure, consider market imperfections as largely exogenous and conclude that internationalization leads to a more competitive environment. This conclusion seems to be shared by Vernon, Caves, Graham and Cantwell.

We should also note some key differences here between the market power approach and the internalization theory. Both groups of theories stress market imperfections but the imperfections stressed by the internalization school relate to the existence and level of transaction costs carried by the operations of the market. The other group of theorists, by contrast, stress the oligopolistic structure of the economy. The internalization school stresses efficiency as the main objective of decisions about production, including locational decisions; the other approach stresses strategic behaviour. The internalization school, in contrast to the other theorists, is led to the conclusion that the behaviour of firms leads the system towards equilibrium.

Most economists in the market power tradition stress strategic behaviour towards their rivals. We should note that strategic behaviour could also be directed towards labour and governments. Sugden (1991), drawing on his earlier work with Cowling, develops the theme of a 'divide and rule' approach towards labour in the context of strategic behaviour by TNCs towards rivals. Ietto-Gillies (1988, 1992 Chapter 14, 1996) sees the issue of strategies towards labour as contributing to the explanation of the growth and pattern of FDI. The thesis is that the fragmentation of production in many countries puts companies in the position of facing a fragmented labour force. This strategy of fragmentation can be considered a reaction to the increase in the power of labour.

The increase in mass production in the 1960s and 1970s and the related internalization on the domestic front put labour in a strong position *vis-à-vis* capital. In reaction to this, various strategies have been adopted towards labour, in particular:

- a strategy of externalization of some non-core activities through subcontracting and similar arrangements; this leads to organizational and ownership fragmentation of production and of the labour force employed;

- a strategy of fragmentation of the labour force through location in various countries; this makes labour organization more difficult.

This approach helps to explain some of the pattern of international production and in particular:

(a)   the increase in FDI in developed countries;

(b)    cross-border investment;

(c)    the large share of intra-industry FDI;

(d)    the increase in sub-contracting including international sub-contracting;

(e)    the increase in the network of operations of TNCs.

A strategy of ownership and geographical fragmentation leads to a weaker position for labour at the level of the company and the macro economy. Moreover, there is a link between strategic behaviour towards labour and towards rivals: success in dealing with labour puts the company in a stronger position against its rivals.

## 5.6 The eclectic approach

As already highlighted in the introduction to this chapter, explaining the many changes in the internationalization of economic activities is far from an easy task. This is partly due to the complexity of the issues to be explained. Internationalization can take the form of trade, which implies home production and foreign markets. It can take the form of foreign production, which can either be direct, through internalization across countries, or can be implemented through external arrangements such as licensing, franchising, sub-contracting. Mixed arrangements such as joint ventures are also possible and are becoming increasingly common.

It is therefore not surprising that no single theory can easily explain all the relevant phenomena. There are of course theories that are more realistic than others and more successful than others in explaining the real world and in making predictions. None the less the complexity of the phenomena to be explained remains, particularly when allowance is made for such elements as: intra-industry direct investment, cross-country investment, investment in developed versus developing countries and different patterns in various industries.

John Dunning has been working on foreign direct investment since the 1950s, well before the subject became very widespread in business schools. Indeed Dunning's work greatly contributed to its dissemination. The beginning of his work coincided with the big wave of American investment in Britain. Indeed Dunning began by puzzling over the industry pattern of such investment, the characteristics of American investor companies and the characteristics of the macro environment in the home and host countries. He began by trying to explain why, within the United Kingdom, labour productivity in United States' subsidiaries, was, on average, higher than the productivity in United Kingdom-owned companies. The traditional explanation given at the time was along conventional neoclassical and macroeconomic lines. Economists were trying to explain it in terms of different factor endowments on the part of the two economic systems. A different explanation focused on the relevance of elements which are specific to the firm and on how firms organized and managed their resources. Dunning used this as the basis for explaining different performance between companies and industries in different countries. As mentioned in section 5.5.2, Hymer also stresses advantages specific to firms operating in oligopolistic markets.

In fact, Dunning (1991) traces the development of his own research agenda and its relationship to other works as well as to criticism of his own work. There is also an extensive reply to his critics in Dunning (1988).

Dunning's work went through various developments and refinements, culminating in Dunning (1977) which tried to explain the 'why', 'where' and 'when' of international production and trade by developing a system for classifying and analysing various advantages likely to influence decisions regarding the type of international activities undertaken as well as their country and industry pattern.

The advantages are grouped into 'Ownership', 'Locational' and 'Internalization' (OLI) advantages. The advantages are specific to, respectively:

(a)    firms;

(b)    countries/locations; and

(c)    the organization of production.

The third type considers the advantages of internal versus external production. Dunning (1980, p.275) explains his *eclectic approach* thus:

> Its principal hypothesis is that a firm will engage in foreign direct investment if three conditions are satisfied: (1) It possesses net ownership advantages *vis-à-vis* firms of other nationalities in serving particular markets. These ownership advantages largely take the form of the possession of intangible assets, which are, at least for a period of time, exclusive or specific to the firm possessing them. (2) Assuming condition (1) is satisfied, it must be more beneficial to the enterprise possessing these advantages to use them itself rather than to sell them or lease them to foreign firms, i.e. for it to internalize its advantages through an extension of its own activities rather than externalize them through licensing and similar contracts with independent firms. (3) Assuming conditions (1) and (2) are satisfied, it must be profitable for the enterprise to utilize these advantages in conjunction with at least some factor inputs (including natural resources) outside its home country; otherwise foreign markets would be served entirely by exports and domestic markets by domestic production.

This approach is 'eclectic' in that it combines elements of various theories in a broad classificatory framework. It allows the analyst to consider all the possible influences on the determinants of the extent and patterns of various international activities. The advantages in each category can be many, as highlighted in Box 5.4. There are also interrelationships between the various categories. Ownership advantages can be enhanced or stifled by locational-specific elements. The distinction between ownership and internalization advantages is not always clear cut. The generality of the theoretical framework can thus become both an asset and a liability for Dunning's approach. He is well aware of this and writes, partly in reply to his critics: 'The eclectic paradigm is to be regarded more as a framework for analysing the determinants of international production than a predictive theory of the multinational firm' (1991, p.124). The eclectic paradigm has been very widely accepted in the international business academic community as an operational, practical framework for researchers into international business problems. For example the United Nation Centre on TNCs has often used this framework to analyse the geographical and industry pattern of FDI.

---

**Box 5.4**  The eclectic theory of international production

(1)  **Ownership specific advantages** (of enterprises of one nationality, or affiliates of same, over those of another).

(a)  Which need not arise due to multinationality.
  Those due mainly to size and established position, product or process diversification, ability to take advantage of division of labour and specialization, monopoly power, better resource capacity and usage.
  Proprietary technology, trade marks (protected by patents and legislation).
  Production management, organisational advantages, market systems, research and development capacity; 'bank' of human capacity and experience.
  Exclusive or favoured access to inputs such as labour, natural resources, finance, information.
  Ability to obtain inputs on favoured terms (due, for example, to size or monopsonistic influence).
  Exclusive or favoured access to product markets.
  Government protection (for example control on market entry).

(b)  Which those branch plants of established enterprises may enjoy over *de novo* firms.
  Access to capacity (administrative, managerial, research and

development, marketing, etc.) of parent company at favoured prices.

Economies of joint supply (not only in production, but in purchasing, marketing, finance, etc., arrangements).

(c) Which specifically arise because of multinationality.

Multinationality enhances the above advantages by offering wider opportunities.

More favoured access to and/or better knowledge about information, inputs, markets.

Ability to take advantage of international differences in factor endowments and markets. Ability to diversify risks, e.g in different currency areas, and to exploit differences in capitalization ratios.

(2) **Internalization incentive advantages** (to protect against, or exploit, market failure).

Reduction of costs (e.g. search, negotiation, monitoring) associated with market transactions.

To avoid costs of enforcing property rights.

Buyer uncertainty (about nature and value of inputs, for example technology, being sold)

Where market does not permit price discrimination.

Need of seller to protect quality of products.

To capture economies from externalities and interdependent activities (see 1(b) above).

To compensate for absence of futures markets.

To avoid or exploit government intervention (e.g., quotas, tariffs, price controls, tax differences etc.).

To control supplies and conditions of sale of inputs (including technology).

To control market outlets (including those which might be used by competitors).

To be able to engage in practices such as cross-subsidization, predatory pricing etc., as a competitive (or anti-competitive) strategy.

(3) **Location-specific advantages.**

Spatial distribution of inputs and markets.

Input prices, quality and productivity (for example labour, energy, materials, components, semi-finished goods).

Transport and communications costs.

Government intervention.

Control on imports (including tariff barriers), tax rates, incentives, climate for investment, political stability etc.

Infrastructure (commercial, legal, transportation).

Psychic distance (language, cultural, business, customs defferences, etc.).
Economies of research and development, production and marketing (e.g. the extent to which scale economies make for the centralization of production).

*Source: Dunning (1981), pp.80–81.*

## 5.7 Conclusions

This chapter has attempted a summary of the main theories of international production by grouping them into broad approaches or paradigms. It should be stressed that the categorization must be taken as a very broad one. Some theories contain elements from various categories.

In terms of the analytical elements mentioned we should highlight the following. Many theories directly or indirectly touch on advantages linked to macroeconomic elements. These elements are related to the relative endowment, on the part of countries, with factors and resources.

Most theories stress market imperfections. However, imperfections can be interpreted as relating to transaction elements and costs, or as relating to the structure of markets in which companies operate. Cantwell (1991, p.25) writes on this point, in relation to the internalization versus the market power theory: 'The emphasis is on achieving profit maximization through the efficient exchange of intermediate products rather than through the exclusion of (potential) rivals in the final product market.' Some theories stress efficiency as the guiding principle of action and as the objective of decisions; others stress strategic decisions and behaviour. While profits play a key role in both efficiency and strategy-driven decisions, we could highlight key differences in the following elements. In the efficiency approach higher profits are achieved through cuts in costs (particularly the transactions costs in the internalization theory). The strategic approach would emphasize issues of market share. There are differences in: the timespan over which the decision is taken (shorter in the case of efficiency-driven decisions); the interplay with other economic agents particularly rivals (stronger in the strategic decisions); the tendency towards equilibrating decisions and outcomes (stronger in the efficiency approach).

In the efficiency/transaction costs approach, it is not clear-cut which institution and mechanism achieves efficiency more easily at any given time. Sometimes it is the market, sometimes it is the hierarchical institution. Usually the institution is identified with the private corporation although there is no reason why the same conclusions should not apply to the public one.

It is interesting to note that the 1950s and 1960s saw a trend towards internalization. Large organizations, including firms, were seen as efficiency-driven organizations that could economize on transaction costs. The 1980s saw the reversal of this trend, however, with large organizations (in both the public and private sector) externalizing non-core activities.

The strategies analysed were usually strategies towards rival companies. It is, of course, also possible to consider strategies towards other players in the economic system such as governments and labour. Reduction in costs of labour gives advantages over rivals whenever a more advantageous position regarding labour is achieved compared to one's rivals. In relation to strategies towards rivals, collusive behaviour may, at times, be considered more appropriate than aggressive behaviour.

Are market imperfections endogenous or exogenous? Does the conduct of firms lead to market power or vice versa? Are TNCs a cause or effect of market failure? Are they a problem or a solution to market failure? These are open questions and different theories provide different answers to them.

It is not clear cut, in theories that stress factor endowments, to what extent the movement of products and capital across frontiers contributes to changes in factor endowments and the macro environment and to what extent these remain fully exogenous.

Some theories stress production and its organization more than others, which lay stress on exchange and on monetary phenomena (such as the conventional neoclassical theory or Aliber's currency areas approach).

The stagnationist elements in some theories may relate to both the determinants of production and the effects of production; there are often also some elements of distribution. Distribution can be analysed in relation to other rivals (distribution of market shares), in relation to labour (distribution between profits and wages), or in relation to the distribution of investment and profits between various countries. In relation to distribution, Baran and Sweezy (1966, p.23) use the Marxian concept of 'economic surplus' which they define as 'the difference between what a society produces and the costs of producing it'. It can be considered here to be approximately equal to total profits plus interest and rent. The distribution of the economic surplus between the companies' sector and governments in various countries could also be seen through the operations of transfer prices.

The various types of distribution highlighted here are often interlinked. A stronger position towards labour gives the company a more profitable position that can then be used to obtain advantages over its rivals, for example, because it allows the firm to penetrate a new market by charging lower prices. A favourable income-distribution position for the company might thus also lead to a favourable market share position for the same company. Similarly a favourable position in relation to the distribution of surplus between the company and governments, through lower taxation bills engineered via the manipulation of transfer prices, may lead to a stronger position *vis-à-vis* the company's rivals.

## 5.8 Further reading

Dicken, P. (1992) *Global Shift. The Internationalization of Economic Activity*, Paul Chapman Publishing Co., London.

(Chapter 5 is particularly relevant.)

Ietto-Gillies, G. (1992) *International Production: Trends, Theories, Effects*, Polity, Cambridge and Oxford.

(This deals with most of the theories touched on in this chapter at greater length. Chapters 6, 7, 8, 9, 11, 12, 13, 14 and 15 are particularly relevant. Students are advised to read these chapters.)

Pitelis, C.N. and Sugden, R. (1991) (eds) *The Nature of the Transnational Firm*, Routledge, London.

(Chapters 2, 3, 4, 5, 8 and 9 are particularly useful.)

United Nations Centre on Transnational Corporations (1992) *The Determinants of Foreign Direct Investment. A Survey of the Evidence*, United Nations, New York.

(This provides a survey of research into the determinants of FDI and into the application of various theories to particular countries and situations.)

Postgraduate students should also be encouraged to read some of the original literature mentioned in this chapter.

## 5.9 Suggestions for group work

Possible questions and tasks

Set A

1.  Give Hymer's main criticisms of the neoclassical theory. Are they still applicable?

2.      On what grounds did Coase criticize the working of the market?

3.      Give three examples of transaction costs drawn from your own experience and three examples from a company of your choice.

Set B

1.      Describe the trade pattern between various types of countries according to the PLC.

2.      Describe the motivations and flows of FDI according to the PLC theory.

3.      Why do different customs or currency areas lead to FDI, according to Aliber?

4.      Why do different growth areas lead to FDI?

Set C

1.      What is the relationship between (a) competition and pricing and (b) competition and flow of FDI in the PLC model?

2.      How does Knickerbocker explain the concentration of FDI in the same locations?

3.      Explain how Cowling and Sugden see that transnationalism affects the competitive structure of the industry and economy.

Set D

1.      Why is Dunning's approach called 'eclectic'?

2.      Define 'ownership', 'locational' and 'internalization' advantages.

3.      List the ownership advantages of a company of your choice.

4.      With reference to your chosen company and its activities, what do you consider to be its internalization advantages?

5.      What are the locational advantages of Britain?

6.      List the locational advantages of a developing country of your choice.

## 5.10 Mini case studies

The work on each of these three cases should again be group work with a plenary report-back session at the end. The tutor should allow at least one hour for this group work on each case.

---

**Box 5.5**  Volvo truck plant for Poland

Volvo, the Swedish car and commercial vehicle maker, is to establish a truck assembly plant in Poland. The plant, which will be located in Wroclaw, will have a capacity to assemble up to 1000 heavy and medium-duty trucks a year. Volvo trucks have been assembled hitherto in Poland by Jelcz, the Polish truck maker, but this agreement expires at the end of the year. The Swedish group said that it would be moving equipment, tools and personnel from the Jelcz facilities to Wroclaw, where it planned to produce more than 700 trucks in 1995. Volvo is the leading importer of heavy-duty trucks to Poland and expects to deliver around 550 units this year. It has established a new marketing and finance company during 1994 and has a network of 10 dealers selling exclusively Volvo vehicles.

*Source:* The Financial Times, *21 November 1994.*

---

Task

Students should use either the PLC model or the eclectic approach to analyse the motivations, sequence, and effects of Volvo's activities in Poland.

---

**Box 5.6**  Chinese roads paved with gold

It was an invitation the world's car makers could hardly refuse. When China's Ministry for Machinery Building asked for ideas for a 'people's car' to be submitted in conjunction with a small-car exhibition in Beijing, most large international car manufacturers obliged.

As a representative of General Motors, which was displaying its Opel/Vauxhall Corsa among other models in Beijing, said: 'When they say jump – people jump.'

China, which last year produced 234 000 cars from its own plants, currently has fewer than 2 million cars in use, of which fewer than 5 per cent are privately owned. The ministry's 'Strategic Development Research Team of China's Family Car' forecasts a steep rise to 22 million by 2010. It predicts that by the year 2010, China will be producing 3.5 million cars a year, two-thirds sold privately.

It is this prospect of an ever-widening circle of car owners in the world's most populous country that is proving such a magnet. China's urban population alone is 300 million, which compares to continental Europe and exceeds that of the US. 'Who can ignore an opportunity in a market that could be the world's largest in 20 years?' asked Mr Toshiake Yasuda, Nissan's chief representative in China.

Under a new car industry policy unveiled earlier this year, China plans to raise production by 2000 to between 1 million and 1.5 million, based on output from 'three or four' large conglomerates that will be developed over the next few years. This production would account for 90% of demand from the Chinese market by 2000–2003.

The foreign participation being sought by the government will help to rationalize a motor industry that is highly fragmented.

'Consolidation is badly needed, if the sector is to benefit from economies of scale,' according to a recent study by the Economist Intelligence Unit. 'The government's blueprint is to accelerate the natural process of rationalization in the industry over the next few years, in order to create a few large and strong producers.'

China has set its sights on mass-producing a 'people's car' designed specifically for the Chinese market. The question for Beijing – no less than for foreign carmakers – is whether existing models that have been tried and tested would fit China's requirements best, or whether a completely new car is required. At last week's motor show for small cars in Beijing, most of the world's leading producers displayed cars form their existing ranges: Ford showed its Fiesta, General Motors the Corsa, Nissan the Micra, Toyota the Tercel and PSA Peugeot Citroen The Citroen ZX, which is already being produced in China.

But it was the concept cars, specially designed for the Chinese market, that captured most attention (see below). These included Porsche's C88 prototype, a 1.1 litre five-seater that hogged the limelight, the Mercedes-Benz FCC (Family Car China), and Mitsubishi's X-concept study derived from its Chariot/Space Wagon small multi-purpose vehicle.

At stake is the right to build a low-cost, fuel-efficient car for the standard Chinese family, that could have sales running into the millions and would provide a solid platform for growth in a market with enormous growth potential.

With market growth sluggish in Europe and North America, the world's leading car makers are fighting to establish a presence in the world's emerging markets.

According to Mr Alex Trotman, chairman and chief executive of Ford, the world's second largest vehicle maker, about 80 per cent of the world's population live outside the traditional automotive markets of West Europe, North America and Japan, but the number of cars and trucks sold in these regions represents only about 8% of the world's total.

The motor industry believes that the Asia/Pacific region holds the brightest prospects, with sales in Asia (excluding Japan) expected to triple during the next 15 years.

Japanese car makers already have a stranglehold on most of Asia with as much as 90 per cent of car markets such as the Philippines, Indonesia and Thailand. In China, however, the Japanese producers have been held at bay, and it is the European industry that has taken the early lead – its one success story in the region.

Volkswagen, Europe's largest car maker, was a pioneer among Western car makers in entering China, having signed its first joint venture in 1984. It claims that by 2000 it will have a capacity to produce 660 000 cars and 830 000 engines a year - 3 000 000 cars a year at Shanghai Volkswagen and 360 000 a year at FAW–Volkswagen, its joint venture with First Automobile Works in north-east China.

VW claims that it has made 'huge strides' in developing the supplier industry in China. Local content at the Shanghai plant now exceeds 80 per cent, and it estimates that about 40 joint venture contracts and approximately 100 production and know how licences have been agreed between foreign – predominantly German – suppliers and local Chinese partners. An additional 30 joint ventures are under negotiation.

'With our commitments in China, we are pursuing a strategic objective of capturing a long-term leading market position in the region,' said Mr Martin Posth, VW director for Asia/Pacific. 'China is envisaged as the main production site with smaller satellite operations elsewhere in Asia.'

Ford is setting up a series of components joint ventures in China in the hope that this will open the way for it to begin assembling vehicles in the near future. 'We are eager to establish vehicle assembly projects in China at the earliest opportunity", said Mr Frank Macher, Ford vice-president and general manager of its automotive components division.

Chinese officials responsible for deciding which foreign manufacturer will build the family car expect a decision by 1996, but are not committing themselves as to whether one or more car makers will be chosen. Mr Zhang Xiaoyu, director of the Department of Automotive Industry in the Ministry of Machinery Building, said that China would be guided in its decisions by which of the companies 'provided the best terms for us". Mr Zhang said one issue that would influence the Chinese decision would be whether the applicants' proposals complied with automotive policy, including technology transfer and the development of the local components industry.

Foreign car producers say that even if a decision is made on the family car proposal by 1996, production would not start before 1998-99 at the earliest. This timetable suggests that China will have difficulty meeting its production target of at least 1 million cars by 2000.

The prospect of participating in the birth of a Chinese small car has appeared too daunting for some companies in the world motor industry. BMW, for example, considered participation through Rover, the UK car maker it acquired early this year, but held back.

'We have investigated it but we think one would lose a lot of money', said Mr Bernd Pischetsrieder, chairman of the BMW management board. 'Whoever does this people's car project will not be successful financially.'

Mr Posth of VW acknowledges that two contradictory arguments confront all industrial investors. The first says: 'You will certainly lose at the start, if not in the long run as well. The initial phase will last much longer than you ever thought it would.

'It will take far longer than you ever imagined to learn the rules in China. You will be constantly hindered by your Chinese partner from doing the right thing – they profess to know everything better, even though they had invited you because of your technical superiority and managerial know-how . . . And where are those billions of consumers.?'

On the other hand, said Mr Posth, 'by not being in China, you are perhaps missing out on the chance of a lifetime. If your competitors are investing in China and exporting from there, they will be able to beat you wherever they like anywhere in the world.

'It may or may not be the end of the Deng Xiaoping era . . . but then where can you invest without incurring some sort of risk? And don't forget what people said in the 1950s about getting involved in Japan.'

The stampede by the world's carmakers into Beijing last week suggests that few are prepared to be absent, however great the risks.

*Source:* The Financial Times, *23 November 1994.*

Tasks

1. List at least three advantages of China as a location for international motor manufacture.

2. Give the main ownership advantages for VW and Ford respectively.

3. Is the behaviour of motor manufacturers in China affected by the oligopolistic structure of the industry? If so, how?

**Box 5.7**   Market imperfections and TNC's strategies

- IBM, the world's largest computer firm and a pioneer among multinationals, established a dominant position in the world market for mainframe computers by the late 1960s, which lasted until personal computers and workstations took over in the past five years. In theory, this offered IBM the chance to organize its manufacturing on a global scale, maximizing its efficiency and minimizing its costs. But, it did not do that; instead it spread its factories around the world in order to limit imbalances in its trade between its main markets and to ensure that in most markets it was a big employer as well as a big seller. Why? Because IBM felt it had to keep governments friendly. It needed to avoid regulatory attacks on its market dominance, and governments were among the biggest buyers of mainframe computers. Now that IBM has lost its dominance and computers have become a commodity business, this structure is one of Big Blue's worst headaches.

- The world's six biggest accountancy firms are in the top rank in virtually every country in the world except where they are barred by law. Yet auditing and accounting are intensely local affairs, requiring detailed knowledge of local rules and regulations. Arthur Andersen or Price Waterhouse ought not, in theory, to have an advantage over domestic competitors except with multinational clients – which, though large, are almost always a minority. Why, then, have these firms themselves become such successful multi-nationals?

  One answer may lie in their ancillary businesses such as consulting, in which they have special skills; another may lie in their ability to buy and organize information technology. But these are not enough to explain such widespread dominance. Reputation, the power of the brand name, must play the biggest part. The market for accounting and auditing is an imperfect one: buyers lack the information to tell a good accountant from a bad one, or find it costly to find out, which comes to the same thing. They also seek the accountant's brand name as a means to convince others about their own worth, especially investors and creditors, who are similarly short of information.

- The EC's single-market programme is supposed to be removing barriers to trade between its 12 members, allowing companies to organize themselves on a regional basis. Why, then, does Ford have car factories in Britain, Belgium, Spain and Germany? You might expect it to consolidate wherever manufacturing costs proved the lowest. One reason could be history: Ford had been making cars in Britain since 1908, and it is costly to close factories down in order to consolidate them. That is probably important, but it should become less so over time. The biggest reason may well be risk diversification. If there is a strike in Belgium, or a rise in German wage rates, or a 20% devaluation of sterling, then a spread of plants gives Ford the chance to cover a risk or exploit an opportunity.

- Recently Intel, America's top chip maker, announced plans to build a chip factory in Ireland. On the face of it, this makes little sense. Irish labour costs are low, but such costs play little part in the manufacture of memory chips. Ireland has no unique reserve of skills for technology industries. Transport costs matter hardly at all for chips, since they weigh little and are worth a lot. To a chip maker, automation and quality control matter the most, so it make sense to centralize. Why, then, is Intel investing? The likeliest explanation is a mixture of pre-emption of trade barriers and the matching of a competitor's move. If Intel produces inside the EC, then it will be able to cope if the Community raises barriers against imported chips. And a competitor, Texas Instruments (TI), has already been lured by Italian subsidies to build a factory in Italy. By establishing itself in Ireland, Intel may help to limit future Italian subsidies to TI, since it could appeal to the European Commission on grounds of unfair competition; and if there were to be general, Community-wide support for the sort of chips TI and Intel make, then Intel would qualify too.

- A common slogan in recent years has been that if a company is to succeed in international competition it needs a presence in each of the richest areas: Japan, the EC, North America. Many firms believe this, as they are certainly following the advice. But is it right? A strategy which sought to establish dominance in just one of these markets, or in two could be just as profitable. The cost of building a presence in a market where a firm is weak can be astronomical, as many have discovered in Japan.

    This 'triad strategy' as it was called by one of its main advocates Kenichi Ohmae, a consultant at McKinsey, is often so costly that it endangers a firm's strengths elsewhere. But the best reason for adopting it is nevertheless an important one: to counter competitors' moves. It is a strategic game: a presence in a rival's home market might distract the rival or might lower the rival's profits; it might also yield valuable information about tactics or technology, say.

*Source:* The Economist, *27 March 1993, pp.13–14.*

Tasks

1.  How does the oligopolistic structure of the motor car industry explain the possible 'triad strategy'?

2.  List the main factors that account for the success of Price Waterhouse.

3.  What were IBM's main ownership advantages in the 1960s? How do they differ from the main ownership advantages in the 1990s?

4.  How do you account for Intel's international strategies?

5.  Compare the elements of competition that are specific to the three industries (computer manufacturers, accounting and chips manufacturers) in terms of Porter's approach.

# 6

# International trade and global competition

## 6.1 Introduction

Chapter 4 set out the international trading environment within which the multinational firm operates. This chapter will look at how the existence of multinational firms can affect the theoretical determinants of trading patterns and trade flows. It will also consider the implication for trade policy of the increasingly global nature of competition in many industries.

The chapter begins with a survey of conventional neoclassical trade theory and discusses its drawbacks and limitations as a framework for explaining trade flows in the real world. It will be seen that neoclassical trade theory was developed within an essentially static framework in which goods moved freely between countries but in which factors of production, most notably capital, were assumed to move much less freely between countries than between regions within countries. The firm was assumed to be largely domestically based, its international involvement being essentially confined to arms-length trading between unrelated buyers and sellers in other countries. Although neoclassical theory may not be entirely redundant when it comes to explaining trade in a modern dynamic framework in which internationally based firms predominate, its usefulness has necessarily become more limited as firms have undertaken international investment.

This chapter continues with a survey of some of the attempts subsequently made to overcome the limitations of neoclassical trade theory. These include attempts to incorporate demand-side factors such as differences in consumer preferences and supply-side factors such as increasing returns to scale and dynamic change arising from new technologies. More recently, the growing importance of intra-industry trade has led trade economists to develop models of trade premised on the assumption that markets are imperfectly competitive. All of these approaches have done much to make trade theory correspond more to the real world. Nevertheless, few, if any, of these newer theories adequately incorporate the reality that a growing and possibly dominant share of trade in the modern world is conducted by companies whose productive activities are no longer confined to a single nation.

The modern large firm is typically a multinational corporation (MNC) not merely in the sense that it operates in more than one country but increasingly because the ownership and control of such organizations transcends national boundaries. One important feature of this transnational structure is that much of the cross-border trade that MNCs undertake actually involves transactions between different overseas branches of the same company. Such intra-firm trade is known to constitute a significant proportion of trade, especially in manufactured goods.

The next part of the chapter examines the importance of intra-firm trade and its possible implications for trade theory. A central question concerns the extent to which trade theories need to be revised to take account of the multinational firm.

To what extent can existing theories be modified to incorporate the multinational or do they need to be jettisoned altogether? As we shall see, a major problem is the absence of any wholly satisfactory theory that can take their place. Although the recent trade theory literature does include some important new developments in this respect, no new theory bringing together trade and international production has emerged. Perhaps one of the most satisfactory approaches is the eclectic theory of John Dunning (discussed in Chapter 5) which seeks to develop a typology of trade and production in which different theories each have a role to play as explanations for particular types of trade and investment.

A new approach has recently been suggested by Michael Porter in his pioneering work entitled *The Competitive Advantage of Nations* (1990), and the remainder of this chapter is devoted to a discussion of the insights which this approach opens up. Porter has called for a fundamental adjustment in thinking about international production which switches the emphasis from country-specific to firm- and industry-specific considerations. The key players in the real world are not individual nations competing on the basis of essentially static endowments of different factors of production (or even fixed consumer preferences) but firms operating in global industries whose operations frequently straddle national boundaries. These firms make decisions about where to locate their productive activities in the light of the particular advantages that different countries may offer at any given time. It follows that if nations wish to succeed internationally they must attract such firms to locate value-enhancing activities within their own borders by developing an environment that is conducive to competitive success.

## 6.2 The limitations of neoclassical trade theory

Neoclassical trade theory regards the basis for international specialization as residing in differences between nations in comparative costs resulting from their pattern of factor endowments. All countries are viewed as possessing differing quantities of the various factors or inputs used in production, namely, land, labour and capital. In any particular country there will be one factor that is relatively abundant and therefore cheap, while the other factors will be scarce and therefore relatively expensive. The production of any particular good requires different proportions of each of these factors. The factor proportions used to produce a particular good are shown by a country's production function. It follows therefore that nations will enjoy a comparative cost advantage in those products which use relatively large amounts of the country's most abundant factor of production. So, nations that are well endowed with labour will enjoy a comparative cost advantage in labour-intensive activities. Likewise, those that are relatively well endowed with capital will specialize in capital-intensive activities.

It is important to realize that this factor proportions theory (sometimes named after its originators as the Heckscher-Ohlin Theory) is based on certain implicit assumptions regarding methods of production and patterns of consumption. One assumption is that the production functions for particular goods will be identical between countries. This rules out the possibility of 'factor-intensity reversal', the possibility that the factor proportions or intensities used to produce a particular product might vary across countries due to different factor prices. A good might thus be produced using capital-intensive methods in a country where labour is expensive but by labour-intensive methods in other countries where labour is cheaper. We know that, in the real world, factor-intensity reversal does take place but the important question is whether or not it is sufficiently important to render the factor proportions theory invalid.

Another implicit assumption is that consumer preferences are identical in all nations. If this assumption was invalid factor prices might differ even in countries that had identical factor endowments since the relative prices of the capital-intensive products will be higher in countries where demand is skewed towards capital-intensive goods. Such a domestic pattern of demand could raise the cost of capital sufficiently to offset any cost advantage in capital-intensive goods arising from relative capital abundance. Again, the empirically important question concerns the extent to which consumer preferences differ sufficiently to influence relative prices in different countries. Even if the preferences of households with a similar income do not vary much, aggregate preferences will differ between countries with different per capita income levels and demand factors may therefore influence trade patterns. In fact, post-neoclassical theories of trade have treated demand-side factors with a greater amount of respect (Linder, 1961).

Perhaps one of the biggest drawbacks of neoclassical trade theory is the essentially static framework in which it is couched. If this was appropriate for explaining nineteenth and early twentieth century trade it is clearly unsatisfactory for the fast-moving conditions in which we currently live. There are two aspects of this that are of special importance.

First, factor endowments and hence factor prices and comparative costs can change over time. Neoclassical theory does not assume that factors of production are entirely immobile internationally. It does, however, assume that labour migration and capital flows are not generally sufficient to significantly alter a country's stock of factors and hence the source of its comparative advantage. This is clearly unsatisfactory. Both labour and capital can become scarcer or more abundant over time. For example, slower demographic growth combined with rapid capital accumulation has meant that, in many newly industrializing countries, labour has become relatively dearer and capital relatively cheaper as the economy has grown. Capital flows between countries can similarly alter the stock of capital in different countries and hence alter factor prices over time.

Second, the process of technological change may alter the source of comparative advantage over time. The neoclassicists were aware of the role played by technological change in determining trading patterns. Clearly, a country that was the originator of a new method of production or a new product could enjoy a comparative advantage that was unrelated to factor endowments. It was thought unlikely that this would last for any length of time because the new technology would quickly be imitated by producers in other parts of the world. This assumed an implausibly short time lag in which knowledge was more or less instantly diffused internationally. Subsequent empirical work has shown there to be a much longer time lag in the spread of new technology so that a country may enjoy a comparative advantage based on innovation for much longer. It is equally important, however, that a country's comparative advantage in a particular product can at any time be eliminated by innovation in another country. Comparative advantage, particularly in the context of technology, is therefore a shifting phenomenon in which the distribution of advantage at any point in time is nothing more than a snapshot of what in reality is an evolving picture. Most recently, economists have begun to consider the way in which the internationalization of firms has affected the international distribution of technical expertise (Cantwell, 1993; Pearce, 1992). The ability of MNCs to locate operations in any part of the globe has promoted a degree of locational-specificity in the international pattern of research and development. Certain parts of the world, for example Silicon Valley in the United States, have emerged as centres for particular forms of technological competence and MNCs' research operations have gravitated to these places. Where such forms of locational-specificity are important, then forms of learned, rather than inherited, comparative advantage, based on accumulated technological expertise, can provide a country with an enduring advantage.

In terms of trading patterns in the world economy, neoclassical trade theory predicts that trade will be greatest between countries with differing factor endowments. Since capital is relatively abundant in developed countries and labour is relatively cheap in developing countries this points to much trade taking place between countries at different stages of development. While this may have accounted for much of the trade that was undertaken before the Second World War it most certainly fails to accurately describe the principal patterns of trade during the past half-century. As Chapter 4 demonstrated, the experience of the past 50 years has been that trade has been greatest between the developed countries, in other words between countries at roughly the same stage of development.

One of the fastest growing areas of trade has been between the developed countries of West Europe, all of which possess relatively similar factor endowments. Moreover, it is striking that much of this trade has taken the form of intra-industry trade in essentially similar goods. In Chapter 4 intra-industry trade was defined as the export and import of goods belonging to the same industry. Now, since industries normally constitute a group of products with similar input requirements or factor intensities, intra-industry trade does not readily emerge from within a neoclassical framework. If a country possesses a comparative advantage in some of the products belonging to a particular industry it will possess a similar advantage in all of these products! It would therefore make no sense to be a net exporter of some products but a net importer of other products within the same industry. Neoclassical trade theory thus failed to anticipate some of the trends in world trade that have been most apparent in the last 50 years.

One of the reasons for this inadequacy is that neoclassical trade theory is still couched in the framework of perfectly competitive markets. Like the rest of neoclassical thought, costs were assumed to increase with output in such a way that the possibility of market concentration was excluded except in the cases of the natural monopolies. If, however, average costs decrease significantly with high volumes of output the possibility exists that production may become concentrated in the hands of a small number of oligopolistic producers. At the same time, so long as demand-side factors were played down, little importance was attached to product differentiation. Goods were assumed to be largely homogeneous in such a way that no single producer could exert much, if any, influence over the price of their own product. Firms were passive price takers able to sell as much as they wished at the going price but nothing at all at a price even slightly above the market price. Neither of these assumptions hold up well in today's world. Producers often enjoy considerable market dominance, even under conditions of product homogeneity (oil is an example) and because they control a large share of the market they have the power to influence the market price. In many markets, moreover, the products they sell are typically differentiated from those of rival firms enabling a producer to sell some output, albeit normally a lower amount, at a price higher than that of its competitors. It is thus the existence of product differentiation, coupled with economies of scale, which creates a basis for intra-industry trade.

## 6.3 Trade theory and the growth of firms

The conventional theory of comparative advantage was originally developed during an era when international trade was largely separate from industrial production and undertaken by merchant organizations that operated independently from the actual producers. Most of the goods traded were primary commodities and semi-manufactured goods and international specialization reflected much more faithfully the factor endowments of the countries concerned. Indeed, in the colonial age, which in much of Africa drew to a close as recently as the 1960s, a nation's colonies were viewed as sources of raw materials and captive markets for manufactured exports. The structure of the international economy during the colonial era therefore afforded the relative factor cost approach to international trade a substantial degree of explanatory power. The development that most clearly cut across the country-centred, factor proportion approach to international trade was the emergence, during the last quarter of the nineteenth century, of large-scale corporations, many of which engaged in FDI. Breakthroughs in transport and communications, and an increased application of scientific principles to the manufacturing process, ushered in a period of rapid industrial concentration around the turn of the century in Britain, Europe and, especially, in the United States (see Chapter 1). Mass production and mass distribution systems needed new forms of management organization if the economies of scale and scope were to be successfully exploited. The development of managerial capitalism thus provided the means to effect a transition from small-scale to large-scale industrial enterprise and brought forth growth-oriented firms that were prepared to engage in much greater levels of investment, including mergers and acquisitions of domestic rivals.

The corporate strategies emanating from among this new breed of firms quickly turned beyond the domestic economy and, as a result of their willingness to engage in FDI, MNCs emerged in a number of the key industries. In some cases overseas investment was designed to secure sources of supply and reap the benefits of backward vertical integration. Investments in raw material exploitation, whilst generating flows of FDI, actually did little to change the pattern of international trade. They did, however, act to bring these transactions within the compass of a single firm. Meanwhile, international investments in manufacturing industries, such as sewing machines and cigarettes, meant that FDI began to replace exports of final goods in certain industries. This growth of FDI, and the consequent growth of MNCs which arose from it, heralded a new phase in the international economy: the evolution of global industries.

In neoclassical economics, capital movements between countries had been assumed to take the form of portfolio investments, with international capital transfers responding to differences in the rate of return on money capital (Caves, 1982, pp.31–67). Differences in the return on money capital reflected differences in the level of savings relative to investment. As such, capital flows were substitutes for trade. Capital flowed from capital-abundant countries to capital-scarce countries in response to differences in the rate of return on capital. These capital flows, however, served to make capital-scarce countries less capital scarce and capital-abundant countries less capital abundant, thus, in theory, reducing the incentive for these countries to trade.

A new approach to the question of international capital flows was developed in Vernon's product life-cycle theory, reviewed in Chapter 5. In this theory, capital flows between countries were envisaged to take the form of direct investment by companies. Although the incentive to move production from the innovating country first to other developed countries and then to developing countries was based on the attraction of lower production costs and hence effectively to differences in the return on capital, such differences in rates of return were not the result of the relative scarcity or abundance of financial capital in different countries. Rather the rate of return was the return on productive capital, that is risk capital productively invested, as opposed to the interest rate, which is the return earned by money capital invested in financial markets. Thus Vernon's work allowed for the possibility of international capital flows that were driven by real (productive) rather than financial economic incentives.

Where overseas production replaces exporting as the method of servicing the foreign market, such investment would be trade-displacing. It could, on the other hand, also be trade-enhancing. This would be the case if, especially in the early stages of operations, the overseas subsidiary needed to import more components and parts from the parent company. It would also be the case if, subsequently, the overseas subsidiary began exporting a significant proportion of its output.

Vernon's approach represents an early attempt to link together the international growth of the firm and the changing patterns of trade in the world economy. A parallel development among neoclassical trade economists was to consider the implication of industrial concentration for models of trade that had hitherto been based upon the conceptual model of perfect competition. This has been one of the most productive branches of trade theory in recent years. A large number of, in many cases, mathematically complex models have been developed to see what happens if product markets (at home or abroad) are not perfectly competitive.

One form of imperfect competition is monopolistic competition. This is mainly found in manufactured consumer goods industries where firms compete by producing differentiated versions of the same good. As we have already seen, one possible outcome for international trade of such competition is intra-industry trade. The fact that such goods are normally produced under conditions of decreasing average costs may explain why any given producer does not seek to make all varieties of the goods that consumers demand. It is also partly the case that producers are each consciously seeking to distinguish their goods from those of rivals in an effort to increase their market share. The existence of strong local preferences in such markets will exert a major influence on which products a country specializes in, and the existence of decreasing average costs means that producers in countries where there exists a large domestic demand will enjoy a cost advantage which can be exploited in foreign markets.

Of particular importance for these new 'imperfectly competitive' models of international trade has been the growing significance of oligopolistic competition. In such markets, the number of sellers is few because of the existence of sizeable barriers of entry into the industry. The product may or may not be differentiated. Oligopolistic markets have always interested economists because it is much more difficult to define any long-run equilibrium position in such markets. Perhaps the simplest case is where domestic firms collude to maximize their joint profits. In this case, they act like a single monopolist. One of the most important results of such a model is the prediction that local producers will charge a higher price for the same good when sold domestically than that charged on export sales.

This gives rise to the phenomenon of 'dumping' which has attracted much attention in trade policy debates. The logic behind the idea of dumping is that, by restricting sales in the domestic market, where the colluding producers have monopoly control over output, price can be raised by proportionately more than the reduction in the amount sold and profits can thereby be increased. Export sales, by contrast, can only take place at the price prevailing on the world market where, in many industries, producers face a horizontal demand curve. In practice, of course, price discrimination of this kind may not be possible. Anti-trust laws in the exporting country may render such arrangements (whether formal or informal) illegal. Dumping may risk provoking an anti-dumping complaint by producers in the foreign market which could lead to anti-dumping duties being imposed on future imports.

A feature of competition under conditions of oligopoly is that firms become caught up in a game of second-guessing. Each firm needs to anticipate the likely reaction of rival producers to any decisions that are made to alter output levels and prices. Thus, in oligopolistic industries, firms behave strategically. There are only a few sellers, so the actions of any one firm will affect the market conditions facing its rivals. Models of trade that have been developed under the assumptions of oligopolistic competition have produced some interesting results. Once again, intra-industry trade is invariably an outcome.

In the particular case of a duopoly (two producers only), Brander and Krugman have shown that, on certain assumptions about how firms will behave, two-way trade in identical commodities is possible (Brander, 1981; Brander and Krugman, 1983). Once again, a result of this model is that each producer sells its product for a lower price abroad than the price that it charges at home, a phenomenon which Brander and Krugman termed 'reciprocal dumping'. Unfortunately, none of these models tell us anything more about what products various countries will specialize in. Rather, they are theories which seek to show how orthodox conclusions about equilibrium must be modified in oligopolistic markets.

One aspect of the introduction of models of industrial structure into the 'new trade theories' has been the conclusions which it leads to concerning trade policy. In particular, the new trade theories have contradicted the conventional belief that trade intervention by the authorities will invariably be harmful. Neoclassical theory favours minimal intervention on the grounds that free trade will ensure the best use of global resources. Countries will automatically specialize in producing those goods in which they enjoy a comparative cost advantage. Attempts by governments to restrict trade by erecting import barriers or to artificially boost exports through subsidies not only damage trading partners but inflict costs on their own citizens. New trade theory shows that, where markets are less than perfectly competitive, these arguments are not always valid. Thus, in oligopolistic industries, where firms act strategically, interventions by national authorities may give producers in one country an important advantage over rivals. Since producers in such industries earn economic rents over and above the normal return from taking risks (profits which cannot be competed away by the entry of new rivals to the industry) increased domestic production of the good ensures that these rents accrue to the local economy rather than the foreign economy (see Krugman, 1987).

These new developments in trade theory, based upon imperfect competition, represent a useful step forward. They all suffer from one particular weakness, however, which is the failure to acknowledge the multinational company as an increasingly dominant institution through which trade is undertaken. In this respect, neoclassical theories were inadequate not simply in their assumption of perfect markets but also in developing models that assumed that trade was conducted between independent, essentially domestically owned firms on an arms-length basis. Modern trade theory is little better. Before the emergence of the new trade theory, Vernon's product life-cycle theory was the only theory to make any attempt to incorporate the multinational company as a driving force. Even the new trade theory is more concerned with the structure of markets than with the structure of the firm. It is not just that the structures of many product markets differ in reality from the models used in textbooks; the firm as the organization through which trade is conducted has changed significantly. A great deal of modern international trade now takes the form of intra-firm trade: transactions across international boundaries which remain within the compass of a single MNC.

What is significant about the growth of intra-firm trade is that it reflects a tendency for production to become increasingly internationally integrated. The modern, large multinational corporation organizes its production on a global basis. Direct investment abroad which merely replicates production in the home country is now much less common. Much direct investment in the earlier decades of the post-war era was of this kind. Multinationals set up subsidiaries abroad to produce the same goods which were previously exported. In the Vernon product life-cycle model such investment occurred in the maturity phase of a product's life as manufacturers of new products faced increasing competition in foreign markets from local producers able to imitate their innovation. Such investment took place mainly in other developed countries and was the first stage in which companies that were previously essentially domestically based expanded internationally. The output of the overseas subsidiary was, initially at least, largely intended for the local market. At a later stage, however, a proportion of output might be exported. The aim of such investment was to eliminate transport costs and to jump tariff or non-tariff barriers. Lower production costs or generous incentives offered by the host country government were other factors that could induce multinationals to undertake such investment. Such investment was largely trade-displacing because its object was to substitute for exports. As previously noted, however, the need to import more components and parts from the parent company might mean that exports from the home country would continue and even increase following the establishment of the foreign subsidiary. Trade in final goods was hence simply replaced by trade in intermediate products.

Although investments that simply replicate domestic production in foreign markets still take place, most large companies originating from one or other of the advanced industrialized countries have already established extensive overseas operations covering most of the major regions of the world. There is little incentive for these companies to engage in further market-oriented investment. Instead, they have reached a stage in their international expansion when the concern is to bring about the most efficient global rationalization of their production possible. They have sought to achieve this through both vertical and horizontal rationalization of production on either a global or regional basis or both.

Vertical rationalization involves individual plants located in different countries specializing in particular stages or processes of production. Each plant becomes a highly specialized producer of a small range of components and parts which are then shipped to one or more specialist plants for assembly before being exported to the final market. The car industry aptly depicts this process, with specialist plants producing components such as car batteries, engines, carburettors, fan belts, gear boxes, exhausts and radiators. The advantage of such specialization is that it enables each plant to achieve efficiency gains from long production runs. Casson has explained this process as being in part the result of a technological revolution that transformed many manufacturing industries shortly after the end of the Second World War, radically changing the way in which products were designed (Casson, 1986). As a result, most manufacturing products could be described as 'multi-component goods' in that they are essentially assemblages of a large number of standardized components, each of which is itself an assembly of a set of sub-components. This utilization by MNCs of a 'new international division of labour' has promoted a massive growth of largely intra-firm trade in intermediate products (Frobel, Heinrichs and Kaye, 1980).

Horizontal rationalization takes place when multinational companies reorganize the production of finished products within a given industry in such a way as to permit greater plant specialization. For example, a white goods producer may concentrate production of fridges in a plant in one country, washing-machines in another, freezers in a third and microwave ovens in a fourth. Previously, these goods may have all been produced in one or two plants for sale largely in the domestic market where the subsidiary was located. Nowadays, a single plant is liable to supply several different national markets. Such highly specialist plants can obtain considerable cost savings from producing a single product in large quantities. This concentration in production may lead to increased intra-firm trade if, for example, the finished product is exported to a distribution subsidiary owned by the company in the foreign market. It clearly does give rise to increased intra-industry trade, however.

Given these trends in international specialization which have been promoted by MNCs, the products that a particular nation produces and exports are no longer simply a function of factor endowments or even the nature of consumer preferences. Rather, they depend on the ability of a nation to offer itself as a favourable location for the international production of a particular good. What is desperately needed, therefore, is a model of trade which can incorporate these kinds of activities by multinational companies.

In developing a critique of conventional trade theory, however, some degree of caution must be exercised. The globalized nature of manufacturing production does not render factor endowments or consumer preferences completely irrelevant for explaining patterns of trade. Indeed, there is a sense in which globalization may even strengthen the relevance of these factors as explanations for trade. Thus, the decision as to where a multinational is to locate a particular process or stage in the production of a good may depend on factor-intensities (UNCTAD-DTCI, 1995). For example, certain low-wage countries have been successful in attracting labour-intensive operations. In a similar manner, the existence of a strong local preference for a particular good in a country provides an incentive to locate production in that country. It is clear, however, that the process whereby multinationals rationalize their global or regional operations is more complex than this. Multinationals typically operate in oligopolistic markets in which strategic behaviour plays an important role. For example, the need to reduce risk by keeping abreast of rivals plays an important role in foreign investment decisions. A company may thus set up a subsidiary in a particular region of the world simply because a rival has done so and it does not want to be left behind. Moreover, the speed with which multinationals can shift assembly-type operations from one country to another will mean that international competitiveness is much more dynamic than in the past. Placing reliance on the purely static advantages bestowed by a particular pattern of factor costs may therefore provide only a temporary source of national competitive advantage in the face of global investment decisions by MNCs.

The main problem for conventional trade theory, however, may simply be that it is defining the problem in the wrong way. Trade economists still tend to talk in terms of countries that are assumed to be made up of large numbers of firms, industries and consumers. Trade is seen as the process whereby these entities called 'countries' exchange different products. The growth of world trade and production, however, has meant that countries have become much more economically interdependent and this feature is now a hallmark of the modern global economy. At the same time, most industries have come to be dominated by a diminishing number of ever bigger companies whose operations frequently straddle many national boundaries. Whether or not a country is a net exporter or importer of a particular product then depends on the competitive decisions of these leading firms. Within the context of the globalization of many of the world's industries, therefore, the debate concerning a country's comparative advantage needs to be reconsidered in the light of theories that explain the factors that account for a firm's competitive advantage. This may necessitate the trade economist borrowing some tools from the business economist. To explain patterns of international specialization and trade it will be necessary to understand the forces that dictate decision-making by MNCs because, increasingly, it is these firms that dictate the international dispersion of economic activity, and much international trade is conducted under their direction. A step forward in providing such an approach is the work undertaken by Michael Porter (Porter, 1986; 1990) to which we now turn.

## 6.4 From comparative advantage to competitive advantage

In his major study, *The Competitive Advantage of Nations* (1990), Michael Porter put forward the case for a new approach to the theory of international trade. In calling for a 'new paradigm' in which to study the structure of international trade, Porter argued that existing approaches were no longer adequate as explanations of international trading patterns within the modern global economy. More significantly, he questioned whether the policy implications of the traditional comparative advantage theory of trade could still be considered appropriate as a guide to government action.

Approaches to international trade within the dominant neoclassical paradigm have focused on the issue of country-specific endowments. This in turn has led to an analysis of comparative advantage in international trade which takes as its point of reference the geographical nation states through whose boundaries trade is conducted. The natural tendency of this country-specific, macro-economic approach is to treat 'success' in international trade as a characteristic of particular nations in the aggregate (for example in terms of a country's balance of trade performance) and this is then contrasted with the 'failure' of other countries. Specific factors are then sought by way of explanation and rationalization. Improving a nation's trading performance according to such an approach involves identifying those features of the national economy that mitigate against international trading success (such as excessively high wage levels) and adopting appropriate responses to them at the level of macro economic policy.

This notion of success and failure at the level of the nation as a whole provides Porter with the first element of his critique of the existing paradigm of international trade. For him, the nature of the issue at stake is not 'why do some nations succeed and others fail in international competition?' but rather 'why does a nation become the home base for successful international competitors in an industry?' The point of this reformulation is to place international trade in the microeconomic framework of industrial competition; firms engage in international economic activity as part of their strategic efforts to gain a competitive advantage against their actual and potential industry rivals.

The traditional tendency of trade theories to concentrate on the relative factor endowments of countries has served to direct ideas regarding international trade performance along particular channels. Success in international trade has been construed as an outcome of country-specific factors such as:

- macroeconomic policy (exchange rates, interest rates);

- average wage levels;

- natural resource endowments.

Governments have therefore been encouraged to develop approaches towards international trade policy that have concentrated on influencing the structure of relative costs facing their own nations' firms compared with their foreign-based rivals. This approach towards international trade leads to inappropriate policy conclusions and fails to explain many of the patterns of international trade that have emerged over the course of the last two or three decades, as we saw earlier in this chapter. Examples abound of firms succeeding in industries for which the domestic economy clearly has inappropriate resource endowments. An example is the success of firms in capital intensive industries such as shipbuilding and steel in capital-poor Korea (Amsden, 1989).

In the long run the significance of differences in national factor endowments for shaping patterns of international trade have been progressively undermined by three forces:

- the process of worldwide economic development which has led to a convergence among nations of many of the basic factors of production such as the availability of a workforce with sufficient education and skills to perform adequately in many industries, and the basic infrastructure (telecommunications, ports, roads) required to enable firms to successfully operate there;

- technological progress, which has given firms the power to circumvent scarce factors by using new products and processes. In many modern industries, access to state-of-the-art technology is now more important than low labour costs, while the materials and energy requirements have been reduced or synthetic substitutes developed. Modern materials such as engineering plastics, ceramics, carbon fibres, and the silicon used in making semiconductors are made from raw materials that are very widely available;

- the process of globalization, both of firms, which has served to free them from the resource constraints of their own nation, and of markets. The international capital market is now sufficiently developed to allow firms from capital constrained countries such as Korea to obtain the necessary funds to finance domestic investment.

Rather than being an outcome of factor endowments, success in the field of international trade increasingly relies upon the same considerations as success in industrial competition; the two are an outcome of the same set of forces. For Porter, the key to industrial success lies in the question of productivity. To achieve competitive success, firms from a nation must possess a competitive advantage in the form of either lower costs or differentiated products that command premium prices. To sustain an advantage, firms must achieve more sophisticated competitive advantages over time by providing higher-quality products and services or producing more efficiently. This translates directly into productivity growth (Porter, 1990, p.10). Increasing productivity in this way lies at the heart of Porter's notion of competitive advantage expounded in his earlier work (Porter, 1980, p.1985) and is something for which firms continually strive through the formulation and refinement of competitive strategies.

This focus on productivity growth within the firm links considerations of industrial efficiency together with national prosperity since a rising national standard of living depends upon the capacity of a nation's firms to achieve high levels of productivity and to increase productivity over time. At the same time, productivity is the force that provides Porter's approach with its essential dynamism. Competitive success (domestic and international) grows from the constant attempts by firms to improve their performance; a nation's firms must relentlessly improve productivity in existing industries by raising product quality, adding desirable features, improving product technology, or boosting production efficiency. The factors that support the success of a nation's firms in international trade are increasingly those that relate to innovation and change rather than the static considerations of relative factor cost.

To understand how this process operates within the context of a national economy, Porter has introduced the idea of the 'diamond'. The determinants of a nation's industrial success relies on the four interrelated conditions shown in the boxes of Figure 6.1 acting together in a mutually self-reinforcing way. Factor conditions represent one element in this equation. Porter distinguishes between a nation's factors of production in two ways:

- he makes the distinction between basic factors versus advanced factors: the former include natural resources, climate, physical location, unskilled and semi-skilled labour, and debt capital; the latter include the communications infrastructure, highly skilled personnel and research institutes;

- generalized factors versus specialized factors: the former can be employed in a range of industries whilst the latter represent the key to industry-specific innovation.

The point of the distinction is that the advanced/specialized factors are created rather than endowed and evolve gradually over time. Compared with the basic/generalized factors, they cannot be easily matched by other countries that happen to possess similar resource endowments. They therefore provide a nation with a source of competitive advantage that can be continually developed. The advanced and specialized factor conditions represent the foundation on which many of a nation's competitive advantages are built.

National advantage within particular industry sectors will also be supported by the three other elements of the 'diamond'. Firm strategy, structure and rivalry within an industry segment will be critical in determining the degree of competitiveness and innovation that is generated and thus to the process of stimulating productivity gains.

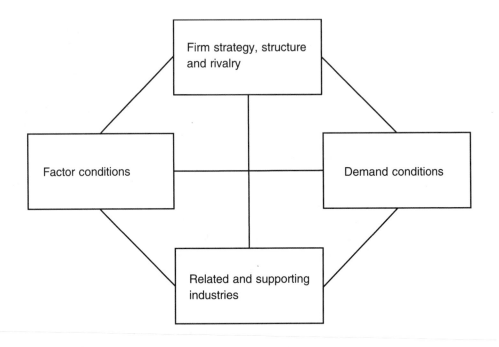

**Figure 6.1**  The determinants of national advantage. Source: M. Porter, *The Competitive Advantage of Nations*, Figure 3.1.

Competitive strength in a nation's industry will be further advanced if it is coupled with sophisticated demand conditions in the domestic market and the parallel development of a set of related and supporting industries. This structure of national advantage means that the economy of a country will be characterized by deeply embedded and highly innovative clusters of expertise within a number of industrial sectors. The greater the number and complexity of these clusters, the stronger will be a nation's competitive advantage. The economic growth and the trading performance of a nation's economy are therefore the outcome of progressive improvements undertaken by the firms (including the foreign subsidiaries of MNCs) that operate there.

National competitive advantage stems both from improving the existing products and processes that comprise a nation's economic activities at a point in time, and from decisions by the firms who operate in a nation to create and compete in new and more sophisticated industry segments where productivity will generally be higher. Porter refers to this ongoing process as 'upgrading' and it involves a two-pronged approach by firms to economic growth:

- implementing productivity increases that have the effect of freeing labour in existing industries or segments;

- developing new industries or segments that absorb the labour freed elsewhere.

Successful economies are thus in a process of becoming increasingly complex and specialized: adding value rather than simply growing in size. Hence, in summarizing his argument, Porter states: 'All this should make it clear why cheap labour and a "favourable" exchange rate are not meaningful definitions of [national] competitiveness. The aim is to support high wages and command premium prices in international markets' (Porter, 1990, p.7).

Another aspect of Porter's critique of the neoclassical 'factor cost' approach is that it assumes all forms of industrial specialization to be equally desirable from the point of view of trade, because any export industry is capable of earning foreign exchange revenue. In contrast, Porter argues that the rate of productivity that any given industry can achieve will vary; some industries will only register low levels of productivity growth while others will, through the process of upgrading, continually enhance their level of productivity both in absolute terms and relative to other industries. It is these high productivity industries that hold the key to a nation's prosperity.

The internationalization of economic activity causes the absolute level of productivity in given industries to converge towards the highest that modern industry can achieve. Without international competition the rate of productivity in any given industry could vary from one country to another. Domestic firms in industries that are subject to the forces of international competition (for example global industries) must achieve comparable levels of productivity to ensure their long-term survival. A nation that is losing competitive strength in those industries that have relatively high levels of productivity will achieve much slower rates of economic growth than nations whose domestically based firms emerge as leaders in these industries.

International trade plays a vital role in enabling nations to enhance their levels of productivity by eliminating the need to produce all goods and services within the nation itself. A nation's firms may specialize in those industries or segments in which they have acquired a productivity advantage and use this value, created through high productivity exports, to purchase goods and services from foreign firms that have gained the highest levels of productivity in other industry segments. By allowing national specialization in areas of high productivity, trade raises the average productivity level in an economy. The difference between Porter's approach and earlier theories of comparative advantage is that the key areas of specialization are those which a nation's firms (including foreign subsidiaries based there) have created rather than inherited.

Outward FDI by a nation's own firms will also contribute to increasing domestic productivity as long as it represents part of the process of upgrading (shifting its lower productivity activities to other nations) or entails performing selected activities that lead to enhanced competitive advantage in foreign markets (such as local servicing or product modification). Such investment, as part of a firm's competitive strategy, will tend to result in higher exports and foreign profits, boosting domestic earnings. Foreign investment by a nation's firms will only undermine the national economy if the activities transferred abroad involve higher levels of productivity growth than those that are retained at home.

Firms seeking competitive advantage will thus employ strategies embodying both international trade and foreign direct investment as they seek to continually upgrade their activities to achieve higher levels of productivity. International trade has helped to support this process by allowing increased specialization in narrowly defined industries and in segments within industries, hence generating the phenomenon of intra-industry trade. In many industries, and especially in distinct segments of industries, Porter's empirical research has discovered many examples where those firms that have successfully captured international competitive advantage are based in only a few nations. This phenomenon, referred to as 'clustering', suggests that the 'diamond' of national advantage applies to industries and segments within a nation, rather than to the economic environment which the national economy provides for its firms in general. In any given national economy, firms in certain industries blossom while firms in others decline in the face of international competition.

The globalization of industries and internationalization of companies has hence not served to make national-specific factors irrelevant as a determinant of industrial success but rather has changed their nature. To boost a nation's competitive advantage governments should encourage initiatives that support the objective of productivity enhancement in those industries and segments that are able to attain the highest levels of value creation, rather than implementing defensive policies designed to improve a nation's factor cost profile compared with that of other nations. In contrast to the static benefits bestowed by a nation's factor endowments, Porter's work has placed much greater emphasis on the dynamic factors that enable firms to enhance productivity. In doing so, Porter has linked the trade performance of a nation much more closely to the activities of those firms whose operations occur within its boundaries but whose competitive orbit is defined in global terms.

## 6.5 Conclusion

This chapter has considered the implications of the growth of MNCs and global industries for theories of international trade. Although this debate is by no means concluded, it is clear that in the modern international economy, theories of international trade need to explicitly accommodate the competitive activities of multinational firms. Both the international location of economic activity, and the international trade that arises as a result of this pattern of specialization are now largely the result of strategic decisions made at the corporate headquarters of MNCs.

As we have shown, two key developments that have characterized the increasingly international nature of industrial competition in recent years have been the growth of horizontal and vertical integration within MNCs of production facilities which span national boundaries. Internationally integrated production is now one of the principal features of global industries. Horizontal integration has led to international specialization, designed primarily to achieve economies of scale in plant size, and has stimulated a rapid expansion of intra-industry trade. Vertical integration, which was the main motivation behind the early growth of MNCs, has meanwhile led to the production process itself becoming internationally segmented in many industries. This has been an important factor promoting the growth of intra-firm trade.

Economists studying international trade have not been oblivious to the changes taking place. The work of the new trade theorists and international business analysts has led to significant progress in the field, principally through an application of the insights gained from theories of oligopolistic competition and internalization. More recently, writers in the area of business strategy have also begun to consider the relationship between international trade and the decision-making of firms. The importance of productivity gains through various forms of technical innovation has been emphasized in their writings, and these have been shown to rely more on the environment in which firms operate than the cost advantages bestowed by a particular endowment of factors of production. The skills and flexibility of a workforce, for example, coupled with the technological infrastructure that a particular location provides, may be critical in determining the international location decision of a MNC looking to site a new manufacturing plant. On such considerations are built the competitive advantages of nations and, hence, many of the patterns of international trade specialization that characterize the modern global economy.

## 6.6 Further reading

Greenaway, D. and Winters, A. (1994) *Surveys in International Trade*, Basil Blackwell: Oxford.

Grimwade, N. (1989) *International Trade*, Routledge, London.

Helpman, E. and Krugman, P. (1992) *Trade Policy and Market Structure*, MIT Press, Cambridge MA.

Markssen, S., Melvin, J., Kaempfer, W. and Maskus, K. (1995) *International Trade – Theory and Evidence*, McGraw-Hill, New York.

Neilsen, S., Madsen, E. and Pedersen, K. (1995) *International Economics: The Wealth of Open Nations*, McGraw-Hill, London.

Pomfret, R. (1991) *International Trade: An Introduction to Theory and Policy*, Basil Blackwell: Oxford.

Porter, M.E. (1990) *The Competitive Advantage of Nations*, Macmillan: London.

On Intra-firm Trade, see:

OECD (1993) *Intra-Firm Trade, Trade Policy Issues*, OECD: Paris.

## 6.7 *Questions for further discussion*

1. Why would we expect the issue of factor-intensity reversal to be more important in the textile industry than in the car industry?

2. How can we explain the fact that international trade in the post-war period has grown rapidly between countries whose factor endowments are quite similar?

3. Is the transfer abroad of assembly operations by a manufacturing firm likely to be trade displacing or trade enhancing? Why?

4. What is meant by the term 'dumping'? Why is it linked to the growth of oligopolistic competition?

5. Distinguish between, and give examples of, vertical and horizontal rationalization. Which is more important for generating intra-firm trade?

6. How according to Porter does the need for firms to enhance their levels of production affect their international location decisions?

7. What are the implications for economic policy of a shift in the focus of performance from the 'comparative advantage of countries' to the 'competitive advantage of firms'?

# Part Two

# International business strategy and management

# 7

# *Strategic planning and management in international firms*

## *7.1 Introduction*

> The two most important tasks that top managers in an MNC have to carry out are determining the firm's overall strategic direction, and building an organisational form that delivers the performance required by the strategy. (Taggart and McDermott, 1993, p.49.)

In Part Two, this book changes its emphasis and considers the tasks identified in the above quotation, that is the strategies, structure and decision-making of the international firm. This chapter explores the first of the tasks: defining and analysing the various components of the strategic management process in multinational corporations. It starts by seeking to define international strategic management and to ask why it is of increasing importance to the international firm. The main part of the chapter considers the key elements of this process.

Later chapters explore the specific components in much greater depth, dealing with issues such as international market entry decisions and developments in MNC organizational structure. It is important to take into account strategic analysis concepts which are significant to firms whatever the extent of their international involvement and to consider what the distinctive features of corporate strategy in the multinational corporation are.

## 7.2 *The definition of strategy*

James Brian Quinn (1980, p.3) defines strategy as:

> . . . the pattern or plan that integrates an organisation's major goals, policies and action sequences into a cohesive whole. A well-formulated strategy helps to marshal and allocate an organisation's resources into a unique and viable posture based on its relative internal competencies and shortcomings, anticipated changes in the environment and contingent moves by intelligent opponents.

Most definitions of strategy emphasize that it involves the overall direction in which the business enterprise is developing, addressing general questions like where the enterprise is going, as well as more specific ones such as what business or businesses the enterprise is in, or should be in? For the multinational corporation this needs to be extended to include locational questions such as 'what countries is the enterprise in, or what countries should it be in?' The form of the MNC's presence is also a strategic question; for example should it have a manufacturing subsidiary rather than servicing a particular country through exports?

Johnson and Scholes (1993, p.10) define strategy very much in terms of this concept of development direction:

> Strategy is the direction and scope of an organisation over the long term: ideally which matches its resources to its changing environment . . .

An immediate issue that arises for the multinational corporation is the question of scope; by virtue of operating internationally the MNC enjoys much wider geographic scope than the purely national domestic corporation. In consequence the MNC faces more complex, multiple operating environments than does the domestic firm. This makes strategic decision-making in the international firm more complex and increases the range of strategic options or choices of strategic direction available to the firm. Michael Porter (1985, 1986) defines strategy in terms of the achievement of competitive advantage; by virtue of its international scope of operations, the MNC is likely to have greater choice in ways of achieving competitive advantage when compared to the domestic firm (this issue is examined at greater length in Chapter 8).

Wheelen and Hunger define the term 'strategic management' as '. . . that set of managerial decisions and actions that determine the long-run performance of a corporation' (Wheelen and Hunger, 1995, p.3). This adds an additional factor to our understanding of strategy: strategic decisions are not disembodied but are taken by the managers of multinational firms and are influenced by their personalities, values and abilities. The strategic decisions of major multinational corporations such as Ford, IBM, Toyota or Sony have historically been intimately connected with the personalities and qualities of their founders and chief executives. As Mintzberg (1987) has pointed out, the term 'strategy' has Greek origins in the word *strategos* meaning 'generalship'. The military origin of the concept helps us to identify that one important influence on corporate performance is strong or weak corporate generalship, in addition to the organization's internal resources and external environment.

## 7.3 The need for strategic management and planning

Strategic management and planning are necessary for the following reasons:

- To achieve a clear sense of direction for the business enterprise. To take a forward view and establish a clear set of objectives and goals.

- To provide an important integrating and co-ordinating function for the MNC on geographic, functional and product bases as the MNC has grown more diverse in its operations.

- Through this co-ordination role to minimize intra-organizational conflict including tensions in headquarters/subsidiary relationships.

- To serve as a guide to action, providing a framework for the MNC's operating and administrative decisions. To maximize corporate performance by maximizing strengths and opportunities, minimizing weaknesses and threats.

- To respond successfully to the uncertainty, complexity and competitiveness of the international business environment encountered by firms of increasingly global scope.

## 7.4 The international strategic management process

Figure 7.1 sets out the main components of the international strategic management process. Conceptually the process involves four key stages: international strategic analysis, strategy formulation, strategy implementation, and strategy evaluation, monitoring and control.

### 7.4.1 International strategic analysis

Strategic analysis involves investigating the position of the international firm with respect to its external environment, industry context,

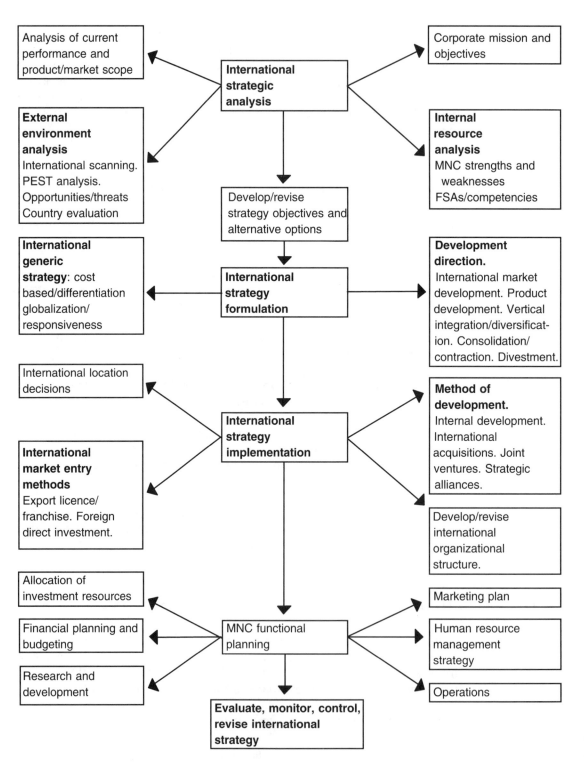

**Figure 7.1** International strategic management process.

objectives, power relationships, performance, resources and competencies.

## (a) External environment

The analysis of the firm's external international business environment is designed to identify the strategic opportunities and threats it faces; these are key forces of change in the business environment that are likely to result in a change of strategy either positively by presenting new strategic growth opportunities to the firm, or negatively by posing threats to the continuation of present strategies. PEST analysis (Political, Economic, Social and Technological Environmental analysis) is a simple method of carrying out an environmental audit of these influences in order to identify which factors (if any) pose these strategic challenges.

## (b) Political environment

As already noted, by virtue of its operation across frontiers, the international firm inevitably interacts with many governmental systems and regulatory regimes. Environmental scanning needs to take account of the stability of host government regimes and the degree of political risk exposed (for example risk of civil war, expropriation, fundamentalist political and religious ideology, and so forth). The liberalization of world trade, privatization programmes and deregulation of markets have brought about new market opportunities in Central and East Europe and China, but new competitive threats have arisen in previously protected markets, for example telecommunications.

## (c) Economic environment

Many of the above factors have both an economic and a political dimension. A key economic factor, however, has been the deepening of the business cycle after the long post-Second World War economic boom, with the emergence of major phases of world economic recession in 1980–1 and 1990–3.

## (d) Social environment

More discerning customers, the emergence of environmentally concerned consumers, the segmentation of mass markets, the globalization of markets – these have all been important social and marketing changes, as have important demographic factors such as population growth rates in southern countries and ageing populations in northern countries.

## (e) Technological environment

Changes in communications technology are important in making the operation of the modern MNC possible. Technological change, manifest in new products and processes, is generally an important source of specific advantage and disadvantage for a firm.

Many of these environmental factors, such as deregulation, will have different consequences in different sectors; PEST analysis will assess their relative importance for the firm or industry under consideration.

### (f) Internal analysis

This seeks to analyse the strengths and weaknesses of the international firm, the quantity and quality of resources available, its firm-specific advantages, core competencies and the sources of competitive advantage. These will be examined at greater length in section 7.7 below.

### (g) Objectives and power

An analysis of the firm's *objectives and power* relationships is a key element of strategy formulation; an important component of strategy evaluation is to examine whether existing strategies are achieving the firm's objectives, whether measured in terms of profits, growth or wider, social measures of performance such as environmental impact or employment conditions. Power relationships in international firms tend to be complex with multiple stakeholders, whether internal (for example headquarters/subsidiary relationships) or external (as a result of the need to achieve legitimacy with a range of organizations such as government bodies, trade unions and consumer groups in different countries). Such complex power and stakeholder relationships often result in complex and multiple business objectives.

### (h) SWOT analysis

The identification of internal strengths and weaknesses, and external opportunities and threats, is usually referred to as *SWOT analysis*. It must not degenerate into a simple descriptive listing of internal and external factors. Its purpose is to assist the firm to understand the nature of the forces of change at work and to aid strategy formulation through the choice of appropriate and effective strategies from available alternatives.

## 7.4.2 Strategy formulation

The model outlined in Figure 7.1 identifies two key aspects of strategy formulation and choice: international generic strategy and development direction. International generic strategy concerns the overall strategic positioning of the firm, how it chooses to compete and to achieve competitive advantage. As well as key choices between cost-based competition (for example the achievement of worldwide economies of scale) and differentiation (for example brand building), international generic strategy includes the determination of the correct balance between global standardization and integration on the one hand, and national/local responsiveness on the other. A further level of strategic choice concerns the issue of development direction; as a result of its strategic analysis the multinational corporation may decide to withdraw from certain countries, to enter new countries (market development) or to concentrate its efforts on research and innovation (new product development). Issues of development direction will be discussed in section 7.9 below and international generic strategy will be the focus of Chapter 8.

## 7.4.3 Strategy implementation

Strategy implementation is concerned with the way in which the desired strategy is to be achieved and made to work. Figure 7.1 indicates that there are several components to strategy implementation:

- International location decisions involve the spatial dimension of international business strategy: the countries in which specific activities should be located. These decisions are influenced by evaluating particular countries and scanning in the first analytical stage of the strategic management process.

- International market entry methods: choices about the method of foreign market entry including exporting, licensing and foreign direct investment.

- Methods of development: choices regarding whether to carry out the strategy (for example product development) through internal means, through acquisition or through the use of strategic alliances and joint ventures.

- Organizational structure: implementation of strategy works through the management of people in the international organization. Changes in strategy can have significant organizational consequences and can result in important structural changes.

- Functional planning: the discussion so far has concerned the strategic decisions of the business as a whole or corporate level strategy. Implementation very much involves the need to create functional plans and strategies in order to achieve the overall strategy; for example financial planning, marketing planning and strategy, human resource management strategy.

### 7.4.4 Strategy evaluation, monitoring and control

The final stage of the international strategic management process is concerned with evaluating the chosen strategies and methods of implementation, monitoring corporate performance, and managing and controlling the process. Evaluation may involve a number of criteria; Johnson and Scholes suggest that three of the most important criteria are suitability, acceptability and feasibility (Johnson and Scholes, 1993, pp.244–6). Suitability concerns the appropriateness of the strategy; does it match and address issues identified in the internal and external analysis? Acceptability is concerned with the objectives of owners, managers and other stakeholders in the international firm; is the chosen strategy achieving stakeholder objectives? Feasibility concerns whether the strategy is realizable within financial and other resource constraints; is it over ambitious, can it be financed, could competitor reactions destroy the strategy?

Although portrayed as a linear procedure in Figure 7.1, international strategic management is in fact an interactive process, the monitoring and control stage providing feedback for strategic analysis in the next time period.

This section has set out the main components of the strategic management and planning process in international firms. It is not possible here to explore all of these elements in greater depth. The remainder of this chapter examines three topics: competitive analysis, internal analysis and strategic choice. Later chapters are concerned with international generic strategy, strategy implementation, and international organizational structures.

## 7.5 Competitive environment and industry characteristics

Multinational companies do not inhabit an economics textbook world of theoretical market structures such as perfect competition and pure monopoly. In some instances, firms operate in highly competitive conditions as a result of the interplay of world market forces of supply and demand; examples include many commodity products such as coffee, copper or paper. Characteristics of such products include lack of product differentiation and frequent swings in volumes, often resulting in quite wild fluctuations in world price levels.

In many cases multinational companies operate in market structures dominated by a few large firms: what economists term 'oligopoly'. Many consumer durable goods such as automobiles or washing machines are produced under conditions of international oligopoly in which a few large multinational companies, such as General Motors and Toyota, or Whirlpool and Electrolux, dominate the international industry. Often such firms have a degree of market power but not complete market dominance. Although the market structures involved are far removed from the textbook world of perfect competition, competition in the form of direct rivalry can be very intense under oligopolistic conditions, taking a range of forms. Firms involved often compete in a variety of ways including product differentiation through product design, advertising and branding, new product development and innovation, and a range of pricing policies. The search for competitive advantage becomes a vital aspect of firms' strategy under such oligopolistic conditions, although as both Michael Porter (1985) and John Kay (1993) demonstrate, there are few sources of competitive advantage that cannot ultimately be eroded or imitated.

Industrial economists such as F.M. Scherer (1980) emphasize the extent to which industrial behaviour by firms in such situations is the outcome of structural factors such as the number and size distribution of firms, the possibility and extent of product differentiation, the nature of cost conditions including transport costs and economies of scale, and the extent and height of barriers to entry for new competitors.

Michael Porter's 'five forces' framework builds on this structural approach to oligopoly behaviour by providing a useful conceptual tool for analysing 'The key structural features of industries that determine the strength of the competitive forces and hence industry profitability' (Porter, 1980, p.4).

The five competitive forces illustrated in Figure 7.2 are:

- intensity of rivalry among existing competitors;

- threat of new entrants;

- bargaining power of buyers;

- bargaining power of suppliers;

- threat from substitute products.

### 7.5.1 Intensity of rivalry

There are several factors determining the degree and intensity of industry rivalry.

*The degree of industry concentration and the size distribution of competitors.* Where an industry is highly concentrated and one firm is clearly dominant, rivalry is likely to be low and the firms concerned engage in leader/follower behaviour. In concentrated international oligopoly situations such as the supply of colour film by firms like Fuji, Agfa and Kodak, price competition is often low and competition often takes the form of advertising and product development. In contrast, where

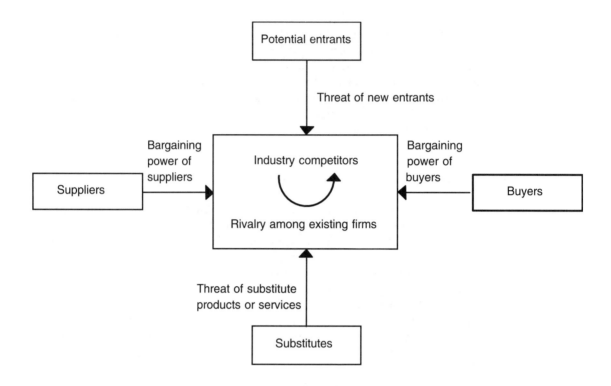

**Figure 7.2** The five competitive forces that determine industry profitability.
Source: Porter (1980), p.4.

there are numerous or equally balanced competitors, rivalry is likely to be high. Even where there are only a few firms, but they are quite equally balanced in size, the battle for market share may become intense. The 'cola wars' between Coca Cola and Pepsi illustrate this.

*Competitor diversity* refers to the degree of similarity or difference between firms in the industry. Diversity is likely to be high where firms are themselves highly diversified in terms of product range and have different origins, objectives, management styles and cost structures. Porter's proposition is that such diversity is likely to lead to more intense rivalry than in industries where competitors are quite similar in terms of these factors. Often in protected markets, such as the United States steel industry until the late 1980s, the producers enjoy a 'quiet life' and have similar cost structures. In an international context, foreign competitors are likely to increase diversity and hence rivalry.

*Industry growth rate.* Where this is high, rivalry is likely to be low, as was the case in the young personal computer industry of the early to mid-1980s, which experienced a growth rate of over 30 per cent per annum. Presumably if the industry is growing rapidly, the firms' sales growth comes out of industry growth; they do not need to fight for market share. Rivalry is likely to be more intense in mature and saturated markets; ultimately a firm can only increase its sales at another's expense. In the personal computer industry a reduction in industry growth rates in the 1990s, which was due in part to the industry product life cycle and in part to the recession, resulted in much more intense rivalry among major competitors such as Apple, IBM, Hewlett Packard and Compaq.

*The degree of product differentiation.* The lower the degree of product differentiation, the greater the intensity of rivalry. Where products are clearly differentiated, there is likely to be less emphasis on price competition and more competition through methods such as branding and marketing. In the young personal computer industry there was considerable differentiation in terms of design, components and differences in operating systems. By the early 1990s many of these differences had disappeared; the personal computer had increasingly become a commodity product, facing considerable competition from 'clone' suppliers, which augmented the more intense rivalry identified above.

*High exit barriers allied to excess industry capacity.* Entry barriers are a familiar concept; exit barriers are less so. They are factors that prevent firms from leaving an industry. Porter defines them as '. . . economic, social and emotional factors that keep firms competing in businesses even though they may be earning low or even negative returns on investment' (Porter, 1980, p.20). The factors involved include specialized assets, fixed costs of exit such as labour redundancy agreements, emotional barriers such as management values and objectives, and government restrictions, for example concern over job losses and regional policy. In the world shipbuilding industry, the response of European shipbuilders to the successful rise of Japanese and Korean producers exhibited many of these factors. For example, shipyard equipment represented specialized assets with little alternative economic use; they were valuable in shipbuilding but otherwise only of scrap value. In these circumstances rivalry may become extremely intense, and the producers (and governments) involved may be prepared to withstand a long period of losses before leaving the industry.

*High strategic stakes.* MNCs may have high strategic stakes in certain countries but regard others as relatively marginal to their worldwide strategy. They are likely to compete much more aggressively in the former category, accepting a long period of losses in order to maintain a presence in the countries involved.

Other factors influencing the level of rivalry according to Porter include high fixed costs, lumpiness of incremental capacity increases and high switching costs; arguably the world airline industry exhibits a number of these features. If, for example, most of an airline's planes are Boeings, there may be high switching costs (such as maintenance and retraining costs) in ordering future aircraft from Airbus.

## 7.5.2 Threat of entry

According to Chan Kim and Mauborgne (1988), in evaluating international industry competition, it should be borne in mind that the threat of entry comes not so much from new businesses as from two significant groups which multinational corporations should regard as potential competitors: existing companies that operate in related business segments, either abroad or in the MNC's home market, and companies that operate in the same business segment but in different parts of the world. Relatively simple diversification and locational moves can transform both groups from potential competitors to actual competitors. More generally Porter (1980) identified seven main factors giving rise to entry barriers: economies of scale; product differentiation; capital requirements; absolute cost advantages; access to distribution channels; government policy and expected retaliation.

*Economies of scale.* Economies of scale occur where unit costs fall as the volume of production increases. They act as an entry barrier by requiring a new entrant to either come into the market with sufficient volume to achieve economies of scale, or encounter a cost penalty depending on the extent of the scale economies in the industry. From Adam Smith's *Wealth of Nations* we can see that one of the determinants of economies of scale is the size of the market. For European MNCs originating from small home countries, such as Sweden's SKF in ball bearings, internationalization in the early twentieth century was partly driven by the need to obtain sufficient market size to achieve economies of scale in production, this helping to consolidate SKF's market position in relation to smaller-scale European producers. The achievement of scale economies can be seen as a significant factor in the globalization of industries such as consumer electronics since 1960, as discussed in the next chapter.

*Product differentiation.* In industries where product differentiation is important, for example chocolate confectionery, existing firms have an advantage based on brand identity and customer brand loyalty. A new entrant has the additional expense (and risk) of attempting to build new brands from scratch, in addition to setup and production costs. The greater attraction and certainty of international brand buying over brand building as a method of market entry has been an important factor in corporate acquisition behaviour. Unfortunately, by the end of the 1980s the popularity of this acquisition method had resulted in the inflated prices which had to be paid for the value of some brands, such as international drinks brands.

*Capital requirements.* The sheer cost of entering some industries in terms of setup costs and capital requirements is sufficiently high to deter new entrants. This is particularly the case in industries like aerospace where the costs of research and development and capital intensity are high.

*Absolute cost advantages.* Established firms in some industries may have cost advantages over new entrants irrespective of the scale of output. Such absolute cost advantages have included favourable access to raw materials in industries like aluminium, and proprietary product technology and know-how in industries like pharmaceuticals.

*Access to distribution channels.* Access to distribution channels may favour the established firm over the new entrant, particularly for consumer goods. This is particularly the case where the manufacturers are vertically integrated and own or control the main distribution channels, as was the case until recently in the British and German brewing industries. Even in grocery foodstuffs, the limited availability of supermarket shelf space may favour the familiar, established brand over the new entrant.

*Government policy.* Whether in the form of patent protection (pharmaceuticals) or the regulatory framework (banking and financial services) government policy may create an absolute barrier for a time, deterring the entry of new firms.

*Expected retaliation.* A significant type of entry barrier is behavioural rather than structural in nature. It is based on anticipated retaliatory behaviour, such as aggressive price cutting, by established firms if entry were to occur. Allegations of anti-competitive behaviour of this type have been made against international airlines like British Airways.

## 7.5.3 Bargaining power of buyers

The number and size distribution of buyers is an important determinant of buyer power; the higher the level of buyer concentration the higher their level of buying power in relation to the firms in the industry. We tend to think that buyer power is low for many products, with millions of individual consumers acting as ultimate buyers. There are many types of products and services, however, where a degree of monopoly buying power (monopsony) may exist; examples include defence equipment suppliers where ministries of defence are purchasers, or telecommunications equipment suppliers when state telecommunications monopolies were buyers in the era before deregulation. A further determinant of buyer power is the absence or presence of switching costs; where it is easy for the buyers to switch orders between rival suppliers, buyer power is likely to be higher than in a situation where the buyer is 'locked in' to a particular supplier and where significant costs may occur in switching to an alternative industry supplier.

Given the chain of intermediaries between producers and the individual consumer, buyer power may exist at wholesale or retail level, particularly where a further determinant, the possibility of backward integration by the buyer, is present. The changing balance of power in Europe between branded grocery food manufacturers and grocery supermarkets is partly the result of increased retailer concentration and partly the result of the success of supermarkets' own brands.

### 7.5.4 Bargaining power of suppliers

Similar factors influence both buyer power and supplier power. Supplier concentration, switching costs and the ability to vertically integrate forward, help to determine the level of supplier power. In the personal computer sector, for example, a successful marketing campaign has made consumer awareness of the microprocessor manufacturer Intel greater than that of many of the personal computer brands that use it.

### 7.5.5 Threat from substitute products

The final force influencing industry competition and profitability is the extent of the possible threat from substitute goods and services. One problem is that from the consumer's viewpoint all products are ultimately substitutes for one another in terms of expenditure. Porter is concerned here with the possibility of substitutes whose price/performance characteristics make them a real threat to the products of the existing firms. Technological change and product innovation are clearly important factors influencing this force; an example is steel and concrete partially displacing the use of brick in the building industry.

In general, the way the five forces model works is that the stronger the five forces (intensity of rivalry, threat of new entrants, bargaining power of buyers and suppliers, and threat from substitute products) the weaker will be the ability of the existing competitors to earn profits and the less attractive the industry will be. Conversely, the weaker the five forces, the greater the profit potential and attractiveness of the industry. The five forces are not simply a given; they are likely to change through time. One role of business strategy is to actively influence the size and impact of the five forces over time; for example through measures such as differentiation, vertical integration or mergers and acquisitions.

## 7.6 Strategic group analysis

Firms operating under conditions of international oligopoly may find considerable variation in the identity, number and size distribution of competitors internationally; for example Burger King and McDonalds may be direct rivals worldwide but they face significant differences in terms of national and local competitors in the burger market segment, and from food and restaurants generally, from one country market to another. Strategic group analysis is a method of segmenting or classifying different groups of competitors within an industry on the basis of strategic dimensions such as geographic spread or degree of product diversity. Porter states:

> A strategic group is the group of firms in an industry following the same or a similar strategy along the strategic dimensions. An industry could have only one strategic group if all the firms followed essentially the same strategy. At the other extreme, each firm could be a different strategic group. Usually, however, there are a small number of strategic groups which capture the essential strategic differences between firms in the industry. (Porter, 1980, p.129.)

The 'strategic dimensions' that could be used to analyse an international industry include geographic scope (the number of countries/regions the different firms are operating in), product range and diversity, number and extent of brands, size, nationality, product quality, pricing (high/moderate/low), degree of vertical integration, and types of distribution channel used.

Figure 7.3 illustrates a strategic group analysis of the international brewing industry using the simple dimensions of geographic scope and product range. Each strategic group brings together firms with a similar level of geographic coverage and product range. It is shown from a United Kingdom perspective; the local, regional and national groups involved are all British; global players like Heineken and Anheuser-Busch compete against one another worldwide but face different local, regional and national competitors in countries such as Spain, India and Japan.

One limitation of the method is its essentially two-dimensional nature: an MNC using it might need to conduct numerous analyses for the different countries and the different strategic dimensions but the contrasts involved could be very useful in helping to determine where to choose offensive strategies and where to employ defensive ones. Used dynamically the technique could indicate the extent to which a particular firm is repositioning itself and moving from one strategic group to another. The concept of entry barriers, normally used at industry level, can be extended to this context in terms of mobility barriers or obstacles preventing mobility of firms from one strategic group to another. Historically, industrial evolution has often exhibited such mobility; even

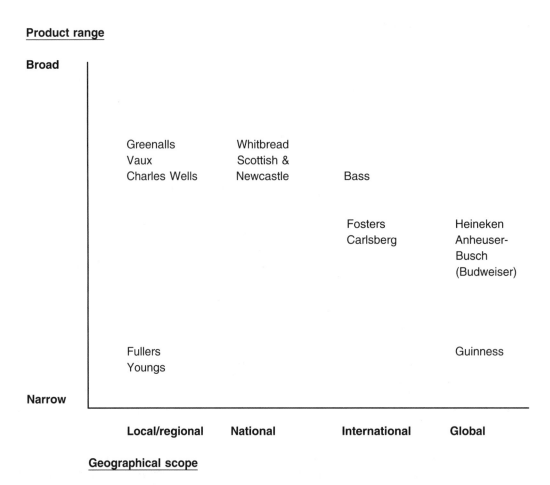

**Figure 7.3** Strategic group analysis: international brewing.

the iron and steel industry was, until this century, quite localized within regions before becoming national and eventually international in scope.

Chapter 2 identified the significance of foreign direct investment and economic growth in Asia, in particular in the 'tiger' economies and Japan. One consequence is the extent to which the world economy has now become dominated by Europe, north America and Asia. At the level of the most internationalized firms, the truly global players, it is important to establish a business presence in all three of these international areas, either directly or indirectly via strategic alliance or joint venture (as British Airways has done with Quantas in Australasia). As Chan Kim and Mauborgne pointed out in *Becoming an Effective Global Competitor*:

> . . . MNCs need not only to identify actual and potential global competitors but also to establish a market presence in their competitors' profit sanctuaries. By expanding operations into their global rivals' key

geographic markets, MNCs can gain several benefits. (Chan Kim and Mauborgne, 1988, p.34.)

Extending their analysis, these benefits can be identified as:

- widening the scope of geographic areas they can choose from when launching an offensive or defensive strategy against their competitors;

- denying their rival a profits sanctuary that could be used to cross-subsidize products in the MNC's home country through international transfer pricing;

- forcing their rivals to redirect management time and resources to the protection of a previously secure domestic market base;

- achievement of strategic intelligence as a result of entry to rivals' home markets, for example information on technology, production expertise and the rivals' new product development as well as clarification of their 'strategic intent';

- achievement of wider benefits of internationalization like increased sales revenues, greater economies of scale and lower per unit costs.

One example Chan Kim and Mauborgne give of this type of global competitive strategy is Kodak's response to Fuji's successful erosion of its domestic market share in the United States in the mid 1980s. Rather than tackling Fuji head on in the United States where a price-cutting war would have done more damage to Kodak than to Fuji (in terms of their respective market shares) it decided to retaliate by increasing its market presence in Fuji's Japanese domestic market by creating a new Japanese subsidiary with research facilities and a much-enhanced advertising budget (Chan Kim and Mauborgne, 1988, p.37).

## 7.7 Internal resource analysis

An internal analysis of the international firm helps to identify the firm's specific strengths and weaknesses and its sources of competitive advantage. According to Robert Grant, through internal analysis we can investigate '[w]hat the firm does *better* than its competitors' (1991, p.105) and what others have termed the firm's 'core competencies' (Prahalad and Hamel, 1990) or 'strategic capabilities' (Lenz, 1980). Prahalad and Hamel define core competence as;

> . . . the collective learning in the organization, especially how to coordinate diverse production skills and integrate multiple streams of

technologies . . . it is also about the organisation of work and the delivery of value. (Prahalad and Hamel, 1990, p.281.)

Examples of such competencies and capabilities include Philips' continuing expertise in lighting, Sony's competence at miniaturization, Honda's in small engine manufacture and 3M's innovations in sticky tape including self-adhesive 'post-it' note pads.

A very useful method of conducting internal analysis is to examine the various functional activities of the business organization to identify key strengths and weaknesses. Below are some of the major functional departments and questions which could arise:

*Marketing.* A primary issue here is the size and significance of the marketing function. This partly involves a cultural question: to what extent is the organization's culture marketing- and customer-oriented? Some technology-oriented companies have a culture dominated by the research scientist and engineer at the expense of profitable marketing opportunities.

To what extent has the firm engaged in effective international market planning and undertaken rational decisions about the extent of marketing standardization and adaptation in different countries? A further issue is the extent to which the firm involved is carrying out market research on its customer base.

*Operations* involve the production and delivery of goods or services. Issues here include the age and adequacy of the capital stock, whether there is sufficient productive capacity, and productivity (the efficiency with which the assets are being used).

*Finance.* Is the firm adequately financed? What are the sources of finance? What is the relationship between the level of borrowing and share capital? Further questions concern the adequacy of the firm's financial controls and budgetary planning procedures. The use of financial ratios to analyse an MNC's performance is discussed in Appendix One.

*Human resource management.* There are quantitative and qualitative issues concerning the size of the labour force and the suitability of its skills and qualifications. The quality and depth of management is also an issue here. The organization of the personnel function itself is a potential problem area.

*Research and development.* The significance of this function varies enormously from industry to industry. In sectors like clothing and beverages it is relatively unimportant (when measured as research and development expenditure as a percentage of sales turnover for example) whereas in sectors like aircraft and pharmaceuticals it is much more significant and may be the core competency of the business organization.

The effectiveness of the research and development function is difficult to measure; arguably research and development expenditure is simply an input measure and tells us little about how successful the research and development function is, although inter-firm comparisons may be quite useful. (For example, is the firm matching or exceeding the industry average expenditure?) Output measures, such as the number of drugs patented in the pharmaceuticals industry, are unreliable, as many drugs never reach the market. For multinational drugs companies like Glaxo, having a portfolio of very successful drugs like Ventolin and Zantac is the key to commercial survival but this is arguably the result of successful manufacturing, marketing and distribution strategies as well as the effectiveness of their research laboratories in discovering and developing the drugs in the first place.

## 7.8 Value chain analysis

An investigation of the international firm's internal strengths and weaknesses based on a functional study is useful for analytical purposes but needs to be supplemented by techniques such as Michael Porter's value chain analysis (1985), illustrated in Figure 7.4, if we are to understand a firm's strategic capability. The value chain examines productive activity as an interrelated set of value-creating activities from the supply of raw materials and components on the left hand side of the diagram to the consumer beyond the right hand arrow. Porter states:

> A systematic way of examining all the activities a firm performs and how they interact is necessary for analysing the sources of competitive advantage. (Porter, 1985, p.33.)

This is particularly important for analysing the geographically wide-spread activities of the international firm where many of the linkages involved not only cross national frontiers but may be thousands of miles apart and may involve a range of suppliers, partners and distributors.

Value-chain analysis recognizes that the consumer, in purchasing a consumer durable product like a motor car, is not simply purchasing the car itself but is also buying a bundle of product characteristics which include a variable range of extras and incentives linked to marketing and sales, such as a financing package which includes trade-in on the purchaser's existing vehicle, after-sales service and a warranty. Both here and at earlier points in the value chain there may be opportunities to create competitive advantage over rivals either through cost advantages (for example a more efficient, lower-cost distribution system for the finished products) or through differentiation (for example in the retailing sector through shop design and layout). Porter classified the two types of value creating activities, primary and support, as follows:

### (a) Primary activities

*Inbound logistics* involve supplier relationships and refer to all the processes involved in receiving, storing and distributing the inputs, components and raw materials used in the production process. Process innovations by Japanese car manufactures, in particular 'just-in-time' supply methods, have been important in this sector. The possible extent and complexity of inward logistics in a multinational firm is examined by Preece, Fleisher and Toccacelli in their 1995 study of Levi Strauss's value chain; in supply terms they found that Levi Strauss was sourcing blue denim jeans and other garments from more than 600 contractors in over 50 countries (Preece, Fleisher and Toccacelli, 1995, p.91).

*Operations* are the processes of manufacturing and assembly of inputs to produce the final product form. Operations also make up the central activities of delivering a service whether we are considering the operations of an airline, a supermarket chain or a bank.

*Outbound logistics* relate to storage, processing orders, transport and distribution of the product to the final consumer.

*Marketing and sales* involve activities like advertising and promotion, organization of the sales force, selecting the distribution channels, managing relationships with potential customers and pricing. In contrast

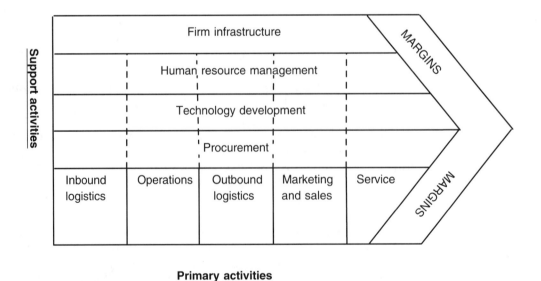

**Figure 7.4** The generic value chain. Source: Porter (1985), p.37.

to its worldwide sales and distribution systems, Levi Strauss has continued to centralize its very successful advertising and brand-building activities in San Francisco, California (Preece, Fleisher and Toccacelli, 1995, p.93).

*Service.* This enhances the value of the product in terms of installation and training, maintenance, repair and after-sales service.

## (b) Support activities

*Procurement.* Whilst the primary activity, inbound logistics, concerns inputs of raw materials and components, the procurement support activity runs right through the value chain and occurs in many parts of the organization.

*Technology development.* The role of technology is not limited to the research and development department or manufacturing but also runs right through the value chain. For Levi Strauss the use of information technology is very important in its retailer links and outbound logistics; electronic data interchange permits direct communication with electronic point-of-sale information from major retail outlets, allowing automatic restocking and invoicing from the company's distribution system.

*Human resource management.* Those activities involving the recruitment, training, development, promotion, and payment of people working for the organization. Preece, Fleisher and Toccacelli point out that the degree of labour intensity in garment manufacture makes human resource management a vital support function for Levi Strauss's clothes manufacturing/operations activities.

Levi Strauss appears to carefully nurture its reputation as a progressive employer, both in its own plants and in its partnership relationships with suppliers in low labour-cost countries in Asia and Latin America, where its 'Sourcing Guidelines' govern responsible employment practices, health and safety standards, and environmental requirements (Preece, Fleisher and Toccacelli, 1995, p.91). More generally, in industries like advertising and computer software, skilled human resources are a key source of competitive advantage. The human resource management support function has a key role to play in retaining and motivating the staff involved.

*Firm infrastructure* involves the structures and routines of the organization and its management, planning, accounting, finance and quality control mechanisms.

## 7.9 Strategy formulation: strategic options

Moving beyond the strategic analysis stage of the strategic management model, Johnson and Scholes (1993, p.204) provide a useful conceptual framework linking together different aspects of strategic choice; decisions over strategic positioning, development direction and method of implementation. Figure 7.5 identifies the various components of these different strategic options.

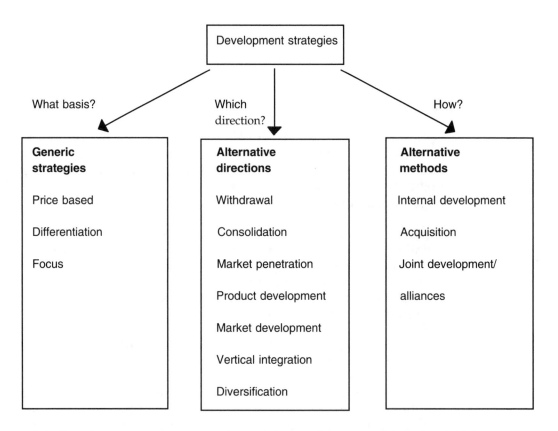

**Figure 7.5** Development strategies. Adapted from Johnson and Scholes (1993), p.204.

### 7.9.1 Generic strategy

The Johnson and Scholes model follows Michael Porter's analysis in conceiving generic strategy as the achievement of competitive advantage either through the choice of price/cost leadership, differentiation or focus (Porter, 1985, pp.11–16). This is explored at greater length in an international context in Chapter 8. Hill and Jones (1995) suggest that these generic strategies are themselves based on four factors that they term the 'generic building blocks of competitive advantage': efficiency, quality, innovation and responsiveness, illustrated in Figure 7.6.

- Efficiency. Important factors influencing efficiency include labour productivity, capital intensity, economies of scale, learning-curve effects and a company's cost culture generally. Efficiency directly underpins a price/cost leadership generic strategy.

- Quality. The quality of a product or service refers to its standard of excellence and reliability. Hill and Jones point out that high product quality has a twofold impact on a firm's competitive advantage. First, it helps the firm to build a brand name and reputation for quality and enables the firm to charge a premium price for its products, as we find with Marks and Spencer's St Michael brand clothes and foodstuffs. Second, production runs with fewer defects and faults in need of rectification have beneficial effects on labour productivity and efficiency. The 1990 MIT study of the world automobile industry found that quality was an important contributor to the superior productivity of Toyota and other Japanese car manufacturers when compared to the Americans and Europeans (Womack *et al.*, 1990, pp.85–7).

- Innovation. The introduction of new products and processes may contribute to competitive advantage both in terms of reducing costs and achieving differentiation. Innovation may take a variety of forms including new or improved products, production processes, management systems, organizational structures and use of design and information technology. Examples include Toyota's 'lean' production system, Levi Strauss's logistical use of information technology, Xerox's development of the photocopier and Marks and Spencer's supplier relationships.

- Customer responsiveness. Wolfgang Muller has suggested that, in the conditions of the 1990s, customer responsiveness is the ultimate basis of competitive advantage and other factors such as efficiency, quality and innovation enhance both a product's value and the firm's ability to respond to customer needs with superior service (Muller, 1991). Hill and Jones point out that important components of customer responsiveness include ability to customize goods and services to the requirements of individual consumers, customer order response time, superior quality and design and superior after-sales service and support (Hill and Jones, 1995, p.110).

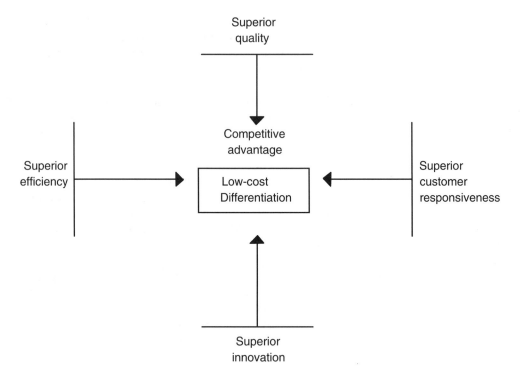

**Figure 7.6** The generic building blocks of competitive advantage. Source: Hill and Jones (1995) p.107.

### 7.9.2 Development direction

A second order of strategic choice encompasses the variety of development directions that a business organization can select.

*Withdrawal.* Starting with the negative end of the range of potential choices available to the business organization, the result of strategic analysis may point to the need for a company to withdraw from a particular product or market. The extent to which many multinational companies grew by diversification in the 1970s and 1980s has forced many to engage in asset disposals and sell businesses in the more difficult and complex environment of the 1990s. The shock of a period of low profits or even losses has forced many companies to focus on those parts of the value chain that are most successful: to concentrate on core activities and to dispose of or contract out activities that can be performed more efficiently by others. The reorganization at the Dutch electrical giant, Philips, in the early 1990s saw a focus on its core consumer electronics and lighting businesses, and the disposal of Philips white goods (kitchen appliances such as washing machines and fridges) to Whirlpool and telecommunications to AT & T (*Financial Times*, 25

February 1992). For the multinational company, withdrawal may relate to a decision to withdraw from particular country markets, as Rover was forced to do in its long period of retrenchment in the car industry, or to withdraw from manufacturing in a particular country, as Volkswagen was forced to do in the United States.

*Consolidation.* As a strategy, consolidation implies internal reorganization and rationalization as opposed to the external orientation of a strategy of withdrawal from particular products or markets discussed above. British Airways consolidation strategy in the 1990s has focused on quality improvement, better asset utilization (each aircraft flying longer passenger miles) and improvements in efficiency such as higher labour productivity through changes in working practices. In other international firms consolidation strategies have resulted in significant managerial and organization changes and in companies like IBM this has been accompanied by redesigning or re-engineering many of the business systems and functional departments (Lloyd and Phillips, 1994).

*Market penetration.* This occurs where a company concentrates on expanding its market share in existing product markets. The discussion of Porter's five forces model suggested that this strategy is likely to be easier in expanding markets rather than mature or static markets where the struggle for increased market penetration can become intense. Ability to increase market share in declining industries may depend on the rate at which other firms leave a particular industry (Johnson and Scholes, 1993, p.226).

*Market development.* Market development, in contrast to market penetration, is where the firm's strategy concentrates on expanding into new markets and new market segments. In terms of the different development directions, it is this option that clearly embodies a firm's internationalization strategy and can take a range of forms, from exporting to foreign direct investment.

*Product development* involves a strategy of introducing new or improved products. In certain industries such as consumer electronics or pharmaceuticals this type of innovation is the key to competitive advantage.

*Vertical integration.* A strategy of backward vertical integration involves the expansion of the firm's scope upstream into the value-creating activities of its previously external suppliers; an example might be the case of a motor car manufacturer that acquires one of its electrical component suppliers. Forward vertical integration expands the firm's scope towards its customers by, for example, taking over distributors and retailers. We refer to a firm as being vertically integrated when it is present in most of the stages of production from the supply of raw materials to retailing. For example, Laura Ashley Plc, the clothing and fabrics multinational, was involved in fabric and clothing design, manufacture and retailing until the early 1990s. The benefits of vertical integration include co-ordination, control and planning advantages, and internalization of the profit margin held by the supplier or distributor. Disadvantages include the probability that certain activities will fail to achieve economies of scale and could be performed more efficiently externally. It may result in inflexibility and a failure to be responsive to changing markets and competitive conditions. Whatever the advantages of co-ordination and control, Laura Ashley found it increasingly difficult to reconcile its increasingly worldwide retailing activities with the extent of its vertical integration. Like many firms in the 1990s it has been forced to become less vertically integrated and to concentrate on certain core activities, increasingly outsourcing the manufacture of clothing.

*Diversification* occurs where the firm expands beyond its present product markets to both new products and new markets. Related diversification occurs where there is some linkage to existing activities, such as similar technology or marketing knowledge. Unrelated or conglomerate diversification occurs where there is no linkage at all to present activities. Companies like Lonrho or Hanson (often termed 'conglomerates') are groups of apparently unrelated businesses. Many international firms grew by acquisition and diversification in the 1970s and 1980s but have been forced by the difficult trading conditions of the 1990s to become less diversified and dispose of these acquisitions. Kodak, for example, diversified into pharmaceuticals in the 1980s with the purchase of Sterling-Winthrop. Management changes and refocusing on Kodak's core photographic business resulted in the disposal of Sterling-Winthrop in the early 1990s.

Figure 7.7 is an adaptation of H. Igor Ansoff's corporate strategy matrix, and classifies these various strategic options according to whether they involve existing products and markets or new ones. It would be a mistake to conceive of these different strategic directions as mutually exclusive; an international firm like Philips, in devising a new strategy, is likely to select a package of measures involving some degree of withdrawal and consolidation combined with elements of product development (CD Interactive and Digital Audio Tape) and market development (targeting the Indian and Chinese markets).

### 7.9.3 Development method

The third component of the Johnson and Scholes model indicates a variety of methods by which development direction can be achieved. A strategy of product development could be achieved in the pharmaceuticals industry through internal development (the discovery, testing and

| Product Market | Present | New |
|---|---|---|
| Present | Market penetration | Product development |
| New | Market development | Diversification |

**Figure 7.7**  Ansoff's growth vector. Source: Ansoff (1987).

commercial development of a new drug from its own laboratories), through acquisition (the takeover of a rival drugs company with its range of products), or through a policy of collaboration in the form of a strategic alliance or joint venture with another firm in the industry.

## 7.10 Summary

This chapter has explored a number of issues concerning strategic management and planning in international firms. Strategic decisions are those that involve the long-term direction and scope of the international firm. The international strategic management process is conceived as a four-stage process involving strategic analysis, both internal and external, strategy formulation and choice, strategy implementation and the monitoring, control and evaluation of strategy. A number of conceptual frameworks underpinning strategic management have been explored in greater depth; these include the five forces model of competitive structure, strategic group analysis, the value chain and the different types of strategic choice. These concepts are applicable to the domestic firm as well as the international firm. We have also attempted throughout to show where strategy processes in the international firm are different from those of the domestic firm in terms of geographical scope, environmental complexity, the number of variables that influence its behaviour and the greater range of decision-making choices.

## 7.11 Further reading

Ellis, J. and Williams, D. (1993) *Corporate Strategy and Financial Analysis*, Pitman, London.

Ellis, J. and Williams, D. (1995) *International Business Strategy*, Pitman, London.

Grant, R.M. (1991) *Contemporary Strategy Analysis*, Blackwell, Oxford.

Gray, S. (1995) Cultural perspectives on the measurement of corporate success. *European Management Journal*, Vol. 13(3), 269–75.

Hill, C.W. and Jones, G.R. (1995) *Strategic Management; An Integrated Approach*, 3rd edn, Houghton Mifflin, Boston MA.

Johnson, G. and Scholes, K. (1993) *Exploring Corporate Strategy*, Prentice Hall International, London.

Kay, J. (1993) *Foundations of Corporate Success*, Oxford University Press, Oxford.

Mills, R. and Robertson, J. (1991) *Fundamentals of Managerial Accounting and Finance*, 2nd edn, Mars, Lechlade.

Porter, M.E. (1985) *Competitive Advantage; Creating and Sustaining Superior Performance*, Free Press, New York.

Porter, M.E. (1986) Competition in global industries: a conceptual framework, in *Competition in Global Industries* (ed. Porter, M.E.), Harvard University Press, Boston MA.

Prahalad, C.K. and Hamel, G. (1990) The core competence of the corporation. *Harvard Business Review*, May–June, 79–91.

Root, F.R. and Visudtibhan, K. (1992) *International Strategic Management; Challenges and Opportunities*, Taylor & Francis, New York.

Taggart, J.H. and McDermott, M.C. (1993) *The Essence of International Business*, Prentice Hall, New York.

## 7.12 *Questions for further discussion*

1. With reference to Box 8.3 in Chapter 8, analyse Ford of Europe's strategic position in 1992 making use of SWOT analysis.

2. Chapter 7 applied strategic group analysis to the international brewing industry. Select an international industry (such as pharmaceuticals or automobiles) and research the main competitors. Determine at least four ways in which they can be divided into strategic groups. What are the uses and possible limitations of this method?

3. Table 7.1 contains financial information for IBM. Calculate the key time series and financial ratios for IBM and analyse its performance over the period covered. What are the probable main causes of the variations in performance you have observed?

4. Table 7.2 provides sales turnover and profit information for IBM in different regions of the world. Analyse the differences between profit and sales in the different areas and comment upon the possible causes of the differences observed.

**Table 7.1** IBM selected financial data (dollars in millions except per share amounts)

|  | 1995 | 1994 | 1993 | 1992 | 1991 | 1990 |
|---|---|---|---|---|---|---|
| Total revenue | 71 940 | 64 052 | 62 716 | 64 523 | 64 766 | 68 931 |
| Total cost | 41 573 | 38 768 | 38 568 | 35 069 | 32 073 | 30 715 |
| Gross profit | 30 367 | 25 284 | 24 148 | 29 454 | 32 693 | 38 216 |
| Operating expenses: selling, general and administrative | 16 766 | 15 916 | 18 282 | 19 526 | 21 375 | 20 709 |
| Research development and engineering | 6010 | 4363 | 5558 | 6522 | 6644 | 6554 |
| Restructuring charges | – | – | 8945 | 11 645 | 3735 | – |
| Total operating expenses | 22 776 | 20 279 | 32 785 | 37 693 | 31 754 | 27 263 |
| Net earnings (loss) before changes in accounting principles | 4178 | 3021 | (7987) | (6865) | (598) | 5967 |
| Per share of common stock | 7.23 | 5.02 | (14.02) | (12.03) | (1.05) | 10.42 |
| Effect of accounting changes | – | – | (114) | 1900 | (2263) | – |
| Net earnings (loss) | 4178 | 3021 | (8101) | (4965) | (2861) | 5967 |
| Per share of common stock | 7.23 | 5.02 | (14.22) | (8.70) | (5.01) | 10.42 |
| Cash dividends paid on common stock | 572 | 585 | 905 | 2765 | 2771 | 2774 |
| Per share of common stock | 1.00 | 1.00 | 1.58 | 4.84 | 4.84 | 4.84 |
| Return on stockholders' equity | 18.5% | 14.3% | – | – | – | 14.8% |
| Total current assets | 40 691 | 41 338 | 39 202 | 39 692 | 40 969 | – |

| | 1995 | 1994 | 1993 | 1992 | 1991 | 1990 |
|---|---|---|---|---|---|---|
| Net investment in plant, rental machines and other property | 16 579 | 16 664 | 17 521 | 21 595 | 27 578 | 27 241 |
| Working capital | 9043 | 12 112 | 6052 | 2955 | 7018 | 13 313 |
| Total assets | 80 292 | 81 091 | 81 113 | 86 705 | 92 473 | 87 568 |
| Total current liabilities | 31 648 | 29 226 | 33 150 | 36 737 | 33 951 | – |
| Long term debt | 10 060 | 12 548 | 15 245 | 12 853 | 13 231 | – |
| Total debt | 21 629 | 22 118 | 27 342 | 29 320 | 26 947 | 19 545 |
| Stockholders equity | 22 423 | 23 413 | 19 738 | 27 624 | 36 679 | 42 553 |
| Second quarter stock price ($) high | 99.38 | 65.00 | 54.38 | 98.63 | 114.75 | – |
| Second quarter stock price ($) low | 82.25 | 51.38 | 47.13 | 81.63 | 96.63 | – |

*Source: IBM annual reports and accounts.*

**Table 7.2** IBM geographic analysis (dollars in millions)

|  | 1995 | 1994 | 1993 | 1992 |
|---|---|---|---|---|
| **United States** | | | | |
| Revenue – customers | 26 789 | 24 118 | 25 703 | 24 633 |
| Inter-area transfers | **10 553** | **6336** | **7297** | **7524** |
| Total | 37 342 | 30 454 | 33 000 | 32 157 |
| Net earnings (loss) | 599 | 969 | (5566) | 5545 |
| Assets at 31 December | 38 584 | 37 156 | 38 333 | 42 109 |
| **Europe/Middle East/Africa** | | | | |
| Revenue – customers | 25 238 | 23 034 | 21 779 | 24 971 |
| Inter-area transfers | **2530** | **1787** | **1071** | **1154** |
| Total | 27 768 | 24 821 | 22 850 | 26 125 |
| Net earnings (loss) | 2271 | 1086 | (1695) | (1728) |
| Assets at 31 December | 24 066 | 25 816 | 24 566 | 26 770 |
| **Asia/Pacific** | | | | |
| Revenue – customers | 13 892 | 11 365 | 10 020 | 9672 |
| Inter-area transfers | **2698** | **1876** | **1452** | **1875** |
| Total | 16 590 | 13 241 | 11 472 | 11 547 |
| Net earnings (loss) | 1098 | 567 | (443) | 126 |
| Assets at 31 December | 12 789 | 12 619 | 12 778 | 12 837 |
| **Americas** | | | | |
| Revenue – customers | 6021 | 5535 | 5214 | 5247 |
| Inter-area transfers | **5333** | **4257** | **3458** | **3452** |
| Total | 11 354 | 9792 | 8672 | 8699 |
| Net earnings (loss) | 324 | 498 | (251) | 157 |
| Assets at 31 December | 7530 | 7783 | 7359 | 6990 |
| **Eliminations** | | | | |
| Revenue | (21 114) | (14 256) | (13278) | (14 005) |
| Net (loss) earnings | (114) | (99) | (32) | 125 |
| Assets | (2677) | (2283) | (1923) | (2001) |
| **Consolidated** | | | | |
| Revenue | 71 940 | 64 052 | 62 716 | 64 523 |
| Net earnings (loss) | 4178 | 3021 | (7987) | (6865) |
| Assets at 31 December | 80 292 | 81 091 | 81 113 | 86 705 |

*Source: IBM annual reports and accounts.*

## Appendix A: *International performance analysis*

Assessment of the performance and effects of multinational corporations can be considered from two perspectives: from the point of view of the macro economy and from that of the micro economy. Indicators such as investment flows, balance of payments data and employment statistics allow us to evaluate the social and economic impact that MNCs make on the macroeconomy of a country but a wider cost/benefit analysis is problematic and it is debatable whether such indicators are an adequate guide for host government policies and strategies. This is particularly important in the case of multinational corporations that operate within the sphere of many countries with different accounting conventions and rules. This issue is extensively dealt with in Bailey *et al* (1994), where the specific case of Glaxo is considered and a variety of performance indicators are calculated. At the microeconomic level we need to consider indicators and types of analyses that allow the monitoring of a company's performance through time and which enable some comparison with other companies. This is the primary issue here.

Published financial data including company annual reports and accounts provide important information for analysing the performance of an MNC and have particular relevance for a student's international corporate project. It is beyond the scope of this book to attempt a full treatment of international accounting and ratio analysis. Instead we seek to identify some of the most important and easily available statistics that a student could use to make an initial evaluation of financial and market performance. Performance analysis needs to be approached with caution for a purely domestic company; this caution should be all the greater for an international company operating worldwide. A recent paper by Sidney Gray concluded:

> Performance measures related to profits are not reliable indicators of the comparative success of large companies in an international context. Such measures are strongly influenced by national cultural differences and can only be interpreted within their own cultural and business context . . . Given the variety of corporate objectives and priorities across countries it would seem desirable to adopt a more holistic approach to the measurement of corporate success, incorporating both financial and non-financial indicators. (Gray, 1995, p.274.)

One very important factor involves differences in international accounting conventions, despite the efforts of bodies such as the International Accounting Standards Committee (IASC) to achieve greater harmonization. The layout of the accounts and actual terminology used, for example 'profits' and 'net earnings', vary considerably internationally. The use of transfer pricing by the international firm may result in significant distortions. Transfer prices are the internal prices used in intra-firm trade: they are the internal prices at which components and finished products are transferred between the headquarters of an organization and subsidiaries, and from one subsidiary to another (c.f. Chapter 2). The manipulation of transfer prices can misstate both the overall profits of the MNC and the amounts of profits made in different countries thereby affecting the MNC's worldwide taxation liability. For example artificially high costs and hence prices on goods outbound from a particular country subsidiary will transfer profit and cash flow to that subsidiary.

In addition to the ethical implications, this could make inter-firm comparison more difficult. It is possible that the worst abuses of transfer pricing may have disappeared, however, partly for external reasons. In order to enjoy good host–government relations MNCs have become increasingly anxious to avoid undue scrutiny and well-publicized action by government revenue authorities. For internal control purposes, undue manipulation of transfer prices makes budgetary and financial control procedures more difficult; the setting and monitoring of financial targets for different companies in the group may become impossible. We need to consider three approaches to international performance evaluation:

- Historical (time series) analysis of the company itself. This is perhaps the most useful approach in a performance analysis constrained by time and resources. Calculation of percentage changes and ratios in an MNC's own accounts minimizes the difficulties caused by different international accounting conventions. Time series analysis over, say, five to seven years enables significant trends to be identified and evaluated and may be linked to the internal resource analysis of the company. It is still the case that the company may decide to change its accounting conventions or the end of its financial year, making simple year-by-year analysis more difficult.

- Comparisons of performance with other MNCs in the same industry or sector, for example profitability and growth comparisons, give an important indication of the performance of a corporation in relation to similar companies. Such comparisons, whilst useful, should be approached with care. In the world automobile industry a comparison of Toyota, Volkswagen, Fiat and General Motors would involve differences between Japanese, European and American accounting conventions in such matters as profits and depreciation and would be distorted by differences in product ranges and in the geographic spread of the firms concerned. Given the degree of diversification of many MNCs, it may be very difficult to make a like-for-like comparison between two or more MNCs, except in the crudest terms.

- Comparison of MNC performance with industry benchmarks. For example in the United Kingdom it is frequently suggested that a return of 18–20 per cent on capital employed represents an average to good return, and 33 per cent is seen as a benchmark threshold for long-term liquidity. Below 33 per cent we may refer to a company as being low geared, significantly above that, for example at 80 per cent, we may refer to the company as moderately to highly geared. Profits and rate of return benchmarks may be strongly influenced by the stage of the business cycle and by industry risk. We would expect rates of return to be lower in recession years and in relatively safe sectors like public utilities than in boom years and in higher risk sectors such as biotechnology.

International differences in corporate finance and culture may have a significant impact on profit and long-term liquidity benchmarks. Whereas British and American companies make considerable use of capital markets and equity finance, Japanese and continental European companies have traditionally made much more use of long-term borrowing (debenture or bond) finance and bank finance. One consequence is that gearing benchmarks tend to be higher for a Japanese or German MNC than an American one. In terms of business culture there is more pressure on British and American companies to maximize short-run profit performance and dividends whereas continental European companies may run on lower profit margins as a result of long-term investment priorities and conservative financial policies in relation to, for example, depreciation. Gray (1995) summarized a number of research studies on the degree of 'optimism' or 'conservatism' in accounting policies in different countries and found that the profits declared by United States' and United Kingdom companies are prepared on a much more optimistic basis and have a more short-term orientation than those of German or Japanese companies.

Given these various qualifications, Box 7.1 identifies four areas where the student of international business can do some useful work on an MNC's annual reports and accounts:

- *Product/market/country scope.* An important but easily overlooked initial stage of analysis is to examine the horizontal and geographic scope of the MNC under scrutiny. What are its main products and areas of activity? How diversified is it? What are its strengths and weaknesses in terms of country coverage? Simple percentage comparisons of what the main products and country markets are in relation to both the proportion of sales and profits can sometimes be very revealing.

- *Growth performance.* It is very useful to construct short time series of the percentage per annum behaviour of the firm's sales turnover and profits, both overall and for particular business headings if they are available. A company whose turnover is growing at 30 per cent per annum or more is doing very well in growth terms but such growth may bring its own problems; how is the growth being financed, and is the management team being expanded to manage the growing organization? Growth and market share information for specific products may be helpful in drawing inferences about product life-cycle stages. Changes in resources such as physical assets and employment may be useful clues in identifying the directions of strategic change in the organization.

- *Profitability.* Box 7.1 identifies two important performance measures that can usually be calculated from the information in the annual accounts: profitability measured as a percentage of the equivalent year's sales turnover, and return on capital employed. In the United Kingdom it is usual to take profit before interest and taxation as the profit measure for these calculations. Some limited comparison with industry profitability benchmarks may be possible. However profitability trends for the specific company are frequently interesting; for example, is the 'return on capital employed' (ROCE) stable, rising, or falling over time.

- *Liquidity.* The current ratio is calculated by dividing current assets (stocks and debtors) by current liabilities (creditors and bank overdraft); it is a measure of the company's ability to meet its short-run (less than one year) financial obligations. As has been pointed out by Mills and Robertson (1991, pp.86–7), a standard rule of thumb for many years was that current assets should be double current liabilities; in other words the current ratio should have a value of 2.0. This not only ignored significant differences between sectors such as retailing and, say, railway equipment manufacture but also implied that a higher current ratio value was better than a lower one. A high current ratio may indicate idle resources, however, such as too much cash tied up in inventories.

Longer-term liquidity and financial risk are measured by the company's gearing or gearing ratio; the relationship between the company's longer term debts and total assets or shareholders' funds. There are many ways the gearing ratio can be calculated; one is the simple debt/equity ratio, another is long-term debt/total shareholder funds. One advantage of corporate debt finance is that the interest payments on it are charged before pre-tax profits whereas the dividend payments on equity finance are made out of post-tax profits. Multinational companies like Hanson PLC have been very astute in using financial structure to reduce corporate tax liabilities. Too high a gearing ratio (subject to the earlier international comparison caveat) may, however, indicate financial risk; interest payments on debt still need to be made in a period of declining profitability, even though the company may be making losses.

**Box 7.1** Multinational performance analysis

1. Product/market/country scope

2. Growth performance (percentage per annum)

   A. Turnover

   B. Profits

   C. Capital assets

   D. Employment

3. Profitability

   A. Return on capital employed: $\dfrac{\text{profits}}{\text{capital employed}}$ %

   B. Profitability: $\dfrac{\text{profits}}{\text{turnover}}$ %

4. Liquidity

   A. Short run: $\dfrac{\text{current assets}}{\text{current liabilities}}$

   current ratio

   B. Long run: $\dfrac{\text{long term debt}}{\text{shareholders' funds}}$

   gearing

# 8

# *International business strategy*

## *8.1 Introduction*

International business literature has become less interested in the reasons why internationalization occurred in the first place and more concerned with the strategic analysis of the established multinational corporation operating in a number of countries. Bruce Kogut for example argued:

> The fundamental change in thinking about global competition in the 1980s has been the shift in interest over the decision to invest overseas to the strategic value of operating assets in multiple countries. (Kogut, 1989, p.386.)

This chapter is concerned with the analysis of strategies of multinational corporations that operate assets in several countries. The previous chapter has suggested that the concept of strategy in international business can be interpreted in various ways at different levels of decision making: the overall strategic posture or positioning of the multinational corporation, the MNC's developmental strategies, its market entry strategies and its use of different strategic methods such as international acquisitions and strategic alliances. This chapter is concerned with the first of these levels in exploring international business strategy: the MNC's overall strategic posture. Other dimensions of the strategies of international firms will be considered in Chapter 9.

In the literature of the 1980s and 1990s, the fundamental international strategic choice was the extent to which the MNC's posture was one of global integration and standardization, or one of differentiation and responsiveness to national and local differences. Kobrin (1991) and others have pointed out that the origins of this observed tension in the decision making of the international firm go back at least as far as John Fayerweather in 1969 who contrasted pressures for unification (implying uniformity and standardization) with the fragmentation influences of different national environments. Other writers, notably Martinez and Jarillo (1989) and Bartlett and Ghoshal (1989), have argued that this fundamental tension may be transcended by the adoption of more complex global or 'transnational' strategies, that are multidimensional and seek to achieve both global efficiency and local responsiveness. The emergence of such transnational strategies is a relatively recent phenomenon and is itself the subject of some controversy.

The chapter commences with Michael Porter's (1985) analysis of generic strategy and competitive advantage and examines his (1986) global/multidomestic industry framework. Factors promoting or retarding the globalization of international business are then discussed, as well as some of the empirical evidence on global integration. The chapter goes on to examine the impact of these forces on international generic strategy, contrasting the work of Leontiades (1985), Porter (1986), and Prahalad and Doz (1987).

Different international strategies have important implications for the location of economic activities, the need to co-ordinate international subsidiaries and the extent of MNC centralization/decentralization. These issues are examined in the context of Peter Dicken's (1992) work which adds an important economic geography element to the analysis. The chapter concludes with consideration of the concept of transnational strategy.

## 8.2 Generic strategy and competitive advantage

Michael Porter holds that firms, whether operating in national or international markets, face a key choice of strategic posture in relation to 'generic strategy' which he explains as follows:

> The notion underlying the concept of generic strategies is that competitive advantage is at the heart of any strategy, and achieving competitive advantage requires a firm to make a choice – if a firm is to attain competitive advantage, it must make a choice about the type of competitive advantage it seeks to attain and the scope within which it will attain it. (Porter, 1985, p.12.)

The basic generic strategy choice is illustrated in Figure 8.1, and involves competing either on the basis of low cost/price or through differentiation, in other words through factors that emphasize the distinctiveness of the individual company's product or service. Porter argues that the firm's position within its industry is determined by its competitive advantage and its competitive scope. The latter refers to the breadth of the firm's target market. This varies between a broad scope (a mass market) or narrow scope (targeting a specific market segment or market niche). The combination of competitive advantage and competitive scope produces a two-by-two strategy choice matrix as illustrated.

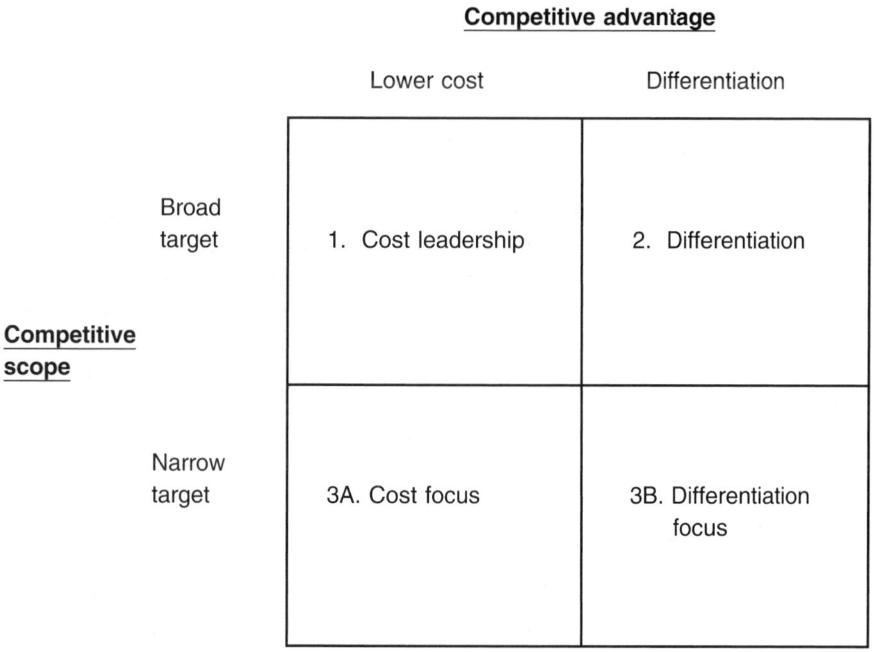

**Competitive advantage**

|  | Lower cost | Differentiation |
|---|---|---|
| **Broad target** | 1.  Cost leadership | 2.  Differentiation |
| **Narrow target** | 3A. Cost focus | 3B. Differentiation focus |

**Competitive scope**

**Figure 8.1**  Three generic strategies. Source: Porter.

## 8.3 Global industries and multidomestic industries

In analysing international generic strategy, the extent of choice facing the international firm is significantly enhanced because of differences in the competitive scope of the industry in which the firm is operating. Porter argues:

> The pattern of international competition differs markedly from industry to industry. Industries vary along a spectrum from multidomestic to global in their competitive scope. (Porter, 1986, p.17.)

In multidomestic industries the international firm operates in what is effectively a series of separate national markets segregated by tariffs, trade barriers, differences of culture, and buyer behaviour; hence the term 'multidomestic'. Competitive strategy emphasizes the advantages of what Doz (1986) terms national responsiveness: differentiating and adapting the product to respond to country differences. This is a country-centred strategy. Hout *et al.* argue:

> Typically these (multidomestic) businesses have products that differ greatly among country markets and have high transportation costs, or their industries lack sufficient scale economies to yield the global competitors a significant competitive edge. (Hout, Porter and Rudden, 1982, p.99.)

Examples of multidomestic industries traditionally include consumer packaged goods (for example washing powder), retailing, consumer finance and insurance.

In global industries, by contrast, the firm needs to co-ordinate or integrate its activities on a worldwide basis. The firm will seek to achieve competitive advantage through integrated international operations whether based on costs as a result of international economies of scale, or based on differentiation, for example by creating a global brand. Examples of such global industries include commercial aircraft, colour TV sets, automobiles and digital watches. Box 8.1 contrasts multi-domestic and global industries in terms of their competitive characteristics and strategies.

Both Doz (1986) and Leontiades (1985) emphasize that multidomestic or nationally responsive strategy tended to be typical of multinational corporations until the 1960s. Figure 8.2, adapted from Leontiades, indicates that 'national' strategies are most appropriate in conditions of high national barriers and small national market size (as for example in the extreme case of the economic nationalism of the 1930s) whereas global strategies are appropriate in conditions of low national barriers and large national market size. Michael Porter similarly puts the issue in a developmental context, arguing that the first global competitors, firms such as Gillette, Singer, Ford, Otis, and National Cash Register, appeared in the 1890s and early 1900s, but:

> The burst of globalization soon slowed . . . Most of the few industries that were global moved increasingly towards a multidomestic pattern. Multinationals remained, but between the 1920s and 1950, many evolved toward becoming federations of autonomous subsidiaries. The principal reason was a strong wave of nationalism and resulting high-tariff barriers, partly caused by the world economic crisis and world wars. (Porter, 1986, p.43.)

Box 8.1

| Multidomestic industries | Global industries |
|---|---|
| Competitive characteristics: | Competitive characteristics: |
| • Competition in each country is essentially independent of competition in other countries. | • An industry in which a firm's competitive position in one country is significantly affected by its position in other countries and vice versa. |
| • The international industry is essentially a collection of national domestic industries. | • The industry is not merely a collection of domestic industries but a series of *linked* industries in which rivals compete worldwide. |
| Strategy: | Strategy: |
| • The firm should manage its international activities as a portfolio. | • The firm must integrate its activities on a worldwide basis to capture linkages between countries. |
| • National strategies should enjoy a high degree of autonomy. | • The global competitor must view its international activities as an overall system but must still maintain some country perspective. |
| • Country-centred strategy determined by competitive conditions in each country. | |
| • International strategy collapses to a series of domestic strategies. | |

*Source: Dicken (1992), p.143.*

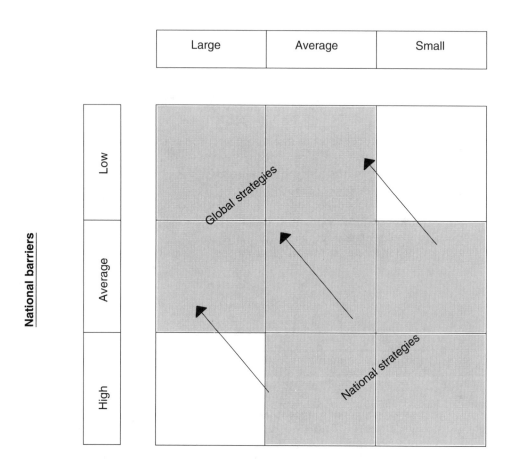

Note: world countries classified by size of national market and national barriers in a given industry.

**Figure 8.2** Conceptual view of the distribution of global and national competitive strategies in an industry. Source: adapted from Leontiades (1985), p.58.

## 8.4 Reasons for globalization

There is a strong theme running through the writings cited above taking the view that multidomestic strategy represented a type of dominant paradigm in international business strategy until roughly the late 1950s. Since then, and with accelerating pace, globalization has become increasingly important. A number of reasons have been suggested for the growth of globalization forces since the mid-1960s.

- Worldwide convergence (homogenization) of consumer tastes. This was identified as a key feature of globalization by Theodore Levitt in his famous 1983 Harvard Business Review article. To some extent such changes in consumer behaviour were supply-led; product innovation and technology effectively created global markets for consumer electrical goods such as the Sony Walkman.

- Creation of global brands such as Marlboro, Coca Cola, and Levi 501, reinforced the convergence of consumer tastes, erected product differentiation barriers to entry, and permitted the achievement of major advertising and marketing economies.

- Global standardization and simplification of products.

- Manufacturing economies of scale. The production of standard products for world markets permitted significant manufacturing economies of scale which were not available to the national producer.

- Achievement of cost reductions. The scale advantages mentioned above permitted major cost reductions which could in turn achieve important price advantages for the global competitor.

- Facilitating conditions, such as the revolutions in transport, tele-communications and information technology, 'world shrinking' technologies, radically reducing the time and cost of communication and travel between the geographically distant subsidiaries of a multinational company. A further set of facilitating conditions are those relating to the reduction and removal of international trade barriers through the successive rounds of the General Agreement on Tariffs and Trade (GATT).

- Technological intensity. The increasing pace of innovation and escalating research and development costs meant that, in industries like aircraft production, the supply of standard products to world markets permitted the spreading of these types of initial fixed costs across greater volumes, for example by Boeing and the European Airbus Consortium.

- Strategic response to global competitors. This occurs when a company responds to global competitors by globalizing itself. It fits with the observed tendency for imitative behaviour under conditions of oligopoly, including international oligopoly; the international car industry provides a good example here (see below).

The achievement of multiple competitive advantages is implicit in many of the above factors. In contrast with Michael Porter's analysis, Theodore Levitt (1983) cautioned:

High quality and low costs are not opposing postures . . . If a company forces costs and prices down, and pushes quality and reliability up – while maintaining reasonable concern for suitability – customers will prefer its world standardized products.

A complementary analysis of globalization factors is provided by Yip *et al.* (1988) who identify a number of external 'drivers of globalization', (see Figure 8.3), classifying them into competitive, economic, market and environmental factors. The international automobile industry and the pressures to develop a 'world car' concept are used by Yip *et al.* to exemplify these drivers of globalization. In relation to market factors, globalization forces include similar demand trends across markets (safety, reliability and fuel efficiency), shorter product life cycles interacting with rising product development costs to dictate worldwide spreading of development expenditure, marketing economies as a result of transferable brands and advertising. In relation to environmental factors for the car industry, converging government regulations on safety and emissions and rapid technological change (new production methods, materials, robots) are important globalization forces (Yip *et al.*, 1988, pp.102–3).

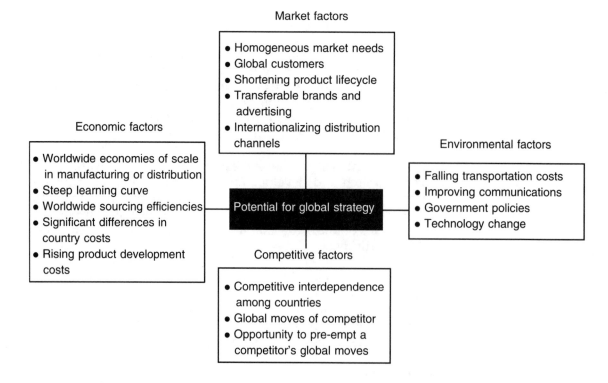

**Figure 8.3** External drivers of industry potential for globalization. Source: Yip, Loewe and Yoshino (1988), pp.37–48.

## 8.5 *Critique of the globalization thesis*

There is a significant body of literature, including Susan Douglas and Yoram Wind's (1987) riposte to Theodore Levitt, which cautions that the globalization thesis has been overstated.

- Few industries or indeed corporations are truly global; only a relatively small group of companies have the size and resource base to become 'true' global competitors.

- The cost of building 'global brands' is high (Richard Lynch 1994, p.58). Lynch estimated it would require an advertising and promotions budget of at least US $60 million for three years to build a successful European or global brand. This implies sales of at least US $600 million per year in order to finance this level of advertising expenditure.

- Customer needs differ. Whilst global standardization is possible for some products, diverse customer needs often exist which are more successfully met by a nationally responsive strategy.

- Segmentation of markets indicate that consumer behaviour and tastes are becoming more discriminating rather than less (although a strategy of global segmentation rather than standardization could address this issue).

- There are significant country differences in marketing and distribution channels.

- Flexible manufacturing systems and economies of scope (economies resulting from the linkage of complementary products and processes as in the chemicals industry) may reverse the cost advantages of world-scale plants. Evidence on this point is contested (see Kobrin, section 8.6 below). Theodore Levitt, for example, whilst acknowledging the importance of such developments as computer assisted design and manufacturing (CAD/CAM) argues: 'There is no conceivable way in which flexible factory automation can achieve the scale economies of a modernized plant dedicated to the mass production of standardized lines' (Levitt, 1983).

- The continuing importance of government regulations and activities in creating national or regional markets rather than global markets, as reflected in the advent of the Single European Market in January 1993, the North American Free Trade Area, and the ASEAN group of countries.

Chakravarthy and Perlmutter (1985, pp.30–2) provide a useful overview of the twin processes of globalization and adaptation in terms of two forces driving international strategy. They term these forces economic and political imperatives. The economic imperative involves the various globalization pressures discussed above, such as efficiency and scale. The political imperative involves counterpressures towards national responsiveness arising from the role of home and host governments as important external stakeholders:

> . . . both have begun to regulate MNC activities with increasing sophistication . . . in coping with powerful external stakeholders such as the host government, the MNC requires strategies that are tailored to each national context. (Chakravarthy and Perlmutter, 1985, p.32.)

## 8.6 *The empirical measurement of global integration*

Stephen Kobrin (1991) sought to measure the extent and determinants of global integration empirically. The research sought to operationalize integration as the proportion of intra-firm flows of resources. Using this criterion, he calculated an index of integration for 56 US manufacturing industries with significant international involvement, for which data was available in 1982.

In 10 industries intra-firm sales accounted for 25 per cent or more of international sales; these included motor vehicles (44 per cent), communications equipment, electronic components including semiconductors (39 per cent), photographic equipment, scientific instruments (29 per cent) and industrial chemicals (26 per cent). The list, Kobrin suggested, was consistent with an intuitive case-based classification of the group of most globally integrated industries.

At the other extreme were 14 least-integrated industries where the index value of intra-firm trading was less than 10 per cent. These included paper boxes, leather products, ferrous metals and forgings, food products including dairy products, beverages and non-electrical machinery. As Kobrin pointed out:

> . . . the least integrated industries (i.e. those in which the index is lowest) . . . appear to be those one would expect to be nationally responsive. (Kobrin, 1991, p.21.)

Given that integration appeared to be increasing rapidly, one limitation of the study identified by Kobrin himself was that 1982 represented the last date for which reasonably complete data existed; his partial updating to 1986 found some 'dramatic' increases in integration among the already most globally integrated industries. One further limitation of this and many other MNC studies was the exclusive concentration on manufacturing industries and firms. Contrasts to include non-manufacturing, service sector strategy would be interesting.

Kobrin's other significant finding concerned the causes or determinants of globalization. The main variables he tested were technological intensity, manufacturing economies of scale and advertising intensity. He found that technological intensity was the most important structural determinant of globalization whilst manufacturing economies of scale appeared to have been 'overstated' as a determinant of global integration. Realization of the minimum efficient scale at the level of the national economy and possible scale reductions due to flexible manufacturing appeared to be important in reducing the significance of economies of scale as a determinant of globalization. (On this point see the questions for discussion at the end of the chapter and Box 8.2.)

Both the cost and the pace of technological change appeared to be relevant to technology as a primary determinant of globalization. Kobrin concluded:

> At some point it becomes impossible for even the dominant firm in the dominant market to remain in the industry on a uninational basis. Companies must integrate transnationally to support the level of R & D expenditures and to obtain mastery of the complex technology needed to compete. (Kobrin, 1991, p.29.)

## 8.7 International generic strategy

The previous sections have explored aspects of the tension between the forces of globalization and responsiveness, as well as the measurement of global integration. In the light of this discussion, we return to the issue of generic strategy choice in international business. This section examines three models of generic strategy choice: those of Michael Porter (1986), James Leontiades (1985) and C.K. Prahalad and Yves Doz (1987).

### 8.7.1 Michael Porter's model

Michael Porter's (1986) international strategy choice model, illustrated in Figure 8.4, brings together his analysis of competitive advantage based on low costs or differentiation with the concept of geographic scope and the extent to which the strategic posture is global or country centred. The alternative choices are outlined below:

*Global strategies*

- Global cost leadership. This is the broad scope strategy that seeks to obtain competitive advantage by cost reductions achieved through standardization and worldwide economies of scale, for example colour TV production.

- Global differentiation. This is still a broad scope strategy but one that seeks to achieve advantage through product differentiation, for example through the creation of global brands such as IBM.

- Global segmentation. This, by contrast, is where an international firm focuses on a segment but serves that segment worldwide. Cray in supercomputers and Porsche's luxury sports car segment are examples of this strategy.

*Country-centred strategies*

- Protected markets. This, again, is a broad scope strategy. The MNC actively seeks out havens from global competition such as India, Mexico and Argentina, where government protectionist policies such as local content requirements and tariff barriers have in the past protected international firms already operating there.

- National responsiveness. This is the narrow scope strategy at a polar extreme from global differentiation. The product is differentiated and adapted from one country to another.

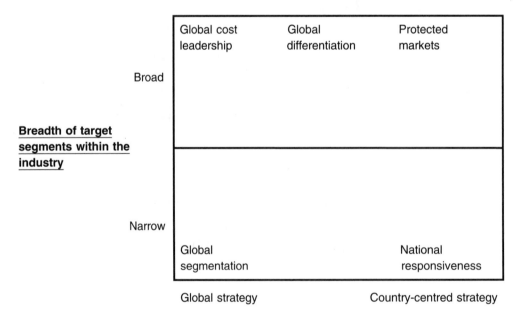

**Figure 8.4** Strategic alternatives in an international industry. Source: adapted from Porter (1986).

## 8.7.2 Leontiades (1985) international portfolio model

Leontiades' analysis shares many similarities with the Porter approach but is located instead within the Boston Consulting Group portfolio product planning choice framework. Figure 8.5 illustrates Leontiades' four 'generic international competitive strategies' distinguished by scope and market share objectives. The two national strategies, national high share and national niche, correspond respectively to Porter's protected markets and national responsiveness strategies. In distinguishing between global high share and global niche strategies Leontiades (1985) identifies a number of interesting characteristics.

*Global high share strategy*

The firms adopting this strategy are usually industry giants such as IBM, Shell, General Motors and Electrolux:

- The product marketing mix is geared to mass markets and is usually characterized by a high degree of international standardization.

- A high priority is placed on the firm's international market share position.

- Production facilities are operated as part of a regional or global network, where possible, to reduce unit costs.

- Design and research expenditures are high by industry standards but are low on a per unit basis, reflecting the ability to defray costs across markets.

- Such firms have historically tended to avoid coalitions with other partners such as joint ventures and alliances.

*Global niche strategies*

Leontiades makes the point that relatively few MNCs will have the size and resources to be broad scope global competitors; instead many may choose to focus on a niche or segment that is served world wide. The characteristics of this strategy include:

- Focus on a selected global speciality.

- Avoidance of head-on competition with global high-share competitors.

- Choice of a specialization that is relatively insensitive to price competition.

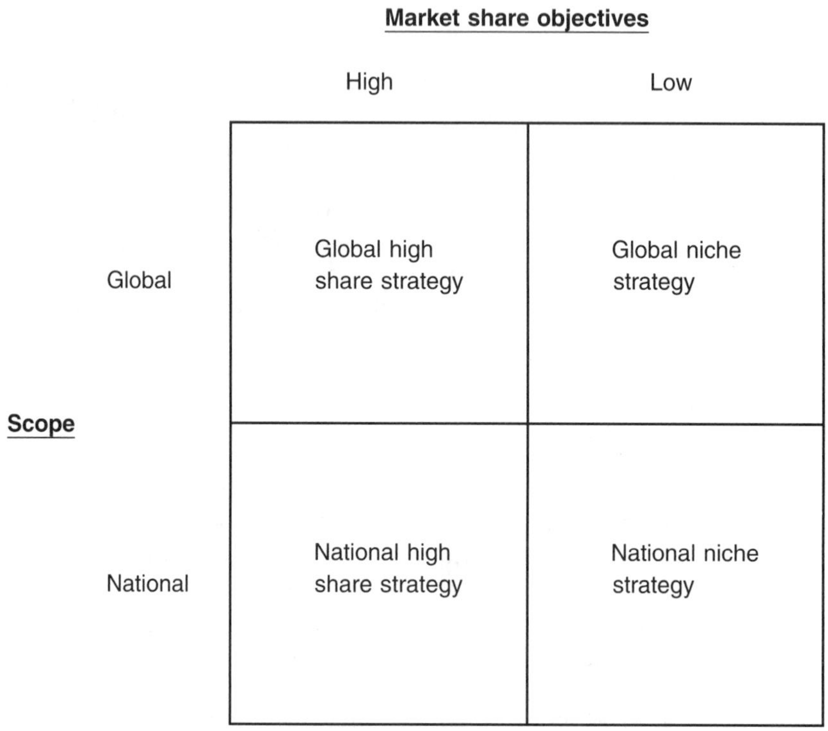

**Market share objectives**

| | High | Low |
|---|---|---|

Scope

| | Global high share strategy | Global niche strategy |
|---|---|---|
| Global | | |

| | National high share strategy | National niche strategy |
|---|---|---|
| National | | |

**Figure 8.5** Four generic international competitive strategies. Source: Leontiades (1953) p.53.

- Capitalization on complementing the products and technologies of larger competitors (such as the use of 'IBM compatible' technology in the computer equipment field).

- Extensive use of co-operation and alliances with other firms to build a global presence.

The bases of segmentation upon which such specialization may occur include geography, product type, technology, customer/user characteristics, stage of production, and product life-cycle stage.

## 8.7.3 Prahalad and Doz

C.K. Prahalad and Yves L. Doz in *The Multinational Mission: Balancing Local Demands and Global Vision* (1987) explored international business strategy choice in terms of pressures for global integration and local responsiveness which could be plotted on an integration–responsiveness grid as illustrated in Figure 8.6. They argued:

> The Integration–Responsiveness (IR) grid provides us with a way of capturing the pressures on a given business – pressures that make strategic coordination and global integration of activities critical, as well as the pressures that make being sensitive to the diverse demands of various national markets and achieving local responsiveness critical. (Prahalad and Doz, 1987, p.18.)

They suggest that the model has important implications for global competition, organizational structure and strategy; at the polar extremes an industry such as semi-conductors which is high on integration and low on responsiveness will be run by most global competitors on a worldwide basis, whereas industries such as processed foods which are high on responsiveness and low on integration will involve significant local autonomy.

Businesses such as telecommunications, computers and pharmaceuticals which are high on both dimensions will be in the central region; Prahalad and Doz suggest that such businesses may require more complex structures that can accommodate both types of pressure.

Ghoshal and Noria (1993) further explored this central area of the integration/responsiveness grid, pointing out that the two forces are not necessarily 'opposite ends of a spectrum'. As well as industries like computers with simultaneous strong demands for global integration and responsiveness, 'weak–weak' combinations could be conceived. Cement products, for example, are highly standardized, hence local responsiveness is weak, yet global integration is also weak because of the nature of economies of scale and transport costs in the cement industry (Ghoshal and Noria 1993, p.26).

## 8.8 The international value chain

The next stage in our analysis of international business strategy is to return to Michael Porter's concept of the value chain which was introduced in the previous chapter. Figure 8.7 reproduces the value chain diagram with primary value creation divided into upstream and downstream activities. Industries with an emphasis on upstream activities are those such as civil aircraft and automobile production where technology, research and development, purchasing economies and manufacturing economies are important. Industries with an emphasis on downstream activities, by contrast, include many consumer goods industries where marketing, brand image, sales and service are important to the achievement of competitive advantage.

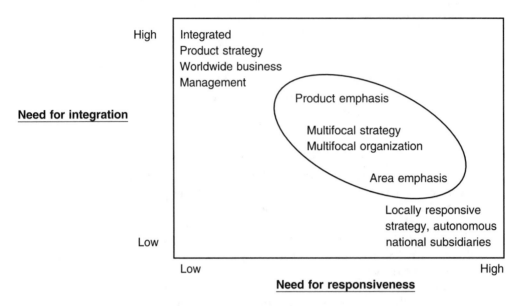

**Figure 8.6** Integration–responsiveness grid: strategic focus and organizational adaptation. Source: adapted from Prahalad and Doz (1987) p.25.

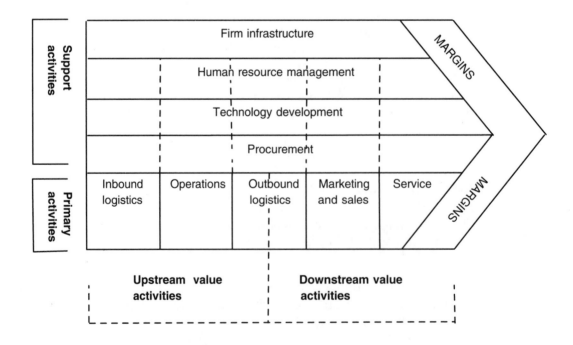

**Figure 8.7** Upstream and downstream activities in the value chain. Source: Porter (1986) p.24.

Downstream activities need to be located close to the consumer. Such industries are therefore likely to be towards the responsiveness end of the Prahalad and Doz grid (Figure 8.6). Industries with an emphasis on upstream activities are likely to be towards the integration end. Michael Porter writes:

> In industries where downstream activities or other buyer tied activities are vital to competitive advantage, there tends to be a more multidomestic pattern of international competition. In many service industries, for example, not only downstream activities but also upstream activities are tied to buyer location, and global strategies are comparatively less common. In industries where upstream and support activities such as technology development and operations are crucial to competitive advantage, global competition is more common. In global competition the location and scale of these potentially footloose activities is optimized from a world wide perspective. (Porter, 1986, p.23.)

## 8.9 Configuration and co-ordination of international activities

So far the integration/responsiveness dichotomy has been applied to the MNC as a totality. The next stage is to break the value chain into its different activities. Certain of these, for example research and development, are centralized and located in the MNC's home country, whereas others, for example after sales service, are by their nature decentralized and adapted to local differences. Kogut argues:

> This trade-off was largely focused on end-products and the problems of market access . . . It was a minor but non-trivial adjustment to alter this framework so that the global integration and country adaptation trade-off may be resolved by standardizing some links in the value added chain and differentiating other links. Not surprisingly the differentiated links frequently entail downstream activities . . . there is an important implication of this adjustment that is often not reflected in current empirical work, namely, a standardization and differentiation typology is too simple and inaccurate if focused only at the market for final goods. (Kogut, 1989, p.386.)

A vertically integrated firm may hence be able to use different strategies for different parts of the industry's value chain. This is all the more important where the MNC chooses to be in certain sections of the value chain itself but uses external relationships such as licence agreements and strategic partnerships to encompass other parts of the chain. An example is Coca Cola's integration and standardization of the global brand, although it takes a multidomestic approach to production and distribution through the use of licensing agreements.

Michael Porter (1986) develops this issue by introducing the concepts of 'configuration' and 'co-ordination' of the value chain. By 'configuration' he means 'location': where a particular value activity is located as well as in how many locations it is situated. By 'co-ordination' Porter means how the same activity performed in different countries is linked together and how it is co-ordinated with the rest of the value chain. For example, in the case of the operations function, the main configuration issues are likely to be where production facilities are located and how many locations there should be. The co-ordination issues might include the allocation of production tasks amongst the different facilities, the co-ordination of component flows between the facilities, the transfer of technology and experiential learning. The configuration of activities may be concentrated or dispersed; for example, within the same international firm, technology development might be concentrated in a single location whereas procurement and service activities might be geographically dispersed.

Figure 8.8 presents Peter Dicken's adaptation of Porter's analysis of different types of international strategy using the co-ordination/configuration framework.

- Simple global strategy would involve both geographically concentrated configuration and a high level of co-ordination. Porter argues that many Japanese firms in the 1960s and 1970s used the simplest possible global strategy, concentrating as many value activities as possible in one country, the 'home base' and tightly co-ordinating the downstream activities in the countries in which they were operating through standardization.

- Multidomestic strategy represents the other polar extreme: Porter's country-centred strategy with the value chain highly geographically dispersed, autonomous subsidiaries and low levels of co-ordination. The traditional federal structures of some European multinationals like Philips exhibit many of these characteristics.

- Export-based strategy involves geographically concentrated configuration but low levels of co-ordination; it is characteristic of the MNC at an early stage of internationalization, with most foreign markets being serviced by exports.

- Complex global strategy is what Porter termed 'high foreign investment with extensive subsidiary co-ordination'. Arguably this has characterized the more complex international strategies of the 1980s and 1990s, with MNCs operating in an increasingly 'borderless world' (Ohmae, 1990). The functions of the headquarters as well as those of operating divisions are dispersed in various international locations, as in pharmaceuticals companies such as Glaxo, where research laboratories have been dispersed worldwide. Disadvantages include duplication of effort and the additional co-ordination costs imposed by these dispersed central functions.

Peter Dicken suggests a number of possible development paths for international firms in the 1980s and 1990s through the use of the arrows in Figure 8.8 (Dicken, 1992, pp.194–5).

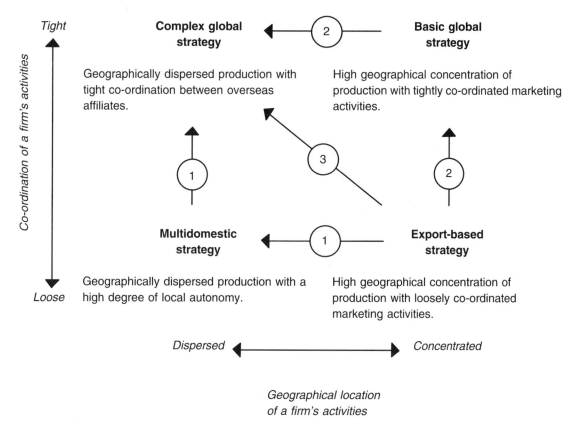

**Figure 8.8**  A typology of international competitive strategies.
Source: Dicken (1992) p.195.

## 8.10 Configuration of operations and production

Peter Dicken, in *Global Shift*, extends this analysis by focusing on the configuration of the production function (see Figure 8.9). The four quadrants of each diagram represent national boundaries; the international economy is simplified to four countries:

- Globally concentrated production. Diagram (a) corresponds to the simple global strategy of Figure 8.8, with the concentrated location of

a. Globally concentrated production

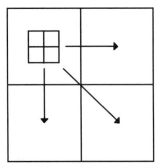

All production occurs at a single location. Products are exported to world markets.

b. Host-market production

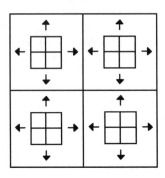

Each production unit produces a range of products and serves the national market in which it is located. No sales across national boundaries. Individual plant size limited by the size of the national market.

c. Product specialization for a global or regional market

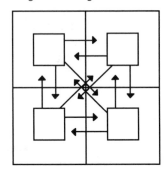

Each production unit produces only one product for sale throughout a regional market of several countries. Individual plant size very large because of scale economies offered by the large regional market.

d. Transnational vertical integration

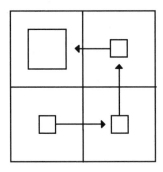

Each production unit performs a separate part of a production sequence. Units linked across national boundaries in a 'chain-like' sequence – the output of one plant is the input of the next plant.

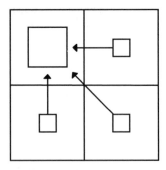

Each production unit performs a separate operation in a production process and ships its output to a final assembly plant in another country.

**Figure 8.9** Some major ways of organizing transnational production units. Source: Dicken (1992) p.202.

production in the home country, tightly co-ordinated marketing and the servicing of foreign markets through exporting.

- Host-market production. Diagram (b) portrays multidomestic organization of production in which each subsidiary is a clone or 'miniature replica' of the parent. As a result of tariff or non-tariff barriers, each subsidiary only produces and sells within the national market in which it is located.

- Global product specialization. In recent times horizontal integration has become increasingly important as a way of organizing international production. Diagram (c) portrays a situation where each plant specializes in the production of a specific product which is then sold throughout the group of countries or regional market. Arguably, in the field of white goods production, manufacturers such as Electrolux and Whirlpool are specializing in this way, with a particular plant producing a particular type of washing machine, another fridge freezers, another dish-washers, and so on. The products are then distributed by the firm's sales subsidiaries throughout the group of countries concerned. Horizontal specialization and integration of this type makes extensive economies of scale possible. Dicken suggests that the increasing importance of regional economic groupings such as the European Union after the Single European Market and the North American Free Trade Area, will make product specialization of this type increasingly important.

- Transnational vertical integration. This comes in two variants illustrated in diagram (d). In the first version there is a 'chain like' sequence in which 'materials, semi-finished products, components and finished products are transported between the geographically dispersed production units' (Dicken, 1992, p.204). The output of one unit becomes the input of another stage in the chain. In the second version each production unit specializes in a particular operation or component, then ships the component to the left-hand quadrant country for final assembly. In both versions, following final assembly, the finished product is re-exported worldwide, including the component production countries. Dicken suggests the pioneers of transnational vertical integration from the late 1960s onwards were United States multinational corporations in fields like electronics which established component export platforms of this type in East and South-East Asia and Mexico.

Hybrids of the various models can often be found; for example Ford of Europe between 1967 and 1994 organized production with a degree of horizontal specialization: Ford's plant in Genk, Belgium, specialized in Sierra production and the plant in Valencia, Spain, specialized in Fiesta production. At the same time elements of transnational vertical integration were found in Ford's 'component commonization and sourcing' policy; this meant that specific plants specialized in particular components (engines in south Wales, axles in Bordeaux) which were then transported to the car assembly plants. Against the scale advantages of this integrated system could be set co-ordination, logistics, and transport costs, as well as the potential vulnerability of the system to disruption, for example as a consequence of industrial relations problems.

One important aspect of transnational vertical and horizontal integration is the extent to which such systems of organizing production require the growth of intra-firm trading and transfers of components and finished goods compared to the earlier models. One empirical finding of relevance to Dicken's analysis is Kobrin's (1991) study cited earlier. Kobrin, following Casson (1986), broke intra-firm trade down into two components:

- 'Hub-and-spoke' configuration; that is intra-firm trade involving headquarters/subsidiary trade in either direction.

- 'Networked' configuration; that is intra-firm trade taking place between the affiliates.

He found that a majority of intra-firm trade in 1982 (61 per cent on an unweighted basis) was of the 'hub-and-spoke', subsidiary to head-quarters, type. Only five industries could be classified as 'networked' with 55 per cent or more of intra-firm trade between the subsidiaries. The industries involved were textiles, pharmaceuticals, soaps, foods and plastics (Kobrin, 1991, pp.22–3).

Finally Yves Doz, in discussing the benefits of integration, writes as follows:

> In integrating their operations, the MNCs have added several layers of competitive advantage to the internalization of intangible assets and to strength in global rivalry . . . they have increased their oligopoly power by exploiting scale and experience effects beyond the size of national markets and therefore, raised the barriers to entry to the industries in which they participate. They have also made it increasingly difficult for national firms (i.e., producing and selling only in one country) to survive in global industries . . . MNCs can, more easily than national firms, exploit differences in labour cost among countries . . . Integration thus provides MNCs with the potential to maximize their total system-wide margin between prices and costs, to exploit imperfections in labour and financial markets, and to improve bargaining power with host governments. (Doz, 1986, pp.3–4.)

## 8.11 The transnational strategy epoch

The chapter's discussion of international strategy to this point has been explicitly centred around the trade-off between integration and adaptation. In contrast to this, a number of writers have suggested that the international firm has reached a stage in its evolution in the 1990s in which the integration/adaptation trade-off has been transcended. Martinez and Jarillo in their 1989 article, for example, identify three distinct chronological phases:

- Period 1: 1920–50: 'multinational', 'multidomestic'.

- Period 2: 1950–80: 'global', 'pure global'.

- Period 3: 1980 onward: 'transnational', 'complex global'.

They list the strategic characteristics of Period 3 as:

> Decentralization of production in many places in the world, each specialized in processes and/or products, with a strong interdependence among them. Interorganizational transfer of technology and ideas. Simultaneous response to national interests and local needs, and to economic forces towards globalization. (Martinez and Jarillo, 1989, p.505.)

Bartlett and Ghoshall's work (1987 and 1989) provides the fullest elaboration of the transnational concept as a new form of international business integration which transcends the global concept. Their research was based on interviews with 236 managers in the worldwide operations of nine international firms: Procter & Gamble, Unilever and Kao in branded packaged goods, General Electric, Philips and Matsushita in consumer electronics, ITT, Ericsson and NEC in the telecommunications switching industry.

Bartlett and Ghoshal's starting point is the distinction between global, multinational and international industries and strategies. In global industries such as consumer electronics, efficiency is the key driving force, firms like Matsushita are able to produce standardized colour televisions for a global market with massive economies of scale. In multinational industries such as branded packaged goods, like soap powders, national responsiveness was found to be the key driving force. In international industries such as telecommunications switching, organizational learning, 'the ability to transfer knowledge and expertise from one part of the organization to others world wide' appeared to be the key to competitive advantage (Bartlett and Ghoshal, 1987, p.7).

Figure 8.10 summarizes the strategic positioning of the nine companies in relation to the dominant strategic requirements of the

**Dominant strategic**
**requirements of**
**industry**

**New organizational challenge**

| | Responsiveness (multinational) | Efficiency (global) | Transfer of knowledge and competencies (international) |
|---|---|---|---|
| Responsiveness (branded packaged products) | Unilever | Kao | Procter & Gamble |
| Efficiency (consumer electronics) | Philips | Matsushita | General Electric |
| Transfer of knowledge (telecommunications switching) | ITT | NEC | Ericsson |

**Dominant strategic capability of company**

**Figure 8.10** Industry requirements and company capabilities.
Source: Bartlett and Ghoshal (1989) p.21.

industry. For example, in the case of consumer electronics the dominant

strategic requirement of efficiency was best achieved by Matsushita. The research found that 90 per cent of the company's production was supplied from modern, world scale plants in Japan. The remaining 10 per cent of production was largely assembly type operations in Taiwan and Singapore. From its production base, Matsushita served its world markets with fairly standardized products through export (Bartlett and Ghoshal, 1989, p.23). In Porter's terms it was following a simple global strategy which had good strategic fit with the requirements of the industry. By contrast both Philips and General Electric had a poorer strategic fit, Philips competing with a multinational strategy whilst

General Electric's consumer electronic's group used an international strategy which exploited its parent's technological capability.

In the intensive competitive conditions of the 1980s, however, Bartlett and Ghoshal argue that such 'unidimensional' competitive advantage is not enough to maintain corporate success; strategic requirements have instead become multidimensional:

> In the emerging international environment . . . there are fewer and fewer examples of industries that are pure global, textbook multinational, or classic international. Instead, more and more businesses are being driven by simultaneous demands for global efficiency, national responsiveness, and worldwide learning. These are the characteristics of what we call a transnational industry. (Bartlett and Ghoshal, 1987, p.12.)

The simultaneous nature of this imperative characterizes transnational industry and strategy, and Bartlett and Ghoshal suggest that this is a relatively recent phenomenon. In the more popular literature on international business the same type of concept is described by Kenichi Ohmae as 'global localization' (1990, p.93) and by Arvind Phatak as 'glocalization', Phatak argues:

> . . . the parent company plays a central role in coordinating its network of globally dispersed affiliates, and in making the network operate as one integrated, collective global unit. Global companies, however, must be careful that in their zealous pursuit of an effective global strategy they do not neglect managerial initiative at lower levels in the organizational hierarchy . . . Glocalization, which means thinking globally but acting locally, includes an optimal mix of parental control where it counts, and local initiative at regional and subsidiary levels. (Phatak, 1992, p.127.)

One approach is to see a transition in the focus of international business strategy taking place over time, from multidomestic to global to transnational (Martinez and Jarillo, 1989). Critics of the Bartlett and Ghoshal thesis point out, however, that it may be dangerous to generalize from a sample of nine firms when only a handful of international firms may be at this transnational stage. An alternative approach, synthesizing earlier frameworks, is that of Hill and Jones (1995) illustrated in Figure 8.11, which emphasizes the continuing relevance of matching strategy to the environment: a transnational strategy is relevant where cost and responsiveness pressures are both strong; in other environments alternative international strategies may be more appropriate. A fuller critique of the transnational strategy model, and its organizational implications, is examined in Chapter 10.

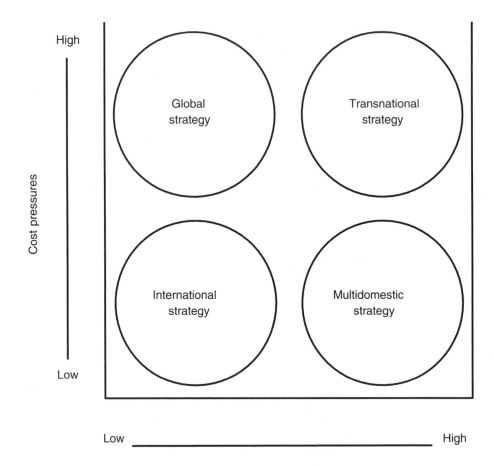

**Figure 8.11**  Four basic strategies. Source: Hill and Jones (1995) p.233.

## 8.12 *Summary*

This chapter has explored a number of the central issues in international business strategy regarding the overall strategic positioning of the international firm. Bruce Kogut raised an important question for any analysis of global strategy: 'What is really different when we move from a domestic to an international context?' (Kogut, 1989, p.383). The answer we initially provided involved the integration/adaptation framework and the extension of the choice of geographic scope in relation to international generic strategy. Later versions of the trade-off model involved the integration and standardization of some aspects of the value chain and the adaptation of others, as well as the configuration and co-ordination of activities involving concentration or dispersal choices.

In addition to a static trade-off framework between aspects of integration and adaptation, with some industries classified as global and others multidomestic, we found the international business strategy literature also dealt with the issue in terms of a dynamic dominant paradigm. In the first half of the twentieth century this dominant paradigm was that of the multidomestic/nationally responsive strategy. From approximately 1950 onwards the dominant paradigm shifted to global integration as a result of the interplay of the various forces of globalization identified in this chapter. According to certain authors, a further paradigm shift has been taking place in the 1980s and 1990s, moving towards the dominance of transnational strategy.

## 8.13 Further reading

Bartlett, C.A. and Ghoshal, S. (1989) *Managing Across Borders; The Transnational Solution*, Century Business, London.

Dicken, P. (1992) *Global Shift: The Internationalization of Economic Activity*, 2nd edn, Paul Chapman, London.

Ellis, J. and Williams, D. (1995) *International Business Strategy*, Pitman, London.

Hill, C.W. and Jones, G.R. (1995) *Strategic Management: An Integrated Approach*, 3rd edn, Houghton Mifflin, Boston MA.

Kobrin, S.J. (1991) An empirical investigation of the determinants of global integration. *Strategic Management Journal*, 12, 17–31.

Levitt, T. (1983) The globalisation of markets. *Harvard Business Review*, May–June, pp.92–102.

Martinez, J.I. and Jarillo, J.C. (1989) The evolution of research on coordination mechanisms in multinational corporations. *Journal of International Business Studies*, Fall, pp. 489–514.

Ohmae, K. (1990) *The Borderless World; Power and Strategy in the Global Marketplace*, Harper Collins, London.

Porter, M.E. (1986) Competition in global industries: a conceptual framework, in *Competition in Global Industries* (ed. Porter, M.E.) Harvard University Press, Boston MA.

Prahalad, C.K. and Doz, Y.L. (1987) *The Multinational Mission: Balancing Local Demands and Global Vision*, The Free Press, New York.

Root, F.R. and Visudtibhan, K. (eds) (1992) *International Strategic Management: Challenges and Opportunities*, Taylor & Francis, Washington DC.

Taggart, J.H. and McDermott, M.C. (1993) *The Essence of International Business*, Prentice Hall, Englewood Cliffs NJ.

Yip, G.S. (1992) *Total Global Strategy*, Prentice Hall, Englewood Cliffs NJ.

## 8.14 *Questions for further discussion*

1.  With the use of examples distinguish between multidomestic and global industries.

2.  What do we mean by 'globalization'? Why is globalization increasing?

3.  Is the globalization trend irreversible? What forces act against it?

4.  In relation to Michael Porter's international value chain, distinguish between upstream and downstream activities. Under what circumstances are global or multidomestic strategies more appropriate?

5.  With reference to Box 8.2, why have economies of scale become increasingly important as a globalization force in consumer electronics? Compare and contrast the views expressed by Bartlett and Ghoshal with the findings of Stephen Kobrin's empirical research (section 8.6).

6.  Why is advertising intensity an ambiguous measure of global integration?

7.  Read the account of Ford's 1994 reorganization (Box 8.3) and answer the following questions:

(a)  In general, what are the main international strategic and organizational issues raised in the article?

(b)  What specific globalization forces are exemplified by the reorganization?

(c)     In Porter's terms, identify the main changes proposed to the configuration and co-ordination of Ford's value-creating activities.

8.      In relation to production and operations, what are the main advantages and disadvantages of transnational vertical integration as analysed by Peter Dicken?

9.      Outline and critically evaluate Bartlett and Ghoshal's concepts of the transnational corporation and transnational strategy.

10.     With the use of conceptual frameworks discussed in this chapter, analyse the international strategy of your corporate project MNC.

---

**Box 8.2** Globalization and economies of scale in consumer electronics

The development of the transistor by the Bell Laboratories in 1947 signalled a new era in consumer electronics. The replacement of vacuum tubes by transistors greatly expanded the efficient scale for production of key components and the subsequent development of printed circuit boards made mass production feasible by reducing both the amount and the skill level of labour required to assemble radios, televisions, tape recorders, and similar equipment.

The introduction of integrated circuits in the late 1960s further reduced the number and cost of components and increased optimum manufacturing scale. The use of automated insertion machines allowed manufacturers to reduce costs and increase quality dramatically. On-line testing, materials handling, and final assembly and packaging were also automated. As a result, the efficient level of production of colour televisions rose from 50 000 sets per year in the early 1960s to 500 000 sets in the early 1980s.

Meanwhile, scale economies in research and development and in marketing were also increasing. No single market could generate the revenues needed to fund the required state-of-the-art skills in micro-mechanics, micro-optics, and electronics. Similarly, the emergence of giant retail chains was changing the rules of marketing consumer electronics products. Their bargaining power squeezed the margins available to manufacturers; at the same time they had to be supported with a heavier advertising budget since companies could no longer rely on knowledgeable store personnel to educate the consumer and communicate product benefits. Again, the effect was to raise break-even volumes. Given the new manufacturing, research and marketing economies, some industry observers estimated that a total annual volume of 2.5 million to 3 million sets was needed to remain viable as a global player in the colour TV business – at least 20 times the volume required just two decades earlier . . .

... Among the three consumer electronics companies we studied, only Matsushita built its strategy primarily on manufacturing scale economies. In 1980, over 90 per cent of the company's production, valued at $13 billion, was concentrated in specialized, highly efficient plants in Japan, although foreign sales accounted for over 40 per cent of total revenues.

Source: Bartlett, C.A. and Ghoshal, S. (1989) *Managing Across Borders: The Transnational Solution,* Century Business, London, pp.22–3.

**Box 8.3** Ford's 1994 restructuring

Ford, the world's second-largest vehicle maker, yesterday threw down the gauntlet to its rivals in the auto industry. For the first time in its history it is seeking to become a global corporation, breaking down the national and regional barriers that have blocked its drive to create common vehicles for the world market. 'This is a worldwide business that requires the broadest thinking and execution,' Mr Alex Trotman, Ford chairman and chief executive, said yesterday.

In a bold move aimed at freeing it from the shackles of its corporate history, Ford is planning to move to a single set of processes and systems throughout its product development, manufacturing, supply and sales activities. If it succeeds, Ford will set new benchmarks that will be hard for most of its competitors to match.

All the world's carmakers face the same challenge of trying to increase the efficiency of their enormous investment programmes, while at the same time producing a greater diversity of products. They must increase the speed at which they can bring products to the market while jumping into emerging markets, be it for multi-purpose vehicles, sport-utility vehicles or micro cars. They must squeeze their massive materials purchasing bills by moving to global sourcing for parts and systems.

What they can no longer afford in a world of overcapacity and shrinking margins is the luxury of duplication. It is too wasteful, for instance, to develop an Escort-sized car for Europe, and in parallel to develop a similar but yet entirely different vehicle for North America. With its deeply entrenched traditions of independent regional fiefdoms that is exactly what Ford has been doing, but now it is calling a halt.

Ford's problem – and one that it has in common with General Motors, its arch domestic rival and the world's biggest vehicle maker – is that it carries a much heavier burden from its history than its more agile Japanese rivals. The big Japanese players, Toyota, Nissan and

Honda, have only been moving into world markets in a significant way in the past 20 years. With the benefits of modern communications, their organizations have been more streamlined. Essentially the same car has been sold in all markets around the world. A Toyota Corolla is little different whether it is sold in North America, Europe or Japan. In its main features it is designed and engineered only once, even though it is assembled in four continents. By contrast, Ford of Europe and General Motors Europe have developed as fully fledged independent vehicle makers. For many years most of their products have been designed, developed and engineered solely for the European market, perhaps with some exports to the rest of the world. They have duplicated rather than complemented their parent organizations in North America.

In its corporate revolution Ford plans to create Ford Automotive Operations, which will effectively merge its European and North American operations as well as its automotive components group into a single operating unit. In place of its largely independent regional companies, Ford is reorganizing itself along global product lines through five vehicle programme centres (VPCs), four in North America and one in Europe. The European VPC, with its research and engineering centres split as now between the United Kingdom and Germany, is to become responsible for small and medium front-wheel drive cars. This will be a worldwide responsibility and will include the manufacturing plants around the world building such vehicles, whether in the United States, Mexico or Europe. It will cover the development of Fiesta, Escort and Mondeo-sized cars in Europe and in North America.

Headquartered in the US at Ford's research and engineering centre in Dearborn, near Detroit, Michigan, will be the other four vehicle programme centres:

- for large front-wheel drive cars, such as the Ford Taurus;

- for rear-wheel drive cars such as the Ford Crown Victoria, but ultimately, too, the Jaguar range, though Jaguar will maintain resources in the United Kingdom;

- for personal-use trucks, such as the Ford Windstar multi-purpose vehicle; and

- for commercial trucks. This VPC in North America, for example, would take over responsibility for the development of the highly successful Ford Transit van from Europe.

'By integrating all our automotive processes and eliminating duplication of effort, we will use our creative and technical resources most effectively,' said Mr Trotman yesterday. He claimed that Ford's new way of doing business would provide customers with a broader array of vehicles in most markets and would ensure that the group was fully competitive in quality and value against the best in the world.

At the same time the simplification of engineering, purchasing and other processes would 'substantially reduce the cost of operating the automotive business'. Ford estimated the potential cost-saving from the reorganization of at least 2–3 billion dollars a year by the end of the decade.

The group has been feeling its way for more than a decade towards ways of increasing the global punch of its organization. Its top management has long been tantalized by the holy grail of the so-called world car, and by the savings that should be achieved by developing a product once for both manufacture and sale in different continents. It tried in the late 1970s with a common programme for Ford Escorts in Europe and in North America, but the cars launched at the beginning of the 1980s ended up with little more in common than the name and the blue FORD oval badge on the bonnet.

Ford has come closer in the past few years with the Mondeo world car programme, a six billion dollar attempt to develop a largely common car to replace both the Sierra in Europe and the Ford Tempo/ Mercury Topaz in North America. This car, launched in Europe early last year and this year in North America, is the biggest roll of the dice in Ford's history in terms of the financial resources it has consumed. The six-year Mondeo programme was the most ambitious and costly programme undertaken by the United States vehicle maker.

Ford had to reform its engineering and manufacturing infrastructure in America and Europe to break down entrenched barriers between the two in order to develop in Europe a mainstream car acceptable in both markets. The Mondeo/Ford Contour/Mercury Mystique is being assembled at Ford's Genk plant in Belgium, at Kansas City in the United States, and in Mexico.

The same family of four-cylinder engines is being made at plants in Bridgend in the United Kingdom and at Cologne in Germany for Europe, and at Chihuahua in Mexico for North America. A top-of-the-range aluminium V6 engine is being made at Cleveland, Ohio, for both the United States and European-produced cars. Manual transmissions are being made in Europe at Halewood, Merseyside, in the United Kingdom, and at Cologne, while an electronically controlled, four-speed automatic gearbox is being made in the United States. After a global search, common component producers have been chosen to supply both the European and North American assembly plants.

Mondeo was the one-off programme that began to show the way forward for Ford. Now the lessons are to be institutionalized throughout its organization. Product development in North America and Europe will become fully integrated with the five-vehicle programme centres. They will have specific worldwide responsibilities and will report to one product development executive. Supporting the changes in the product development process, Ford's manufacturing, purchasing and marketing and sales operations will each become integrated worldwide. An automotive strategy office will co-ordinate strategic planning.

These are huge steps and will take several years to complete, but they are still only the first steps. Looming on the Ford agenda are the issues of how it should integrate Mazda into this new organization, its loss-making 25 per cent-owned affiliate in Japan. And how it should tackle the integration of its Latin American operations, where the group owns 49 per cent of Autolatina, with Volkswagen of Germany controlling 51 per cent. In both cases it must take into account the sensitivities of its partners, and they must wait for tomorrow. The merger of Ford Europe and North America is more than enough for today.

*Source: Kevin Done,* The Financial Times, *1994.*

# The implementation of international business strategy

## 9.1 Introduction

This chapter explores the question of strategy implementation, the methods used by MNCs to achieve their international strategy, at greater length. It begins by discussing the use of international joint ventures and strategic alliances, it briefly examines international acquisitions and mergers and concludes by discussing alternative methods of foreign market entry and development.

## 9.2 Strategic alliances and joint ventures

An important feature of the growth of international business has been the extent to which multinational corporations have developed commercial relationships intermediate between the internalization of activities within their own organizational hierarchies and arm's length, external market transactions (cf. Lorange and Roos, 1992, pp.3–4). These intermediate relationships have taken a multitude of forms and are frequently referred to as strategic alliances, joint ventures or global coalitions. Figure 9.1 seeks to distinguish between these and outright corporate acquisitions and mergers.

The degree of formalization, hierarchy and internalization increases as one goes from left to right in the figure. Formalization refers to the extent to which formal structures, legal entities and written rules are present, and hierarchy refers to the existence of a ranked administrative and managerial infrastructure. Strategic alliances are the least formalized of the collaborative links identified here; they are co-operative links between firms that are competitors in other respects. Often the alliance exists for a specific purpose (a technology agreement, for example) and may take the form of a written contract with a defined termination date. These international strategic alliances or global coalitions are defined by Porter and Fuller as '. . . long term alliances between firms that link aspects of their businesses but fall short of merger' (Porter and Fuller, 1986, p.315).

**Form of relationship**

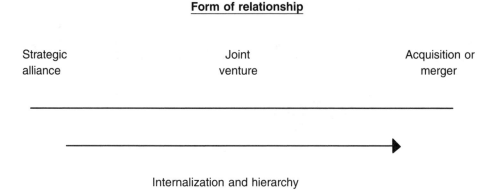

Strategic                       Joint                       Acquisition or
alliance                        venture                     merger

Internalization and hierarchy

**Figure 9.1** Acquisitions, joint ventures and alliances.

Some strategic alliances start as simple contractual technology agreements but evolve over time to include equity participation. The Honda/Rover alliance, for example, started in 1979 as a limited licence agreement for Rover to assemble a Honda model badged as the 'Triumph Acclaim'. By 1986 they were engaging in joint development and co-production (the Rover 800/Honda Legend) and in 1990 Rover and Honda (UK) exchanged 20 per cent minority shareholdings. The alliance effectively dissolved with BMW's takeover of Rover in 1994.

The traditional equity joint venture is a more formal partnership where the firms involved establish a new, separate business entity owned jointly by the two parents which retain their independent identities. These joint ventures were frequently used as a method of entering overseas markets, particularly in less developed countries such as India where national laws often required partnership with local firms. There is an equivalent requirement in China in the 1990s. Joint ventures were, until recently, a necessary mode of entry to the Japanese market owing to Western firms' ignorance of the Japanese consumer, language and business practices and the possible extent of the Japanese economy's non-tariff barriers.

Since the 1960s the globalization of international business has seen an enormous increase in the number and type of coalitions and alliances, these being more informal collaborations than traditional joint ventures. These 'new' alliances were increasingly undertaken for strategic reasons to achieve competitive advantage in terms of technology and product development, cost reduction, or product differentiation and marketing. Examples of this include Rover/Honda, Volvo/Renault and Ford/Mazda from the many instances in the world automobile industry, NEC/Honeywell/Bull in the computer industry and the strategic alliance of Philips and Matsushita of Japan for the joint development and manufacture of new electronics products such as compact discs and video-cassette recorders. Indeed, diversified multinational corporations like Philips and Siemens are increasingly involved in a multiple network of alliances corresponding to various aspects of their business operations.

Some studies have pointed to the speed at which the number of inter-firm agreements has grown since 1980. David Connell (1988) estimated that during the first half of the 1980s the number of international co-operation agreements signed each year by companies from the United States, Japan, and the European Community increased by more than five times. The empirical analysis of strategic alliance data in Chapter 2, Table 2.5, shows significant growth in the formation of strategic alliances in the period 1985–9 compared to 1980–4. Glaister and Buckley (1994) similarly found that the rate of international joint venture formation rose significantly between 1987 and 1990 compared to the earlier years of the decade.

There was a large increase in strategic partnerships across frontiers in the European Community after 1986 as businesses developed corporate strategies in preparation for the planned completion of the internal market in 1992. Christopher Lorenz pointed to the range of agreements, partial mergers and proposed full mergers in electronics and electrical engineering which involved GEC, General Electric of America, Siemens, Thomson and Plessey.

There have also been considerable partnership developments in European manufacturing sectors such as automobiles and trucks, computer software, food and packaging, and in property and financial services (*Financial Times*, 16 March 1989). Glaister and Buckley found that half of the total joint ventures formed were concentrated into four sectors: financial services, telecommunications, aerospace and other manufacturing (Glaister and Buckley, 1994, p.49).

## 9.3 Types of joint ventures and strategic alliances

It is possible to distinguish a number of types of joint venture according to the power relations between the constituent parts:

- Dominant parent. A venture in which one of the joint parents is clearly dominant in terms of attributes such as size and market share.

- Independent child. Here the joint subsidiary operates at arms length from the parents.

- Multi-parent. Here there are several parent companies. A good example of this in Europe is the multinational ownership of Airbus Industries.

Porter and Fuller (1986) employ the value chain concept to analyse different types of strategic alliance. They argue that coalitions can be formed at any point of the firm's value chain:

> Coalitions arise when performing an activity with a partner is superior to performing the activity internally on the one hand, and to reliance on arm's length transactions or (full) merger with another firm on the other. (Porter and Fuller, 1986, p.322)

They employ a simplified value chain to group coalitions into four main types:

1. Technology development.

2. Operations and logistics.

3. Marketing, sales and service.

4. Multiple activity.

Porter and Fuller identify two distinct types of coalition that involve any value activity: the X and Y types. In X-type coalitions the firms share complementary activities by dividing the industry's value activities among themselves as might be the case, for example, if one aircraft manufacturer specialized in research, development and design work on an aircraft while another carried out the manufacture. It implies that the firms involved have asymmetric strengths and weaknesses. In Y-type coalitions the firms involved co-operate in the same basic activity within the value chain, for example joint production or joint research and development, in order to achieve economies of scale or to spread risks.

International partnerships have become increasingly diverse in type. As well as formal equity-sharing joint ventures, companies have formed licensing agreements, technology agreements, co-production arrangements, component supply agreements, joint marketing arrangements, and have become involved in consortia formation, turnkey projects, contracting and subcontracting arrangements.

## 9.4 Reasons for the use of joint ventures and strategic alliances

Brooke (1986, p.103) suggests the following reasons for the formation of traditional joint ventures:

1.  To acquire market knowledge/expertise/distribution channels in an unfamiliar overseas market.

2.  Expansion with limited capital outlay. The use of a joint venture shares the costs (and risks) of international expansion; the use of multiple joint ventures may make simultaneous expansion in a number of markets possible.

3.  To improve sales prospects, particularly in terms of government contracts and the public sector.

4.  They are sometimes essential to gain access to certain markets, for example where government legislation requires local participation.

In contrast Bernard M. Wolf (1992) suggests a threefold classification of reasons for strategic alliances, based on Bruce Kogut's (1988) methodology, shown in Box 9.1. According to Wolf, 'learning' has three components; first, organizational or tacit knowledge such as knowledge of lean production methods; second, the transfer of technology relating to a specific product or process; third, geographic learning: acquisition of knowledge about a specific country or area in relation to consumer behaviour and institutional structures.

Various types of cost and risk factors are identified, many of which have time components; some collaborations reduce development time or the time involved in achieving additional capacity. Wolf's third category is termed 'Market positioning – market seeking' and includes market entry reasons, as well as competitive factors; where the collaboration has the effect of changing the nature of competition in the industry, for example the alliance creates a stronger competitor than the two or more

**Box 9.1** Motivations for strategic alliances

I.    *Learning*

   1. Organizational

   2. Hard technology

   3. Geographical

II.    *Cost minimization and risk reduction*

   1. Sourcing and production economies

   2. Development economies

   3. Research economies

   4. Marketing economies

   5. Financial economies

   6. Regulatory economies

   7. Project economies

   8. Equity economies

III. *Market positioning – market seeking*

   1. Market access

   2. Changing nature of competition

*Source: Wolf (1992), p.1.*

firms involved acting separately. Porter and Fuller similarly emphasize the importance of strategic alliances in shaping competition: '. . . coalitions can influence who a firm competes with and the basis of competition' (Porter and Fuller, 1986, p.325). The growing role of international strategic alliances can be related to the globalization factors discussed in Chapter 8. The following causes seem to be important:

- David Connell (1988, p.4) identified a range of globalization forces in the development of international collaboration: growing internationalism of world markets, decline in relative transport and communications costs, the growing similarity of patterns of consumption and the opportunity of larger markets in turn creating new cost pressures through greater economies of scale with scope for market-and-production-oriented coalitions.

- Kenichi Ohmae (1989) emphasized the importance of coalition formation for creating a corporate presence in the component parts of the Triad (North America, Western Europe, and East/South-East Asia). The achievement of a global spread has been an important motive for world airline alliances such as British Airways/Quantas and British Airways/US Air, the increasing complexity and costs of technical change making it less likely that a single company can command adequate technical skills and resources.

- The speed of the innovation process itself and the potential of global technology transfer through alliance formation.

A related technological issue is the competitive role strategic alliances may play in the struggle for industry standards, such as JVC's success in establishing VHS as the worldwide standard for video cassette recorders at the expense of Sony's Betamax standard. In the technology of digital video discs (DVD) Sony and Philips have formed an alliance to create a common format, whilst Toshiba, Time-Warner and the French group Thomson have allied around a rival format. Matsushita, despite other strategic links with Philips, decided in 1995 to opt for the Toshiba DVD format; the likelihood is that this will be a deciding factor in ensuring that this, rather than the Sony–Philips alliance, becomes the industry standard (*Financial Times*, 25 January 1995).

## 9.5 The continuing role of joint ventures

During the last 20 years the types of, and motivations for, strategic alliances have increased enormously. At the same time the rationale for traditional equity-sharing joint ventures has extended significantly beyond purely market access factors, frequently sharing a rationale which overlaps the list of factors identified above. In the United States motor industry in 1984, for example, General Motors formed the 50–50 joint venture, New United Motor Manufacturing Incorporated (NUMMI), with Toyota to produce the Chevrolet Nova in a redundant General Motors car plant at Fremont, California. The oil price rises of 1973 and 1979 had contributed to the successful import penetration of the United States car market by Japanese and German small cars. General Motors' range primarily consisted of large, high fuel-consumption models. Negotiations between the United States and Japanese governments resulted in the imposition of voluntary export restraints (VERs) on the Japanese motor manufacturers. General Motors gained important learning and time advantages from the NUMMI joint venture: expertise in small car technology, access to the Toyota lean production system and an 'off-the-shelf' small car to extend its product range, since the Chevrolet Nova was based on an existing Toyota car design. Toyota gained a production foothold in the United States market (to counteract its growing concern over United States protectionism) and geographic learning concerning the United States market, United States labour/management relations and component supply (Sasaki, 1993, pp.45–6).

A different rationale is illustrated by the 1995 Asea Brown Boveri (ABB)/Daimler Benz joint venture to supply locomotive and railway equipment. The European industry was experiencing excess capacity and was quite fragmented; the 'big three', Asea Brown Boveri, Siemens of Germany and the Anglo–French joint venture, GEC/Alsthom, only accounting for 10 per cent of industry output. Daimler Benz was concerned to find a solution for its loss-making railway equipment subsidiary whilst Daimler's subsidiary offered complementary skills for ABB: ABB was strongest in heavy locomotives, high-speed trains and signalling, whilst Daimler was strongest in light and urban transport systems, and airport transportation (*Financial Times,* 20 March 1995). Asea Brown Boveri calculated that this joint venture would create a stronger group to compete for international contracts as Central and Eastern Europe, and some of the larger developing countries like India and China, modernized their rail systems. The new group is to be a 50–50 owned joint venture but Daimler Benz is to pay ABB $900 million in cash to compensate for its subsidiary's smaller size and poorer performance.

## 9.6 Disadvantages and costs of international collaboration

In addition to the benefits and advantages of international collaboration there are many practical problems and disadvantages. As a result, few strategic partnerships appear to be long lasting. Kathryn Harrigan's research study found that only 45 per cent of international co-operative agreements were judged as successful by their participants, only 60 per cent of formal agreements lasted more than four years, and 14 per cent more than 10 years (Harrigan in Contractor and Lorange, 1988). This section investigates the costs and disadvantages involved in strategic collaboration; it also examines whether strategic alliances and joint ventures are prone to identical problems and which type is the more enduring.

As long ago as 1972, Stopford and Wells identified an inherent tension in joint venture formation involving an implicit trade-off between 'the drive for unambiguous control' and 'the quest for additional resources' (Stopford and Wells, 1972, p.75). One immediate consequence of sharing is some degree of control loss compared with 'going it alone'. Policies operating in a parent company, for example accounting policies and financial controls, may have to be modified in a subsidiary in order to suit the other parent, imposing adaptation and co-ordination costs. Similarly there appears to be an inherent tension with strategic alliances in that they involve co-operation between firms that are competitors in other respects.

One set of problems concerns conflicts of interest, strategic objectives and culture and the support or opposition of the major stakeholders involved. In the case of joint ventures this might arise from the division of interest which can occur between the parents and between the parents and their subsidiary. Such conflicts of interest may relate to such issues as profits and dividend policy, sourcing, production and pricing policies. Conflicts may, however, also result from fundamental differences in the strategic objectives and culture of the partners.

In relation to strategic alliances in the European car industry, initial collaboration commenced in the late 1980s between Swedish-owned Volvo and French state-owned Renault. A formal strategic alliance was concluded between them in 1990 with the exchange of minority shareholdings. The collaboration was expected to result in joint development programmes, joint sourcing of parts and exchange of parts, including engines, for use in both companies' trucks and cars. The emphasis was on the sharing of development costs and the reduction of unit costs as a result of components, such as Volvo's new 1.4 litre engine, being manufactured at higher volumes for both car producers (Wolf, 1992, p.156). Pehr Gyllenhammar, Volvo's chairman, encouraged the collaboration's development over the next three years into a formal proposal to merge the two companies. In December 1993 a revolt by Volvo shareholders and senior management led to the abandonment of the merger talks, the strategic alliance's collapse and Gyllenhammer's resignation after over 20 years in charge of the company.

The causes of this crisis included conflict over the long-term strategic objectives of the collaboration among the various stakeholder groups and an apparent clash of corporate cultures, with Renault's managers being accused of arrogance towards the Swedes and a fear that Volvo would be relegated to branch plant status (*Financial Times*, 27 April 1994). Stakeholder opposition seems to have been a crucial factor, complicated by Renault's state ownership, the possible influence of the French government in the future group and the absence of an open capital market valuation of Renault's shares.

> The merger plans collapsed because shareholders and managers were concerned that Volvo had been undervalued in the deal, and that the partnership was turning into a takeover by Renault, a company that would still be under French state control. (Kevin Done, *Financial Times*, 2 February 1994.)

A further issue illustrated by the collapse of advanced strategic alliances like Volvo/Renault and Honda/Rover, is the downside risk, the risk of failure, presented by the alliance, particularly where the different firms' value chains are linked together as in the case of co-manufacturing. Despite Honda's anger at its treatment during the BMW/Rover takeover, it was forced, in the short-term at least, to maintain elements of its contractual links with Rover. This analysis suggests that an MNC planning alliance formation needs to have an exit strategy should the alliance fail in order to minimize the downside risk.

International alliances may lead to *decision-making rigidity*; flexibility of response and rapid policy changes could be made more difficult by international collaboration. The establishment and maintenance of international coalitions may be extremely costly of scarce management time. Doz, Prahalad and Hamel suggest that in practice the least formal, contractual strategic alliances may offer less flexibility than joint ventures:

> Purely contractual agreements offer little flexibility, unless they are constantly renegotiated, a cumbersome and often irritating process. Contracts, though, by limiting the partners' commitment, can be terminated at a relatively low cost . . . joint ventures, which create a common optimization structure between partners, allow for more flexibility, provided the conflicts between partners' strategic control and joint venture autonomy do not stifle such flexibility. (Doz, Prahalad and Hamel, 1990, p.141.)

Strategic alliances and joint ventures may result in a surrender of competitive advantage; there may be potential 'hidden agendas' where one partner is using the coalition to acquire the other's proprietary knowledge and expertise. David Lei points out that the partner also gains access to the company's strategic thinking and policy:

> Although joint ventures have considerable appeal as a means to share risks and markets, they could constrain the company's future strategy if the venture involves a leakage of either proprietary knowledge or some critical corporate core skill. (Lei, 1989, p.103.)

Reich and Mankin (1986) argue that United States joint ventures, particularly with the Japanese, have been used by the foreign partners to prevent the US company moving further down the experience curve and introducing further product innovation, putting it into a position of extreme dependency on its Japanese partner. Similarly Lei (1989, p.105) points out that Honeywell's joint venture with Bull of France and NEC of Japan resulted in the United States company eventually becoming simply the US marketing and distribution arm of its foreign partners and led to its disengagement from the computer industry in 1988.

## 9.7 The balance of advantage

It could be argued that the balance of advantage seems to have moved against formal joint venture agreements which appear to be organizationally ineffective, expensive in terms of management time and could involve the loss of core corporate skills and strengths. Less formal arrangements such as strategic alliances, involving short-term contractual agreements, minimize the need for costly administrative superstructures, and maximize collaborative benefits.

By contrast Doz, Prahalad and Hamel concluded that in some respects contractual strategic alliances offered less flexibility than a joint venture that has developed organizational autonomy. The above analysis suggests that in a strategic sense global coalitions can produce long-term competitive disadvantages as well as benefits. Doz, Prahalad and Hamel conclude:

> Our tentative examination of (strategic) partnerships as an alternative to organic or acquisition internalization yields mixed results. While, in principle, strategic control, strategic redirection and flexibility issues can be addressed in partnerships, the added difficulties brought about by partnerships, in particular partnerships between competitors, lead us to question the viability of partnerships as a durable alternative to fully-owned growth. Our tentative evidence suggests that most partnerships may be intrinsically unstable, bound to fall back towards mere OEM (Original Equipment Manufacturing) relationships between buyers and sellers, or to evolve into a single operating entity . . . Whether this single common entity results from a merger between operations, or from the existence of a stable, relatively autonomous joint venture, it is characterized by strategic unity and flexibility. (Doz, Prahalad, and Hamel, 1990, pp.141–2.)

In sum the factors determining the effectiveness and success of strategic alliances include the following:

- complementarity;

- agreement on objectives;

- compatible strategies;

- compatible cultures;

- no surrender of core assets/competencies;

- comparable contributions/rewards;

- stakeholder blessing;

- thorough and lengthy planning process.

## 9.8 International acquisitions

Acquisitions and mergers involve changes in corporate ownership. In essence a merger is a corporate marriage such as that between the Swedish company Asea and the Swiss company Brown Boveri in the European engineering industry. Both Asea's shareholders and Brown Boveri's shareholders received shares in the new corporate identity, Asea Brown Boveri. An acquisition or takeover, by contrast, occurs where one firm purchases another from its shareholders and control of the enlarged group passes to the acquirer: for example the 1988 acquisition of Rowntree by Nestlé, in which the Rowntree shareholders received Nestlé shares plus a cash element in return for their existing shares. An acquisition may be agreed by the managements involved ('friendly') or contested by the target company's management ('hostile').

Chapter 2 has identified the extent to which international acquisitions and mergers have become the dominant mode of foreign direct investment in recent years. Examples include the Asea Brown Boveri merger already mentioned, Hong-Kong and Shanghai Bank's acquisition of the British Midland Bank, Japanese Bridgestone's takeover of the United States company Firestone in the tyre industry, and Matsushita's diversificatory acquisition of the American firm MCA in the entertainments industry. In addition to these very large international acquisitions, each involving the takeover of billions of American dollars of assets, there were countless small acquisitions by MNCs in all sectors of economic activity. The reasons for international acquisitions and mergers include the following:

- Strategic objectives and corporate growth. Many international acquisitions are motivated by the desire to reinforce competitive advantage and to achieve enhanced profits. Acquisitions and mergers are a much more rapid method of corporate growth than growth by organic, internal means; a company may be able to more than double its size as a result of a single deal.

- Pursuit of size, synergy and scale. The financial resources and scale advantages resulting from increased size have traditionally been advanced as important factors in merger activity. In relation to horizontal mergers (those between firms in the same product market), efficiency gains through the achievement of economies of scale have had an important place in the literature. This benefit does not occur automatically, however; many mergers in the past have simply placed existing plants under a single ownership, and the costs of the merger have been such as to absorb funds that would otherwise be available for investment in larger production facilities. Arguably this is all the more likely in the case of international acquisitions where the need for geographic market presence may make the acquiring company reluctant to rationalize production facilities.

- Market dominance/defence of market share. The pursuit of market power, concentration and the elimination of competitors have frequently been advanced as reasons for acquisitions and mergers. At national level an international acquisition may change the ownership of a competitor but leave the total number of competitors in the national market unaffected. In some international industries such as aircraft production or personal computers, world market share may have significance and may be directly increased by absorbing a competitor. International competition may promote mergers as a defensive response; another type of defensive manoeuvre occurs where a company undertakes acquisitions to make itself bid-proof; by becoming larger the firm seeks to prevent itself becoming an acquisition victim.

- Foreign market entry. Sections 9.10 and 9.11 below elaborate the alternative modes of entry into foreign markets and the importance of acquisitions in relation to the investment entry mode. A significant component of the increased cross-border acquisition activity in the European Union appears to have the intention of increasing European market presence in the context of the Single European Market. This has involved cross-entry by European (including Swiss and other non-European Union) multinational companies and further market entry through acquisition by American and Asian MNCs, attracted by the size of the European market but potentially concerned by the emergence of a fortress Europe mentality. Brand buying; in a number of sectors, brand ownership is a key factor for success. It may be more cost effective to acquire brands, for example international food and drink brands, through purchase of the businesses involved than to engage in the cost and risk of attempting to build an international brand from scratch.

- Divestment. Acquisition resulting from MNCs divesting themselves of peripheral activities, thus making them available for acquisition by other companies, is important numerically but not necessarily in terms of asset value. Under the competitive conditions of the 1990s there has been a tendency to focus on core activities, resulting in considerable sales of subsidiaries between firms.

## 9.9 Problems and disadvantages of international acquisitions

A number of studies have pointed to the mixed results of acquisitions and mergers in performance terms. Whilst acquisitions and mergers achieve positive results in growth terms, Ravenscroft and Scherer (1987) and Auerbach (1988a) found a significant deterioration in post-merger corporate profitability and share prices compared to the profitability of the pre-acquisition or merger constituent companies. Michael Porter (1987) investigated the effectiveness of diversification through acquisition of 33 United States corporations such as Procter and Gamble, 3M and General Electric over the period 1950 to 1986. Porter's findings were predominantly negative; on average the corporations subsequently divested themselves of 60 per cent of their acquisitions in entirely new fields and 74 per cent of their acquisitions in unrelated activities (Porter, 1987, p.48). Although the studies quoted included international acquisitions, none specifically examined international acquisitions *per se*. The following are some important problems and issues involved in acquisition and merger behaviour:

- Partner selection and poor pre-acquisition planning. Haspeslagh and Jemison's (1991) study of acquisition management emphasized the extent to which poor pre-acquisition screening and planning was an important factor in explaining acquisition failure. This was all the more important in international acquisitions compared to purely national mergers because the degree of knowledge about the potential takeover victim or merger partner was likely to be significantly lower. Even in relation to diversification in United States' industry, Porter (1987) found that many US corporations diversified into industries that research would have found to be relatively unprofitable and unattractive in industry structure terms, suggesting a serious absence of pre-merger research and analysis. One of the most serious cases of poor pre-acquisition screening and partner selection was British Ferranti's £420 million agreed acquisition of the United States company International Signal and Control (ISC) in 1987 in the defence electronics sector. By 1989 Ferranti discovered that ISC had defrauded it of assets valued at £215 millions in the form of fraudulent defence contracts and stocks that did not exist (Booth 1993, pp.272–3). The acquisition seriously weakened Ferranti and forced it to engage in asset disposals from its main United Kingdom operations in order to try to forestall bankruptcy.

- Costs of acquisition. It has been argued that the purchase price paid by acquiring companies in the late 1980s and early 1990s was excessive, reflecting takeover bid battles and the soaring valuation of brands. Examples include the £1.6 billion paid by Ford to acquire Jaguar, and the £2.5 billion paid by Nestlé in its bid battle with Jacob Suchard for control of Rowntree. Assessing an acquisition with the methodology of investment appraisal and comparing the discounted stream of future revenues with the costs of acquisition, one may find that in some cases it produces low or even negative returns.

- Management failure. Ravenscraft and Scherer (1987) have suggested that poor post-acquisition performance is primarily the result of managerial failure, particularly where the management involved has seen the acquisition as an end in itself and has failed to achieve post-acquisition integration of the companies involved.

- Strategic mismatch. This includes the extension of the MNC beyond the area of its core competence. Taggart and McDermott suggest that the international diversification of Japanese electronic companies such as Matsushita and Sony into the Hollywood movie industry through their acquisition of MCA and Columbia Pictures respectively provide an example of this type of strategic mismatch (Taggart and McDermott, 1993, p.193).

- Branch plant status. From the viewpoint of the acquisition victim, one important issue is the fear that acquisition will involve the removal of higher value activities such as design, research and a role in strategy formulation and that the organization will be relegated to branch-plant status. This was clearly a concern in the proposed 1993 Renault/Volvo merger discussed earlier, as well as in the 1988 Nestlé/Rowntree acquisition. In practice Nestlé appears to have been sensitive to this problem, providing Rowntree with an enhanced role in managing the combined group's confectionery business.

- Anti-trust and competition policy. One issue in international acquisitions and mergers is the possible impact of host government mergers policy and its policy stance towards foreign takeovers. Two levels of merger control have existed within the European Union since 1989: a European Commission regulatory power for acquisitions and mergers which involve a worldwide turnover of ECU 5 billion or more, and national controls with varying thresholds (for example worldwide turnover of ECU 430 million in Sweden, and ECU 1.04 billion in Germany) (Commission of European Communities, 1996). National governments have sometimes opposed foreign takeovers in principle; for example the British and French governments with proposed Ford/Rover and Fiat/Citroen takeovers respectively. Brussels may make asset disposals a condition of merger approval as occurred with Nestlé's acquisition of Perrier in the mineral water sector. None the less only a very small minority of international acquisitions have been affected in these ways.

## 9.10 Foreign market entry and development

An important dimension of international strategy implementation is the choice of method (mode) of foreign market entry and development. Root (1994) defines an international market entry mode as

. . . an institutional arrangement that makes possible the entry of a company's products, technology, human skills, management, or other resources into a foreign country. (Root, 1994, p.24.)

Root classifies entry modes into three main types: export, contractual (or knowledge based) and investment entry modes; various permutations of the three types are identified in Box 9.2. The next sections consider the advantages and disadvantages of the different entry methods.

**Box 9.2**  Classification of alternative entry modes

*Export entry modes*

Indirect

Direct agent/distributor

Direct branch/subsidiary

Other

*Contractual entry modes*

Licensing

Franchising

Technical agreements

Service contracts

Management contracts

Construction/turnkey contracts

Contract manufacture

Counter-trade arrangements

Other

*Investment entry modes*

Sole venture: new establishment

Sole venture: acquisition

Joint venture: new establishment/acquisition

Other

*Source: Root (1994), p.26.*

## 9.11 Export entry modes

We saw in Chapter 2 that many multinational enterprises commenced their internationalization through the use of export strategy; advantages include high levels of control, low levels of risk and co-ordination effort and the possibility of production economies. Japanese consumer electronic companies like Matsushita and Sony were able to achieve significant economies of scale and experience curve effects in the 1970s by servicing world markets through exports from their factories in Japan. Disadvantages of the export entry mode include the possibility of tariff barriers, high transport costs, especially for products with a high weight/value ratio like cement or beverages, and a lack of adaptation and responsiveness to local consumer tastes.

The following represent a range of different methods of exporting:

*Indirect export.* This is where the firm itself does not engage in international trade but uses export houses or other types of intermediaries to serve foreign markets. In Asia, a very important form of indirect export has traditionally been the trading company such as the Japanese *Sōgō Shōsha*, which specialized in trade with the rest of the world on behalf of Japanese manufacturing firms. The most passive type of exporting is where a foreign buyer takes the initiative in approaching a supplier for products it cannot obtain in its home market.

*Direct export.* Direct exporting is where the firm itself undertakes the work of exporting. A number of organizational tasks are involved including market research and taking decisions regarding the marketing mix; foreign market pricing, product policy, promotional strategy and distribution channels in the foreign markets, export documentation and the logistics of the movement of goods to consumers in the foreign market. James Dudley (1993) identifies the following organizational requirements for exporting:

- providing a marketing and distribution structure in each foreign territory;

– setting up a management team to handle exports; and
– organizing to handle documentation and logistics.
(Dudley, 1993, p.205.)

*Use of agents and distributors.* In the foreign market itself, supply frequently takes place through a foreign agent or distributor. The traditional difference between these two is that the agent acts contractually on behalf of the firm selling the products on commission, whereas the distributor takes legal title to the goods, covering overheads, costs and profits from the difference between the manufacturer's supply price and the price charged by the distributor in the foreign market. Michael Brooke (1986, pp.59–60) emphasizes the importance of foreign agent and distributor selection and the extent of problems resulting from poor choice. An agent may also carry competitors' lines and not market the firm's products sufficiently strongly or have insufficient financial resources to become a significant market presence; alternatively an agent may be so concerned with earning commission that quality of product and customer service may be sacrificed. Such problems occur less frequently in the case of distributors, who may be able to offer the firm an existing distribution network, but major difficulties occasionally occur as Nissan discovered with its United Kingdom distributor in the early 1990s.

*Direct export through the firm's own branch or subsidiary.* Whilst agents and distributors have the advantage of country-specific knowledge, a logical next step is for the firm itself to set up its own jointly or wholly owned sales or marketing subsidiary in the foreign market. Any deficiency of market knowledge may be compensated for by the recruitment and employment of local staff. Direct export through a branch office or subsidiary company involves a greater degree of commitment and accompanying risk in the foreign market, but overcomes the potential problems of using foreign agents and distributors and internalizes the stream of profit which would otherwise be paid to the external agent.

## 9.12 Contractual entry modes

Root defines these as 'long term non-equity associations between an international company and an entity in a foreign target country that involve the transfer of technology or human skills from the former to the latter' (Root, 1994, p.27). Contractual entry modes take a number of forms including licensing, franchising, technical agreements, management and service agreements, construction and turnkey contracts.

*International licensing.* Under a licence agreement the firm grants rights to a foreign company to manufacture the company's products or to use some other type of proprietary knowledge gained from the firm such as patents, copyright, brands and trademarks. In return the foreign firm makes licence payments to the parent company, usually in the form of royalties. The licence holder bears the costs of setting up the manufacturing process and distributing the product in the foreign market. International licensing may therefore permit the parent firm to expand very fast in international markets without having to finance this growth itself. Licensing may be particularly appropriate where the goods involved are bulky or costly to transport, for example Whitbread's licence to brew Heineken in Britain, or Pilkington's worldwide licensing of its float glass process for manufacturing sheet glass.

Disadvantages of international licensing include the loss of direct control over the industrial property, its manufacture and quality. Its worldwide reputation could suffer from poorly manufactured products licensed in one or two countries. The loss of the stream of profits to the licence holder needs to be set against the financial benefits of international expansion through licensing. Finally the firm risks the surrender of competitive advantage through the loss of proprietary technology to foreign competitors (what Hill, Hwang and Kim (1990, p.119) term 'dissemination risk').

*International franchising.* This is essentially a type of licence agreement where, in addition to granting rights to use the firm's patents, brand, trademark and technology, the parent firm frequently provides assistance with the design, equipment, organization and marketing of the business. The franchise agreement frequently includes a lump sum payment and a share of the franchisee's profits. Whilst licence agreements take place primarily in manufacturing industry, international franchises are common in retailing and services. Examples include Benetton in fashion retailing, McDonalds, Burger King, Hertz car rental and Hilton Hotels. Franchising has the advantage of providing the parent company with greater control over the international use of its proprietary technology and expertise but, like licensing, it offers the opportunity of international expansion with substantial financial costs borne by its partners. Where there are significant numbers of franchisees, as in the examples quoted, the parent company frequently needs to establish a regional organization structure in order to service its partners and supervise product quality.

## 9.13 Investment entry mode

Investment entry involves the control of manufacturing plants or other productive assets in the foreign market itself through whole or part ownership. This has been explored at some length in Chapter 2. The investment entry mode may involve a green field development (for example Ford's manufacturing plant at Valencia in Spain), the acquisition of an existing company (for example Volkswagen's partial acquisition of Skoda in the Czech Republic) or a joint venture (for example the Toyota/General Motors joint venture, New United Motor Manufacturing Incorporated, in California). Foreign market entry through direct investment maximizes control and protects the firm's proprietary technology and knowledge. It internalizes the stream of profits earned by agents, licensees and franchisees in other types of entry mode but it involves the maximum degree of commitment, financial investment and risk compared to the other entry modes.

## 9.14 Determinants of foreign market entry mode

The previous section outlined the advantages and disadvantages of various entry modes. These different methods of market entry and development are not necessarily alternatives given the complexity of contemporary global strategies. The large international firm might engage in foreign direct investment in some markets, licence production in others and serve some countries through exports, whilst the firm itself contributes to international trade flows as a result of intra-firm trade between its various worldwide subsidiaries. None the less it is important to explore the determinants of broad choices of entry mode. It is clear from the earlier discussion that many factors affect foreign market entry mode decisions. Root (1994, p.29) classifies these into two types: external/environmental variables and internal company-specific factors.

### 9.14.1 External factors

- Size and growth rate of foreign market. In terms of country selection, market size and growth potential tend to be important locational variables. Root (1994) suggests they will also influence entry mode: small foreign markets tend to favour modes with low break-even volumes (for example indirect exporting, direct exporting through agents or distributors and licensing) whereas large markets may favour modes with greater resource commitments, high break-even sales volumes and the potential to achieve economies of scale, such as direct export through the company's own branch or subsidiary, or the investment entry mode. Alternatively the firm may be uncertain of the level of potential demand in the target market; again this would point to entry strategies with low resource commitments.

- Competitive intensity. Chan Kim and Hwang (1992) suggest that intense competitive conditions in the foreign market discourage investment entry modes;

... other things being equal, the greater the intensity of competition in the host market, the more MNCs will favour entry modes that involve low resource commitments. (Chan Kim and Hwang, 1992, p.36.)

Root points out that competitive conditions in the MNC's home country may also influence the entry mode. In sectors with low levels of industrial concentration, firms may well be smaller in absolute terms (fashion clothing firms are an example) and enter foreign markets by exporting. Under oligopoly conditions firms may be larger and have greater financial resources and, as we saw in Chapter 7, imitative, leader/follower behaviour tends to be high. 'Because oligopolists are unlikely to view a rival's exporting or licensing activities as a competitive threat, oligopolistic reaction is biased towards investment in production' (Root, 1994, p.33).

- Country risk. Firms will generally prefer exporting and licensing to investment entry modes where country risk and uncertainty are high.

- Geographical distance. This refers both to physical distance and also what could be termed 'psychic distance'. Chan Kim and Hwang (1992, p.35) refer to this as 'location unfamiliarity'. The greater the psychic distance, the more likely is the use of export entry methods. Familiarity with the foreign market in terms of language, consumer behaviour, tastes, culture, and distribution structures is likely to favour investment entry modes. Host government policies may have significant influence over the firm's choice of entry mode. Tariff barriers and import restrictions may deter export strategies whilst exchange controls may deter investment entry modes particularly because of controls over the repatriation of profits. Host government regulations may dictate local participation in the entry method by requiring the use of joint ventures.

## 9.14.2 Internal factors

- Product characteristics. Product characteristics such as value/weight ratios have an important influence on entry strategy. In the international brewing industry, licensing and investment (acquisition) strategies have generally been preferred to exporting although some premium beers are successfully exported, the fact that they are 'home bottled' being part of the brand identity. In the area of kitchen white goods it is interesting to note that Japanese suppliers such as Mitsui have made greater inroads in the European market with relatively high value/weight products like microwave ovens than with heavier gas or electrical cookers.

- Services. In general, manufactured goods can be physically exported; services like construction, retailing and management consultancy need to be directly produced in the foreign market. The establishment of sales offices, branches and subsidiaries or joint ventures with local companies may be the initial steps in foreign market entry.

- Degree of product differentiation. Root (1994) suggests that highly differentiated products are more likely to be exported than less differentiated ones because they can achieve premium pricing in the foreign markets and can more easily absorb the transport costs involved. Less differentiated products compete more directly on price, hence they may move more rapidly to local production in order to forego the transport costs.

- Technology and dissemination risk. According to Hill, Hwang and Kim (1990, p.119) dissemination risk 'refers to the risk that firm-specific advantages will be expropriated by a licensing or joint venture partner'. This risk will be least where a wholly owned subsidiary is established as a result of an investment entry strategy.

- Resource/commitment factors. As we proceed down Root's list of entry modes (Box 9.2) the resource demands, dedicated assets and the level of commitment required of the MNC increase. Whilst the full range of entry mode choices may be available to the large MNC, a firm with limited resources, or one engaging in international activity for the first time may be limited to the export entry mode.

### 9.14.3 International business strategy and foreign market entry mode

Hill, Hwang and Kim (1990) argue that the existing literature on entry mode decisions is fragmentary and makes insufficient provision for strategic variables in determining the choice of entry mode. They seek to integrate a number of the key internal, external and strategic variables in an 'eclectic' theory of the entry mode decision focusing on the choice between licensing, joint ventures and wholly owned subsidiaries.

The model in Figure 9.2 initially identifies three 'constructs' or foundations: control, resource commitment and dissemination; for example, entry via wholly owned subsidiaries involves a high level of control, high resource commitment, but low dissemination risk. Hill, Hwang and Kim (1990, p.120) argue:

> The theory developed herein suggests that strategic variables influence the choice of entry mode primarily through the control requirements that they entail. Different strategies require different degrees of control over the operating and strategic decisions of foreign affiliates, and thus different entry modes.

The characteristics of different entry modes

| Entry mode | Constructs | | |
|---|---|---|---|
| | Control | Resource | Dissemination risk |
| Licensing | Low | Low | High |
| Joint venturing | Medium | Medium | Medium |
| Wholly owned subsidiary | High | High | Low |

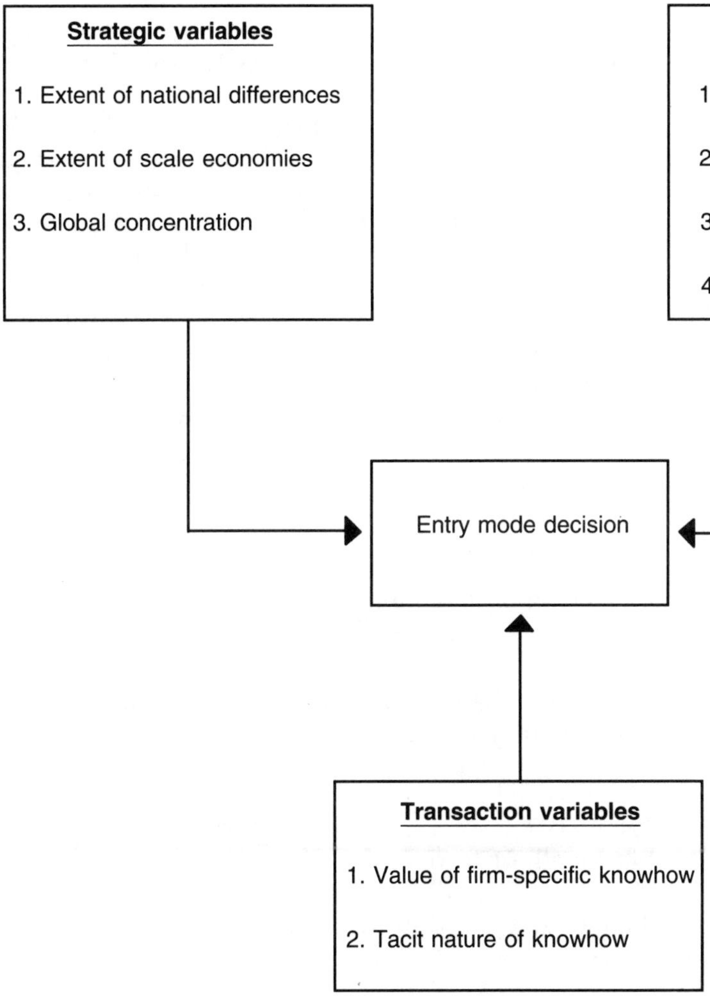

| Strategic variables | Environmental variables |
|---|---|
| 1. Extent of national differences | 1. Country risk |
| 2. Extent of scale economies | 2. Location familiarity |
| 3. Global concentration | 3. Demand conditions |
| | 4. Volatility of competition |

Entry mode decision

| Transaction variables |
|---|
| 1. Value of firm-specific knowhow |
| 2. Tacit nature of knowhow |

**Figure 9.2** The decision framework. Source: Hill, Hwang and Kim (1990), p.120.

Among the propositions they advanced was the view that, all other things being equal, firms that pursue a multidomestic strategy will favour low-control entry modes whilst firms that pursue a global strategy will prefer high-control entry modes; this reflects competitive (international oligopoly) conditions in global industries and the greater needs for integration and co-ordination. These propositions were supported in a separate research paper by Kim and Hwang (1992).

## 9.15 Summary

This chapter has examined a number of issues concerned with strategy implementation; the methods used by MNCs to achieve their international strategy. International firms have increasingly used international collaborative agreements, strategic alliances, joint ventures, international acquisitions and mergers to achieve their strategic objectives. Foreign market entry and development remains an important factor motivating these developments but international collaboration is now undertaken for various reasons and involves all aspects of the MNC's value chain.

Significant problems characterize international collaboration. Alliances need careful partner selection and management to succeed. Similarly, acquisitions offer the quickest method of international growth but many have experienced mixed results in performance terms.

## 9.16 Further reading

Bleeke, J. and Ernst, D. (1993) *Collaborating to Compete,* John Wiley, New York.

Hill, C.W.L., Hwang, P. and Chan Kim, W. (1990) An eclectic theory of the choice of international entry mode. *Strategic Management Journal,* 11, 117–28.

Lorange, P. and Roos, J. (1992) *Strategic Alliances: Formation, Implementation and Evolution,* Blackwell, Oxford.

Ohmae, K. (1989) The global logic of strategic alliances. *Harvard Business Review,* 67(2), 143–54

Porter, M.E. and Fuller, M. (1986) Coalitions and global strategy, in *Competition in Global Industries,* (ed. M.E. Porter) Harvard Business School Press, Boston MA.

Root, F.R. (1994) *Entry Strategies for International Markets,* Lexington Books, Lexingon MA.

Taggert J.H. and McDermott M.C.(1993) *The Essence of International Business,* Prentice Hall, Hemel Hempstead, Herts.

Young, S. *et al.* (1989) *International Market Entry and Development,* Hemel Hempstead, Herts.

## 9.17 Questions for further discussion

1. What appear to be the main determinants of success or failure in international strategic alliances?

2. Examine the use of strategic alliances and joint ventures by your corporate project MNC. Identify the main reasons why these alliances have been undertaken. Overall, do you consider them to have been successful?

3. To what extent has the corporate project MNC engaged in international acquisitions and mergers? Identify the benefits and disadvantages of one specific acquisition or merger. What steps has the MNC taken to integrate the acquired company? How successful has it been?

# 10

# *International organizational structure*

## *10.1 Introduction*

The three previous chapters have referred to a number of issues regarding organizational structure in their analysis of international strategy. This chapter seeks to examine some of the key organizational questions facing the international firm at greater length. The chapter begins by placing our contemporary interest in organizational issues in an historical and comparative context. In placing these issues in a historical context it refers back to the analysis in Chapter 1 and the evolution and development of the international firm. In taking a comparative perspective it contrasts the similarities and differences in MNC structure between Europe, Asia and the United States.

The following section looks at the choice between international organizational alternatives, examining the advantages and disadvantages of the different structures. The relationship between international business strategy and structure is explored in the next sections. Finally the chapter seeks to go beyond an analysis of formal structures and to take account of informal processes, values and culture, the influence of 'administrative heritage' and leadership.

It is important to identify at the outset the variety of factors which influence and determine the shape of international organizational structure. These are:

1. Age, history and origins of the company.

2. Size, sales, employment.

3. Product type as such (extractive, services and so forth).

4. Product diversity.

5. Geographic diversity.

6. Technology and production methods.

7. International business environment/competitive conditions.

8. International business strategy.

## 10.2 Historical development of international organizational structure

Samuel Humes (1993) argues that there was considerable diversity in the organizational structuring of international companies originating in different continental traditions in the first half of the twentieth century. These earlier divergent traditions are highlighted in the first column of Figure 10.1.

| Continent | Earlier divergent traditions (thesis: divide by territory) | Recent converging transitions (antithesis: divide by product) | Prospective emerging trends (synthesis: bridging the divide) |
|---|---|---|---|
| American | International divisions manage foreign affiliates | Global multifunctional product divisions manage overseas affiliates – trend evident from 1960s | |
| European | 'Daughter' companies report to corporate board | Product divisions expand global and multifunctional roles – trend evident by 1970s | Global operating divisions supported by corporate-wide continental (marketing/sales/service and/or management support co-ordinating organizations |
| Asian | Trading companies manage business overseas | Production division as well as sales divisions develop their own overseas affiliates – trend develops in 1980s | |

**Figure 10.1** Successive organizational phases of prototypical leading multinationals. Source: Humes (1993), p.24.

### 10.2.1 United States

Alfred Chandler, in exploring the historical links between strategy and organizational structure, chronicled the evolution of United States Corporations from functional or unitary structures to multidivisional structures as they grew and diversified (Chandler, 1962). It was entirely consistent with their product-based divisional structures that early phases of internationalization should involve the creation of an international division to manage activities abroad, particularly where this involved operations in other parts of the American continent. Humes points out that General Electric formed an international division in 1919 and Standard Oil did likewise in 1927 whilst General Motors grew by international acquisition, taking over the United Kingdom's Vauxhall Motors in 1925 and Adam Opel in Germany in 1929 (Humes, 1993, p.21).

### 10.2.2 Europe

European companies such as Philips, British Petroleum or Nestlé tended to develop decentralized 'daughter' companies or 'clones' of themselves to manage their international activities. For multinationals such as Philips, founded in 1890, with small home markets like the Netherlands, foreign sales soon became much larger than domestic sales. Foreign subsidiaries were run with considerable autonomy, partly due to the international business environment of the 1920s, 1930s and 1940s, with the extreme economic nationalism and high tariff barriers of the 1930s and the dislocation caused between 1939 and 1945 by the Second World War. Despite being separated by the war and attendant occupation, subsidiaries of Philips in Germany, Czechoslovakia, France, Britain and North America, as well as the home company in the Netherlands itself, continued in existence as virtually independent entities.

### 10.2.3 Japan

There was little direct involvement in international activities by Japanese firms before the Second World War. In contrast to European and American firms, the Japanese operated through intermediary trading companies, the *Sōgō Shōsha*, such as Mitsui, Mitsubishi and the Sumitomo Corporation. Many of these had their origins in the 1870s when the industrializing Meiji government encouraged their development in order to counteract the dominance of Japan's trade by Western merchants and trading companies and to compensate for Japan's relative ignorance of international trade (Ozawa, 1987). During the first half of the twentieth century these Japanese trading companies dominated Japan's trade with the rest of the world, not only acting as middlemen but also exporting and importing on their own account. It is a relatively recent phenomenon for Japanese manufacturing companies in sectors like motor vehicles or electronics to act independently in the international economy, whether through export or foreign direct investment (*Economist*, 11 February 1995).

## 10.3 Choice of international organizational alternatives

The previous section has indicated the diverse origins and experience of multinational corporations in different parts of the world and the extent to which this is reflected in differences in organizational structure. In this section and following sections, alternative international organizational structures are examined more formally and recent developments are discussed.

### 10.3.1 International division structure

Figure 10.2 illustrates a multidivisional organizational structure with an international division for foreign operations. Whilst it has the advantage of grouping together all the firm's foreign specialists, arguably there is tension between the organization's primary specialist product divisions and a multiproduct, multidisciplinary international division.

Despite these disadvantages, Stopford and Wells (1972, p.72) found that, in 1966, 106 or 65 per cent of their sample of 162 United States multinational corporations were employing international division structures. Taggart and McDermott suggest that this was because, even in the 1960s, many United States multinational corporations were still primarily reliant on their domestic market, overseas sales were a small proportion of total sales and the international division structure remained appropriate. A significantly different situation existed in Europe:

> European MNCs by contrast – especially those from the smaller countries (e.g. the Netherlands, Sweden, Switzerland) – did not have a large domestic market and thus were more disposed to internationalization. Thus international sales often accounted for the bulk of their turnover, rather than a small proportion as was the case in the 1960s for many US MNCs. The international division was thus largely redundant for European MNCs. (Taggart and McDermott, 1993, p.156.)

As their international scope and activities grew, multinational corporations of all types turned increasingly to global structural arrangements. As Samuel Humes has pointed out (1993, pp.10–11) the organizational challenge is to reconcile three structural perspectives: functional, product and geographic:

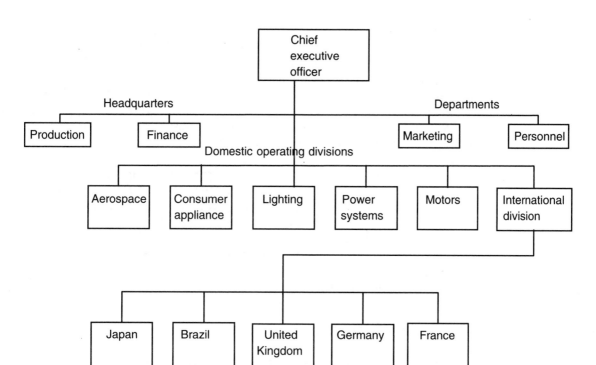

**Figure 10.2** International division structure.

- Functional perspectives are based on the needs of the different functional departments of the international firm such as production, research and development, marketing, finance and human resources.

- Product perspectives are based on the need for organizational divisions to take responsibility for specific products, particularly where product diversification is high.

- Geographical perspectives are based on the need for area, national or regional structures particularly where the extent of geographic diversification was high.

The structural solution used by many MNCs was to prioritize one of these dimensions and to subordinate the other two; the solution was in consequence a compromise with a mixture of advantages and costs which are explored in the sections below.

### 10.3.2 Global area division structure

This structure prioritized the geographic or territorial dimension and the MNC's primary divisions are based on area; for example Europe, North America, Asia. The general manager in each area is responsible for all the firm's products and functional activities in that territory (see Figure 10.3). The structure is relatively decentralized, with economies of scale largely achievable within the region and relatively little intra-firm trading across the regions. On the integration/responsiveness grid the structure is likely to be much more responsive to local differences and tastes than other structures.

Hodgetts and Luthans (1994, p.192) suggest global area structures are most often used by MNCs in mature industries with relatively narrow product lines, such as automobiles, containers, cosmetics, foods, beverages and pharmaceuticals. Humes (1993, p.11) points out that the area-driven structure was particularly favoured by the older European multinational corporations, with large overseas sales not dominated by any single geographic territory, such as British Petroleum, Philips, Imperial Chemical Industries, and Royal Dutch/Shell.

### 10.3.3 Global product division structure

This structure is illustrated in Figure 10.4. Here the MNC is primarily structured on product divisions which operate worldwide. It appears to be particularly suitable for diversified MNCs with wide product ranges where technology and user markets may be quite different from one product group to the next. The structure achieves a high degree of global integration and co-ordination for the specific product with efficiency gains and economies of scale. It facilitates global planning and strategy for the product but, compared to the area division structure, it is likely to be much less responsive to local conditions and differences in consumer behaviour and tastes.

Other disadvantages include the degree of duplication likely in the business functions (marketing, finance, human resources and so forth) for the different product divisions. Moreover, whilst product/strategic business unit strategy may be enhanced, co-ordination across product divisions and corporate level strategy may be weak. Many American multinational corporations, such as General Electric and Mobil evolved their international division structures into global product divisions.

### 10.3.4 Global functional structure

Here, by contrast, the business functions (production, marketing, finance, human resources and so forth) hold worldwide responsibilities and the general manager for marketing will be responsible for marketing

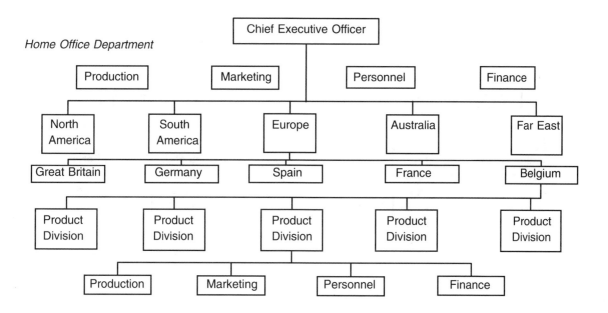

**Figure 10.3** Global area structure.

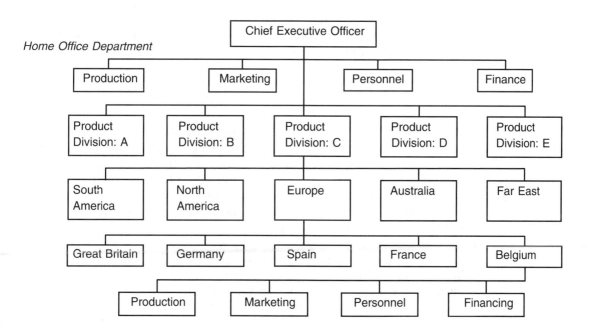

**Figure 10.4** A global product structure.

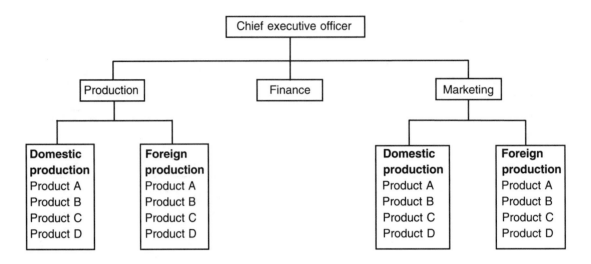

**Figure 10.5** Global functional structure.

all the MNC's products on a worldwide basis (see Figure 10.5). It has the benefit of creating a tight, highly centralized organization, removing much of the functional duplication implicit in the global product division structure. Co-ordination across functions, for example between production and marketing, however, may be very difficult. Some Japanese companies, such as Nissan and Hitachi, have adopted this solution; elsewhere it is mainly to be found among extractive companies such as oil and mining companies.

### 10.3.5 Mixed and global matrix structures

In practice few of these structures are found in a pure form and various mixed or hybrid structures exist. There was considerable experimenta-tion in the 1970s and 1980s with global matrix structures that sought to overcome the disadvantages of the previous global structural models with three dimensional structures in which the MNC was organized simultaneously on dual product, functional or area lines, and no single dimension was prioritized. A possible matrix structure is illustrated in Figure 10.6.

In line management terms, such structures tended to be very difficult with two or even three ways reporting. Decision-making frequently became slower and bureaucracy increased with the need for committees to resolve conflicts and achieve co-ordination. Bartlett and Ghoshal write:

> Most companies that experimented with this structure encountered the same problems. The matrix amplified the differences in perspectives and

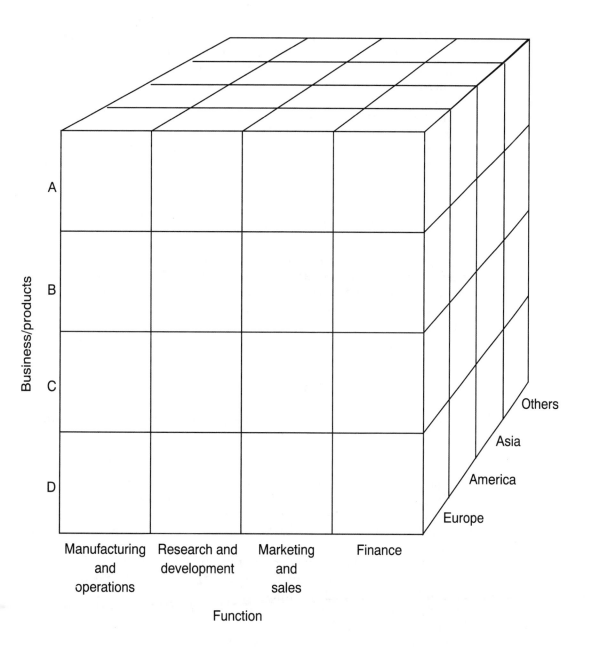

**Figure 10.6**  A three-dimensional matrix.

interests by forcing all issues through the dual chains of command. Even a minor difference could become the subject of heated disagreement and debate. But the very design of the global matrix prevented the resolution of differences among managers with conflicting views and overlapping responsibilities. Barriers of distance, time, language and culture impeded the vital process of confronting and resolving differences. (Bartlett and Ghoshal, 1989, pp.31–2.)

In the competitive, cost-conscious environments of the late 1980s and 1990s, matrix structures imposed costs and delays that could not be afforded. Many such experiments, for example at Dow Chemicals, Shell and Citibank, were dismantled in favour of simpler, leaner structures.

## 10.4 Stopford and Wells' empirical study of structure

In this section we return to the question of the choice of international organizational structure and the relationship between strategy and structure. Stopford and Wells' (1972) structural stages model was based on an empirical investigation of the strategy/structure linkages in 187 large United States corporations. The model defined the relationship in terms of two variables:

- the number of products sold internationally ('foreign product diversity', shown vertically in Figure 10.7) and

- the proportional importance of foreign sales to total sales ('percentage foreign sales', shown horizontally).

International division structures tended to be used where both product diversity and percentage foreign sales were low. With an increase in product diversity, companies in the sample tended to adopt global product divisions. Where product diversity remained relatively low, but the percentage of foreign sales increased significantly, global area divisions tended to be adopted, as we discussed earlier in relation to European MNCs. Whilst few companies in Stopford and Wells' sample were classified as having a matrix structure, the authors speculated that the combination of high product diversity and high percentage foreign sales, the question mark region in the figure, would be associated with the adoption of matrix structures.

In view of the international differences in MNC structures discussed earlier, one limitation of the Stopford and Wells model was that it generalized from a sample that only included United States corporations. Some debate has also taken place over the positioning of the international division boundary (the point at which the international division structure ends and a more globally oriented structure begins).

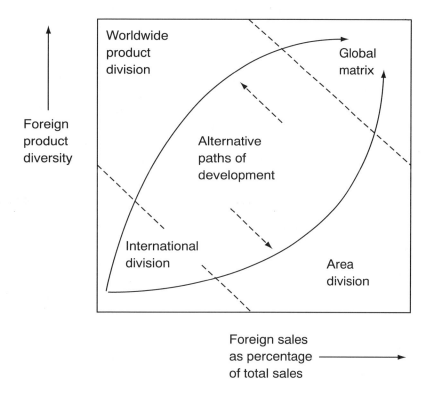

**Figure 10.7** The Stopford and Wells model of MNC organizations. Source: adapted from Stopford and Wells (1972) p.72.

Recent writers such as Ghoshal and Nohria argued that whilst the structural stages model retained descriptive usefulness, reducing the determinants of MNC structure to two variables was a considerable oversimplification (1993, pp.23–4).

Egelhoff (1988) published a revised version of the Stopford and Wells model using a sample of 34 European and US MNCs. He argued that a further variable needed to be added to the original model, reflecting the increasing importance of foreign direct investment: the percentage of foreign manufacturing. This would create a three-dimensional framework (see Figure 10.8).

For low percentages of foreign sales the two studies had similar predictions; low product diversity associated with international divisions and high product diversity associated with global product divisions. Similarly global product divisions are appropriate where there is a high percentage of foreign sales and high product diversity but a low percentage of foreign manufacturing; in this situation the foreign markets are serviced by the use of substantial exporting from the parent to the foreign subsidiaries. However:

When the strategy involves manufacturing a high percentage of the goods needed to support foreign sales abroad, foreign subsidiaries become relatively more interdependent with each other, and interdependency between the foreign and domestic operations of the company decreases for operational matters. The revised model shows that area division structures provide the type of coordination and information processing needed to handle the interdependency associated with this strategy. Such strategies and structures are not global but regional, and therefore more responsive to regional and national interests than global product strategies and structures. (Egelhoff, 1988, p.11)

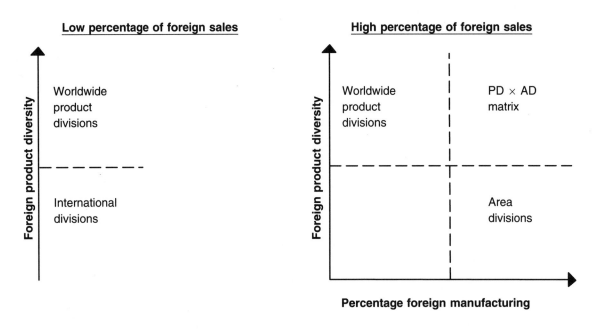

**Figure 10.8** Revised model showing the relationship between strategy and structure in multinational corporations. Source: Egelhoff (1988) p.12.

Finally Figure 10.8 suggests that a combination of a high proportion of foreign manufacturing with high foreign product diversity is likely to be associated with a product division and area division matrix structure (PD x AD matrix). It is interesting that despite the growth of diversified MNCs with significant overseas manufacturing, both studies found relatively low instances of the use of matrix structures in their samples (three in Stopford and Wells' and two in Egelhoff's). This is consistent with the earlier observation of rapid adoption and rejection of matrix structures during the period in which the two studies took place. If the research evidence found little support for the use of matrix structures, an open question is raised concerning what type of organizational structure (if any) occupies the top right hand boundary in the two models. The next sections explore one solution to this question proposed by Bartlett and Ghoshal (1989).

## 10.5 International strategy and structure

The analysis of international business strategy in Chapter 8 discussed the work of Bartlett and Ghoshal (1989) in relation to different types of international industry and strategy. This section outlines Bartlett and Ghoshal's corresponding organizational typology and details one empirical test of their work. They identify four types of organizational structure (see Table 10.1):

1.  *The multinational organizational model.* This is reflected in the decentralized organization of, for example, pre-war European companies with relatively autonomous subsidiaries and high responsiveness to local market differences. An important characteristic of these firms (for example British companies operating in imperial markets) was the extent to which the firm was run on the basis of personal relationships and family ownership links. Franko, in his 1976 study of European multinational companies, referred to these as 'mother–daughter' relationships, where subsidiary heads reported personally to the company's president. Very simple financial reporting procedures were often used and the need for co-ordination was low.

2.  *The international organizational model.* Bartlett and Ghoshal argue that this type of structure became common in the early postwar decades when

    The key task for companies that internationalized then was to transfer knowledge and expertise to overseas environments that were less advanced in technology or market development. (Bartlett and Ghoshal, 1989, p.49.)

    It was the form of organization that best reflected the technological causes of Vernon's international product life-cycle theory (see Chapter 5). Some functions in the international model are centralized and others are decentralized; in particular knowledge and research and development take place at the centre and are subsequently transferred to the subsidiaries.

3.  *The global organizational model* emphasizes efficiency, centralization and control; it is a 'hub and spoke' model typical of Japanese internationalization in the 1980s.

**Table 10.1**  Organizational characteristics of the transnational

| Organizational characteristics | Multinational | Global | International | Transnational |
|---|---|---|---|---|
| Configuration of assets and capabilities | Decentralized and nationally self-sufficient | Centralized and globally scaled | Sources of core competencies centralized, others decentralized | Dispersed, interdependent and specialized |
| Role of overseas operations | Sensing and exploiting local opportunities | Implementing parent company strategies | Adapting and leveraging parent company competencies | Differentiated contributions by national units to integrated worldwide operations |
| Development and diffusion of knowledge | Knowledge developed and retained within each unit | Knowledge developed and retained at the centre | Knowledge developed at the centre and transferred to overseas units | Knowledge developed jointly and shared worldwide |

*Source: Bartlett and Ghoshal (1989) p.65.*

4.   The transnational organizational model. In Bartlett and Ghoshal's analysis the transnational corporation is a new organizational form which has developed in response to the increasingly turbulent international business environment. The transnational involves a globally integrated network structure

> . . . in which increasingly specialised units worldwide . . . [are] . . . linked into an integrated network that ... [enables] . . . them to achieve their multidimensional strategic objectives of efficiency, responsiveness and innovation. The strength of this configuration springs from its fundamental characteristics: dispersion, specialization and interdependence. (Bartlett and Ghoshal, 1989, p.89.)

The features of the transnational include:

1.   A complex configuration of assets and capabilities in which some functions and resources are centralized, others decentralized, creating an interdependent network of specialized units.

2. Flexibility in the role of overseas subsidiaries with differentiated contributions by national units to integrated worldwide operations.

3. Knowledge developed jointly and shared worldwide; this contrasts with the centralization of development and diffusion of knowledge in the global and international organization models, and its dispersal in the multinational organizational model.

In the area of new product development, for example, the transnational is characterized by the use of multinational, multidisciplinary project teams. Christopher Lorenz cites the example of the Swedish white goods conglomerate, Electrolux, and its development team for a new generation of fridge freezers, the 'Quattro 500':

> Under the leadership of Heiki Takanen, a Finn based in Stockholm, the product was designed and developed for 'global' markets by a multidisciplinary task force from Europe and the United States, meeting sometimes on one side of the Atlantic and sometimes on the other. Much of the design work was done in Italy, but the product was engineered in Finland with Swedish assistance, and with particular marketing input from Britain. Initial production is in Finland, but . . . it may also be manufactured in the United States. (Lorenz, *Financial Times*, 21 June 1989.)

The speed of adoption of the transnational structure and the extent to which this structure provides a 'universal solution' are important sources of controversy. Ghoshal and Nohria, for example, argue that Bartlett and Ghoshal (1989) have frequently been misinterpreted; that the 'transnational integrated network organization should be used only for MNC'S operating in highly complex environments' and that companies elsewhere 'must simplify wherever possible' (Ghoshal and Nohria, 1993, p.24). In fact Ghoshal and Nohria's article argued the continuing relevance of structural fit, of matching organizational structure to environment and strategy, indicated by their article's title 'Horses for Courses: Organizational forms for Multinational Corporations'. Figure 10.9 summarizes their four organizational environments corresponding Bartlett and Ghoshal's (1989) structures. Comparing it with the Stopford and Wells model (Figure 10.7) transnational structures, responding to strong global integration and local responsiveness pressures, take the place of matrix organizations in the outer right quadrant.

Kenichi Ohmae in *The Borderless World* (1990) sets out his own five-step evolutionary stages model of internationalization:

- Stage 1. Early internationalization. In this stage foreign markets are served by arms-length exporting through the use of local agents and distributors.

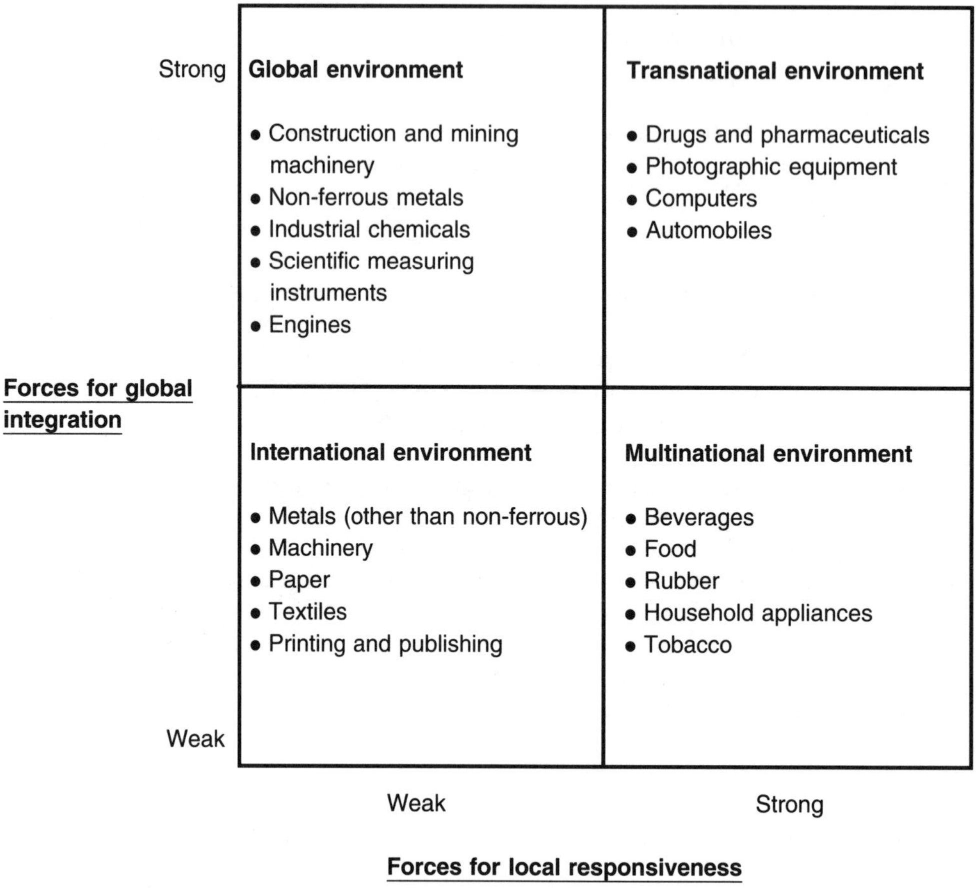

| | | |
|---|---|---|
| | **Global environment** | **Transnational environment** |
| Strong | • Construction and mining machinery<br>• Non-ferrous metals<br>• Industrial chemicals<br>• Scientific measuring instruments<br>• Engines | • Drugs and pharmaceuticals<br>• Photographic equipment<br>• Computers<br>• Automobiles |
| | **International environment** | **Multinational environment** |
| Weak | • Metals (other than non-ferrous)<br>• Machinery<br>• Paper<br>• Textiles<br>• Printing and publishing | • Beverages<br>• Food<br>• Rubber<br>• Household appliances<br>• Tobacco |

**Forces for global integration** (vertical axis: Strong to Weak)

Weak          Strong

**Forces for local responsiveness**

**Figure 10.9** Environment of MNCs: classification of business. Source Ghoshal and Noria (1993) p.27.

- Stage 2. Exporting is still the primary mode of entry but international involvement increases with the company setting up or taking over its own foreign distribution network.

- Stage 3. This is where the company begins to carry out its own manufacturing, marketing and sales in key foreign markets.

- Stage 4. This stage involves a complete set of business functions, a full replica of the parent company, being established in key foreign markets. Many headquarters functions are decentralized with the headquarters retaining a number of support functions such as personnel and finance for the subsidiary operations. Ohmae refers to this as the 'complete insiderization' stage, with the legitimacy of the

MNC subsidiary fully accepted in the host country (IBM Japan, for example, is regarded in the first instance as a Japanese company).

- Stage 5. Ohmae terms this the 'true globalization' stage where the MNC attempts to lose its nationality and to treat all its customers as if they were equidistant; for example a Japanese company would try to treat a Belgian customer with the same degree of attention as a Tokyo customer (1990, pp.17–18).

This clearly illustrates a difference in terminology. Ohmae's true or genuine globalization stage corresponds to Bartlett and Ghoshal's transnational organization, and not to their global organization structure with its connotations of centralization and domination by the company's headquarters.

According to Ohmae, the challenge is to 'get rid of the headquarters mentality' and achieve global localization, 'a new orientation which simultaneously looks in both directions' (Ohmae, 1990, p.93). Ohmae also suggests that many multinational companies are operating in a Stage 4 organizational mode and he cites United States companies with a long history of international involvement, such as Coca Cola, and many modern Japanese firms. The nature of the transnational organization is examined further in the next section.

## 10.6 The transnational corporation, heterarchy and informal processes

Bartlett and Ghoshal's concept of the transnational corporation goes beyond the creation of a 'globally integrated network organization' and other changes in terms of the MNC's formal structure. It involves significant changes to informal organizational processes and the 'mind sets' of international managers. In their 1990 Harvard Business Review article they discuss two managerial 'traps' that confronted MNCs in the 1980s and 1990s – one strategic and one structural. The strategic trap involved adopting static, unidimensional strategies to deal with an increasingly dynamic, complex environment. The structural trap was that, in responding with more complex strategies, MNC managers frequently adopted much more complex matrix-style structures which, as we saw in section 10.3 above, were costly and cumbersome. Bartlett and Ghoshal, however, argued that environmental complexity was a fundamental reality to which multinational companies needed to respond and developed an interesting biological metaphor to identify the change processes taking place:

> For those companies that adopted matrix structures, the problem was not in the way they defined the goal. They correctly recognised the need for a multidimensional organization to respond to growing external

complexity. The problem was that they defined their organizational objectives in purely structural terms. Yet formal structure describes only the organization's basic anatomy. Companies must also concern themselves with organizational physiology – the systems and relationships that allow the lifeblood of information to flow through the organization. And they need to develop a healthy organizational psychology – the shared norms, values and beliefs that shape the way individual managers think and act. (Bartlett and Ghoshal, 1990, p.140.)

From their MNC interview research base they found that the companies that were most successful in managing change and improving their organizational capability were those that started by trying to change organizational psychology, individual managerial attitudes and informal processes, rather than the organization's structure. The ideal starting point was 'organizational psychology and physiology' rather than 'anatomy'. They quote one of their executive interviewees as stating: 'The challenge is not so much to build a matrix structure as it is to create a matrix in the minds of our managers' (1990, p.145).

Martinez and Jarillo (1989) examine this issue in terms of the evolution of co-ordination mechanisms in MNCs. Their analysis of the international business research literature's changing foci suggests that the 'globalization phase' (from approximately 1950 to 1980) was accompanied by the formalization of co-ordination mechanisms compared to the largely personal relationships of the earlier multidomestic phase. Such formalization included centralization and departmentalization, with standardization using written procedures, formal job descriptions, etc. In the 'transnational period' since 1980, the emphasis in the literature has shifted to the use of 'more informal and subtle' co-ordination mechanisms to supplement the above, such as:

1.    Lateral relationships cutting across formal structure (such as the use of temporary project teams, task forces and committees).

2.    Informal information systems and channels of communication among the international managers.

3.    A strong, unifying organizational culture integrating the organization through a system of shared values and beliefs.

They suggest that the evolution and adaptation of strategy during the period since 1950 has resulted in increased co-ordination demands and they hypothesize:

Simple strategies need little coordination and therefore are implemented by using structural and formal mechanisms. Complex strategies (those resulting from interrelated, multiplant, multimarket policies) need an enormous coordinating effort, and so are implemented through both types of mechanisms: structural and formal, plus informal and subtle. (Martinez and Jarillo, 1989, p.492.)

In providing an analysis of the multinational corporation which goes beyond formal organizational structure, Hedlund and Rolander (1990) similarly define the emerging transnational in informal process terms. Their starting point is a critique of the strategy structure paradigm in which causal linkages run from environment to strategy to structure, the organization/environment link is seen as 'symbiotic' with strategy in the modern MNC, determining its environment as much as it is determined by it. In place of MNC organizational hierarchy, Hedlund and Rolander (1990, p.22) contrast an organizational structure based on heterarchy 'where many centres of many different kinds (e.g. in terms of functional, geographic or product responsibility) are coordinated increasingly through normative means.' They identify the following characteristics of the 'heterarchical MNC':

- *Many centres of different kinds.* With the dispersal of headquarters functions to locations in various countries, the organizational structure is multidimensional and flexible with no single dimension (product, functional or geographic) prioritized. Foreign subsidiaries play a strategic role in relation to the company as a whole.

- *Integration primarily by normative means.* Integration occurs through company culture, mission and management style rather than through financial control or coercive measures.

- *A wide range of governance modes.* A variety of institutional arrangements from market to hierarchy are used to govern the internal and external networks operated by the firm, for example the strategic importance of coalitions with other firms.

- *Information is replicated throughout the MNC.*

- *Strategy as action;* learning, innovation and experimentation are seen as important, the many centres involved allowing such experimentation to take place in various foreign subsidiary locations, and the lessons learnt to be replicated throughout the organization.

Hedlund and Rolander found empirical evidence for the heterarchic model in their analysis of Swedish/Swiss multinational corporations such as Electrolux (white goods), Asea Brown Boveri (electrical engineering) Tetra Pak (packaging) and SKF (ball bearings). Geographic dispersal of the functions of headquarters was frequently observed but there was less support for other elements of their model.

## 10.7 *Strategic predisposition and EPRG profile*

Chakravarthy and Perlmutter (1985) provide an important integrative typology which they term 'strategic predisposition'. This links together the MNC's mission and culture, strategy, structure and functional orientation (see Table 10.2).

Building on the work of Perlmutter (1969) they identify four distinct types of 'primary attitude':

- *Ethnocentric.* This is a predisposition where the values and culture of the parent and its home country dominate. Home country nationals tend to occupy key managerial positions throughout the world exemplified by the European 'tour of duty' by the executives of many United States and Japanese corporations. The product tends to be standardized in terms of home country marketing, a global integration strategy followed through a centralized, global product division structure.

- *Polycentric.* This means literally 'many centred' and is the opposite of an ethnocentric predisposition. Strategy and marketing tend to be nationally responsive, adapting to the countries where the MNC operates. It tends to use an area division structure, with local nationals recruited and promoted to key positions in their own country.

- *Regiocentric.* This is a predisposition in which the parent tries to blend its values and interests with those of its subsidiaries on a regional basis. Marketing and strategy tend to be integrated and standardized regionally but not across regions. Ford of Europe between 1967 and 1994 was to some extent an example of this type but Chakravarthy and Perlmutter suggest that the ideal type of this structure is likely to involve product and regional organization tied through a matrix and the appointment of local staff to key regional positions, whereas at Ford personnel practices tended to be ethnocentric in nature.

- *Geocentric.* World oriented, defined in terms of a global systems approach to decision making. In contrast to the global strategy and structure of an ethnocentric predisposition, geocentrism is a type where 'Headquarters and subsidiaries see themselves as parts of an organic worldwide entity. Superiority is not equated with nationality . . . Good ideas come from any country and go to any country within the firm' (Heenan and Perlmutter, 1979, p.21). Similarly, personnel practices will involve 'the best people everywhere in the world developed for key positions everywhere in the world.' Strategy and marketing will involve both global integration and adaptation.

Perlmutter (1969, p.14) suggests that these predispositions are rarely found in a pure form. There may, for example, be variation by functional

**Table 10.2**  Orientation of the firm under different EPRG profiles

| Orientation of the firm | Ethnocentric | Polycentric | Regiocentric | Geocentric |
|---|---|---|---|---|
| Mission | Profitability (viability) | Public acceptance (legitimacy) | Both profitability and public acceptance (viability and legitimacy | Same as regiocentric |
| Governance | Top down | Bottom up (each subsidiary decides on local objectives) | Mutually negotiated between region and its subsidiaries | Mutually negotiated at all levels of the corporation |
| Strategy | Global integration | National responsiveness | Regional integration and national responsiveness | Global integration and national responsiveness |
| Structure | Hierarchical product divisions | Hierarchical area divisions with autonomous national units | Product and regional organization tied through a matrix | A network of organizations (including stakeholder and competitor organizations) |
| Culture | Home country | Host country | Regional | Global |
| Marketing | Product development determined primarily by the needs of home country | Local product development based on local needs | Standardize within region but not across regions | Global product, with local variations |
| Finance | Repatriation of profits to home country | Retention of profits in host's country | Redistribution with region | Redistribution globally |
| Personnel practices | People of home country developed for key positions throughout world | Local people developed for key positions in their own country | Regional people developed for key positions anywhere in the region | Best people throughout the world developed for key positions throughout the world |

*Source: adapted from Chakravarthy and Perlmutter (1985) pp.5–6.*

department: finance might retain an ethnocentric outlook, whilst the marketing department, in responding to customers' needs, might be polycentric in outlook, whereas research and development might be geocentric in attitude. In consequence Perlmutter, and subsequently Chakravarthy and Perlmutter (1985), term the MNC's dominant predisposition its EPRG (ethno-, poly-, regio-, geocentric) profile. The terms ethnocentric, polycentric and geocentric broadly coincide with the global, multinational (-domestic) and transnational organizations identified earlier. Chakravarthy and Perlmutter conclude: 'An ethnocentric or polycentric EPRG profile is very common, while a regiocentric or geocentric EPRG profile is relatively new among MNCs' (Chakravarthy and Perlmutter, 1985, p.4). They suggest that the major obstacle to moving towards more geocentric structures is the difficulty of altering the 'mind set' of the international managers involved; the difficulty in giving them a world orientation.

Kobrin (1994, p.494) suggests that one important implication of this is that the multinational corporation may be defined not only in terms of geographic scope but also the degree of global integration or local responsiveness, and in terms of the mind set of its managers. Kobrin's research concluded that whilst a geocentric mind set did appear to be positively correlated with an MNC's geographic scope, 'it did not appear to be a function of length of international experience, strategy or organizational structure' (Kobrin, 1994, p.507). In contrast, Chakravarthy and Perlmutter concluded:

> The most important instrument available for changing the predisposition of an MNC is human resource management . . . It is important, therefore, that the personnel policies of an MNC ensure: 1) that the proper mix of attitudes is nurtured through job rotation, promotion and placement; and 2) that job assignments are carefully made in keeping with the manager's attitudes. The critical determinant of an MNC's successful adaptation to its environment is its ability to nurture relevant attitudes in its managerial work force. (Chakravarthy and Perlmutter, 1985.)

## 10.8 Critique of the transnational solution

To sum up the previous sections, an overview of the transnational corporation is developing in a varied literature which discusses the emergent TNC as much in terms of management processes and mind sets as in terms of formal organizational structures. Concepts representative of this thinking already mentioned include the 'matrix of the mind' (Bartlett and Ghoshal), and 'heterarchy' (Hedlund and Rolander). Similarly concepts of the MNC as an 'organizational tent' (Hedberg et al., 1976) and the 'virtual' transnational corporation (Byrne, 1993) belong to this framework. Pursuing Bartlett and Ghoshal's biological metaphor further, recent emphasis on the MNC's physiology and psychology understates the precise nature of the organizational structure skeleton holding the whole thing together. In addition, Taggart and McDermott conclude their review with important qualifications:

> It is uncertain . . . whether many MNCs will in fact make the transition to 'transnational' or 'heterarchical' status. First, proponents of the 'transnational' concept have based their hypothesis on a very small sample, which may not be representative. Second, existing studies which suggest that MNCs will increasingly devolve headquarters decision-making powers have been based on MNCs from one small home country – Sweden – giving a quite different perspective of internationalization from that which may be obtained by examining MNC'S from several, large home countries. (Taggart and McDermott, 1993, p.163.)

One direct piece of empirical research on the 'transnational solution' is Leong and Tan's (1993) study. This sought to test the validity of the Bartlett and Ghoshal organizational typology by a questionnaire survey of 151 MNC executives. The survey asked the respondents to categorize their own firm into one of Bartlett and Ghoshal's four organizational types and to indicate the degree of fit with the three sets of organizational characteristics summarized in Figure 10.9 above. The results partly corroborated Bartlett and Ghoshal's typology:

> Multinational corporations dominated, followed by the international and global forms. The transnational form as expected, was found to be the least evident structure. Second, the evidence in general furnished partial support for the differences in characteristics predicted across the four organization types of Bartlett and Ghoshal 1989 . . . however, it was found that executives who typed their organizations as being international and transnational in nature did not appear to endorse many of the behaviours predicted by the typology. (Leong and Tan, 1993, pp.457–8.)

One of the explanations for the findings advanced by the researchers was that most MNCs are at present operating with either multinational, international or global structures, hence the transnational represented an ideal form 'most companies are attempting to adopt' in the future; in consequence the precise characteristics of a future structure were unclear for the executives involved. A more critical stance in relation to these findings could conclude that there was a lack of support for the emergence of the transnational phase as proposed by Bartlett and Ghoshal.

Turner and Henry in their 1994 study sought to identify the extent of 'transnationalism' in a sample of 10 United States and European MNCs. The Bartlett and Ghoshal characteristics tested were dispersal, specialization and interdependence. There was very little evidence to support the adoption of these organizing characteristics and even where there was some support for the geographical dispersal of assets (Unilever, Nestlé and Asea Brown Boveri) this was primarily the result of corporate origins and 'administrative heritage'. They concluded:

> It is clear for most international companies the transnational model is more of an aspiration than a reality. [Globalization trends] . . . have induced many companies to organize around world wide product divisions. This trend was anticipated in the 1970s by Stopford and Wells. However from the evidence available we would hypothesize that the world wide product division is becoming the 'standard' model in most situations, with the other three ideal-typical structural solutions increasingly marginalised. (Turner and Henry, 1994, p.427.)

Turner and Henry's hypothesis is supported in other work. Samuel Humes (1993) important study of organizational change in European, American and Asian multinational corporations reached similar conclusions. Compared with the diversity of approaches evidenced in the first half of the twentieth century, Humes found significant evidence of convergence in organizational trends on all three continents, with widespread adoption of global product divisions with multifunctional roles:

> On all three continents, multinationals, conscious of the increasing pressures for change and the continuing need to improve their organizations, are developing a wider range of management dynamics. Some of the reorganizational steps that multinationals are taking appear more cautious and more piecemeal than others, but their cumulative impact upon corporate organizational traditions has been revolutionary. They have already led to converging transitions and pointed to prospective organizational trends. (Humes, 1993, pp.24.)

## 10.9 Summary

Important sources of controversy concern the speed of adoption of the transnational structure and the extent to which this structure provides a 'universal solution'. As we have seen, Ghoshal and Nohria argued that Bartlett and Ghoshal (1989) have frequently been misinterpreted that the 'transnational integrated network organization should be used only for MNCs operating in highly complex environments' and that elsewhere 'companies must simplify wherever possible' (Ghoshal and Nohria, 1993, p.24). At one level this does appear to reconcile the Bartlett and Ghoshal work with Samuel Humes' (1993) hypothesis of continental convergence around global product division structures, as well as Turner and Henry's similar (1994) conclusions. The environment facing almost all international companies in the 1980s and 1990s is highly complex and dynamic, however, and many have responded by simplifying rather than embracing complexity.

## 10.10 Further reading

Bartlett, C.A. and Ghoshal, S. (1989) *Managing Across Borders; The Transnational Solution*, Century Business, London.

Bartlett, C.A. and Ghoshal, S. (1990) Matrix management: not a structure, a frame of mind. *Harvard Business Review*, July–August, 138–45.

Bartlett, C., Doz, Y and Hedlund, G. (1990) *Managing the Global Firm*, Routledge, London.

Dicken, P. (1992) *Global Shift*, Paul Chapman, London.

Ghoshal, S. and Nohria, N. (1993) Horses for courses: organisational forms for multinational corporations. *Sloan Management Review*, Winter, 23–35.

Hendry, C. (1994) *Human Resource Management Strategies for International Growth*, Routledge, London.

Humes, S. (1993) *Managing the Multinational; Confronting the Global – Local Dilemma*, Prentice Hall, London.

Leong, S.M. and Tan, C.T. (1993) Managing across borders: an empirical test of the Bartlett and Ghoshal (1989) organisational typology. *Journal of International Business Studies*, 3, 449–64.

Martinez, J.I. and Jarillo, J.C. (1989). The evolution of research on coordination mechanisms in multinational corporations. *Journal of International Business Studies*, Fall, 489–514.

Taggart, J.H. and McDermott, M.C. (1993) *The Essence of International Business*, Prentice Hall, New York.

Turner, I and Henry, I, (1994) Managing international organisations; lessons from the field. *European Management Journal*, December, 12(4), 417–31.

## *10.11 Questions for further discussion*

1.  What were the main similarities and differences between the dominant forms of MNC organizational structure in the United States, Europe and Asia in the period up to 1950? How do you account for these differences?

2.  Under what circumstances are each of the following structures appropriate?

    • Global functional division structure.

    • Global product division structure.

    • Global area division structure.

    Give examples of each type of structure.

3.  What are the main advantages and disadvantages of international matrix structures?

4.  Outline and critically evaluate the Stopford and Wells structural stages model

5.  What are the main features of Bartlett and Ghoshal's 'transnational solution'. What do you consider to be the main criticisms of the model?

6.   Explain the following concepts:

    (a) heterarchy;

    (b) ethnocentrism;

    (c) geocentrism.

7.  Analyse the main organizational structure changes at Royal Dutch Shell in 1995 (Box 10.1). What are the main causes of the changes proposed?

8.  Analyse the organizational structure changes in 1994 at Ford (Box 8.3). To what extent, if at all, is Ford moving towards a Bartlett and Ghoshal transnational organization?

**Box 10.1** Organizational restructuring at Royal Dutch Shell (1995)

The special characteristics of Shell are its sheer size (it is Europe's largest multinational corporation) and its multinational (Anglo-Dutch) ownership, reflected in the split of the corporate headquarters between London and the Hague. Historically this has reinforced the tendency of European MNCs (Philips, Nestlé) to structure their organizations on primarily geographic lines. At Shell the regional bosses have been the primary power in the organizational structure. However, over time a number of matrix structure elements have been added, including professional services such as legal services and functions such as exploration.

At the top of Shell was a four member committee of managing directors, each responsible for one of Shell's four world regions. Under these directors were regional co-ordinators, business functions such as exploration, refining, the selling and marketing of petrol and oil products, and central companies providing legal, financial, information and other services. Under the central organization were the operating companies themselves; in matrix terms, a particular operating company could be defined by its geographic region, its business sector and its line of business.

The *Financial Times* reported:

> The proposed changes, which will be shaped in detail through consultation with staff over the next six months, are radical because they do more than attack the overstaffing and bureaucracy that threaten to weigh Shell down. They will also eliminate many of the regional fiefdoms through which Shell runs its worldwide empire, and which allow local barons to wield a great deal of power . . . With growing global competition and unforgiving shareholder pressure for better performance, few organizations can any longer afford an elaborate structure in which important decisions require laborious debate between several sets of executives with overlapping responsibilities. (*Financial Times*, 30 March 1995.)

Ironically Shell's organizational restructuring was not forced upon it by its immediate financial performance. In 1994 Shell achieved record profits of £4 billion, a 24 per cent increase on the previous year. The pressures for change included Shell's strategic analysis of the changing competitive conditions in the oil industry, the need to reduce overheads and administrative costs for future competitive advantage and the need to be more responsive, market driven and closer to the consumer. Initial cost-cutting measures had already taken place in Shell's operating companies but these were quite small-scale measures compared with the fundamental reorganizations that had occurred at Shell's competitive rivals such as British

Petroleum, Exxon, Amoco and Mobil, stimulated by the twin effects of the early 1990s recession and weak oil prices.

The new structure is to be organized around five centralized business organizations covering Shell's main activities: exploration and production, oil products (refining and marketing), chemicals, gas and coal. Each of the first three organizations is headed by a new business committee with up to eight members representing the largest companies in each business organization. Whilst the committee of managing directors is retained at the corporate centre, it will the business organization committees that will take the key strategic and investment decisions for their sectors, leaving as much executive authority as possible for the operating companies at the local level.

> Shell hopes to encourage maximum local initiative within a structure that keeps the group as a whole heading in the chosen direction, and provides the right checks and balances.

It was estimated that ultimately the organizational changes at headquarters level and subsequent changes across Shell's hundreds of operating companies would achieve as much as a 30 per cent reduction in costs.

*Adapted from Lascelles, D. (1995) Barons swept out of fiefdoms. Financial Times, 30 March and Lascelles, D. and Corzine, R. (1996) Prised out of its Shell. Financial Times, 16 February.*

# 11

# *Globalization and human resources management*

## *11.1 Introduction*

This chapter examines the impact that globalization is having on human resources management (HRM) policies and practices within firms that operate internationally. The chapter begins by examining some definitional and conceptual problems. In particular, it examines different models of HRM and identifies the limits to the development of a universally acceptable model. In doing so it explores some of the key factors that act as constraints on the activities of global businesses in applying HR practices at host country level. The role of organizational culture as an instrument for integrating the diverse operations of international firms is considered in detail and, in particular, the extent to which management of such firms are able to fashion a comprehensive and unifying culture is examined. The chapter indicates why the truly multicultural global business still seems a distant prospect and examines some of the practical steps that international firms are taking to reconcile the culturally diverse nature of their operations.

## *11.2 Globalization*

There is an increasing amount of circumstantial evidence to suggest that the globalization of business is generating similarities in the ways in which firms manage their employees and design the processes by which they manufacture products and provide services. The widespread adoption of team-based working in manufacturing industries, the popularity of various techniques to improve quality, the standardization of working procedures and formal behaviour patterns in service industries and the growth of a shared language regarding organizations and people management all seem to point to an inexorable process of international business integration. These developments appear to suggest that employees' experience of work will become increasingly similar irrespective of national boundaries but does it amount to a coherent set of phenomena from which clear implications can be drawn for HRM? In finding an answer to this we need to pose two further questions: 'what type of organization are we considering here?' and 'is there a coherent model of HRM which can be applied universally when comparing practice in different international organizations?'

Closer examination reveals significant differences in interpretation of the concept of globalization. The sustained expansion of international trade during the past 40 years and its domination by a core group of corporations is seen by some as representing the most significant development in the world economy (Perlmutter, 1969; Dicken, 1992). Other observers focus on the evidence that an increasingly international division of labour has the greatest potential influence on labour force structure, job opportunities and education and training through the optimization of production location (Reich, 1991; Harzing, 1995). For others it is the homogenization of consumer tastes and the development of similar markets that are of greatest significance, in particular because this implies a high degree of integration and centralized management control (Levitt, 1983). Some researchers have endeavoured to define more narrowly the concepts of 'multinational', 'global' and 'transnational' as applied to firms in order to generate more specificity in this increasingly diffuse debate (Bartlett and Ghoshal, 1989; Spivey and Thomas, 1990). These differences in both definition and focus suggest a need for caution in drawing broad conclusions about the significance for HRM and in particular the notion of convergence to any particular model of HRM. The following sections explores this in more detail.

## 11.3 Alternative models of human resources management

While advances in technology and information systems have facilitated the increased internationalization of organization functions, such as finance, manufacturing and marketing, this process has been much slower when applied to the management of human resources. As a corporate practice and an area of academic enquiry and research, international HRM is relatively underdeveloped. The internationalization of business witnessed a major expansion in the number of expatriate managers and in the problems, such as cost and cultural sensitivity, of managing them (Brewster, 1991). It is only in recent years, however, that the focus has shifted from the practical or logistical difficulties associated with an elite management cadre to the strategic significance of human resource management as a factor in competitive advantage. Human resource management is certainly considered a source of advantage in the generic literature on competitiveness but it is not prioritized as such (Porter, 1985, 1991).

Other commentators suggest that as the advanced industrial economies lose their previously privileged access and control of technology and natural resources, and as the newly-industrializing economies (particularly the four Asian 'Tigers': South Korea, Singapore, Taiwan and Hong Kong) outstrip the West in labour-intensive manufacturing industries, the quality of human resources is the critical factor in competitiveness and the one less easily duplicated by competitors (Reich). In the new 'knowledge-based' industries, the key to competitiveness lies in people-based assets such as education, innovation, commitment to quality, and intellectual property.

Human resource management as an ingredient of corporate strategy has generally been associated with the distinctively American model of HRM (Beer *et al.*, 1985), a model which places a premium on management autonomy, the weakness or absence of trade unions and the individualization of employee relations (individualized payment systems, such as performance-related or merit pay, for instance, instead of collective agreements). The American model of HRM, however, does not correspond to corporate policy and practice in other advanced industrial economies. In West Europe, in particular, there are highly regulated labour markets and collectivist institutions and procedures, including relatively strong unions, employers associations and collective bargaining persist. Again, attention is drawn to the significance of the cultural underpinning of HRM practice: European nations share a markedly different set of values from those prevalent in the United States. Management and corporate governance, for instance, tend to be characterized by a pluralist and inclusivist approach to management – accepting the existence and legitimacy of various interests within the firm (employees, managers, suppliers, customers, host communities as well as shareholders are deemed to be 'stakeholders') in contrast to a unitary, and exclusivist philosophy of management characteristic of the Anglo-Saxon economies of the United States and the United Kingdom (Thurley and Wiedenhuis, 1991).

The structures and philosophies of ownership are critical determinants of HRM within individual firms and nations. Stakeholder theory informs the corporate governance of European business and, in a different form, the Tiger Economies of the Pacific Rim (Hutton, 1995). The dominance of institutional shareholders such as banks, pension funds and insurance companies over smaller, individual shareholders is less important in such regimes of corporate governance than their long-term orientation. A preoccupation with short-term returns and profitability has been seen as an institutional constraint on human resource development within United States and British firms. Managers in such firms are more likely to regard training as a cost rather than an investment given the difficulties of costing its benefits or proving its contribution to competitive advantage (Keep, 1989). Moreover, European HRM is conditioned by an environment and culture that is tolerant or even supportive of state intervention. Whether this takes the form of legally enforceable employment rights or state-subsidized training systems, the political constraints on corporate autonomy and managerial prerogatives in West Europe are considerable in comparison with the United States. A basic model for examining the particularity of HR strategies within the European context has been developed by Brewster and Bournois (1991) and has since been further developed by Brewster (1995).

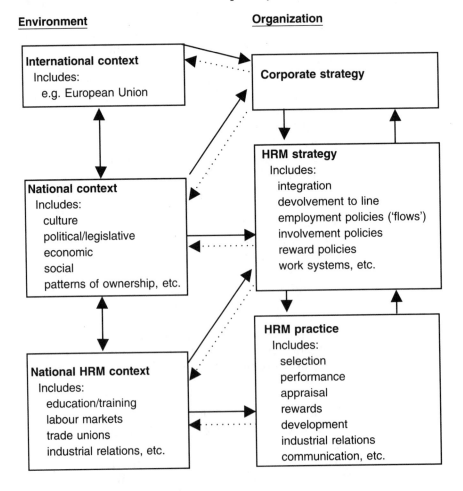

Figure 11.1 European model of HRM. Source: Brewster (1995) p.14.

In addition to the significant differences between the United States and West European countries referred to above, there are also substantial differences within West Europe itself. In fashioning human resource strategy, global companies must be sensitive to the significant variations in local conditions. The constellation of interests, values and cultural differences that confront the global company is, perhaps, best illustrated by comparing the roles and influence of different parties involved in the employment relationship.

## 11.4 Employee relations and statutory employment rights

Even within the advanced industrialized economies, major differences in the legal, political and social contexts of employees relations will influence or even determine a firm's strategic options. American or British firms establishing operations in France or Germany, for example, might generally expect to invest greater resources in training since such 'high skill, high wage' economies demand corporate commitment to developing human resources. In France, companies are legally compelled to invest a fixed percentage of turnover in training while Germany's 'dual system' of training requires firms to jointly fund training provision in partnership with the state (Lane, 1989; Lynch, 1993; Larsen, 1994). Where employee relations are highly regulated, companies are more likely to encounter higher labour costs and more restrictions on management prerogatives – on the right of managers to manage. Regulations confer rights on employees, such as trade union membership and recognition of trade unions for collective bargaining. Employees may also be granted statutory entitlement to various benefits which can significantly increase non-wage labour or 'social' costs. Table 11.1 below indicates the contrast between the regulated European labour market and the American labour market where state intervention is minimal and employee benefits are in the main a matter of employer discretion in response to local labour market conditions.

Such factors are also influential in corporate location or relocation decisions. One survey (International Management, April 1994) found that 74 per cent of senior executives considered labour costs to be very or fairly important in investment decisions. In 1992, Hoover, the US white goods multinational, closed its plant in Dijon, France, rather than its facility near Glasgow, Scotland. Whilst basic costs were broadly similar, the firm's French operations had significantly higher non-wage labour costs due to French employees statutory rights to longer holidays and training. The episode raised considerable controversy as an example of 'social dumping', the practice whereby multinational firms relocate to countries offering cheaper labour at the expense of employment standards and employee rights.

**Table 11.1** Statutory regulations covering employee benefits and rights in Europe* and the United States, 1991

| Benefits and rights | Europe | United States |
|---|---|---|
| Public holidays | 12 | 8–10 |
| Annual vacation | 4 weeks | no statutory rights |
| Sick leave | | |
| – maximum weeks' leave | 54 | no statutory rights |
| – % of earnings paid | 62% | |
| Maternity leave | | |
| – maximum weeks' leave | 18 | 13 |
| – % of earnings paid | 89% | 0 |
| Severance pay | | |
| – % of workers with severance pay | 72% | no statutory rights |
| Unemployment insurance | | |
| – months covered | 16 | 6 |
| – % earnings paid during unemployment | 47% | 50% |

*Source: Freeman (1993).*

* European figures apply to EEC members in 1991 weighted by 1988 employment.

Different value systems and cultural variables will also constrain corporate human resource strategy. A strong collectivist ethos pervades the political and industrial cultures of Nordic economies and new entrant firms pursuing largely individualized employee relations policies, rejecting union representation and collective bargaining for example, are likely to encounter resistance. In 1995, Toys'R'Us, the American retail multinational, refused to recognize unions in its Swedish subsidiary in line with corporate policy. It was forced to accept and bargain with the Swedish workers' union following a concerted campaign of union action, consumer boycotts and political pressure, however. Japanese car manufacturers such as Nissan, and Toyota, which have vigorously resisted unionization of their plants in the United States, have adopted a different strategy in setting up manufacturing operations in Britain. In Britain, unions have been invited to submit applications to be considered for sole recognition rights. This enables the Japanese companies to select their preferred union candidates and these, in turn, are required to accept limitations on their role at plant level. This has formed one element in a strategy based on avoidance of multi-unionism, restricted recognition rights, rigorous selection procedures, mechanisms for employee involvement and relatively high remuneration levels. It has enabled these companies successfully to preserve much of their Japanese approach to the management of employees while adapting to a higher trade union presence in the British car industry (Wickens, 1987; Garrahan and Stewart, 1992). Global firms must adapt their human resource strategies to suit the terrain in which they operate. At the very least, this approach requires consideration of the broad differences in the structures and practices of employee relations in various countries. We will now consider some of these factors.

## 11.5 *National and regional variations in collective bargaining*

Collective bargaining refers to the way in which employers and trade unions negotiate to set the basic terms and conditions of the workforce within a particular company or sector. Terms and conditions include basic wages and salaries, benefits such as pensions and sick pay, working conditions, including working hours, holidays and shift systems. In some countries, collective bargaining is centralized, taking place at sectorial or national level.

In Germany, for example, the pay and conditions of most workers within the engineering industry are negotiated by Gesamtmetall, the national engineering employers' association, and IG Metall, the national metalworkers' union. Individual companies may also negotiate locally, at the level of the enterprise or firm but they are still obliged to accept the minimum standards agreed at national level. In recent years, however, such systems have become more centralized as firms have opted out of national negotiations, resigned from national employers' associations (see below) or otherwise simply refused to implement nationally agreed terms and conditions (Baglioni, 1990; Hegewisch, 1993). In some European countries, such as Germany, France, Italy and Belgium, there is a system of 'bargained legislation'. Agreements between employers and unions are enshrined in legislation. In countries such as the United Kingdom, on the other hand, collective agreements are entirely voluntary and are not legally enforceable.

In some respects, the question of centralization or decentralization tells us little about the industrial relations system or the balance of bargaining power between employers and unions. Italy, for instance, has a mixture of centralized national pacts alongside a plethora of plant-level or firm-specific agreements. Japan has decentralized, locally organized company unions and performance-related pay systems but still maintains the annual central wage negotiations (Soskice, 1990). In contrast to many other European countries, the United Kingdom has a markedly decentralized industrial relations system (Crouch, 1993). Most employers, at least in the private sector, have opted out of national-level negotiations, which they found rigid and costly, and have devolved collective bargaining arrangements to the level of the individual enterprise, workplace or profit-centre. This gives managers greater discretion to negotiate agreements that reflect local circumstances and it undermines the bargaining strength of the unions, which tends to be greater at national level than at local level. The United States also has a highly decentralized industrial relations system with most negotiations taking place between individual firms and local union branches (Wheeler, 1993).

## 11.6 Trade unionism

Corporate policies towards organized labour are an important indicator of HR strategy but, with a few exceptions (World Bank, 1995), the globalization literature generally understates the internationalization of labour markets and ignores the role of trade unions. Unionization is a particularly sensitive and strategic issue because unions can limit management's room for manoeuvre, raise costs and disrupt production and in so doing threaten the viability of the local operation. In a multinational corporation reliant on transnational sourcing, for example, an industrial dispute in one subsidiary can sever supplies of important components or services to operations in other countries. Companies can adopt dual-sourcing strategies so that they are never entirely dependent on a single facility for a specific supply but this complicates and raises the cost of rationalizing operations. This is one reason why a fully decentralized approach to human resource strategy – devolving decisions to national subsidiaries – is unfeasible. As two leading commentators have pointed out:

> [Union action] not only delays the rationalization and integration of MNCs' manufacturing networks and increases the cost of such adjustments, but also, at least in such industries as automobiles, reduces the efficiency of the integrated MNC network. Therefore, treating labour relations as incidental and relegating them to the specialists in the various countries is inappropriate. (Prahalad and Doz, 1987.)

Unions' collective bargaining power may also push up labour costs to the extent that they damage company competitiveness. Unions may also delay or veto corporate investments, relocations or closures. A major new investment by Ford, the United States multinational automobile manufacturer, in Dundee, Scotland, was effectively vetoed by unions in the United Kingdom when they insisted that the proposed facility should be covered by the existing 'Blue Book' agreement governing terms and conditions in Ford's other United Kingdom operations.

Unionization may also bring positive economic effects, however. Research suggests that unions are not necessarily a drag on competitiveness and, in some cases, are associated with higher levels of productivity and lower employee turnover than non-union firms (Baleman, 1992; Metcalf, 1989, 1993). Unionized firms also tend to take human resource development more seriously, showing higher levels of investment in training. As a former United States Secretary of Labor has noted, by raising the cost of labour, unions can give companies an incentive to ensure that such labour is skilled and motivated enough to compensate the company through higher productivity (Marshall, 1992). Unions can therefore represent an important factor in promoting competitive strategies based on high quality, productivity and skills-enhancement rather than short-term cost considerations.

Employees have historically formed and joined trade unions in order to protect and advance their interests in so far as they have seen their interests (in higher wages, shorter working hours and better working conditions) to be in conflict with employers' interests (restraining or reducing costs, maintaining control and boosting profitability and competitiveness). Since most individual employees have no power to control their own working environment or negotiate their own pay rises, unions provide what the great liberal economist, Galbraith, called 'countervailing power' to the otherwise unrestrained power of management within the workplace (Galbraith, 1967).

In most advanced industrialized economies, unions represent employee interests through collective bargaining or, less directly, through forms of employee representation such as work councils. Unions and employers do not always have a hostile or adversarial relationship. Japanese trade unions are fairly quiescent and, outside of the annual wage claim – the *Shunto* – they rarely challenge managerial prerogatives and they accept that employers and employees share a common interest in profitability, competitiveness and the success of the firm (Kuwahara, 1993). In fact, it is not unusual to find senior managers assuming control of a company's union and union officials taking up management posts. Although there is not the same level of accommodation or collusion between unions and employers in West Europe, the notion of 'social partnership' has eclipsed historical class conflict. Social partnership denotes a relationship of mutual respect and legitimacy: employers generally recognize the right of the employees to join and be represented by a union and the right of unions to be recognized, engage in collective bargaining and be involved in forums for employee representation (see below). On the other hand, unions recognize the legitimacy of the enterprise, accept managers' right to manage and generally accept a level of flexibility in working arrangements that enhances corporate competitiveness (Streeck, 1992).

By contrast, the Anglo-Saxon' economies, the United Kingdom, the United States, Canada and Australia, have a tradition of adversarial industrial relations. Employees and employers have maintained a polarized and frequently confrontational relationship, based on mutual distrust and the assumption of a basic conflict of interest. Unions have sought to restrict managerial authority either through negotiated job controls, as in the United States, or restrictive working practices, as in the United Kingdom. Similarly, employers have rejected forms of employee participation common in continental Europe, fearing an extension of union power. In some cases, especially in the United States, employers have fought, often illegally and sometimes violently, to resist unionization or to de-organize existing unions (Freeman and Medoff, 1984).

The meaning of trade unionism also differs between countries. In highly politicized labour movements, union membership reflects an ideological commitment as much as a means of improving pay, conditions or employment security. In countries like France, Italy and Spain, trade unions have been divided according to political allegiance: socialist, communist, liberal, Christian democratic and so on (Visser, 1994, 1995). Consequently, if a multinational firm is inclined or required to recognize a union in France, for example, it will prefer to work with a 'moderate' union federation such as the CFDT or CGT-FO, rather than the communist-orientated CGT.

An important indicator of union strength is union density or the proportion of the workforce organized in trade unions. The advanced industrialized economies can be categorized in three broad groups: high union density where over 70 per cent of workers are unionized (Denmark, Finland, Norway and Sweden); medium range density where between a third and a half of workers are union members (Germany, Italy, Britain. Australia, Canada) and low union density where less than 30 per cent of the workforce is organized (United States, Japan, France, Spain) (Bean, 1992). However, union membership is not necessarily a true reflection of union strength. In France and Spain, for instance, union density is low yet collective agreements negotiated at national or sectorial level may be legally extended to firms in which unions have few members even if such firms take no part in the collective bargaining process. In fact, one of the reasons union membership is so low in France and Spain is because of the 'free-rider syndrome': workers gaining the benefits of union-negotiated pay rises and improvements in conditions whether or not they are union members.

## 11.7 Employers' organizations

Differences in employee relations systems are strongly influenced by the perspectives and organization of employers. In Japan and in most of Western Europe employers are generally well organized in powerful employers' associations. In countries like Austria, Germany and Nordic states, such as Denmark, Norway and Sweden, this has tended to centralize industrial relations. Strong employers' groups negotiate directly with powerful central union confederations to establish a basic collective agreement which sets the framework for negotiations within individual sectors or individual firms, including a recommended minimum increase in wages and salaries (Van Waarden, 1995). Where employers associations are weak or unrepresentative, on the other hand, industrial relations tend to focus on the individual firm, allowing companies more independence and the discretion to negotiate, or to unilaterally decide, without reference to unions or employees, whatever conditions suit their particular needs and resources.

Human resources management is subject to a range of influences which constrain the strategies that international firms can pursue. Far from witnessing any process of homogenization in policies and practices in the management of their employees, a striking degree of diversity persists. Even reference to the different HRM in America, Asia or Europe may be misleading. Within the North America bloc, for instance, Canada has stronger trade unions and a more regulated employment regime than the United States. In the United States, trade unions remain relatively influential in the 'rust belt' states of the north-east and within the public sector, but exceptionally weak in the 'sun belt' states of the south where anti-union 'right to work' laws in certain states make union organization particularly difficult. Likewise, within the European Union, the British labour market is markedly more liberal and collectivist institutions are weaker than in other parts of continental Europe (Ulman *et al.*, 1993). Against this context of diversity it is to be expected that, as Pieper (1990) points out, a single, universal model of HRM does not exist. On the contrary, diversity is growing at the expense of uniformity, even within Europe.

## 11.8 Competitive advantage and culture change

In their search to reconcile global direction on the one hand and sensitivity to the kind of diverse local conditions described above on the other, international firms appear increasingly receptive to the idea that culture can play a crucial role in facilitating the integration of their widely dispersed organizations. They have been subjected to a growing chorus of opinion which argues that the means to securing competitive advantage is through realization of the full potential of their employees.

Success, it is asserted, is associated with those firms that have recognized this apparent truth and moreover possess an organizational culture to sustain it (Peters and Waterman, 1982; Porter, 1985; Bratton, 1994; Pfeffer 1994). The language and ideas of culture change encourage an outward orientation by exhorting managers to look to successful organizations, either in their own country or further afield, in order to identify and emulate those practices that appear to explain success. If the proposition is accepted that the culture of an organization can be changed or even deliberately manufactured then there are obvious attractions for those organizations that operate across different national cultures and face quite different sets of indigenous expectations and values in dealing with such matters as commercial contracts, management styles and working practices.

Since the early 1980s corporate culture has thus assumed the status of a key concept both for those who observe and comment on organizations and those who seek to change them. Indeed, for the latter group, in which consultants must be included as well as managers, the culture of an organization has become a crucial variable for explaining success and failure. It has been estimated that there are over 20 000 consultants offering strategies for culture change and, despite the derivative nature of their offerings, their appeal seems undiminished (Hampden-Turner, 1990, p.208). Management consultants Peters and Waterman have been particularly influential both in the United States and elsewhere in stressing that the determination and ability of senior management to modify corporate culture in a changing world constituted an essential ingredient for success. *In Search of Excellence* (1982) was one of the most widely read books in management circles in recent years but attempts to translate their concept of excellence into operational language is frustrated by the reality that, in common with much of the human resources literature in the 1980s, their work confuses description and prescription. In an otherwise trenchant critique of their methodology and evidence, Guest (1992, p.15) acknowledges that Peters and Waterman have '. . . stimulate[d] a greater interest for ideas about symbolic management, human resource management, culture in organizations and, above all, leadership.'

Central to a majority of culture change programmes is the assertion that successful adaptation and change is dependent on identifying and sustaining a set of shared values in order to gain commitment to the organization's objectives. The fact that many managers treat this as problematic is compounded by the process of management delayering and labour force reductions which invariably accompanies such programmes. The ensuing dislocation and climate of uncertainty can create contradictions between corporate value statements and the day-to-day experience of many managers and other employees (Höpfl et al., 1992). It may also mean that employees only pay lip service to the newly espoused values as a necessary condition of retaining employment. Legge (1989) suggests that the stress which HRM places on the development of corporate culture is partly explained by a need to give direction to the organization but also to mediate the tension between an emphasis on individualism on the one hand and a parallel emphasis on team work on the other. As such, she suggests that it indicates internal inconsistency in the model. A process by which the values, beliefs and norms of organizational life are subjected to critical scrutiny is intentionally unsettling in both the work and non-work lives of those affected for it invariably demands a new and pervasive contract between the employee and the organization.

In spite of this relatively recent explosion of interest in organizational culture change, the concept is not new. The literature on organizational research, from the Hawthorn Experiments in 1929 onward, has relied on culture as a crucial explanatory variable (Morgan, 1986). Jaques (1951), in his long-term and pioneering study of the Glacier Metal Company in West London, emphasized the centrality of culture in understanding the social relations of organizations, in particular their reward system. For a large group of American researchers whose work was influenced in the 1950s and 1960s by what was initially called 'structural functionalism' and later 'systems theory', culture and structure became the twin dimensions in the analysis of organizations (see, for example Blau and Scott, 1963). The growing application of this concept, however, has not been accompanied by any uniformity of definition, a problem that remains with us today.

In a comprehensive examination of contemporary definitions of organizational culture, Sparrow and Hiltrop (1994, p.316) point to a confusion which derives from a concept that is imprecise and ambiguous and conclude: 'the concept continues to elude theoretical precision and managerial instrumentality.' Far from being a hindrance, however, this may help to explain the appeal of organizational culture as a concept and instrument of strategic management.

Whereas culture, as applied to organizational life, was essentially the preserve of academic research until the end of the 1970s, it has subsequently entered the day-to-day language of management and in so doing has acquired considerable impetus from increased international competition. Expansion and decline in national productivity and GNP among existing and newly industrialized economies attracted interest in the characteristics of industries and organizations in countries that benefited from faster growth. Initially the focus of interest was the production systems and manufacturing strategies of other countries but in recent years this has given way to an interest in people management and attempts to explain differences in terms of culture (Brewster and Tyson, 1991).

Several reasons have been advanced to explain this widening interest in culture. It has been suggested that the most influential factors were the growth in Japanese industrial and economic power and the consequent loss of confidence in Western economies, particularly that of the United States, which occurred with the growing internationalization of large corporations (Morgan, 1986). In an environment in which there was widespread ignorance about Japanese society in general and industrial organization in particular, those writers who claimed to have found a causal relationship between Japanese cultural characteristics and economic success gained influence out of proportion to the rigour of their research (Guest, 1992). Gow (1988, p.16) suggests that what he calls the 'learning from Japan' literature was motivated by fear and desperation as managers in the West searched for 'quick fix' answers. According to Legge (1989, p.28) the fascination of American managers with the linkages between a stereotyped 'Japanese' employment culture and Japanese economic strength has emphasized the development and management of an appropriate culture as *the* strategic leadership activity. The shift in GDP away from manufactured to service industries in the older industrial economies is also cited as a factor (Thackray, 1982; Paauwe and Dewe 1995). Central to the so-called quality movement of the 1980s was a conviction that delivering better quality services or products was dependent crucially on changing the attitudes and values of everyone within the organization. Culture change thus became an integral part of virtually all quality improvement programmes (Goetsch and Davis, 1994).

## 11.9 The quest for the multicultural global organization

What models offer guidance to international organizations seeking to change or modify organizational culture? The vision and prototype model for the multicultural multinational corporation is not new. As Chapter 10 argued, Perlmutter (1969) devised a classification of multinational enterprises in which he envisaged that by the end of the century a combination of technological, economic, political and social factors would gradually transform multinationals into geocentric, or truly international structures. Since then his vision of the giant corporation of the future has provided an evolutionary ideal type against which strategic objectives and reality could be measured. It has also offered a framework for examining obstacles to globalization. Perlmutter characterized the geocentric multinational as having a fully international management structure with nationality playing no part in determining appointments. He likened the cultural climate of such corporations to that of an international agency of the United Nations in which business objectives would be entirely divorced from national interest. Although Perlmutter identified many obstacles ranging from political and economic nationalism to the more prosaic problems of management inexperience and staff immobility, it seems he considerably underestimated those forces that have made the evolutionary process so painfully slow.

Why has progress been so limited? Bartlett and Ghoshal (1989) maintain that a preoccupation with the relationship between

**Box 11.1** The discreet charm of the multicultural multinational

'There are very few multicultural multinationals; the truly global multicultural company does not yet exist', David de Pury, Co-Chairman of Asea Brown Boveri (ABB), a Swedish-Swiss electrical-engineering giant, flatly informed an international management symposium at St Gallen in Switzerland. He pointed out that few multinationals produce more than 20 per cent of their goods and services outside their immediate or wider home market; that most boards come predominantly from one culture and that few multinationals are ready to let their shareholder base become as global as their business. This dismissal is all the more striking, in coming from ABB, a firm with a board of eight directors from four different nationalities; an executive committee of eight people from five countries; English as its corporate language; and financial results published in dollars. Perhaps only Royal Dutch Shell – another European giant of mixed parentage, which has some 38 nationalities in its London head office – can claim to have advanced so far down the multicultural route. What chance is there then for big American or Japanese firms that think that globalization simply means having occasional board meetings in London or Paris? Would-be multicultural multinationals are struggling to solve a dilemma that has bedeviled their predecessors: the clash between global standardization and local roots.

*Source: The Economist, 30 July 1994.*

organizational structures and strategy explains the failure of many multinational corporations to assume Perlmutter's geocentric form. This, they suggest, was due to a misplaced belief that by changing the structure, the values and behaviour of individual managers would also change. The difference between what Paauwe and Dewe (1995) term first and second generation models of multinational organization is that the latter focus on culture change, emphasizing managing as the intervening variable and the key to successful strategy implementation. This, they contend, makes the management of human resources crucial and while it applies to domestic as well as international enterprises the latter felt the need earlier to change the way in which they are managed because of the turbulent and complex markets within which they operate. A more compelling explanation is offered by Hendry (1994) who suggests that the increased complexity of international firms means that integration and cohesion become less dependent on formal structural controls and more dependent on cultural norms.

This supports Legge's contention that the popularity of team working, possibly one of the most significant examples of cultural imitation in recent years, is partly explained by the need of organizations with flatter structures to substitute internalized peer group control for the external controls which hierarchical organizations impose on their employees (Legge, 1989).

While the above observations may increase our understanding of the changing objectives and priorities of global businesses, on their own they represent an incomplete explanation of the prolonged gestation of the multicultural global enterprise. Whatever an organization's objectives might be, culture is a complex phenomenon shaped by a variety of factors that are often beyond the control of senior management. Morgan (1986) cites several well-known firms to demonstrate how corporate leaders can have a profound impact on shaping the culture of their respective organizations. It is their positions of power, in particular the ability to reward or punish, which give them a special advantage but they do not, he emphasizes, enjoy a monopoly in its creation. Professional, functional or trade union subcultures are present to varying degrees in all business organizations and comprise what Morgan calls 'a mosaic of organizational realities' (p.127).

Unfortunately, there is still evidence of a relatively uncritical acceptance of the extent to which senior managers can manipulate the culture of their organizations. At worst, this is manifest in three interrelated assumptions, namely that culture change can be approached along the lines of a structural reorganization project, that senior managers are detached from the culture of the organization they lead and that relatively straightforward prescriptions can be identified to accomplish change. Carmody (1994) exemplifies such thinking in advocating a three-step approach for changing corporate culture to increase productivity, a recommendation to retain employee trust being tacked on as an addendum to his formula. Both his analysis and remedy succeed in reducing complex phenomena to a few hundred words. In contrast, Thackray (1982), one of the earliest critics of what he called 'the corporate culture rage', argues that corporations do not *have* cultures: they *are* cultures. Moreover, organizations comprise multiple cultures, many of which are inaccessible to senior management.

Schein's (1985) model of organization culture is helpful here. Culture, he suggests, is represented at three levels of descending visibility: behaviours and artifacts, beliefs and values and basic assumptions. Whereas certain behavioural expressions may be shaped by senior management, for example, the tightly prescribed process of greeting and serving customers in fast food restaurants or in corporate dress codes, and while there may be day-to-day evidence of commitment to key organizational values, basic assumptions are much harder to alter or manipulate. According to Schein, these involve such fundamentals as the nature of reality, truth and human relationships. Of particular relevance is his observation that such basic assumptions are shaped by the environment of the organization. From the perspective of a global enterprise this must include the national culture of the host country. As Sparrow and Hiltrop (1994, p.220) observe:

> Multinational organizations may be able to change the upper levels of organizational culture . . . but stand less chance of influencing the fundamental assumptions their employees have about life and work as these are rooted in the broad cultural settings of nations.

## 11.10 The significance of national cultures

Throughout the 1980s there has been a growing awareness of the nature of different national cultures and their potential implications for cross-border businesses. Hofstede (1980) has been particularly influential in drawing attention to this with his model which was based on data from 116,000 IBM employees in more than 50 countries. Hofstede identified four key dimensions of cultural differences: power distance, uncertainty avoidance, individualism–collectivism and masculine–feminine.

- Power distance measures the extent to which members of a society accept that power in institutions and organizations is distributed unequally. This is reflected in hierarchical superior–subordinate relationships.

- Uncertainty avoidance measures fear of the unknown and the extent to which people feel uncomfortable in unstructured or ambiguous situations. Low uncertainty avoidance would be reflected in informality, tolerance of different views, few rules and control of emotions. Thoroughness, order, specialist knowledge and qualifications reflect high uncertainty avoidance.

- Individualism–collectivism. Individualist societies emphasize individual achievement, identity and decision-making. Collectivist cultures have strong extended family units, group protection of the individual, sophisticated networks and alliances and there is an emphasis on achieving harmony at work and group decision-making.

- Masculinity–femininity. In masculine countries gender roles are strictly demarcated and stereotypical male values, such as competitiveness, materialism, strength and a focus on action tend to be appreciated in organizations. In feminine countries stereotypical female values such as co-operation, caring and nurturing are valued and there is less differentiation between male and female roles.

In developing a model based on national cultures, Hofstede does not take into account the significant regional and ethnic diversity of many of the countries in his sample and leaves his work open to the criticism that the analysis generalizes to an unacceptable degree. Nevertheless, he has helped to focus attention on how national cultures influence such matters as hierarchy, management qualifications and styles and preferred forms of decision making. There is considerable evidence to suggest that obstacles in the path of developing a shared international or even 'European' management model are formidable. The concept of management itself does not translate well from one country to another and, as Lane (1989) points out, the word 'manager', which is Anglo–American in origin, does not have the same meaning in, for example, either France or Germany. Not surprisingly factors such as qualifications and the selection and development of managers vary substantially from country to country (Handy *et al.*, 1988).

## 11.11 *Developing cross-border management*

The cultural and historical traditions of countries, even in close geographical proximity, have produced quite different expectations regarding leadership in managers. Tollgerdt-Andersson (1993), in a study of executive recruitment in Scandinavia, France, Germany and Britain, found significant differences in the leadership qualities desired for senior appointments. In Scandinavian countries, for example, several personal and social qualities invariably formed part of the requirements in job advertisements whereas in France no such requirements were stated. Moreover, she found little similarity in leadership requirements between France, Germany and Britain. Her overall conclusion was that such cultural differences may pose a serious problem for closer European industrial integration. The application to an international context of leadership development approaches which are currently widely used in, for example, the United States, is problematic because the theories from which these have derived have overwhelmingly been the product of American academic interest. Indeed, as Durcan and Kirkbride (1994, p.28) contend '. . . leadership research can be taken as the exemplar of American academic hegemony over a topic area in the social sciences.'

A combination of more empirical research and growing awareness among HRM practitioners of these limitations is reflected in more careful and sober analysis of cross-border management problems. One example of this is the Institute of Personnel and Development's (IPD) corporate culture model which is based on a case study of 15 organizations all of which have an international perspective. This recognizes 'that corporate culture is largely determined by the environment in which the organization operates which will include national values and characteristics as well as business, economic and customer considerations' (Baron and Walters, 1994, p.65). The model includes four main determinants of culture: strategy, structure and technology, values and systems, and policies. In order to manage or change corporate culture it suggests that organizations must be able both to identify these cultural

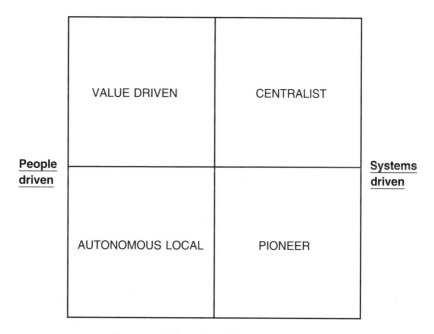

**Figure 11.2** Cross-border management. Source: Baron (1994).

determinants and to understand the way in which they interact with each other.

Centralist organizations develop most of their policies and procedures at the home base, which is usually situated in the country of origin, and disseminate them internationally. They tend to be fairly directive and have a strong identity. Local autonomous organizations allow their various operating units to maintain their own identity and to operate locally developed policies and practices within certain operating parameters. They are also likely to be managed by nationals of the host country. This was seen by many of the organizations in the case study to offer benefits in their approach to cross-border management. Value-driven organizations develop a set of values to which everyone in the organization is expected to subscribe. They shape global strategies but still allow for more detailed local level policies that are adapted to national values. Pioneer organizations make extensive use of expatriate managers who usually have sole responsibility for developing local policies. The values, policies and systems which they apply all tend to reflect the corporate culture of the home base. Theis approach was commonly associated with organizations starting up overseas operations.

There are some obvious similarities with Perlmutter's typology of multinationals although the models differ in several key respects. The most striking difference is that whereas Perlmutter's model may be described as aspirational, the IPD model is based on empirical foundations. More specifically, they have identified two additional dimensions: the closeness or looseness in the relationship of outlying parts of the organization to the home base and the extent to which the organizations are driven primarily by values or systems. They also found evidence of elements of more than one approach in each organization and, while they could see advantages and problems in each approach, unlike Perlmutter's model, there is no implicit advocacy of any one of these. Nevertheless, they did find that many organizations within their sample were moving away from the centralist and pioneer approaches to a more value-driven style of international management. This was because of a need for greater flexibility in translating policies and procedures into forms acceptable to staff in different national cultures. They conclude that there is a dual role for the personnel function in cross-border management, contributing to business strategy on one hand while, on the other, translating policies into processes that are acceptable to local workers and their national culture. They also conclude that the most important quality for success in cross-border management is being open to the notion of cultural difference itself and found that many of the organizations in their sample were replacing expatriates with a more diverse group of managers who possessed what they term 'cultural understanding' (p.68). Their findings are compatible with a growing body of evidence on the high costs and failure rate of expatriate managers (Brewster, 1991; Baumgarten, 1995; Bragg, 1995; CBI, 1995).

Schein (1984) suggests that one of the toughest strategic decisions that management faces in large diversified organizations, particularly if management is unaware of its own cultural assumptions, is whether to enhance diversity in response to local pressures or to create a more homogeneous culture. Given the diversity to be found in global organizations the universal applicability of any one culturally focused model of management and leadership in particular must be in doubt. As Olie (1995, p.142) puts it: 'Behind the facade of superficial uniformity, fundamentally different conceptions of organization and often management are hidden.' This is particularly pertinent to HRM because, if managers are to be selected and developed in ways intended to make them effective in different cultural environments, important strategic choices have to be made about the desired qualities of these post holders and the style(s) of management that they might be encouraged to adopt. Lorbiecki (1993, p.8) notes: 'It is the quality of management, and therefore of managers, that is being put to the test.' Welch (1994) suggests that the HR function can assist globalization by adopting a geocentric orientation to developing a team of international staff who are globally mobile and act as the organization glue while retaining a polycentric orientation at local level. This, however, is merely a point of departure for it is from our conception of management that most other elements within HRM flow, including such key matters as the employment contract, collective and individual relations at the workplace, remuneration and training policies. Such matters represent some of the main manifestations of cultural differences to which HRM must be sensitive when seeking to identify an appropriate balance between global and local needs.

## 11.12 Conclusions

Human resource management cannot be divorced from business strategy, which is itself subject to the constraints of the company's sectoral or cross-sectoral location, organizational characteristics and national culture, the latter profoundly influencing the political, economic and social context of corporate operations. As one commentator recently noted in relation to Japanese HRM, the social embeddedness of the HRM system has been lost in the transition to a view that HRM is something that is designed and implemented by individual firms alone (Moroshima, 1995). There is always an interplay between management choices and the institutional factors which constrain available options. Reference to American, European or Asian models of HRM also obscures the significant divergence of policy and practice within such regional blocs. Furthermore, there will be marked differences within nation states between regions and sectors and between different-sized companies. Not only is globalization a problematic concept but, when applied to HRM, there is only limited evidence of any significant international convergence in management practice. Moreover, as yet, no single, universal model of HRM exists at an international level. Current trends suggest that diversity between nation states or regional blocs will be less significant, and probably less interesting, than diversity across the board between sectors, levels of enterprise and individual companies.

The appeal of a unifying organizational culture is best understood against this background of resilient diversity. It offers the promise of something that might transcend the variability of different operating environments and provide a focus for reconciling global aspirations with local circumstances. Those who have advocated that culture should function as a kind of corporate glue which holds together the global business have, however, been deservedly criticized for their often simplistic analysis. Hendry (1994, p.104) dismisses such corporate culture projects for belonging 'to an ethnocentric worldview, where control and values are determined centrally in the parent country.' Moreover, he argues that this contradicts the basic premise that the international organization benefits from diversity. There is a growing body of evidence, revealed by investigations such as the IPD study, that the more international firms have focused on the phenomenon of organization culture the more they have come to see its complexities. This, in turn, encourages greater sensitivity and openness to cultural differences, a quality which such firms increasingly seek in managers with cross-border responsibilities. In these circumstances the HRM function therefore has a key role to play both in the selection and recruitment of managers with such qualities into the international firm and in the promulgation of these values throughout the organization.

## 11.13 Further reading

Freeman, R.B. (ed.) (1993) *Working Under Different Rules*, Russell Sage/ National Bureau of Economic Research, New York.

Harzing, W.-A. and Van Ruysseveldt, J. (eds) (1995) *International Human Resource Management*, Open University Netherlands, Heerlen, Holland.

Hendry, C. (1994) *Human Resource Strategies for International Growth*, Routledge, London.

Hyman, R. and Ferner, A. (eds) (1994) *New Frontiers in European Industrial Relations*, Blackwell, Oxford.

Prahalad, C.K. and Doz, Y.L. (1987) *The Multinational Mission: Balancing Local Demands and Global Vision*, Free Press, New York.

Sparrow, P. and Hiltrop, J.M. (1994) *European Human Resource Management In Transition*, Prentice Hall, Hemel Hempstead.

Streek, W. (1992) *Social Institutions and Economic Performance: Studies of Industrial Relations in Advanced Capitalist Economies*, Sage, London.

## 11.14 Questions for further discussion

1. To what extent can American ideas and practices in human resource management translate to a European context?

2. How might the labour relations of a particular country or region influence the location or investment decisions of an MNC?

3. Discuss what you consider to be the major factors which can impose constraints on the human resource management practices of international firms at host country level.

4.    Compare and contrast Perlmutter's model of multinational enterprises with the IPD cross-border management model.

5.    Critically examine the evolution of the concept of organization culture and its relevance for international firms.

# References

Abel, C. and Lewis, C.M. (1985) *Latin America, Economic Imperialism and the State: The Political Economy of the External Connection from Independence to the Present*, Athlone Press, London.

Agarwal, S and Ramaswami, S.N. (1992) Choice of Foreign Market Entry Mode: Impact of Ownership, Location and Internalisation Factors. *Journal of International Business Studies*, **23**(1), pp. 1–28.

Aldcroft, D. (1977) *From Versailles to Wall Street 1919–1929*, Penguin, Harmondsworth.

Alford, B.W.E. (1973) *W.D. and H.O. Wills and the Development of the U.K. Tobacco Industry, 1786–1965*, Methuen, London.

Aliber, R.Z. (1970) A theory of direct foreign investment, in *The International Corporation* (ed. C.P. Kindleberger), MIT Press, Cambridge MA, pp. 17–34.

Aliber, R.Z. (1993) *The Multinational Paradigm*, MIT Press, Cambridge, MA.

Amsden, Alice H. (1989) *Asia's Next Giant: South Korea and late industrialization*, Oxford, Oxford University Press.

Anderson, K. and Norheim H. (1993) History, geography and regional economic integration, in *Regional Integration and the Global Trading System*, (eds Anderson K. and Blackhurst R.), Harvester-Wheatsheaf, Hemel Hempstead.

Ansoff, H.I. (1987) *Corporate Strategy, Revised Edition*, Penguin, Harmondsworth.

Aquino, A. (1978) Intra-industry trade and inter-industry specialisation as concurrent sources of international trade in manufactures. *Weltwirtschaftliches Archiv*, **14**(2), pp.275–96.

Auerbach, A.J. (1988a) *Mergers and Acquisitions*, University of Chicago Press, Chicago.

Auerbach, P. (1988b) *Competition: The Economics of Industrial Change*, Basil Blackwell, Oxford.

Baglioni, G. (1990) Industrial relations in Europe in the 1980s, in *European Industrial Relations: The Challenge of Flexibility*, (eds G. Baglioni and C. Crouch), Sage, London, pp. 1–41.

Bailey, D., Harte, G. and Sugden, R. (1994) *Making Transnationals Accountable: A Significant Step for Britain*, Routledge, London.

Baleman, D. (1992) Unions, the quality of labor relations and firm performance, in *Unions and Economic Competitiveness*, (eds L. Mishel and P. Voos), Sharp, New York, pp. 41-107.

Baran, P.A. and Sweezy, P.M. (1966) *Monopoly Capital. An Essay on the American Economic and Social Order*, Penguin, Harmondsworth.

Baron, A. and Walters, M. (1994) *The Culture Factor: Corporate and International Perspectives*, Institute of Personnel and Development, London.

Barnet R.J. and Müller R.E. (1974) *Global Reach: the Power of the Multinational Corporations*, Jonathan Cape, London.

Bartlett, C.A. and Ghoshal, S. (1987a) Managing across borders: new strategic requirements. *Sloan Management Review*, **28,** Summer, pp. 7–18.

Bartlett, C.A. and Ghoshal, S. (1987b) Managing across borders: new organisational responses. *Sloan Management Review*, **29,** Fall, pp. 43–54.

Bartlett, C.A. and Ghoshal, S. (1989) *Managing Across Borders; The Transnational Solution*, Century Business, London.

Bartlett, C.A. and Ghoshal, S. (1990) Matrix management: not a structure, a frame of mind. *Harvard Business Review*, July–August, pp. 138–45.

Bartlett, C., Doz, Y and Hedlund, G. (1990) *Managing the Global Firm*, Routledge, London.

Baumgarten, K. (1995) Training and development of international staff, in *International Human Resource Management*, (eds A.-W. Harzing, and J. Van Ruysseveldt), Sage, London.

Bean, R. (1992) *Comparative Industrial Relations: An Introduction To Cross-National Perspectives*, Routledge, London.

Beer, M. *et al.* (1985) *Human Resource Management*, Free Press, New York.

Bhagwatti, J. (1992) Regionalism versus multilateralism. *The World Economy*, **15**(5), September.

Blau, P.M. and Scott, W.R. (1963) *Formal Organizations*, Routledge & Kegan Paul, London.

Bleeke, J. and Ernst, D. (1991) The way to win in cross-border alliances, *Harvard Business Review*, November–December, pp. 127–35.

Bleeke, J. and Ernst, D. (1993) *Collaborating to Compete*, John Wiley, New York.

Booth, Simon A. (1993) *Crisis Management Strategy*, Routledge, London.

Borys, B. and Jemison, D.B. (1989) Hybrid arrangements as strategic alliances: theoretical issues in organisational combinations. *Academy of Management Review*, **14**(2), pp.234–49.

Bostock, F. and Jones, G. (1994) Foreign multinationals in British manufacturing, 1850–1962. *Business History*, **36**(1), pp. 89–126.

Brag, E. (1995) Overwhelmed, overpaid and over there. *EuroBusiness*, November-December, pp. 40–1.

Brander, James A. (1981) Intra-industry trade in identical commodities. *Journal of International Economics*, 11, pp. 1–14.

Brander, James A. and Krugman, Paul (1983) A reciprocal dumping model of international trade, *Journal of International Economics*, 13, pp. 313–21.

Bratton, J. (1994) Global capitalism and competitive advantage, in *Human Resource Management: Theory and Practice,* (eds J. Bratton and J. Gold), Macmillan, London, pp. 36–56.

Brewster C. and Bournois, F. (1991) A European perspective on human resource management. *Personnel Review,* **20**(6), pp. 4–13.

Brewster, C. and Tyson, S. (1991) *International Comparisons in Human Resource Management,* Pitman, London.

Brewster, C. (1991) *The Management of Expatriates,* London, Kogan Page.

Brewster, C. (1995) Towards a 'European' model of human resource management, *Journal of International Business Studies,* **26**(1), pp. 1–21

Broder, A. (1986) The Multinationalisation of the French electrical industry 1880–1914: dependence and its causes, in *Multinationals: Theory and History,* (eds P. Hertner and G. Jones), Gower, Aldershot.

Brooke, M.Z. (1986) *International Management,* Hutchinson, London.

Buckley, P. and Casson, M.C. (1976) A long-run theory of the multinational enterprise. In *The Future of the Multinational Enterprise,* (eds P.J. Buckley and M.C. Casson), Macmillan, London, pp. 32–65.

Burton, J. (1995) Partnering with the Japanese: threat or opportunity for European businesses? *European Management Journal,* **13**(3), pp.304–15.

Byrne, J. (1993) The Virtual Corporation, *Business Week,* 8 February.

Cain P.J. and Hopkins A.G. (1993a) *British Imperialism: Innovation and Expansion, 1688–1914,* Longman, London.

Cain P.J. and Hopkins A.G. (1993b) *British Imperialism: Crisis and Deconstruction, 1914–1990,* Longman, London.

Cantwell, J. (1989) *Technological Innovation and Multinational Corporations,* Blackwell, Oxford.

Cantwell, J. (1991) A survey of theories of international production, in *The Nature of the Transnational Firm,* (eds N.P. Pitelis and R. Sugden), Routledge, London.

Cantwell, J. (1993) Technological competence and evolving patterns of international production, in *The Growth of Global Business,* (eds H. Cox, J. Clegg and G. Ietto-Gillies) Routledge, London.

Cantwell, J. 1994. The globalisation of technology: what remains of the product life cycle model? *Cambridge Journal of Economics,* 19, pp. 155–174.

Carmody, M.J. (1994) Overhauling corporate culture to improve productivity. *Industrial Engineering,* **26**(5), p. 14.

Casson, M. (1985) Multinational monopolies and international cartels, in *The Economic Theory of the Multinational Enterprise,* (eds P.J. Buckley and M. Casson), Macmillan, London.

Casson, M. (1986) *Multinationals and World Trade,* Allen & Unwin, London.

Caves, R.E. (1971) International corporations: the industrial economics of foreign investment, *Economica,* 38, pp. 1–27. Reprinted in *International Investment,* (ed. J.H. Dunning), Penguin, Harmondsworth, pp. 265–301.

Caves, R.E. (1982) *Multinational Enterprise and Economic Analysis,* Cambridge University Press, Cambridge.

CBI (1995) *Assessment, Selection and Preparation for International Assignments,* CBI, London.

Chakravarthy, B.S. and Perlmutter, H.V. (1985) Strategic planning for a global business. *Columbia Journal of World Business,* summer, **20,** pp. 3–10.

Chan Kim, W. and Hwang, P. (1992) Global strategy and multinationals, entry mode choice. *Journal of International Business Studies,* **23**(1), pp. 29–53..

Chan Kim, W. and Mauborgne, R.A. (1988) Becoming an effective global competitor. *The Journal of Business Strategy,* January/February, pp. 33–7.

Chandler, A.D. (1962) *Strategy and Structure: Chapters in the History of the American Industrial Enterprise,* MIT Press, Cambridge MA.

Chandler, A.D. (1977) *The Visible Hand: the Managerial Revolution in American Business,* Harvard University Press, Cambridge MA.

Chandler, A.D. (1990) *Scale and Scope: the Dynamics of Industrial Capitalism,* Harvard University Press, Cambridge MA.

Chapman, S.D. (1985) British-based investment groups before 1914, *Economic History Review,* 2nd Series, **38**(2), pp. 230–51.

Chapman, S.D. (1992) *Merchant Enterprise in Britain: From the Industrial Revolution to World War One,* Cambridge University Press, Cambridge.

Coase, R.H. (1937) The nature of the firm, *Economica,* **4**(4), pp. 386–405.

Coase, R.H. (1960) The problem of social cost, *Journal of Law and Economics,* **16**(3), pp. 1–10.

Coase, R.H. (1991) The nature of the firm: origin, meaning, influence, in *The Nature of the Firm,* (eds O. Williamson and S. Winter), Oxford University Press, New York, pp. 34–74.

Cochran, S. (1980) *Big Business in China: Sino-Foreign Rivalry in the Cigarette Industry, 1890–1939,* Harvard University Press, Cambridge MA.

Commission of the European Communities (1996) *Community Merger Control Green Paper on the Review of the Merger Regulation,* CEC, Brussels.

Connell, D (1988) *Strategic Partnering and Competitive Advantage,* Paper presented at the eighth annual Strategic Management Conference, 'Winning Strategies in the 1990s'.

Contractor, F.J. and Lorange, P. (eds) (1988) *Cooperative Strategies in International Business: Joint Ventures and Technology Partnership between Firms,* Lexington Books, Lexington MA.

Corley, T.A.B. (1994) Britain's overseas investments in 1914 revisited. *Business History,* **36**(1), pp.71–88.

Cowling, K. (1982) *Monopoly Capitalism,* Macmillan, London.

Cowling, K. and Sugden, R. (1987) *Transnational Monopoly Capitalism*, Wheatsheaf, Brighton.

Crouch, C. (1993) *Industrial Relations and European State Traditions*, Clarendon Press, Oxford.

Daniels, J.D. and Radebaugh, L.H. (1989) *International Business; Environments and Operations*, Addison-Wesley, New York.

Datta, D.F. (1988) International joint ventures: a framework for analysis. *Journal of General Management*, **14**(2), pp. 78–90.

Devlin, G. and Bleakley, M. (1988) Strategic alliances – guidelines for success. *Long Range Planning*, **21**(5), pp. 18–23.

Devos, G. (1993) Agfa-Gavaert and Belgian Multinational Enterprise, in *The Rise of Multinationals in Continental Europe*, (eds G. Jones and H. Schröter) Edward Elgar, Aldershot.

Dicken, P. (1992) *Global Shift; The Internationalisation of Economic Activity*, 2nd edn, Paul Chapman, London.

Done, K. (1994) Tomorrow the world. *The Financial Times*, 22 April 1994, p. 17.

Douglas, S. and Wind, Y., (1987) The myth of globalisation. *Columbia Journal of World Business*, Winter, pp. 19–29.

Doz, Y. (1986) *Strategic Management in Multinational Companies*, Pergamon Press, Oxford.

Doz, Y., Prahalad, C.K., Hamel, G. (1990) Control, change and flexibility: the dilemma of transnational collaboration, in *Managing the Global Firm*, (eds C. Bartlett, Y. Doz, and G. Hedlund), Routledge, London.

Doz, Y.L. and Prahalad, C.K. (1991) Managing DMNCs: a search for a new paradigm. *Harvard Business Review*, **12,** pp. 145–64.

Drummond, I.M. (1987) *The Gold Standard and the International Monetary System 1900–1939*, Macmillan, London.

Dudley, J.W. (1993) *1993 and Beyond*, Kogan Page, London.

Dunning, J.H. (1958) *American Investment in British Manufacturing Industry*, Allen & Unwin, London. Reprinted by Arno Press, New York, 1976.

Dunning, J.H. (1977) Trade, location of economic activity and the MNE: a search for an eclectic approach, in *The International Allocation of Economic Activity*, (eds B. Ohlin, P.O. Hesselborn and P.M. Wijkman), Macmillan, London, pp. 395–431.

Dunning, J.H. (1980) Explaining changing patterns of international production: in defense of the eclectic theory, *Oxford Bulletin of Economics and Statistics*, **41**(4), pp. 269–95.

Dunning, J.H. (1981) *International Production and the Multinational Enerprise*, Allen and Unwin, London.

Dunning, J.H. (1982) A note on intra-industry foreign direct investment. *Banca Nazionale del Lavoro Quarterly Review*, 139, pp. 427–37.

Dunning, J.H. (1983) Changes in the level and structure of international production: the last hundred years, in *The Growth of International Business*, (ed. M. Casson), Allen & Unwin, London, pp. 84–139.

Dunning, J.H. (1988) The eclectic paradigm of international production: a restatement and some possible extensions. *Journal of International Business Studies*, **19**(1), pp. 1–31.

Dunning, J.H. (1991) The eclectic paradigm of International production: a personal perspective, in *The Nature of the Transnational Firm*, (eds C.N. Pitelis and R. Sugden), pp. 117–36, Routledge, London.

Dunning, J.H. (1993) *The Globalisation of Business; The Challenge of the 1990s*, Routledge, London.

Durcan, J. and Kirkbride, P.S. (1994) Leadership in the European context, in *Human Resource Management in Europe*, (ed. P.S. Kikbride), Routledge, London, pp. 11–27.

Egelhoff, W.G. (1988) Strategy and structure in multinational corporations; a revision of the Stopford and Wells model. *Strategic Management Journal*, **9,** pp. 1–14.

Ellis, J and Williams, D. (1993) *Corporate Strategy and Financial Analysis*, Pitman, London.

Ellis, J. and Williams, D. (1995) *International Business Strategy*, Pitman, London.

Enderwick, P. (1989) Multinational corporate restructuring and international competitiveness, *California Management Review*, Fall, pp. 44–58.

Erdilek, A. (1985) *Multinationals as Mutual Invaders: Intra-Industry Direct Foreign Investment*, Croom Helm, London.

Fayerweather, J. (1969) *International Business Management; A Conceptual Framework*, McGraw Hill, New York.

Francks, P. (1992) *Japanese Economic Development: Theory and Practice*, Routledge, London.

Franko, L.G. (1974) The origins of multinational manufacturing by continental European firms. *Business History Review*, **48**(3), 277–302.

Franko, L.G. (1976) *The European Multinationals*, Greylock Press, Greenwich CT.

Freeman, C. (1993) *Technical Change and Unemployment: the Links between Macroeconomic Policy and Innovation Policy*, OECD Conference on Technology, Innovation Policy and Employment. Helsinki, Oct.

Freeman, R.B. and Medoff, J.L. (1984) *What Do Unions Do?* Basic Books, New York.

Freeman, R.B. (1993) How labour fares in advanced economies, in *Working Under Different Rules*, (ed. R.B. Freeman), New York: Russell Sage/National Bureau of Economic Research, pp. 1–28.

Fridenson, P. (1986) The growth of multinational activities in the French motor industry, 1890–1979, in *Multinationals: Theory and History*, (eds P. Hertner and G. Jones), Gower, Aldershot.

Friedman, M. (1953) *Essays in Positive Economics*, University of Chicago Press, Chicago.

Frobel, F., Heinrichs, J. and Kaye, O. (1980) *The New International Division of Labour*, Cambridge University Press, Cambridge.

Galbraith, J.K. (1967) *The New Industrial State*, Allen Lane, Harmondsworth.

Gales, B.P.A. and Sluyterman, K.E. (1993) Outward bound: the rise of Dutch multinationals in *The Rise of Multinationals in Continental Europe*, (eds G. Jones and H. Schröter), Edward Elgar, Aldershot.

Garrahan, P. and Stewart, P. (1992) *The Nissan Enigma*, Mansell, London.

General Agreement on Tariffs and Trade, GATT (1994) *International Trade 92–93, Statistics*, Geneva, 1994.

Geringer, J.M. and Herbert, L. (1989) Control and performance of international joint ventures. *Journal of International Business Studies*, **22**(2), pp. 235–54.

Germidis, D. (ed.) (1980) *International Sub-Contracting. A New Form of Investment*, OECD, Paris.

Ghoshal, S. (1987) Global strategy: an organising framework, *Strategic Management Journal*, 8, pp. 425–40.

Ghoshal, S. and Nohria, N. (1989) Internal differentiation within multinational corporations. *Strategic Management Journal*, **10**, pp. 323–37.

Ghoshal, S. and Nohria, N., (1993) Horses for courses: organisational forms for multinational corporations. *Sloan Management Review*, Winter, pp. 23–35.

Glaister, K.W. and Buckley, P.J. (1994) UK international joint ventures: an analysis of patterns of activity and distribution, *British Journal of Management*, 5, pp. 33–51.

Globerman S. and Dean J.W. (1990) Recent trends in intra-industry trade and their implications for future trade liberalisation. *Weltwirtschaftliches Archiv*, **126**(1), pp. 24–49.

Goetsch, D.L. and Davis, S. (1994) *Introduction to Total Quality: Quality, Productivity, Competitiveness*, Merrill, New York.

Gomes-Casseres, B. (1989) Joint-ventures in the face of global competition. *Sloan Management Review*, Spring, pp. 17–26.

Gow, I. (1988) Japan, in *Making Managers*, (eds C. Handy, C. Gordon, I. Gow and C. Randelsome), Pitman, London, pp.16–50.

Graham, E.M. (1978) Transatlantic investment by multinational firms: a rivalistic phenomenon? *Journal of Post-Keynesian Economics*, 1(1).

Graham, E.M. (1985) Intra-industry direct investment, market structure, firm rivalry and technological performance, in *Multinationals as Mutual Invaders: Intra-Industry Direct Foreign Investment*, (ed. A. Erdilek), Croom-Helm, London.

Grant, R.M. (1991) *Contemporary Strategy Analysis*, Oxford, Blackwell.

Gray, S. (1995) Cultural perspectives on the measurement of corporate success. *European Management Journal*, 13(3), pp. 269–75.

Grimwade N. (1989) *International Trade: New Patterns of Trade, Production and Investment*, Routledge, London.

Grubel H. and Lloyd P. (1975) *Intra-Industry Trade: The Theory and Measurement of International Trade in Differentiated Products*, Macmillan, London.

Guest, D. (1992) Right enough to be dangerously wrong: an analysis of the 'In Search of Excellence' phenomenon, in *Human Resource Strategies*, (ed. G. Salaman) Sage, London, pp. 5–19.

Gugler, P. (1992) Building transnational alliances to create competitive advantage. *Long Range Planning*, **25**(1), 90–9.

Hamel, G. and Prahalad, C.K. (1985) Do you really have a global strategy? *Harvard Business Review*, July–August, pp. 139–48.

Hamel, G. and Prahalad, C.K. (1989) Strategic intent. *Harvard Business Review*, May–June, pp. 63–76.

Hamel, G. and Prahalad, C.K., (1994) Competing for the Future, Harvard Business School Press, Boston MA.

Hamel, G., Doz, Y. and Prahalad, C.K. (1989) Collaborate with your competitors – and win. *Harvard Business Review*, January–February, **67,** pp. 35–9.

Hampden-Turner, C. (1990) *Corporate Cultures: From Vicious To Virtuous Circles*, Hutchinson, London.

Handy, C. *et al.* (1988) *Making Managers*, Pitman, London.

Hardach, G. (1977) *The First World War, 1914–1918*, Penguin, Harmondsworth.

Harrigan, K.R. (1987) Strategic alliances: their new role in global competition. *Columbia Journal of World Business*, **22**(2), pp. 67–70.

Harrigan, K.R. (1988) Strategic alliances and partner asymmetries, in Cooperative Strategies in International Business, (F.J. Contractor and P. Lorange), Lexington Books, Lexington.

Harvey, C. and Press, J. 1990. The City and International mining, 1870–1914. *Business History*, **32**(3), pp. 98–119.

Harzing, A.-W., (1995) Internationalization and the international division of labour, in *International Human Resource Management*, (eds A.-W. Harzing, and J. Van Ruysseveldt), Sage, London, pp. 1–24.

Haspeslagh, P.C. and Jemison, D.B. (1991) *Managing Acquisitions: Creating Value through Corporate Renewal*, Free Press, New York.

Hedberg, B.L.T., Nystrom, P.C. and Starbuck, W.H. (1976) Camping on seesaws, prescriptions for a self-designing organisation. *Administrative Science Quarterly*, **21**.

Hedlund, G. and Rolander, D. (1990) Actions in heterarchies: new approaches to managing the MNC, in *Managing the Global Firm*, (eds S.C. Bartlett, Y. Doz and G. Hedlund), London, Routledge.

Heenan, D. and Perlmutter, H. (1979) *Multinational Organisational Development: A Social Architecture Perspective*, Addison-Wesley, Reading MA.

Hegewisch, A. (1993) The decentralisation of pay bargaining: European comparisons, in *European Development in Human Resource Management*, (eds A. Hegewisch and C. Brewster), Kogan Page, London, pp. 86–100.

Hendry, C. (1994) *Human Resource Management Strategies for International Growth*, Routledge, London.

Hennart, J.F. (1991) The transaction cost theory of the multinational enterprise, in *The Nature of the Transnational Firm*, (eds C.N. Pitelis and R. Sugden), pp. 81–116.

Hertner, P. (1986) German multinational enterprise before 1914: some case studies, in *Multinationals: Theory and History*, (eds P. Hertner and G. Jones), Gower, Aldershot.

Hill, C.W.L. and Jones, G.R. (1995) *Strategic Management; An Integrated Approach*, 3rd edn, Houghton Mifflin, Boston MA.

Hill, C.W.L., Hwang, P., and Chan Kim, W. (1990) An eclectic theory of the choice of international entry mode. *Strategic Management Journal*, **11**, pp. 117–28.

Hinterhuber, H.H. and Levin, B.M. (1994) Strategic networks – the organisation of the future, *Long Range Planning*, **27**(3), pp. 43–53.

Hirsch, S. (1965) The United States electronic industry in international trade. *National Institute Economic Review*, 24, pp. 92–7.

Hobsbawm, E.J. (1987) *The Age of Empire 1875–1914*, Weidenfeld & Nicolson, London.

Hobson, J.A. (1902) *Imperialism: A Study*, 1988 edition, Unwin-Hyman, London.

Hodgetts, R.M. and Luthans, F. (1994) *International Management*, 2nd edition, McGraw Hill, New York.

Hofstede, G. (1980) *Cultures Consequences: International Differences in Work Related Values*, Sage, Beverly Hills.

Hood, N. and Young, S. (1979) *The Economics of Multinational Enterprise*, Longman, London and New York.

Höpfl, H., Smith, S. and Spencer, S. (1992) Values and valuations: the conflicts between culture change and job cuts. *Personnel Review*, **21**(1), pp. 24–38.

Houston, T. and Dunning, J.H. (1976) *British Industry Abroad*, Financial Times, London.

Hout, T., Porter, M.E. and Rudden, E. (1982) How global companies win out. *Harvard Business Review*, September–October, pp. 98–108.

Humes, S. (1993) *Managing the Multinational: Confronting the Global-Local Dilemma*, Prentice Hall, London.

Hutton, W. (1995) *The State We're In*, Jonathan Cape, London.

Hymer, S.H. (1960) *The International Operations of National Firms: A Study of Direct Investment*, Ph.D. thesis, MIT, published 1976, MIT Press, Cambridge MA.

Hymer, S.H. (1971) The multinational corporation and the law of uneven development, in *Economics and World Order*, (ed J.W. Bhagwati), Macmillan, London, pp. 113–40.

Ietto-Gillies, G. (1988) Internationalization of production: an analysis based on labour. *British Review of Economic Issues*, **10**(23), pp. 19–48.

Ietto-Gillies, G. (1992) *International Production: Trends, Theories, Effects*, Polity Press, Cambridge.

Ietto-Gillies, G. (1993) Transnational Companies and UK Competitiveness: does Ownership Matter? in *The Future of UK Competitiveness and the Role of Industrial Policy*, (ed. K. Hughes), Policy Studies Institute, London, pp. 134–55.

Ietto-Gillies, G. and Cox, H. (1996) International production: trends and prospects. *The Business Economist*, **27**(1), pp. 14–24.

Ietto-Gillies, G. (1996) The widening geography of UK international production: theoretical analysis and empirical evidence, *International Review of Applied Economics*, **10**(2), pp. 195–208.

*International Management* (1994) What the Survey Showed, **49**(3), pp. 30–40.

Iversen, C. (1935) *International Capital Movements*. 1967 edn., Frank Cass, London.

Jaques, E. (1951) *The Changing Culture of a Factory*, Tavistock, London.

Jenkins, R. (1987) *Transnational Corporations and Uneven Development: The Internationalization of Capital and the Third World*, Methuen & Co., London.

Johnson, G. and Scholes, K. (1993) *Exploring Corporate Strategy*, Prentice Hall International, London.

Jones, G. (ed.) (1986) *British Multinationals: Origins, Management and Performance*, Gower, Aldershot.

Jones, G. (1993) *British Multinational Banking: 1830–1990*, Oxford University Press, Oxford.

Kalecki, M. (1939) *Essays in the Theory of Economic Fluctuations*, Allen & Unwin, London.

Kay, J. (1993) *Foundations of Corporate Success; How Business Strategies Add Value*, Oxford University Press, Oxford.

Keep, E. (1989) A training scandal, in *Personnel Management in Britain*, (ed. K. Sisson), Blackwell, Oxford, pp. 177–202.

Kindleberger, C.P. (1969) *American Business Abroad*, Yale University Press, New Haven CT.

Kindleberger, C.P. (1974) Origins of United States Direct Investment in France. *Business History Review*, **48**(3), pp. 382–413.

Kindleberger, C.P. (1986) *The World in Depression 1929–1939*, revised edn, Penguin, Harmondsworth.

Knickerbocker, F.T. (1973) *Oligopolostic Reaction and Multinational Enterprise*, Division of Research, Graduate School of Business Administration, Harvard University, Cambridge MA.

Kobrin, S.J. (1991) An empirical investigation of the determinants of global integration. *Strategic Management Journal*, **12**, pp. 17–31.

Kobrin, S.J. (1994) Is There a Relationship between a Geocentric Mind-Set and Multinational Strategy. *Journal of International Business Studies*, **3**, pp. 493–511.

Kogut, B. (1989) A note on global strategies. *Strategic Management Journal*, **10**, pp. 383–9.

Kogut, B. (1988) Joint ventures: theoretical and empirical perspectives, *Strategic Management Journal*, IX, pp. 319–32.

Krugman, P. (1991) *Geography and Trade*, Leuven University Press, Leuven and The MIT Press, Cambridge MA.

Krugman, Paul (1987) Is free trade passé? *Journal of Economic Perspectives*, 1, pp. 131–44.

Kudō, A. and Hara, T. (1992) *International Cartels in Business History*, University of Tokyo Press, Tokyo.

Kuwahara, Y. (1993) Industrial relations in Japan, in *International and Comparative Industrial Relations*, (eds G. Bamber and R.D. Lansbury), Routledge, London, pp. 220–44.

Kuznetz, S. (1953) *Economic Change*, W.W. Norton, New York.

Lane, C. (1989) *Management and Labour in Europe: The Industrial Enterprise in Germany, Britain and France*, Edward Elgar, Aldershot.

Larsen, H.H. (1994) Key issues in training and development, in *Policy and Practice in European Human Resource Management*, (eds A. Hegewisch and C. Brewster), Routledge, London, pp. 107–21.

Legge, K. (1989) Human resource management: a critical analysis, in *New Perspectives on Human Resource Management*, (ed. J. Storey), London: Routledge, pp. 19–40.

Lei, D. (1989) Strategies for global competition. *Long Range Planning*, **22**(1), pp. 102–9.

Lenz, R.T. (1980) Strategic capability: a concept and framework for analysis. *Academy of Management Review*, **5**(2), pp. 225–34.

Leong, S.M. and Tan, C.T. (1993) Managing across borders: an empirical test of the Bartlett and Ghoshal (1989) organisational typology. *Journal of International Business Studies*, **3**, pp. 449–64.

Leontiades, J.C. (1985) *Multinational Corporate Strategy; Planning for World Markets*, D.C. Heath, Lexington MA.

Levitt, T. (1983) The globalisation of markets, *Harvard Business Review*, May, pp. 92–102.

Linder, S.B. (1961) *An Essay on Trade and Transformation*, J. Wiley, New York.

Lloyd, G. and Phillips, M. (1994) Inside IBM: Strategic Management in a Federation of Businesses. *Long Range Planning*, **27**(5), pp. 52–63.

Lorange, P. and Probst, G. (1990) Effective strategic planning processes in the multinational corporation, in *Managing the Global Firm*, (C. Bartlett, Y. Doz and G. Hedlund), Routledge, London.

Lorange, P. and Roos, J. (1991) Why some strategic alliances succeed and others fail. *Journal of Business Strategy*, **6**(2), pp. 25–30.

Lorange, P. and Roos, J. (1992) *Strategic Alliances: Formation, Implementation and Evolution*, Blackwell, Oxford.

Lorbiecki, A. (1993) Unfolding European management development. *Management Education and Development*, **3**(1), pp. 5–13.

Lorenz, C. (1994) Nationality still matters. *Financial Times*, 27 July 1994.

Lorenz, C. (1989) The birth of a transnational: striving to exploit an elusive balance. *Financial Times*, 19 June 1989.

Lundström, R. (1986) Swedish multinational growth before 1930, in *Multinationals: Theory and History*, (eds P. Hertner and G. Jones), Gower, Aldershot.

Luxemburg, R. (1913) *The Accumulation of Capital*, 1971 edn, Routledge & Kegan Paul, London.

Lynch, L. (1993) Payoffs to alternative strategies at work, in *Working Under Different Rules*, (ed. R.B. Freeman), Russell Sage/National Bureau of Economic Research, New York, pp 63–96.

Lynch, R. (1994) *European Business Strategies*, 2nd edn, Kogan Page, London.

Lyons, M.P. (1991) Joint ventures as strategic choice – a literature review. *Long Range Planning*, **24**(4), pp. 130–44.

Magdoff, H. (1966) *The Age of Imperialism. The Economics of US Foreign Policy*, Monthly Review Press, New York.

Marshall, R. (1992) Work organisation, unions and economic performance, in *Unions and Economic Competitiveness*, (eds L. Mishel and P. Voos), Sharpe, New York, pp. 287–315.

Martinez, J.I. and Jarillo, J.C. (1989) The evolution of research on coordination mechanisms in multinational corporations, *Journal of International Business Studies*, Fall, pp. 489–514.

McManus, J. (1972) The theory of the international firm, in *The Multinational Firm and the Nation State*, (ed. Gilles Paquet), Collier-MacMillan, Don Mills, Ontario, pp. 66–93.

Metcalf, D. (1993) Industrial relations and economic performance. *British Journal of Industrial Relations*, **31**(2), pp. 255–84.

Mills, R.W. and Robertson, J. (1991) *Fundamentals of Managerial Accounting and Finance*, Mars, Lechlade.

Mintzberg, H. (1987) Five Ps for strategy. *California Management Review*, **30**(1), pp. 11–24.

Mintzberg, H. (1994) Rethinking strategic planning, part I: pitfalls and fallacies. *Long Range Planning*, **27**(3), pp. 12–21.

Mintzberg, H. (1994) Rethinking strategic planning, part II: new roles for planners. *Long Range Planning*, **27**(3), pp. 22–30.

Mirza, H. (1993) The past, present and future of the Sōgō Shōsha, in *The Growth of Global Business*, (eds H. Cox, J. Clegg, and G. Ietto-Gillies) Routledge, London.

Moran, R.T. and Riesenberger, J.R. (1994) *The Global Challenge: Building the New Worldwide Enterprise*, McGraw Hill, London.

Morgan, G. (1986) *Images of Organization*, Sage, London.

Morikawa, H. (1992) *Zaibatsu: the Rise and Fall of Family Enterprise Groups in Japan*, University of Tokyo Press, Tokyo.

Moroshima, M. (1995) Embedding HRM in a social context. *British Journal of Industrial Relations*, **33**(4), pp. 617–40.

Muller, W. (1991) Gaining competitive advantage through customer satisfaction. *European Management Journal*, **9**(2), pp. 201–11.

Musgrave, A. (1981) Unreal assumptions in economic theory: the F twist untwisted, *Kyklos*, **34**(3), pp. 377–87.

Nicholas, S.J. (1982) British multinational investment before 1939, *Journal of European Economic History*, **11**(4), pp. 605–30.

Nicholas, S.J. (1989) Locational choice, performance and the growth of British multinational firms, *Business History*, **31**(3), pp. 122–41.

Nielsen, S., Madsen, E. and Pedersen, K. (1995) *International Economics: The Wealth of Open Nations*, McGraw-Hill, London.

Nurkse, R. (1933) Causes and effects of capital movements, in *International Investment*, (ed. J.H. Dunning), (1972), Penguin, Hammondsworth, pp. 97–116.

O'Brien, T.F. (1989) 'Rich beyond the dreams of avarice': the Guggenheims in Chile. *Business History Review*, **63**(1), pp. 122–59.

Ohlin, B. (1933) *Interregional and International Trade*, 1967 edn, Harvard University Press, Cambridge MA.

Ohmae, K. (1985) *Triad Power: The Coming Shape of Global Competition*, Free Press, New York.

Ohmae, K. (1989) Managing in a borderless world, *Harvard Business Review*, May–June, pp. 152–61.

Ohmae, K. (1990) *The Borderless World; Power and Strategy in the Global Marketplace*, Harper Collins, London.

Ohmae, K. (1989) The global logic of strategic alliances. *Harvard Business Review*, **67**(2), March–April, pp. 143–54.

Olie, R. (1995) The culture factor in personnel and organization policies, in *Comparative Industrial and Employment Relations*, (eds A.-W. Harzing, and J. van Ruysseveldt), Sage, London, pp. 124–43.

Oman, C (1994) *Globalization and Regionalization: The Challenge for Developing Countries*, Mimeo, OECD Development Centre, January 1994.

Organisation for Economic Co-operation and Development (1994) *The Performance of Foreign Affiliates in OECD Countries*, OECD, Paris.

Ozawa, T. (1987) *The Role of General Trading Companies in Trade and Development*, Asian Productivity Organisation, Tokyo.

Paauwe, J. and Dewe, P. (1995) Human resource management in multinational corporations: theories and models, in *Comparative Industrial and Employment Relations*, (eds A.-W. Harzing, and J. van Ruysseveldt), Sage, London, pp. 75–98.

Panayi, P. (1990) German business interests in Britain during the First World War. *Business History*, **32**(2), pp. 244–58.

Pascalle, R.T. and Athos, A.G. (1982) *The Art of Japanese Management*, Penguin, Harmondsworth.

Payne, P.L. (1980) *The Early Scottish Limited Companies, 1856–1895*, Scottish Academic Press, Edinburgh.

Pearce, R.D. (1992) Factors influencing the internationalisation of Research and Development in *Multinational Enterprises in the World Economy: Essays in Honour of John Dunning*, (eds P.J. Buckley and M. Casson), Cheltenham, Edward Elgar.

Perlmutter, H. (1969) The tortuous evolution of the multi-national corporation, *Columbia Journal of World Business*, 4(1), pp. 9–18.

Perlmutter, H.V. and Heenan, D.A. (1986) Cooperate to compete globally. *Harvard Business Review*, **64**(2), pp. 136–52.

Peters, T.J. and Waterman, R.H. (1982) *In Search of Excellence*, Harper & Row, New York.

Pfeffer, J. (1994) *Competitive Advantage Through People: Unleashing The Power of The Workforce*, Harvard Business School Press, Boston.

Phatak, A.V. (1992) *International Dimensions of Management*, 3rd edn, PWS-Kent, Boston.

Pieper, R. (ed.) (1990) *Human Resource Management: An International Comparison*, De Gruyter, Berlin.

Pitelis, C. (ed.) (1993) *Transaction Costs, Markets and Hierarchies*, Blackwell, Oxford.

Pitelis, C.N. (1991) The transnational corporation: demand-side issues and a synthesis, in *The Nature of the Transnational Firm*, (eds C.N. Pitelis, and R. Sugden) London, Routledge, pp. 194–212.

Pollard, S. (1985) Capital exports, 1870–1914: harmful or beneficial? *Economic History Review*, 2nd ser., **38**(4), pp. 489–514.

Popper, K.R. (1963) *Conjectures and Refutations. The Growth of Scientific Knowledge*. Routledge & Kegan Paul, London.

Porter, M.E. (1980) *Competitive Strategy: Techniques for Analysing Industries and Competitors*, The Free Press, New York.

Porter, M.E. (1985) *Competitive Advantage; Creating and Sustaining Superior Performance*, Free Press, New York.

Porter, M.E. (1986) Competition in global industries: a conceptual framework, in *Competition in Global Industries*, (ed. M.E. Porter), Harvard University Press, Boston MA.

Porter, M.E. (1987) From competitive advantage to competitive strategy. *Harvard Business Review*, May/June, pp. 43–59.

Porter, M.E. (1990) *The Competitive Advantage of Nations*, Macmillan, London.

Porter, M.E. and Fuller, M. (1986) Coalitions and global strategy, in M.E. Porter (ed.), *Competition in Global Industries*, Harvard Business School Press, Boston MA.

Porter, P.G. (1969) Origins of the American Tobacco Company. *Business History Review*, **43**(1), pp. 59–76.

Posner, M.V. (1961) International trade and technical change. *Oxford Economic Papers*, **13**, pp. 323–41.

Prahalad, C.K. and Doz, Y.L. (1987) *The Multinational Mission: Balancing Local Demands and Global Vision*, Free Press, New York.

Prahalad, C.K. and Hamel, G. (1990) The core competence of the corporation. *Harvard Business Review*, May–June, pp. 79–91.

Preece, S. Fleisher, C. and Toccacelli, J. (1995) Building a reputation along the value chain at Levi Strauss. *Long Range Planning*, **28**(6), pp. 88–98.

Pucik, V., Tichy, N.M. and Barnett, C.K. (1992) *Globalising Management; Creating and Leading the Competitive Organisation*, John Wiley, New York.

Quinn, J.B. (1980) *Strategies for Change: Logical Incrementalism*, Richard D. Irwin.

Ravenscroft, D.B. and Scherer, F.M. (1987) *Mergers, Sell Offs and Economic Efficiency*, Brookings Institute, Washington.

Reich, R.B. and Mankin E.D. (1986) Joint ventures with Japan give away our future. *Harvard Business Review*, **64**(2), pp. 78–86.

Reich, R.B.(1990). 'Who is us?' *Harvard Business Review*, January–February, pp. 53–64.

Reich, R.B. (1991a). 'Who is them?' *Harvard Business Review*, March–April, pp. 77–88.

Reich, R.B. (1991b) *The Work of Nations: Preparing Ourselves for 21st Century Capitalism*, Simon and Schuster, London.

Root, F.R. and Visudtibhan, K. (eds) (1992) *International Strategic Management; Challenges and Opportunities*, Taylor & Francis, Washington DC.

Root, F.R. (1994) *Entry Strategies for International Markets*, Lexington Books, Lexington MA.

Roth, K. and Ricks, D.A. (1994) Goal configuration in a global industry context. *Strategic Management Journal*, **15**, pp. 103–20.

Rowthorn, R.E. and Wells, J.R. (1987) *De-Industrialization and Foreign Trade*, Cambridge University Press, Cambridge.

Rubenstein, W.D. (1993) *Capitalism, Culture and Decline in Britain, 1750-1990*, Routledge, London.

Rugman, A.M. (1981) *Inside the Multinationals; the Economics of the Multinational Enterprise*, Columbia University Press, New York.

Rugman, A.M. and Verbeke (1992) A note on the transnational solution and the transaction cost theory of multinational strategic management. *Journal of International Business Studies*, **23**(4), pp. 761–71

Rugman, A.M., Lecraw, D.J. and Booth, L.D. (1986) *International Business: Firm and Environment*, McGraw-Hill, New York.

Sader, F. (1995) *Privatizing Public Enterprises and Foreign Investment in Developing Countries, 1988–93*, World Bank, Washington DC.

Sampson, A. (1993) *The Seven Sisters: The Great Oil Companies and the World they Made*, (new edn), Hodder and Stoughton, London.

Sasaki, T. (1993) What the Japanese have learned from strategic alliances. *Long Range Planning*, **26**(6), pp. 41–53.

Savary, J. (1993) European integration, globalisation and industrial location in Europe, in *The Growth of Global Business*, (eds H. Cox, J. Clegg and G. Ietto-Gillies), Routledge, London.

Schein, E.H. (1984) Coming to a new awareness of organization culture. *Sloan Management Review*, Winter, pp. 3–16.

Schein, E.H. (1985) *Organization Culture and Leadership: A Dynamic View*, Jossey-Bass, San Francisco.

Scherer, F.M. (1980) *Industrial Market Structure and Economic Performance*, Rand McNally, Chicago.

Schröter, H. (1993a) Continuity and change: German multinationals since 1850, in *The Rise of Multinationals in Continental Europe*, (eds G. Jones and H. Schröter), Edward Elgar, Aldershot.

Schröter, H. (1993b) Swiss Multinational Enterprise in Historical Perspective, in *The Rise of Multinationals in Continental Europe*, (eds G. Jones and H. Schröter), Elgar, Aldershot.

Scullion, H. (1994) Staffing policies and strategic control in British multinationals. *International Studies of Management and Organization*, **24**(3), pp. 86–104.

Servan-Schreiber, J.J. (1968) *The American Challenge*, Penguin, London.

Sluyterman, K. and Winkelman, H. (1993) The Dutch family firm confronted with Chandler's dynamics of industrial capitalism, 1890–1940. *Business History*, **35**(4), pp. 152–83.

Soskice, D. (1990) Wage Determination: the changing role of institutions in advanced industrial countries, *Oxford Review of Economic Policy*, **6**(4), pp. 36–61.

Sparrow, P. and Hiltrop, J.-M. (1994) *European Human Resource Management in Transition*, Prentice Hall, Hemel Hempstead.

Spivey, W.A. and Thomas, L.D. (1990) Global management: concepts, themes, problems and research issues. *Human Resource Management*, **29**(1), pp. 85–97.

Stafford, E.R. (1994) Using cooperative strategies to make alliances work. *Long Range Planning*, **27**(3), pp. 64–74.

Stern R. and Hoekman B. (1987) Negotiation on services. *The World Economy*, **10**(1), pp. 39–60.

Stopford, J. and Wells, L.T. (1972) *Managing the Multinational Enterprise*, Basic Books, New York.

Stopford, J.M. (1974) The origins of British-based multinational manufacturing enterprises. *Business History Review*, **48**(3), pp. 303–56.

Stopford, J.M. and Dunning, J.H. (1983) *Multinationals: Company Performance and Global trends*, Macmillan, London.

Stopford, J., Strange, S. and Henley, J.S. (1991) *Rival States, Rival Firms. Competition for World Market Shares*, Cambridge University Press, Cambridge.

Streek, W. (1992) *Social Institutions and Economic Performance: Studies of Industrial Relations in Advanced Capitalist Economies*, Sage, London.

Sugden, R. (1991) The importance of distributional considerations, in *The Nature of the Transnational Firm* (eds C.N. Pitelis and R. Sugden), Routledge, London, pp. 168–93.

Taggart, J.H. and McDermott, M.C. (1993) *The Essence of International Business*, Prentice Hall, New York.

Taylor, B. and Harrison, J. (1990) *Manager's Casebook of Business Strategy*, Heineman, London.

Teece, D.J. (1977) Technology transfer by multinational firms: the resource cost of transferring technological know-how. *Economic Journal*, **87**, pp. 242–61.

Teece, D. (1983) Technological and organizational factors in the theory of the multinational enterprise, in *The Growth of International Business*, (ed. M.C. Casson), Allen & Unwin, London.

Thackray, J. (1982) The corporate culture vultures, *Management Today*, February.

*The Economist* (1993), Multinationals: Survey, 27 March 1993, pp. 13–14.

*The Economist* (1994), The discreet charm of the multicultural multinational, 30 July 1994, pp. 65–66.

*The Economist* (1995), Three ways to go global, 7 January 1995, pp. 60–1.

*The Financial Times* (1994), Tomorrow the world, 22 April 1994

*The Financial Times* (1994), Volvo truck plant for Poland, 21 November 1994.

*The Financial Times* (1994) Chinese roads paved with gold, 23 November 1994.

Thomsen S. and Woolcock, S. (1993) *Direct Investment and European Integration. Competition among Firms and Governments,* The Royal institute of International Affairs and Pinter Publishers, London.

Thurley, K. and Wiedenhuis, H. (1991) Will management become 'European'? Strategic choice for organisations. *European Management Journal,* **9**(2), 127–34.

Tollgerdt-Andersson, I. (1993) Attitudes, values and demands on leadership. *Management Education and Development,* **3**(1), pp. 48–57.

Tomlinson, B.R. (1986) Continuities and discontinuities in Indo-British economic relations: British multinational corporations in India, 1920–1970, in *Imperialism and After: Continuities and Discontinuities,* (eds W.J. Mommsen and J. Osterhammel) Allen & Unwin, London.

Turner, I. and Henry, I. (1994) Managing international organisations; lessons from the field. *European Management Journal,* December, **12**(4), pp. 417–31.

Turner, L. (1973) *Multinationals and the Third World,* Allen Lane, London.

Turrell, R.V. and Van Helten, J.-J. (1986) The Rothschilds, the exploration company and mining finance. *Business History,* **28**(2), pp. 181–205.

Ulman, L., Eichengreen, B. and Dickens, W.T. (1993) *Labor and an Integrated Europe,* Brookings Institute, Washington DC.

United Nations Centre on Transnational Corporations (1988) *Transnational Corporations in World Development. Trends and Prospects,* United Nations, New York.

United Nations Centre on Transnational Corporations (1990) *Regional Integration and Transnational Companies in the 1990s: Europe 1992, North American and Developing Countries,* UNCTC Current Series. Series A, no. 15, United Nations, New York.

United Nations Centre on Transnational Corporations (1991) *World Investment Report,* United Nations, New York.

United Nations Centre on Transnational Corporations (1992) *The Determinants of Foreign Direct Investment,* United Nations, New York.

United Nations Transnational Corporations and Management Division – Department of Economic and Social Development (1992) *World Investment Report,* United Nations, New York.

United Nations Conference on Trade and Development – Programme on Transnational Corporations (1993) *World Investment Report,* United Nations, New York.

United Nations Conference on Trade and Development – Division on Transnational Corporations and Investment (1994) *World Investment Report,* United Nations, New York.

United Nations Conference on Trade and Development – Division on Transnational Corporations and Investment (1995) *World Investment Report,* United Nations, New York.

Urban, S. and Vendemini, S. (1992) *European Strategic Alliances,* Blackwell, Oxford.

Van Ruysseveldt, J. (1995) Growing cross-national diversity or diversity *tout court*? in *Comparative Industrial and Employment Relations,* (eds J. van Ruysseveldt, R. Huiskamp and J. van Hoof), Sage, London, pp. 1–15.

Van Waarden, F. (1995) Employers and employers associations, in J. Van Rusyseveldt, in *Comparative Industrial and Employment Relations*, (eds J. van Ruysseveldt, R. Huiskamp and J. van Hoof), Sage, London, pp. 68–108.

Vaupel, J.W. and Curhan, J.P. (1974) *The World's Multinational Enterprises: a Sourcebook of Tables Based on a Study of the Largest US and Non-US Manufacturing Corporations*, Centre des études Industrielles, Geneva.

Vernon, R. (1966) International investment and international trade in the product cycle. *Quarterly Journal of Economics*, **80**, pp. 190–207.

Vernon, R. (1974) The location of economic activity, in *Economic Analysis and the Multinational Enterprise*, (ed. J.H. Dunning), Allen & Unwin, London, pp. 89–113.

Vernon, R. (1979) The product cycle hypothesis in a new international environment. *Oxford Bulletin of Economics and Statistics*, **41**, pp. 255–67.

Vernon-Wortzel, H. and Wortzel, L.H. (1991) *Global Strategic Management: the Essentials*, 2nd edn, John Wiley, New York.

Viner J. (1950) *The Customs Union Issue*, Carnegie Endowment for International Peace, New York.

Visser, J. (1994) European trade unions: the transition years, in *New Frontiers in European Industrial Relations*, (eds R. Hyman and A. Ferner), Blackwell, Oxford, pp. 80–109.

Visser, J. (1995), Trade unions from a comparative perspective, in *Comparative Industrial and Employment Relations*, (eds W.A. Harzing and J. van Ruysseveldt), Sage, London, pp. 37–67.

Welch, D. (1994) HRM implications of globalisation. *Journal of General Management Studies*, **19**(4), pp. 52–68.

Wheelen, T. and Hunger, J. (1995) *Strategic Management and Business Policy*, 5th edn, Addison-Wesley, London.

Wheeler, H. (1993) Industrial relations in the USA, in *International and Comparative Industrial Relations*, (eds G. Bamber and R.D. Lansbury), Routledge, London, pp. 55–82.

White, R.E. and Poynter, T.A. (1990) Organising for World-wide Advantage, in (1990) *Managing the Global Firm*, (eds C. Bartlett, Y. Doz, and G. Hedlund), Routledge, London.

Wickens, P. (1987) *The Road to Nissan*, Macmillan: London.

Wilkins, M. (1970) *The Emergence of Multinational Enterprise*, Harvard University Press, Cambridge MA.

Wilkins, M. (1974) *The Maturing of Multinational Enterprise*, Harvard University Press, Cambridge MA.

Wilkins, M. (1988) The free-standing company, 1870–1914: an important type of British foreign direct investment. *Economic History Review*, 2nd ser., **41**(2), pp. 259-82.

Wilkins, M. (1989) *The History of Foreign Investment in the United States to 1914*, Harvard University Press, Cambridge MA.

Williamson, O. (1975) *Markets and Hierarchies: Analysis and Anti- trust Implications,* Free Press, New York.

Williamson, O. (1981) The modern corporation: origins, evolution, attributes. *Journal of Economic Literature,* **19,** p. 1537–68.

Wolf, B.M. (1992), Strategic alliances in the European automotive industry, in *Research in Global Strategic Management,* (eds A. Rugman and A. Verbeke), Vol. 3, JAI Press, Greenwich CT.

Womack, J.P., Jones, D.T. and Roos, D. (1990) *The Machine that Changed the World,* Macmillan, New York.

Womack, J.P. and Jones, D.T. (1994) From lean production to the lean enterprise, *Harvard Business Review,* March–April, pp. 93–103.

Wood, A. (1994) *North–South Trade, Employment and Inequality: Changing Fortunes in a Skills-Driven World,* Clarendon Press, Oxford.

Woodall, P. (1994) The global economy. *The Economist,* 1 October 1994, pp. 3–46.

World Bank (1995) *Workers in an Integrating World: World Development Indicators,* Oxford University Press, Oxford.

Wray, W. (1984) *Mitsubishi and the NYK, 1870–1914,* Harvard University Press, Cambridge MA.

Yamin, M. (1991) A reassessment of Hymer's contribution to the theory of the transnational corporation, in *The Nature of the Transnational Corporation,* (eds C.N. Pitelis and R. Sugden), Routledge, London.

Yip, G.S. (1989) 'Global strategy . . . in a world of nations?' *Sloan Management Review,* Fall, pp. 29–41.

Yip, G.S. (1992) *Total Global Strategy,* Prentice Hall, Englewood Cliffs NJ.

Yip, G.S., Loewe, P.M. and Yoshino, M.Y. (1988) How to take your company to the global market. *Columbia Journal of World Business,* Winter, pp. 37–48.

Young, S., Hamill, J., Wheeler, C. and Davies, J.R. (1989) *International Market Entry and Development,* Prentice Hall, Hemel Hempstead.

# Index